APPLIED
RESEARCH
+DESIGN
PUBLISHING

Published by Applied Research and Design Publishing. An Imprint of ORO Editions Inc. Gordon Goff: Publisher

www.appliedresearchanddesign.com
info@appliedresearchanddesign.com

Typeface information if necessary

Text: Gail Peter Borden
Graphic Design: Bruce Mau Design
Project Coordinator: Jake Anderson

10 9 8 7 6 5 4 3 2 1 First Edition

ISBN: 978-1-939621-80-1

Color Separations and Printing: ORO Group Ltd. Printed in China.

International Distribution:
www.appliedresearchanddesign.com/distribution

ORO Editions makes a continuous effort to minimize the overall carbon footprint of its publications. As part of this goal, ORO Editions, in association with Global ReLeaf, arranges to plant trees to replace those used in the manufacturing of the paper produced for its books. Global ReLeaf is an international campaign run by American Forests, one of the world's oldest nonprofit conservation organizations. Global ReLeaf is American Forests' education and action program that helps individuals, organizations, agencies, and corporations improve the local and global environment by planting and caring for trees.

NEW ESSENTIALISM

MATERIAL ARCHITECTURE
GAIL PETER BORDEN

I would like to thank each of the participants who wrote the introductory framing essays for their words here, but more importantly for their years of work, which have served as a beacon.

I would like to thank Gordon Goff and Jake Anderson at AR+D / ORO for their support and work on this project.

I would like to thank Hunter Tura, Sebastian Rodriguez, Luis Coderque, and Patricia Marcucci at Bruce Mau Design for their vision and design in the book's layout.

I would like to thank my wife Brooke, my daughter Frieda, and my son Gail Calvin for their perpetual love and support.

In addition I would like to thank the employees and collaborators including:

Laís Araújo
Luana Barichello
Renata Barros de Albuquerque
Ahad Basravi
Marcelo Bastos
Louise Tedesco Biz
Paula Silva Brizola
Richard Capin
Caroline Cavalcanti
Qian Chun Cheng
Adam Choi
Enoch Chow
Greg Creech
Marianna Alecio De Melo
Elder Felipe
Thais de Freitas
Cristina Gomez
Sarah Hammond
Michael den Hartog
John Hernandez
Yidan Hu
Diana Khotimskaya
Jeffrey Kuruvilla
Yasmin Leite
Hua Li
Jun Liang
Amanda Lima
Wili-Mirel Luca
Isaac Luna
Ana Sara Marcatto
Tristan McGuire
Gabriel Micherif

Aaron Mick
Arsine Mnatsakanyan
Evandro Moura
David Nicholson
Claudia Otten
Nicolas Oueijan
Tamar Partamian
Ashley Peng
Diego Almeida Pereira
Jesse Rabideau
Chris Raimondi
Kevin Reinhardt
Marilia Reis
Hezequias Rocha
Alexandre Salice
Cleyton Santos
Danielle Saunders
Martin Schubert
Darle Shinsato
Shaun Skoog
Alexxa Solomon
George Sovich
Jason Straight
Joyce Tsai
Fernanda Tscha
T.J. Tutay
Aaron Yip
Junru Zheng

Themes:

Thresholds and Propositions: *Precedents and Inquiries*

8

INTRODUCTION

ARCHITECTURE IS EVERYTHING ALL AT ONCE

Where to begin? With an analysis of Chartres Cathedral? Paxton's Crystal Palace? A new study of suburban house typologies? Inflatable weightless structures? Antiquity and architectural gravity? A (economic) material dispersion into contemporary fields? A discourse on material and form? Gail Borden offers many avenues into his work and in this ambitious book places them all on a similar plateau. The sequencing and its interlacing organization is clearly important, but it must—by nature—struggle against the linearity of a book format. The work is the product of a quasi-singular form authorship. Borden is offering not just a range of studies, projects, essays and installations but also a view to a small architectural practice with immense aspirations - the evidence seems the testing of that practice as an instrument to locate architecture. As a form of autobiography the book traces what seems like nearly two decades of work, yet it also traces an architect who is seemingly often alone in the defining of the agenda yet also deeply driven to unearth a multitude of ways to see where architecture is manifest. The landing approach is singular and simultaneously global at once, yet the work is driven by the process - testing mediums, techniques, histories, materials…

Where to begin? Architecture in the work of Gail Borden is all of the above and more. Much more. *New Essentialism* claims a focus on culling a path. Not just Borden's own work but for our field - this is a kind of archive of academic as well as practical work. Some is public and known, others seemingly warm ups or private studies (here shared for the first time) but it is the overall structure of the book that is perhaps the most vivid claim and the one that resonates. It would be easy to see the opposite of the essential in Borden's compendium: in what can seem like a rolling evolution of his past decade's output in the diversity of projects. The halts and stops, and the multiplicity of genres can seem jarring at first. Yet that would be a misreading as it is the ultimate attempt at synthesis that imparts a mode of the essential to the work. It's not the work itself—while often powerful and inventive—what stands out is the persistent testing of inherited claims for architecture. From our vantage, as the reader, we see a kind of academic and material undoing to verify precedents. Some are left unresolved in comparison: what, for example, can we make of a study of the Crystal Cathedral in the same context as a new study for a new suburban tract house? There is a dissonance and an honesty in this that is thrilling to imagine someone willing to take on both. The role of iron in the economy of the 19th century? The role of plywood in our recent decades? I am left to imagine, productively, a conflating of these worlds. I imagine Borden is asking us to imagine some synthetic future of the diverse work here - but that world will require a deeper level of social, economic, and material/scientific work. It will require many authors working in a new simultaneity.

Borden's claim that "architecture is everything all at once" is a stand out passage in the book, but so to is a similarly concise statement about the personal nature of work on architecture. Despite the public and material/economic nature of architecture it is often if not deeply conceived with an immense amount of private and individual concerns. The architect is perhaps more singular and present then we imagine today (when they are part of the work - we often, of course, are not). While it's not stated overtly, Borden's incantation of this condition seems to point to the smallest firms but also SOM or KPF or perhaps even more parametric representative such as SHoP. *New Essentialism* is here not a call for a primary architecture, but instead reads as a testing of the limit conditions that remain today. There is an intense faith that architectural aspirations can be both immediate and material, yet also wildly aspirational. Borden's compendium reveals an architect testing the benchmarks most of us were offered in school, a final version of the architect before they fully dismantle what was given. In the maelstrom of what we encounter in the real (Borden's Houston and Los Angeles)—of current practice's horizon or important histories (Paxton)—we find our new entry. *New Essentialism* seems far less a conclusion or proposal then an attempt to verify a fear and concern about the touchstones of architectural grounds. The energy and drive here is exciting and the faith overcomes the doubts in that regard. But this is also a practice that one thinks cannot stand apart from broader concerns of the city going forward. The book feels like a threshold moment - before it takes on economics or energy or everything else.

At the moment it stands out as a rare practice that, while deeply driven by its author, is also offering a view to our profession.

MICHAEL BELL

Michael Bell is a tenured Professor of Architecture at Columbia GSAPP. At Columbia, Bell is founding Chair of the Columbia Conference on Architecture, Engineering, and Materials, a multi-year research program based at GSAPP and in coordination with Columbia's Fu Foundation School of Engineering and Applied Science and the Institute for Lightweight Structures and Conceptual Design (ILEK) at the University of Stuttgart. He was Director of the Master of Architecture program Core Design Studios between 1999 and 2014 and the school's Housing Design Studios between 2000 and 2011.

Bell has taught at the University of California at Berkeley and Rice University and held visiting professorships at the Harvard University Graduate School of Design, the University of Michigan as the Saarinen Visiting Professor of Architecture, and Berkeley as the Howard A. Friedman Professor of Practice in Architecture. Bell was a Fellow at the Joint Center for Housing Studies at Harvard University between 2011 and 2013.

Bell's architectural design has been exhibited at The Museum of Modern Art, New York, The Venice Biennale, The Yale School of Architecture, and the University Art Museum, Berkeley. Bell has received four Progressive Architecture Awards, and his work is included in the permanent collection of the San Francisco Museum of Modern Art. His Gefter Press / Binocular House is included in American Masterwork Houses of the 20th and 21st Century by Kenneth Frampton.

CONTEXTS

What differentiates humans from animals is exactly this ability to step mentally outside of whatever is happening to us right now, and to assign it context and significance. Our happiness does not come so much from our experiences themselves, but from the stories we tell ourselves that make them matter.

- Ruth Whippman

Rather than opening with a polemical statement of what architecture is, we would like to begin with what it is not. For us, as a practice, we see architecture obviously beyond mere functionality. It is neither the pursuit of the sensational or the spectacular, nor is it a means of semiotic delivery. Defined as none of these, how then do we begin to arrive at an essential understanding of architecture? For us, we start by the simplest observation that we always operate in a given world - a context in the broadest sense. Then we observe that even before architecture is "something" that we assign to it cognitively, it re-presents the world to us in a physical engagement and thus affords the possibility of a direct esthetic experience-a transitory moment when we resonate with the world and ourselves. We are so drawn in this moment that we become detached and just are. Re-entering the given world, we are forced to recreate it subliminally. Through these transformative experiences, we come to look at the given world in a new way.

We would argue that beyond sheltering, signifying, or entertaining ... architecture affords a uniquely human sense of heightened transcendence by setting up a destabilizing relationship with the familiar world - a strangeness that forces a reconfiguration of reality as it was. This is an ephemeral condition that reveals itself to us as part of the architectural engagement, moments perceived directly that resonate with the mind, body, and the world. Do we not come across these experiences in either the colonnades of the mosque at Cordoba, in Kahn's Salk Institute, or in a forlorn walk deep in the woods?

To constantly be in search for an essential understanding of architecture framed as such underlies our praxis - what we could call the meta-project. Operating in the context of clients, contractors and constraints of all sorts, our search is conditioned by an acute pragmatic rationality.

Arriving in the '90s and setting up a practice in the proverbial small pond of Fayetteville, Arkansas—largely contrasted with the more spectacular pursuits of the architects in the coastal playgrounds—we deeply observed our context. What did we see? An eighteen-wheeler truck sporting a larger-than-life Walmart logo blazing through the Ozark forests, the trailers buried deep in the woods resembling an alien landing, the occasional barn in ruin amidst miles of empty country, a pristine rolling landscape dotted with industrial chicken coops - the Ozark outback presented us with a strangeness in itself. Being in such a world, we started to observe the unintended yet curious juxtapositions which revealed absurdities of a high consumerist culture and industrial production beset in a highly natural setting. Through reflecting on this world that was given to us, we

Gentry Public Library

Saint Nicholas Eastern Orthodox Church

Ruth Lilly Visitor Pavilion Indianapolis Museum of Art

Moore Honeyhouse

found ourselves between the natural beauty and the constructed ugliness.

For design inspiration, rather than borrowing fixed stylistic or ideological luggage, we turned to the context itself, both the natural and the cultural. Being empathic to the context allowed us to be free from dogmatic commentary and helped us to be rooted in place looking for possibilities of maximum meaning with minimum means. The discipline of architecture provided a temporal context of its own evolution. Beyond the analytical study of the discipline, architectural experiences through extensive travelling near and far established a personal context to draw from.

The influence of contextual cues in forming a project is not scripted a priori. Each project has certain intrinsic demands which require situational logics, setting up design strategies that try to capture specificities drawn from the local while simultaneously project the universal. Design investigations range from mining the vernacular types for re-calibration, from using the landscape as a repository of familiar figures for abstraction to capturing the material and technological culture. Each project has embedded in itself an entangled web of contextual cues. To illustrate this point, we may take the Shelby Farms Visitor Center (Memphis, TN, 2016), which in its final assemblage has traces of the typical southern porch extrapolated for public use, while alluding to the formal logic of Villa Savoye transmuted with an original formal study of the bullfrog. In the material expression, it borrows from the aluminium grating found in the local industrial buildings. Such transmutations allow for a plurality of analogical reference, all at the service of creating an enriching experience that affords visitors to resonate with the park landscape.

Even though a much earlier project, a similar set of operative logics can be traced in the Keenan Towerhouse (Fayetteville, AR, 2000) resulting in a completely different architectural expression. In that project, the formality derived itself from juxtaposing the commonly found dragonfly with the trailer, raised vertically alluding to the grain silos dotted in the rural landscape around the site, while drawing a connection to the tower typology found in places as far away as Yemen. The materiality was a trans-position of the wood from the surrounding forest, encased in the white panelling common to the silos. From the distance, the Towerhouse is no more than the extension of such a industrial-natural landscape, while only a closer experience reveals the strangeness of its existence.

By constructing a genealogical lineage of investigations in each project, we attempt to create design DNAs that adapt to the particularities of the place. Questioning the typology, formal syntax, materiality, and tectonics opens up logics of gentle transgressions. This trans-logic allows us to move between figuration and abstraction, the sacred and the secular, the natural and the constructed, the ideal and the improvised, and the local and the global. This transgressive shifting between oppositions is not to resolve them but to create a resonance with each. Defying a temporal permanence in any of these states, a new sincerity dictates that we be authentic to the meta-project rather than being stuck in either stylistic dogmatism or post-critical playfulness. We refuse to characterize ourselves as a critical regionalist practice precisely because a local response belies the underlying global diktats, influences, and ideas transmuted from elsewhere. Extrastatecraft has blurred boundaries in a way that erases an autonomous locality. Rather than "local versus global," a glocal condition is the operative reality of the world.

In such a world, we think about architecture with the particulars-at-hand present in the context. In St. Nicolas Eastern Orthodox Church (Springdale, AR, 2010), the abstract profile draws from the figure of the barn as a mediation between the earth and the sky, without bearing any formal resemblance. The Moore Honeyhouse (Cashiers, NC, 1998) explored, in sharp contrast to the steel tectonic, the materiality of honey itself as a mediator of light. Such mediated light affords a sacred experience to be possible even within an ordinary project. When dealing with adaptive re-use/historic preservation projects, rather than negating the past, the trans-logic allows for a simultaneous presence of the new and the old where the old itself is reconfigured in the light of the new, as in the case of the Gentry Public Library (Gentry, AR, 2008). In its materiality, a contemporary metallic tectonic in tandem with the old brick and restored ceiling offers a dualistic experience. Applied at a different scale, as in the case of the Steven L. Anderson Design Center and Renovation of the Vol Walker Hall (Fayetteville, AR, 2013), the formal and material cues from the old building create a deeply resonating experience, where the old and the new inform each other in a synergistic coexistence.

The contextual setting of the project deeply affects the generation of the architectural logic and expression. Located at the Indianapolis Museum of Art's 100-acre Art Nature Park, the Ruth Lilly Visitors Pavilion (Indianapolis, IN, 2010) blends itself into the surrounding forest, and yet retains a gentle autonomy by being raised above the forest floor. In contrast, the Harvey Pediatric Clinic (Rogers, AR, 2016) sits forlorn in its suburban office sprawl context, a stark red formal figure in the rather drab landscape, creating a genius locus around itself. By its autonomous being, it acknowledges the sprawl as the familiar yet is simultaneously disruptive with its formal expression. Such flux between defamiliarization and subsequent refamiliarization is key to real engagement.

This effectual capacity of architecture resides in its inherent need to be experienced through the embodied experience. Beyond naive realism, our search for a more-than-representational realist ontology of architecture fits closely with Gail Peter Borden's timely maneuverings towards an essentialist perspective of re-engagement with physicality, tactility, practicality, and performativity. After the phase of apathy of postmodern relativism followed by the fetishistic post-criticality in architecture, such a manifesto is a helpful guide in an often indifferent world. Against the grip of a capitalist realism, the ephemeral engagement we pursue through a diverse array of material, tectonic, and formal manifestations seeks to resist commodification. Effectively becoming a tool against the attrition of diversity by contemporizing (not universalizing) the local context, we hope to imbue a sense of richness and sublimity, beauty and use, and, hopefully a transformative engagement. We do not believe in the yesteryears' utopia of recreating a garden of Eden as a whole,

Shelby Farms Park

Harvey Pediatric Clinic

Steven L. Anderson Design Center and Renovation of Vol Walker Hall

Keenan Towerhouse

all images courtesy of Marlon Blackwell Architects

we simply offer our efforts in re-making the world by questioning the familiar world we find ourselves in, one project at a time.

1 Michael Benedikt in For an Architecture of Reality speaks of "Such experiences, such privileged moments, can be profoundly moving; and precisely from such moments, I believe, we build our best and necessary sense of an independent yet meaningful reality. I should like to call them direct esthetic experiences of the real."
2 Alva Noë, in Strange Tools: Art and Human Nature, makes the case for thinking of works of art as tools for investigating ourselves based on latest research in cognitive neuroscience and psychology.
3 Hilary Putnam in The Threefold Cord: Mind, Body, and World explores the relationship between our perceptions and reality, projecting his thesis of "natural realism."
4 Keller Easterling's Extrastatecraft is the operating system of the modern world: the subterranean pipes and cables sustaining urban life, free-trade zones, the standardized dimensions of credit cards, and hyper-consumerist shopping malls - the normative global infrastructure that is the Jeffersonian grid of the world.
5 Glocal is a transmodern concept coined by Rosa Maria Magda characterizing the state of the current world.
6 Harry Francis Mallgrave and David Goodman, in An Introduction to Architectural Theory: 1968 to the Present, characterize the post '90's with post-criticality - seizing the capitalist realism rather than resisting it, led from the front by Rem Koolhaas.
7 Mark Fisher, in Capitalist Realism, explores our collective failure of imagination to speculate on an alternative.

MARLON BLACKWELL

Marlon Blackwell, FAIA, is a practicing architect in Fayetteville, Arkansas, and serves as the E. Fay Jones Distinguished Professor in Architecture at the Fay Jones School of Architecture and Design at the University of Arkansas. He served as Department Head from 2009 – 2015 and was named among the "30 Most Admired Educators" by DesignIntelligence in 2015. Work produced in his professional office, Marlon Blackwell Architects, has received national and international recognition with significant publication in books, architectural journals, and magazines, and winning numerous design awards including the 2016 Cooper Hewitt National Design Award in Architecture and a #1 Design Firm ranking by the Architect 50. Blackwell was selected as a United States Artists Ford Fellow in 2014 and received the 2012 Architecture Prize from the American Academy of Arts and Letters. A monograph of his early work, An Architecture of the Ozarks: The Works of Marlon Blackwell, was published by Princeton Architectural Press in 2005. He was selected by the International Design Magazine, in 2006, as one of the "ID Forty: Undersung Heroes" and as an "Emerging Voice" in 1998 by the Architectural League of New York.

TANZIL SHAFIQUE

Tanzil Shafique is a Design Research Specialist at the Office of the Dean of the Fay Jones School of Architecture+ Design at the University of Arkansas. He worked as a Project Designer at the University of Arkansas Community Design Center from 2015-2017 and was a faculty member for the Urban Design Studio, leading the History of Urbanism Seminar. His work as part of the UACDC has been awarded numerous AIA and ASLA awards. He practiced architecture at Roger Ferris+ Partners (2014) and has taught undergraduate studios and conducted research at BRAC University in Bangladesh. His writing on design philosophy has been published both nationally and internationally. In 2016, he co-founded and now co-directs Estudio Abierto / Open Studio, a collaborative think+do tank operating at the intersection of architecture and urbanism. He graduated from Rensselaer Polytechnic Institute in New York in 2014.

THE MATERIAL INQUIRY OF CONSTRUCTION

During the formative years of our practice an unprecedented number of unique work environments were realized in just a few short years. The event of a job coming into the office and its completion occurred with such rapid succession that the energy of the design was naturally sustained through the end of construction, buoyed by the adrenaline that comes from producing at a blistering pace in combination with the direct physical contact with the actual materials of that construction. Our current state of practice is quite different. The size of firm, number of projects, their complexity, and associated duration has all increased. Rather than completing buildings in months, projects now frequently span four, five, or six years from inception to completion. The operative words are now "vigilance," "diligence," and "tenacity."

Despite this shift in the work and process, we remain dedicated to the investigation and exploration of the processes and materials of construction. As philosopher John Dewey described: "inquiry is the controlled or directed transformation of an indeterminate situation into one that is so determinate in its constituent distinctions and relations as to convert the elements of the situation into a unified whole."[1] The inventory of what we engage as the "materials of construction" include differentiated sets from the tactility of sanded oriented strand board (OSB); and far more abstract than re-purposed brooms or ping-pong balls deployed as façades that defined the early work. While previously materials were literally tangible, physical, and visceral, this sensibility has evolved to a broader engagement with social and environmental conditions. The approach declares an optimism and responsibility for materials that are not traditionally about buildings, but nonetheless hold substantial sway over the built environment.

In our earlier projects we brought animation to fairly generic spaces through the use of common materials reinterpreted and transformed beyond their immediate recognition in the service of a practical, typically programmatic goal. These projects operated on the principle that the quality of a design is correlated with the dynamic use of materials for effect. An insistence on simplicity and a confidence that the design is emergent from the course of the experiment with the potential to draw sensual qualities from banal materials (typically otherwise overlooked in the day to day) yields an opportunity for invention.

As projects have grown in scale and complexity, our work continues to emphasize the experience of making things. It does not focus on the object, but the process of making it. This methodology results in an awareness of the material and the experience. Drawing on principle belief that the material of the situation is raw at the outset, the design of a building in service of the public requires an investment in an inclusive and evolutionary process to develop it. "If

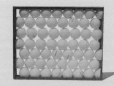

Mock-up for the light wall using ping-pong balls at **Jigsaw Editorial** in Los Angeles.
Photo - Lawrence Scarpa

Large scale mock-up of the glue laminated beam CNC routed wood wall at CoOP Editorial studios in Santa Monica.
Photo - Lawrence Scarpa

Detail of the custom designed and built façade operable screen panels at Cherokee Studios in West Hollywood.
Photo - John Linden

Construction of the twisted brick façade at the Lipton/Thayer House in Chicago.

architecture is completely overwhelmed by politics and absorbed into its processes," writes Hashim Sarkis in his essay "On the Line Between Procedures and Aesthetics," "it cannot transform them. In order to become engaged effectively, architects must maintain the strategic possibility of remaining partly disengaged."[2] One must have the material in hand, to be intimately informed (since disengagement from procedural requirements such as entitlement, permitting, and other approvals is not an option, and worse yet amounts to professional incompetence), but the design lies in the orchestrated transformation of that conditional material. Partial disengagement requires working knowledge and also knowledge that may be usefully "suspended" in the effort to manifest and support our needs as a culture. As Ed Dimendberg writes:

from the single-family home with its elaborate codings of public and private to museums with their implicit and explicit relations to notions of heritage and tradition, architecture can never escape the fate of cultural significance. Acknowledging the radically historicist character of architectural knowledge, that our spatial understandings and predilections have a history, that they ceaselessly change, and that the absolute truth remains elusive constitutes [a] requirement for a culturally reflective practice.[3]

- Ed Dimendberg

The temporary suspension of our architectural and urbanistic inheritance is fundamental to the process of re-envisioning an improved environment as the forces shaping change in American metropolitan centers goes beyond the reaches of the discipline of architecture engaging holistically public policy, transportation, public education, and so on. In this light, it is useful to suspend (at least initially) our claim to disciplinary autonomy, forgoing efforts at aesthetic expression in order to engage with the full scope of the conditional "material" and knowing that both historical knowledge and individual authorship will inevitably return.

The premise and process described as "New Essentialism" and the applied formal manifestation of these methods in the work of Borden Partnership represent a shared sensibility of approach to the issues described. The attention to material, the engagement of type and the fundamental subscription to privileging material and process as a mechanism to advance design provides optimistic inquiries for the future of the discipline. The opportunity that this presents to the discipline provides a path forward that is inclusive, expectant and unique. The conversation provided in these pages challenges us all to pick up the mantle of this framework for the discipline and move forward with its convictions. This emerging practice with the precision of their principles presents an extension of our belief in the opportunity of cultural reflection as a literal material in the design process that must be foregrounded to accomplish the objectives of a contemporary critical practice. Frederick Kiesler once wrote, "Our Western world has been overrun by masses of art objects." What we need are not more and more objects but an objective.

Detail view of the CNC wood wall showing concealed studio doors at
CoOP Editorial Studios in Santa Monica.
Photo - Marvin Rand

LAWRENCE SCARPA

As principal of Brooks + Scarpa Architects, Lawrence Scarpa
FAIA has garnered international acclaim for the creative use
of conventional materials in unique and unexpected ways.
He is also considered a pioneer and leader in the field of
sustainable design.

He is the recipient of the American Institute of Architects
Collaborative Achievement Award, the Smithsonian Cooper-Hewitt National Design Award in Architecture and the
AIA California Council Lifetime Achievement Award. He also
received the lifetime achievement award from *Interior Design
Magazine*. His firm Brooks + Scarpa was awarded the State
of California and National American Institute of Architects
Architecture Firm Award and has received more than fifty
major awards including Record Houses, Record Interiors,
the World Habitat Award, and the Rudy Brunner Prize.

Mr. Scarpa has taught and lectured at the university level
for more than two decades. He is currently on the faculty
at The University of Southern California.

1 John Dewey, Logic: The Theory of Inquiry. (New York: Holt, 1938), p.108
2 Hashim Sarkis, "On the Line Between Procedures and Aesthetics,"
in The Pragmatist Imagination: Thinking About Things in the Making.
(New York: Princeton Architectural Press, 2000), p.103
3 Ed Dimendberg, Excluded Middle: Toward a Reflective Architecture
and Urbanism. (Houston: Rice School of Architecture, 2002), p.39

QUIET MATERIAL

It's tricky to impart a "soul" onto physical objects. To attempt to do so opens a complicated conversation on both an emotional and rational level. The intent here is not to attempt to untangle that conversation, but to reflect upon the powerful effect that I've experienced and observed when humans interact with what some call quiet materials.

Materials found in nature are inherently quiet. They pick up the nature of climatic forces acting on them over time in their unique locations. Natural forces and time are, in fact, soundless. They react and mark unemotionally. It is we who make the noise. Materials allowed to age naturally are the evidence of time and display a sense of history and place. In that spirit, they are authentic. A project that is ten years old is much different than it was when it was ten months old. Allowed to pick up the traces of time and natural forces, buildings become quieter with age.

The power of these materials should come as no surprise, since we are all indeed made of the same matter and subject to the same universal forces. We have a kinship with materials on a molecular level. As humans, however, our unique position of existential, emotional experiencing leads us to deep levels of connection with our material world. And, let's be clear – these connections are more meaningful for us than for the material we are experiencing. Nevertheless, connections with material can be just as meaningful for us as connections with living beings.

I believe the most profound experiences in life are, in fact, subtle moments of internal reflection—sacred moments, if you will—where our souls comingle or touch the physical elements of our world. It should come as no surprise how easy it is to attach emotional significance of such experiences to a quiet material. It becomes, in a sense, an internal conversation about us, a touchstone to that memory or emotion. Quiet materials mark our time and the forces of our lives. Just as a tree from our childhood appears shockingly larger when we return to it later in life, we are humbled by what these quiet materials represent: our extraordinary luck to exist, to experience, and to feel.

The making of architecture is an act of intent, using natural materials and assembling them into an image of our choosing. The Pierre explores this situation with clear purpose by building into ancient stone an object made of reconfigured stone (concrete). In this way, it is a yin of nature to a yang of human intent with all its associated meanings. The hope is that the original aggressive act of carving into the rock quietly ages, thereby marking time. In a sense, that initial move is day one of the architecture. The clock has started, and materials quietly emerge as repositories of our collective story of time and place. It may be a myth, but it is our very human myth.

From certain angles, the house—with its rough materials, encompassing stone, green roof, and surrounding foliage—almost disappears into nature.
Photo - Benjamin Benschneider

The materiality of the built structure—mild steel, smooth concrete, and drywall—create a neutral backdrop for the exterior views to the bay and surrounding landscape.
Photo - Benjamin Benschneider

To design or make something out of quiet materials emphatically implies a responsibility to our experiences of time and nature that, at the root, is about our place in the world. A material so handled will naturally age and get better over time – its patina becoming an authentic marker, like the aging wrinkles or graying of our bodies. Rather than struggle with that reality or deny it as such, we should embrace its natural beauty and its gentle reminder of the cycle of life. Quiet materials remind us that life is about change and that we are supremely fortunate to experience that change.

This sensibility has been a driving force in my work and shared sensibility in the work of Gail Borden contained in the following pages. These projects serve as wayfinding moments in an approach and appreciation of the monumentality offered through the celebration of quiet material.

Ultimately, the idea behind quiet materials is very simple and should be. Without burdening materials with an overreaching "soul," the nature of the materials we experience are deeply meaningful markers of our existence, our life, our soul. And if we are authentic to the nature of the materials we are using, we can move ourselves collectively to a sacred moment that connects us to our existence. A quiet, sacred moment.

The owner's affection for a stone outcropping on her property inspired the design of this house. Conceived as a retreat nestled into the rock, the Pierre (the French word for stone) celebrates the materiality of the site.
Photo - Dwight Eschliman

TOM KUNDIG

Tom Kundig is a principal and owner of Seattle-based Olson Kundig. Over the past three decades, Kundig has received some of the world's highest design honors, from a National Design Award from the Smithsonian Cooper-Hewitt National Design Museum to an Academy Award in Architecture from the American Academy of Arts and Letters. In 2014, Kundig was included in Architectural Digest's AD100 and in 2012, he was inducted into Interior Design magazine's Hall of Fame.

In addition to having received scores of design awards— including ten National Design Awards from the American institute of Architects—his work has appeared in hundreds of publications worldwide including The New York Times, Architectural Record, Financial Times, Architectural Digest and The Wall Street Journal, as well as countless books, and was named to The Wallpaper* 150 as a key individual who influences and inspires the way we live, work and travel. Kundig's current and past work can be found on five continents, including a World Heritage site in Dachstein, Austria.

ITERATIVE FORMS
or the countless charms of repetition

Iterative forms elicit the countless charms of repetition and the inventive versatility of types. I would like to expand on this subject by first offering some recollections from the time I lived in Costa Rica, and secondly via some reflections on Gail Peter Borden's revisions of typology. I recall the intriguing constructions that I saw while growing up in the western coast of Costa Rica, many of them scattered from the port city of Quepos to the inland town of Parrita. Built initially by the United Fruit Company for the workers of their banana plantations (eventually replaced by palm oil cultivation), these repetitive two-story wooden houses would demarcate a large clearing in the midst of their thickly planted fields. I frequently visited and drove by these clusters of houses, their corrugated zinc roofs brightly painted from strident green to red hues. Aligning as a three-sided enfilade, each cluster of houses would form a distinct and common square, sometimes to contain a soccer field, an open market, or a playground. At each open corner and parallel to the main road, a commissariat or a meeting hall would be added to complete and anchor the entire compound. The Royal African palms (the source of palm oil) that surrounded the houses were planted in a similar iterative rhythm unleashing an extraordinary play of light and shade, at times dissolving into endless perspectives anywhere you looked. The regal palm trees produced an enthralling effect as the sunlight streamed from their leafy fronds to the dense ferns and plantings below.

The rudimentary construction system of these houses fascinated me, type was presented as the evolution of an essential vernacular, one adapted to the hot and humid tropical climate. Thus one could trace ingenious cross ventilation details layered or built to attenuate the heat, or one could read the raised verandah and porches as outdoor spaces, often occupied by hammocks or light chairs that also aided in dissipating the heat, or simply understood as another space where living or sleeping areas could spill over from the compact interiors. The house type was preserved not only in the repetition of its primary components but also modified by the personal and contrasting habits of each occupant or family. The combination of serial yet evolving houses, their lack of status consciousness, along with their synchronicity with the Royal African palms that surrounded them, gave the entire setting the aura of an enchanted tropical forest. The adaptability and simplicity of these iterative houses would remain an indelible lesson for me. Since living in the United States I have been able to trace similar traits in a variety of North American housing types, from the Shotgun or Dogtrot houses in Texas to the Saltbox houses in New England, and certainly in Gail Peter Borden's own revisions of typology through his "20 single housing prototypes."

Borden's prototypes outline variants of the modern house as counterpoint to the current anonymity and blandness of suburban houses and sites found aplenty across the United States and the world over. Each of Borden's house types aspires to transform their given site into an effective proposition driven by design engagement. An engagement that entails not only material, spatial, sensorial, and construction considerations, but also more importantly relevant issues of domesticity and their evolving patterns. Borden's investigations offer a malleable alternative to the tyranny of quasi-historical houses that land on a site, not only overblown and clueless, but proud of their indifferent and regressive agendas. At the will of speculative forces and their lending institutions, these houses remain absolute in their dominance of a market where critical design thinking is seldom given any attention or priority. These houses are sold complete with their regalia of superficial and immediate status above everything else. Practically indistinguishable from each other except for the cars on their driveways, these houses march side by side into a landscape of gradual disposability, or engage in an often-futile effort to outlast the value of their mortgage cycle.

The optimistic alternatives proposed by Borden for suburban living, along with the potential of iterative forms, are best captured in a marvelous site model where we see all of the architect's propositions laid out as a neighborhood. As a family of types, from Radial to Bar houses, from Organ to Box houses, from Orchard to Pavilions houses, they exist in this neighborhood individually and collectively, as a field interwoven by diversity and inclusivity. Gone are the ubiquitous double garage doors with their printed wood patterns, the extra wide driveways, the acres of composition shingles, the deaf fencing, the cheapening of standardization. ... The idea of the suburban house, whether it is to fit on a standard 60-foot by 120-foot plot, a smaller or larger plot, is given a lightness, a freedom, and a porosity seldom seen in the suburban landscape. The suburban condition can be imagined as a sustainable garden where type is transformed by a rich and complex set of possibilities. Iterative forms do not have to be deployed in militant seriality but in choral adaptability as Borden's investigations abundantly demonstrate.

CARLOS JIMÉNEZ

Carlos Jiménez was born in San Jose, Costa Rica in 1959 and moved to the United States in 1974. He graduated with honors from the University of Houston College of Architecture in 1981, receiving best thesis and best portfolio awards. He established his own office, Carlos Jiménez Studio, in Houston in 1983. He is a full time faculty member at Rice university and has taught at numerous universities, including Texas A & M University, SCI-ARC, U.C.L.A., the University of Houston, the University of Texas at Arlington, Williams College, the University of Navarra in Pamplona, Spain, Harvard University Graduate School of Design (Eliot Noyes Visiting Design Professor), Tulane University (First Favrot Chair in Architecture), the University of Texas at Austin (McDermott Visiting Professor and Ruth Carter Stevenson Chair in Architecture), the University of California at Berkeley (Friedman Visiting Professor), and the University of Oregon (Pietro Belluschi Distinguished Visiting Professor). He has been and is a frequent lecturer, Juror, and Visiting Critic at universities and cultural institutions throughout the Americas, Europe, Japan, and the Middle East. He is a long-term jury member of the Pritzker Architecture Prize (2001–2012).

Jiménez has won several awards for excellence in design and for his teaching, most notably AIA Houston Educator of the Year 2009, Tecnologico de Monterrey-Queretaro Academic Leader 2009 and 2010, AIA Houston Honor Award (2007, 2008), Charles Duncan Award from Rice University (2006), Chicago Athenaeum Architecture Award (2004), AIA Indianapolis Honor Awards (2003), Architecture (2002), *Architectural Record* Record Houses (1990, 1994, 1996, 2004), Progressive Architecture Young Architects (1987), The Architectural League of New York Young Architects (1988) and Emerging Voices (1994), and Forty under Forty (1995). The work of Carlos Jiménez Studio has been exhibited nationally and internationally at many museums and galleries.

Jiménez's works and writings can be found in *Carlos Jiménez: House and Studio* (2003), *Carlos Jiménez Buildings* (1996), *Crowley* (2009), as well as in monographic issues such as 2-G "Carlos Jiménez" (Barcelona, 2000) and A+U "Carlos Jiménez" No. 306 (Tokyo, 1996), specialized books and catalogues, national and international journals such as *Progressive Architecture, Architecture, A+U, Korean Architect, The New York Times Design Magazine, Taschen Architecture Now, L'Architecture d'Aujourd'hui, Arquine, Arquitectura Viva, A&V, Architectural Record, Phaidon Atlas of World Architecture, Oris, Phaidon's 10 ×10 - 3*, and *Lotus International.*

SPIRIT OF OBJECTS

From a very early age we experience and recognize the spirit of place in the form of objects around us. In nature, in our homes, and in our communities there are moments and things that exude a spiritual aura. We are all born Animist. Animism[1] is the oldest known type of belief system in the world for the simple reason that objects and places house spirits that we are all intimately connected to if we slow down and listen.

There is a Japanese Shinto tradition of signifying a sacred or pure space with an "enclosing rope" known as shimenawa.[2] At times these are similarly used around yorishiro[3] (objects capable of attracting and being inhabited by spirits), which include specific honorific objects from the natural realm: notably select trees, or stones known as iwakura.[4] One such place is the Meoto Iwa in the sea off Futami, Mie, Japan where the relationship of the two rocks serve as symbols of human matrimony. They are coupled with Mount Fuji in the distance as an honorific and resonant act of our place in this world.

Perhaps everything has a spirit if we stop, recognize it, and allow it to be revealed to us. The root word Anima in Latin means "breath, spirit, life."[5] Animism perceives all things: animals, plants, rocks, rivers, weather systems, human handiwork, and even words as sentient and alive.

Objects are defined as something that is material, that can be seen or touched or perceived by the body's senses. These objects can be functional for their spiritual, psychological, and/or physiological functions for our inner well-being as well as our everyday needs. In these capacities objects have the potential to facilitate fundamental connections between us and our world and through this connection to our place and locale provide a humble service as a reverent act of gratitude for what we have.

In colonial America, the Shakers only made things for their intended use and believed that a thing well designed and well made was in itself "an act of prayer."[6] A contemporary extension is the assertion that an everyday object in any culture and any place, that is well conceived—from the chopsticks to the chair—may embody a spirit as a rudimentary act of genius for all humanity. Is this spirit when felt through the engagement with an object that best represents us and our responses to human needs (whether prosaic or transcendent) the root of good design? Was Frank Lloyd Wright correct to change his mentor Louis Sullivan's famous quote to "form and function are one"[7] citing nature as the best example of this integration? Perhaps Anima offers the latent potential trait of all well designed thoughts, theorems, objects, things, and systems.

shimenawa

Meoto Iwa with Mount Fuji in the distance

Chinese chair

Reverence for a simple function and/or for the complex laws of the universe can be expressed in objects spanning from simple handiworks to grand works of art. Walter de Maria created sublime artworks that were concerned with the fundamental laws of our universe. Physics, mathematics, and philosophy emerged through light, weights and measures, rhythm and harmonics, and direct experience in works such as *The Lighting Field* in the northwestern plains of New Mexico near Quemado (1977); *The Earth Room* in New York (1977); as well as *Broken Kilometer* also in New York in 1979. These works speak directly to Hegel's Phänomenologie des Geiste[8] (which can be translated as either "The Phenomenology of Spirit" or "The Phenomenology of Mind" as the German word Geist has both meanings). They confront the opportunity of the phenomena in the philosophical sense through the object of perception examining the differential potential of what the senses and the mind observe of the world.

Material by simple definition means: the matter from which a thing is or can be made. Immaterial implies the spiritual, rather than the physical. Could not both the material and the immaterial interchangeably possess a spirit or presence? The Jazz great Miles Davis reportedly once said by way of the composer Claude Debussy "that the spaces between the notes are just as important as the notes."[9] This offers a clarity that presence is defined both as the state or fact of existing, occurring, or being present in a place or thing but also as a person or thing that exists or is present in a place but is not seen. The tension between the seen and unseen is perhaps the space where we experience the material and the immaterial simultaneously. Or maybe when the essence of something is revealed in-between the physical material we can feel it more powerfully? As Antoine de Saint-Exupery famously said "perfection is achieved, not when there is nothing more to add, but when there is nothing left to take away."[10] This sensibility is overtly witnessed in Donald Judd's boxes. Constructed in ubiquitous natural materials such as concrete, plywood, and aluminum; they project an essential presence at first glance from afar and equally so after hours of direct experience.

Resonance in Physics is a phenomenon in which a vibrating system or external force drives another system to oscillate with greater amplitude at a specific preferential frequency. Resonance between form and function (purpose) creates pleasure and appreciation. Resonance with our imagination (people) stimulates thought and awareness. Resonance with the specifics of our world (place) creates a feeling of belonging. Each of these resonances could be called Spirit. Things resonate and/or are resonant with us due to their meaning on our lives as Objects of Usefulness to our Mind, Body, and Spirit individually and collectively as a society. The Spirit of Objects is a fundamental tenet of Architecture best expressed by Vitruvius's three elements for a well-designed building: firmitas, utilitas, and venustas (firmness, utility, and beauty).[11] As Bernard Rudofsky's canonical book *Architecture without Architects*[12] asserts that a well-designed building is not just the domain of architects. One could now imagine a companion book entitled *Objects with and without Pedigree* that documents objects along the wide-ranging spectrum articulated above. This continuum of design history can teach us much about lost knowledge and the lost respect for fundamental truths about the specificity of our human race on Earth through the Spirit of Objects.

This sensibility threads it way into my own work and the work of Gail Peter Borden. Offered as poetic touchstones in the principles of New Essentialism, and furthered through the projects, methods, and inquiries documented in the ensuing pages, this approach bears witness to the desire to see, engage, and thus understand the primal nature of things. The spirit of objects offers a companion to all of us in our approach and dialogue with making.

Traditional African chair

1 Lonie, Alexander Charles Oughter (1878). Animism in Baynes, T.S. Encyclopedia Britannica. 9th edition, New York: Charles Scribner's Sons, pp. 55–57

2 Encyclopedia of Shinto, Kokugakuin University

3 ibid.

4 ibid.

5 Lonie, Alexander Charles Oughter (1878). Animism in Baynes, T.S. Encyclopedia Britannica. 9th edition, New York: Charles Scribner's Sons, pp. 55–57.

6 Stephen Bowe and Peter Richmond, Selling Shaker: The Commodification of Shaker Design in the Twentieth Century England: Liverpool University Press, 2007.

7 Caesar Cruz, Wright's Organic Architecture: From Form Follows Function to Form and Function are One. Wolkenkuckucksheim – Cloud-Cuckoo-Land – Vozdushnyi zamo, 2012.

8 Georg Wilhelm Friedrich Hegel, Phenomenology of Spirit, Translated by A. V. Miller, Oxford University Press, 1977.

9 Jonathan G. Koomey, Turning Numbers into Knowledge: Mastering the Art of Problem Solving, Analytics Press, 2001, p. 96.

10 Antoine de Saint-Exupery, Terre des Hommes, Gallimard; 1939.

11 Taken from Sir Henry Wotton's version of 1624, translation of the passage in Vitruvius (I.iii.2).

12 Bernard Rudofsky, Architecture without Architects: A Short Introduction to Non-Pedigreed Architecture, University of New Mexico Press, 1987.

Shaker chair

plywood box
Donald Judd

Broken Kilometer
Walter de Maria

WENDELL BURNETTE

Wendell Burnette is a self-taught architect with an internationally recognized body of work. Based in Phoenix for over twenty years, his eponymous studio Wendell Burnette Architects is concerned with space, light, context, and community. He is a native of Nashville who discovered the southwest desert as an apprentice at Frank Lloyd Wright's Taliesin West. His eleven-year association with the studio of Will Bruder culminated in six-year design collaboration on the Phoenix Central Library. He is a Professor of Practice at Arizona State University and lectures widely in the United States and abroad. His projects include residences located locally and nationally, the Palo Verde Library / Maryvale Community Center and the much acclaimed Amangiri Resort in southern Utah, as well as current work in China, Canada, Israel, Saudi Arabia and the UAE. In 2009, Burnette received the Academy Award in Architecture from the American Academy of Arts and Letters in New York City recognizing an American Architect whose work is characterized by a strong personal direction, which was accompanied by an exhibition at the Academy in the same year. Most recently, his first full-length monograph *Dialogues in Space* by Oscar Riera Ojeda Publishers was released worldwide. His design philosophy is grounded in listening and distilling the essence of a project to create highly specific architecture that is at once functional and poetic.

OPEN TECTONICS

Any discussion of architectural intelligence assumes tectonics as the lingua franca. Architectural history is driven by technological progress (forward or backward - witness the difference between the regressive middle ages and the retrogressive renaissance), and tectonics translates this progress into the architectural affect and knowledge that constitute the discipline. With each major technological advance new tectonic terms are introduced, the discipline passes judgement on their utility, and they are incorporated or not. The modern expansion of the tectonic vocabulary can be traced to Semper's re-imagining of the primitive hut fable in the 19th century, when technological advances in both construction and communication (burgeoning material and systems choice, and greater knowledge of non-western building conventions) freed tectonics from its strict association with western trabeated and arcuated construction traditions. A final chapter in this historical saga has potentially opened with the recent digital revolution, which has brought a host of new materials and methods into architecture that move the tectonic discourse beyond the reach of any of the traditions grounding it so far.

To understand how the architectural discipline might survive the test of the digital (which will remove the limits by which the discipline has known itself for millennia) it is necessary to understand the relationship between the architectural intelligence and the discipline, and between them and the discourse of tectonics which give them a voice. The discipline is the straightforward, operative compendium of the relevant history and tradition, the continuous thread which makes that history meaningful. The architectural intelligence is the exportable dimension of that operative knowledge. Tectonics have traditionally been the non-exportable part, what grounds the intelligence in specifically architectural interest.

In his seminal modernist tract, Structure, Construction, Tectonics Eduard Sekler attempts to clarify how the term "tectonics" straddles between architecture and technology. He identifies the importance of expression as key to understanding structure and construction as architectural concerns, illuminating the difference between engineering and architecture. But, while he begins his essay with careful examination of terminology and "precision," the abstraction of the modernist forms he wants to justify does not lead him to understand expression through architecture's longstanding analogy to language. Instead he follows it to psychology, perception and the concept of empathy, where the new vocabulary may operate at a deeper level, prior to any possible linguistic association.

Language became an explicit issue again for architecture only later, when the Post–Modern historicist critique of the sterility of modernism reasserted the connection out of a concern for legibility and meaning. While the debate about whether architecture constitutes a true language remains to be settled, some linguistic concepts can be useful in thinking about the evolution of architectural properties and how the most recent advances may play out.

In linguistic particulars, the technological pacing of architectural history can be productively understood as a tectonic dialectic, swinging between moments when syntax is preeminent, and others when semantics rule. Unlike the exchange of thesis and antithesis, though, a new architectural proposition will be ushered into the field first from the outside, without relation to the existing standards, as the pragmatic consequence of a new technology. This technological innovation will initially be unrecognizable as architecture to the discipline, and so it will be forced into the language of the existing architecture. As it discovers its own tectonic rules, however, it will begin speaking in its own language. Of course, this new language will itself be initially unrecognizable, its forms alien and meaningless to the existing tectonic regime even though they are internally coherent. But as the new stuff gains acceptance and the technology driving/enabling it proves its worth, the new stuff will supplant the existing stuff, assuming meaning outside its own technical parameters, establishing its own semantic regime. From this tectonic perspective, architectural history unfolds through a serial overwriting or abandonment of an existing semantic regime by a new syntactic regime that does not value those semantics and eventually, as it is itself established, introduces new semantic units into the field, which then get overwritten by the next new technology that delivers a new syntactic challenge that cannot be accommodated by the existing semantic regime.

That at least is how it used to be. Modernism's abstract forms pushed out the familiar meaning of the prior classical forms, but the new modern forms were only understood by contrast to that tradition - leaving judgment to rely on the syntactic standards of composition and regulating lines, rather than the semantic content of the prior figures, with its more certain meaning. When the new formalism became established, though, gaining semantic content as form followed—and spoke for—function (eventually disputed by historicism's self-serving critique), it was eventually itself undermined in turn by the new digital technology's even greater abstraction and more complex syntactic expression.

This last development heralds a possible end to the dialectic, though. The survival of the architectural intelligence to date has been guaranteed by the indifference of the syntactic genes which encode it to the semantic load of the units they compose. In contrast, since the semantic genes are charged with conserving their currency or historicity, the knowledge they gather is fixed in time and inherently fragile. But as the new digital tools sharpen the resolution of historically aggregated units into a continuously differentiated smoothness, the syntactical habit that depends on the discreetness of these counters to produce order is confounded and the dialectic stalls. Tectonics melts into the mute folds of the blob, where the semantic dimension has lost its intentionality and the specific architectural intelligence cannot find any syntactic purchase. The discipline fades away, the thread cut.

There is however another side to this new digital technology. Reminiscent of the communication advances that made the rest of the world visible to Semper, the internet has not only expanded that synchronic access, but has opened all of history as well. The deep memory and infinite diachronic reach that makes everything available, and the consequent agnostic attitude about the zeitgeist argument once exemplified by tectonics (which drives the inevitability of the dialectic), means that everything can be authentic and good, in its own way, according to its own rules, playing its own game, referencing its own tradition.

With this, the syntactic impulse of tectonics goes meta and the order-loving architectural intelligence becomes available to all disciplines: no longer tied to specific, physical construction technologies, it may now revel openly in the only limit that still matters. The empathetic compulsion that Sekler identified, which rescued modernist tectonics from the momentary loss of linguistic guidance, is a much more durable assertion of the essential humanity of all willful design. By seeing tectonics, and the architectural intelligence, as "structured empathy" Sekler foreshadows a formula that can connect digital technology's new omniscience with a continuing human program.

This foreshadowing is answered by the program of multimodal "engagement" at the heart of Gail Borden's "New Essentialism," which expands architecture's traditional reverence for tectonics into a holistic lens for refining technology, materiality, and form. Essentially (or New Essentially) this lens focuses the activity of design into an integrative augmentation of modernism's reductive restraint with post-modern narrative. Tectonics are re-informed and critically re-invested with agency. In the writing and thinking of Gail Peter Borden, tectonic logic is featured as a generative mechanism that leads to rigorous meaning as well as seductive form. In the face of cornucopic digital indeterminacy or "undecideability," this New Essentialism grounds conviction in material and process, evaluates outcomes through perception, and reasserts the operative relevancy of "the thing" as emergent from the very matter of its making.

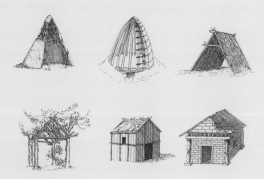

Versions of "the first hut" by a variety of Renaissance architects. Images by Norman Crowe in *Nature and the Idea of a Man-Made World*, courtesy of MIT Press.

Light Frames and Density Frames
Gail Peter Borden

WES JONES

Wes Jones is a partner in Jones, Partners: Architecture, an award-winning, California-based architectural practice known for technologically inspired design. Jones' work has been exhibited widely and can be found in the permanent collections of major museums around the world. Princeton Architectural Press has published two monographs of his work, *El Segundo* and *Instrumental Form*. A third volume, tentatively titled *Alameda*, is in the works. A recipient of the Rome Prize from the American Academy in Rome, and Arts and Letters Award in Architecture from the American Academy of the Arts and Letters, Jones has been named one of the 30 Most Admired Educators in the country in the Design Intelligence Survey of Architectural Education. He currently serves as the Architecture Discipline Head and directs the graduate program of the School of Architecture at USC.

FIGURATION

Composition, ornament, and space. Dialogues in these three key tenets of architecture are of fundamental interest. They offer the essence of experience, organization, and sequence. They orchestrate light, material, and form. These principles are essential considerations for two seminal architects that have shaped the evolution of architecture with an extremity of approach: Andrea Palladio and Adolf Loos. They worked approximately 500 years apart in very disparate locales. Palladio, as a late Renaissance architect, worked primarily in the Veneto region of Italy executing palaces and villas for wealthy clients while Austrian Adolf Loos worked principally in Vienna and Paris. However, their shared examination of these tenets (and a comparative analysis) provides insight into a critical dialogue in architecture.

Though both men were guided by a focus on composition (primarily in relation to symmetry), ornament and space; their work reads extremely differently. Palladio employed serial experimentation through the designs for rural villas, similar to Borden's interest in the single family suburban house. The Villa Barbero, the Villa Emo, and the Villa Rotunda each stretched architecture in new directions through their individuated and focused investigations of a dominant principle. Each as free-standing compositions (as opposed to part of an urban fabric) and thus viewable from all four sides, the Villa Rotunda, in particular, employs serial and symmetrical facades on all four sides, making each elevation identical and creating a nearly perfectly resolved geometric object within the landscape. In contrast, Palladio's urban palaces in Vicenza, such as Palazzo Valmarana and Palazzo Thiene are more restrained, emerging from a respectful approach to the context and the traditions of architecture as well as the culture of the era. Palladio scholar James Ackerman theorizes that Palladio felt more comfortable with experimentation in rural environs because he was far from the judgmental wags of the city. His detachment from the fabric and context of the city provided an opportunity for purity of expression and exaggerated engagement in the object.

Adolf Loos tended to do the opposite. His most radical buildings were located in the city and when he worked in the country, the buildings cultivated a far more conservative approach. Loos designed his iconic urban houses, such as the Villa Moller in Vienna and The House for Tristan Tzara in Paris, with surreal symmetries on the main façade juxtaposed with a freer façade on the back. The Khuner House and the Spanner House, located in remote settings in the Austrian Alps, exhibited a more relaxed attitude and lacked the radical edge that sets Loos' urban efforts apart. Here the urban focus on interiority and

Villa Rotunda
Andrea Palladio

the complexity of space heightened through material and experiential viewing establish themes underlying Borden's investigations through the Spaceframes and the [X]perience Mechanisms.

Underlying each of these architects is a fundamental interest in space and its experience through sequence. Palladio engaging it through the use of order and geometry and Loos through the use of the raumplan. This latter concept was created by Loos to sectionally organize the rooms vertically, rather than merely horizontally. Utilizing function in a very specific way (each room clearly designated for a certain use), there is an interconnected visual dialogue that introduces issues of dominance, complexity, and uncertain hierarchies that set distant spaces in resonating conversation with one another. In contrast, Palladio favored a much freer use of the spaces. His use of function generated rooms dependent upon the season and the time of day.

The approach to ornament was focused but distinct. Palladio, as a Renaissance architect, utilized classical choices employing the rigors of the language's order to reinforce his geometries. In contrast, Loos was known for his denial of non-culturally derived ornament. For example, ornament derivative of Greek and Roman architecture was acceptable, but Art Nouveau (without historical precedent) was not. This rigor allowed for a reductionism that heightened the interest in materiality (the surface and finished material) over the formal articulation of applied imagery. The resonance between geometry and material in Borden's work oscillates between, yet synthesizes these two approaches.

Both Palladio and Loos shared impressive clarity in their approach to these thematics. Their innovation of these foundational mechanisms provided reconsideration through their heightened focus and intent. Both architects allowed location to dictate design decisions and the results were quite remarkable. Architecture fares best when there is constant tension, either from location, program, or theory.

This approach and rigor underscores the work of Gail Peter Borden and is what draws my attention, interest, and respect for his work. Sharing similar beliefs, Borden and I have collaborated under the acronym ABBA (Andrews Borden Borden Andrews) on several projects including our seminal book *Principia: Architectural Principles of Material Form* as well as a series of international competition designs. When Borden and I worked on the 99K House together in 2007, we experienced a particularly rich form of artistic tension. One of us would pose a financial priority and the other would counter with beauty; one would argue structural rationale, the other material sensibility; one would offer programmatic vantage, the other countering with vernacular typological assessments, etc. The process was a constant conversation with each of us providing insight that layered into a balanced solution that considered many aspects of architecture. Borden or I could have provided this on our own, but the magic of those collaborations while working on a project that was measured in inches rather than feet, proved a powerful education for both of us. Architecture can be summed up as a perpetual war between the conservative and the radical. I continue to be grateful for the opportunity to engage in that undertaking with Gail Peter Borden.

The House for Tristan
Tzara in Paris
Adolf Loos

The following pages represent a brief selection of Borden's prolific portfolio. Spanning diverse media, scales, and design opportunities, the combination of built and speculative work offers a precise interest in re-examining and challenging these foundational tenants of symmetry, ornament, and space. In each project, they have been historically examined, expanded, and owned and ultimately translated into uniquely authored projects focusing on material, typology, form, systemic logics, and experience, among others. The argument for a New Essentialism is a foundational return to the promise of the more basic ideals - exquisitely understood and orchestrated to deploy into design thinking and ultimately spatial experiences that are a return to the future of architecture.

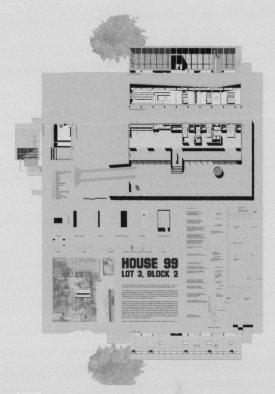

99K House
Borden and Andrews

BRIAN DELFORD ANDREWS

Brian Delford Andrews attended Tulane University and the Architectural Association in London. Upon graduation, Andrews was awarded the AIA Gold Medal and Best Thesis Award. He received his post-professional Masters from Princeton University, where he was also awarded the Skidmore, Owings, and Merrill Travelling Fellowship. Andrews is currently an associate professor at the University of Cincinnati and a visiting professor at the University of Kentucky. He has taught at various institutions including the University of Virginia, Syracuse University, and the University of Nevada, Las Vegas. He was the Robert Mills Distinguished Professor at Clemson University and also the Hyde Chair of Excellence at the University of Nebraska. Andrews' research and practice focuses on drawing and the concept of spatial detritus in society. As a principal in both Andrews/Leblanc and Atelier Andrews, his work has been recognized both nationally and internationally. He has won a Progressive Architecture Award, numerous ACSA awards, Boston Society of Architects UnBuilt, and RADA awards. At University of Southern California, Andrews received an Outstanding Teaching and Mentoring Award. In addition to solo exhibits and publications, Andrews and Gail Peter Borden published Architecture Principia in 2012. Andrews is currently finishing a publication on Guiseppe Terragni's Asilo in Como, Italy.

26

PREMISE:
New Essentialism

MATERIAL ARCHITECTURE
A NEW ESSENTIALISM

Architecture is the process of engagement with material to create effect.

Every design at the point of realization must participate with material and tectonic systems. Physical manifestation requires a dialogue with matter. The boundaries and rules of the natural world, even with man's expanding influence, have governing edges. This juncture with material during making is critical to architecture. The integration of all other factors (from the intellectual to the social, formal to functional) are manifest through the actuality of the building process. This point of transformation from idea to object is where the discourse of space and effect emerges. Moving beyond image and into the reality of things, architecture's presence becomes tactile and its material governance becomes dominant in the design. The physical manifestation of architecture is dependent upon its material sensibilities.

The history of architectural form has moved through a series of major transitions in its history based upon the influences of technology. The response to performance (driving composition and generating experience) has been encircled by intellectual constructs and discourse extending beyond the pragmatic to the philosophical to differentiate architecture from building. The result loads architecture with an overlain intention that informs and develops its intention through a language of form. Highly specific to the discipline, methods and forms (and their associate instincts) have emerged from a dedicated pursuit of newness. Cyclically self-referential while also borrowing and grafting from interdisciplinary fields (to adopt methods, rationales, and sensibilities) architectural form has emerged to define itself through process based techniques and methods. It is time to challenge these methods and reconsider relevance.

Contemporary architectural form must engage a new paradigm. In an era of extreme material and technological complexity the desire for a New Essentialism to drive the formal and perceptual qualities of architecture is paramount. The paradigm of engagement provides direction for architecture. Engagement with the body; engagement with process; engagement with tectonics and materiality; engagement with the environmental and social landscape; engagement with economies and code; engagement with urbanism and place: architecture must confront and respond to all of these with equity and cohesiveness but despite these it must demand a focused return to effect regarded through essential form and logic of construction.

The following text, through five analytical precedents (historical) that demonstrate critical conceptual thresholds in the evolution of the discipline and five experimental design inquiries (projective) unpack the fundamental methodologies of architecture's sensibilities. Each project builds intent into its pro-

Hahatonka Spring,
Camden County
topographic map as a logic
system representing form

Janus
looking forward and
looking backward

log scribe
tools as determinants of
form

cess demanding the unpacking of their legibility through a reflective and methodical examination. Revealing their essential systemic design methods, these projects illustrate the crucial components of a *New Essentialism*, illuminating its characteristics, methods, and the sensibilities that mark its definition.

The collective represents an emergent methodology defining a state of practice offering a means of approaching the looming and increasing complexities facing architecture.

NARRATIVE

The evolution of tools, methods, and material technologies has infused architecture with nearly infinite capabilities. A strategic documentation of the thresholds in this evolution extends architecture's spatial and physical morphologies through pivotal and revelatory innovations in tectonic logics and conceptual considerations. Mapping and unpacking their rationales to systemically document their sensibilities presents a set of design principles transferable to contemporary architectural inquiry. The analytical examination of five critical thresholds in architectural evolution reveals pivotal developments in both conceptual and material systems. These thresholds are marked by innovations during the Greek, Roman, French Gothic, Renaissance, and Early Industrial Eras. These historical thresholds present critical underpinnings of a *New Essentialism*.

New Essentialism has the roots of this thinking in the following sources:

— The investigation of form as a manifestation of ideals through physical objects;

— Materialism responding to the expanding spectrum of capability; commercial production, fabrication tools, and assembly techniques;

— Performance (including diverse rubrics) as a foundational responsibility;

— Expanding technologies of visualization, representation, design processes, information, and systems;

— Social activism rooted in the 1960s but amplified through social media and globalized issues emerging from ongoing strained political, racial, and economic conditions;

— The privileging of experience through the effectual perception of space.

Architecture prior to modernity was rooted in style. Systems (proportional, compositional, ornamental, et cetera) were established through referential methodologies. Like art, which was consumed with a reverence of the natural world and an interest in figuration that related to a descriptive narrative vocabulary, architecture was engaged in the relationship of its rules with its language. Modernism shifted the focus of architecture to include logics of materiality in conjunction with a social agenda to advance the lifestyle, hygiene, and standards of living in an emerging industrialized economy. Composition became grounded in the expression of function and the associative revelation of tectonic systems as a generator of form. In this focused rigor, humanity and place were subordinated. A return to effect and experience is critical to restore their inclusion.

To accomplish and exhibit effect and experience, a reductivism and synthesis is critical. Form must engage with prowess the responsive and combinatory aspiration of diverse concerns, but focus primarily on experience. Individual demands must unify and negotiate into a single compositional result with a dedicated perceptory performance. To accomplish this a reduction to primal essentials leads towards minimalism but remains distinctly different as it must be further endowed with experience. The roots of minimalism, however, are an important point of departure and juxtaposition.

Minimalism, as a term and sensibility, appeared in the mid-1960s in the avant-garde of the fine art world and moved into the western cultural mainstream by the mid-1980s.[1] The historical significance as a uniquely indigenous American style (in combination with its comprehensive adoption across media types) proliferated reductionism. Emerging in an era of heightened intellectual, cultural, social, and technological complexity, the sensibility of minimalism required a reconsideration of all assumptions and focused a re-centering upon the power of less. This opened the opportunity for experience (as perceived and engaged by the body and mind) to be foregrounded. As a result of this process, the intellectual, visual, and, ultimately, material sensibilities emerged as critical collaborating mechanisms to facilitate engagement. Marked by their movement away from the arbitrary and ornamental and towards the essential and systemic allowed for a complexity of relativism that positioned the viewer into a necessitated and meaningful dialogue with the object. The ability to engage and understand something was positioned within the emotive and cognitive relationship with the composition. The refinement of the palette through a reduced engagement allowed for a greater focus on discrete methods and techniques to respond formally. This essentialism naturally weighted the design process with fewer elements and more consideration endowing greater meaning and significance into all aspects.

The minimalist movement endowed an importance upon the means not the ends (a common condition in architecture now in terms of conceptual position, diagrammatic clarity, or simply design intention). New Essentialism varies by:

— While minimalism is a style distinguished by "severity of means, clarity of form, and simplicity of structure and texture;"[2] New Essentialism uses a lavish understanding of tectonics despite a refined compositional palette to accommodate a clarity and singularity of strange form that uses space, texture, and structure and opportunities for pattern and disruption within a system.

— While minimalism is prone to stasis (event free narrative, featureless physicality, monochromatic);[3] New Essentialism engages the movement of the viewer as a body set into the composition and establishes a referential experience to dictate understanding. The featureless becomes the body with moments of disruption and hybridity and distortion within the system to respond to the integration of the moment, its perception, and the resulting effect. Material be-

atonality music score
systemic governing
patterns

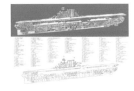

1953 Yorktown Class
Carrier
performative
organizational logics

Elegy
Robert Motherwell
reference and reduction

comes the palette with its physical matter dictating form and deciding honesty of articulation.

— While minimalism is resistant to development (gridded or diagrammatic, repeated modules, harmonic rhythms, and emphasis on a regularity);[4] New Essentialism is bred in the local disruption, the response to nature and opportunity of the predicament within the system.

— While minimalism is non-allusive, non-representational, and non-referential[5] ("Minimalist painting is purely realistic (meaning reflexive) the subject being the painting itself")[6]; New Essentialism emerges from the vernacular reference to history and its legacy of form. It builds complexity out of the association with precedent yet establishes independence from its baggage through a differential evolution of sensibility. Its subject is its own experience but this perception and interpretation always exists relative to memory and history.

— While minimalism flattens perspective through an emphasis on surface and planarity and is anti-illusionistic (neutralization of depth with image as reflection);[7] New Essentialism engages the optical, atmospheric, and emotive to create perceptual effect.

— While minimalism is the reductive element;[8] New Essentialism is the complexity of the simple; the low-fidelity of the elaborate.

— While minimalism is anti-temporality; New Essentialism is dedicated to the fleeting experiential moment of engaging the permanent. As a result of the serious nature of the formal method, the experience requires slowness to its engagement. The result is a foregrounding of one's perception. The composition requires the viewer to load the work with one's own experiences, beliefs, and knowledge through engagement to establish perception. This differs from an object with formal complexity or ornament with directly built-in content, lushly provided to allow the viewer to gorge upon its overtness. The more emaciated sensibility requires baggage to accompany the experience to individually and authorially engage with autobiographical content. The architecture is the interface of the emotive with the physical.

— While minimalism is anti-historical,[9] New Essentialism is trans-historical in its essential quality.

To produce a comprehensive argument about the methodology of New Essentialism, its logic must be inclusive rather than reductive. The complexity of everything is expanding, but New Essentialism must engage a distilled version that through the pixilation of the image reveals its primary traits. The premise of New Essentialism can only be described through its sensibilities as ingredients in a larger approach. Their collective allows for the description of a method. It is beyond minimalism. It is towards a New Essentialism.

New Essentialism is a belief that "things have a set of characteristics that make them what they are, and that the task of science, philosophy, and architecture is their discovery and expression. The doctrine that "essence is prior to existence."[10] is critical to the design process.

New Essentialism / Material Architecture

New Essentialism is the disciplined pursuit of more through the complexity of less. Less however must not rely upon the referential platonic primitives or the even the evolved simplicity of vernacular form. The reduction with complexity comes through tweaking referential origins and expanding their capabilities through disruptions, modifications, and moments of destabilization from the typical. This requires a dedicated understanding and mastery of effectual perception – in New Essentialism the legibility of the eye along with the sensory perception of the body through its scale and movement dictate the experience and orchestration of light and material. These elements become the governing evaluators of the sensibility. New Essentialism emerges from material and form but is evaluated through perception.

New Essentialism is an offering of methodical sensibilities innate in geometry, material, and function combining to create a design methodology. This synthesized logic as an emergent and responsive method is now only just possible through the technological and material capabilities that have allowed for anything but offered nothing. New Essentialism presents a cohesive argument for a solutionism that synthesizes the traditions of architecture with contemporary culture, technology, and practice. It is founded in the following tenants each describing a method and touch point for engagement. New Essentialism is responding to:[11]

— Abstract expressionism and figural sensibility of method rooted in emotive sensibilities with systemic processes of creation. These historically never translated effectively into architecture. New Essentialism pursues the idea of process based on logics of systematized design.

— Minimalism culminated in the rejection of the purification of modernism by reducing the medium to its components and displaying those components overtly: a single pigment or material, a single line, a systemic deployment. New Essentialism pursues the singularity of the idea but through the systematized evolution of the diagrammatic verb or operation. The ability to act upon the figure to iterate and evolve within the system establishes the conceptual methods of systematized design.

— The characteristic reduction to an undifferentiated holism or all-over pattern: the field, the grid, the regularity of the geometric scheme. New Essentialism is marked by the evolution of this system to respond to the local and iterate through the technology of design and production the ideals of mass customization and the founding of responsive rationales within the overall system to provide for localized and individuated moments, or disruptions, within the larger design.

— Repetition as a basic structural component of all classical composition is transposed in modernism to overt and simple repetition as a structural or modular principle. New Essentialism challenges the order to remain within the body as a latent and complex system with hiccups and deviations that introduce the downbeat and individuation of the moment (time) into the overall design.

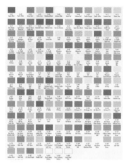

enamel color chart
production of finites

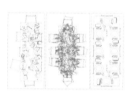

increasing disorder in a dining table
Sarah Wigglesworth and Jeremy Till
action and order

Earth from movie *Noah*
all over weather

flock of birds
responsive systemic logics
of the natural order

— Anti-artifice: New Essentialism eliminates the tyranny of form and iconographic reference to allow for a spatial and effectual domination. The body and our perception and experience are paramount and magnified. Set at the center, the effect of space is the primary driver or perception.

In New Essentialism the complexity of form is rooted in its perception. It is founded upon the sensibility of its intention where the reciprocal user experience marries the idea to the physical. New Essentialism questions the role of composition transitioning form to experience. This offers a new reading on the legacy and potential of architecture.

MANIFESTO: TIME TO
THOUGHTFULLY MAKE[12]

"The search is what everyone would undertake if he were not stuck in the everydayness of his own life. To be aware of the possibility of the search is to be onto something. Not to be onto something is to be in despair."[13]

-Walter Percy
The Moviegoer

The simple task of writing what one believes establishes a vantage of perception. The responsibility and self-reflection to eloquently express and the infrastructure of rules that govern a way of thinking and designing is essential to reflect, analyze, and respond. Advancement is grounded in this cycle. It is an infinitely cyclical process: organically organized as a snapshot of simultaneous arrival and departure. At the moment of this undertaking, the framework of reflection and analysis is a critical interrogation of the self and the work relative to an interpretive reading of the history of architecture within a cultural moment. The method combines the analytical with the self-prescriptive as an intrinsically creative construction. The result is a peripheral glance of a descriptive catalog of thinking. If the manifesto is made, this is an attempt to implement.

The framework for interpretation and engagement is rooted in some critical underpinnings. I am an American architect practicing in the threshold of a new millennium.[14] This work is founded in an engagement with the complexities of architecture and the desire to identify an emergent trajectory founded on (while also advancing) the systemic rationales that have governed the forms and processes of architectural thinking over centuries of evolution. Finding ourselves on the forefront of a technological and information revolution, this is a critical moment in social evolution and architecture has an opportunity and responsibility to define itself and the future of this transition. Change and renewal is occurring and architecture must engage the collective conscious of humankind. This assertion and aspiration has been felt and answered before. It represents too large a responsibility for any one action or undertaking. The premise that a collective movement could bring consensus is a dated and flawed belief. Cultural, political, social, religious, and economic deviations alone have grown too divergent to establish collectivism. The intention for advancement and aspirational intentions to feed to the roots of creative inquiries remains critical nonetheless. This is precisely the purpose of this text: an extension in the chain of my work and its evolution directed towards the discourse of the profession and the evolution of architecture as a whole.

"Philosophy unties knots in our thinking; hence its results must be simple; but philosophizing has to be as complicated as the knots it unties."[15]

-Ludwig Wittgenstein
Zettel #452

constructed perspective
actual form to percieved
form

Pantheon + Villa Savoye
collage

Chema Madoz
interconnected differential
obects

THE NOBLE MEANS OF ARCHITECTURE:
A Definition of Premise

What is architecture? The necessity of such a definition is to establish the specific thinking that governs the ensuing underpinning rationale of motivation and methodology. This establishes the roots of all processes governing both the thinking and the making.

To begin to define such an undertaking it is imperative to address both the complexity and associated baggage of language. The palimpsest layers of historical implementation and the diverse thresholds of interpretation makes projective writing about architecture a nearly impossible task as one quickly becomes read against (and potentially caught within) these legacies. The associative properties of nearly every term requires a re-definition (or at least a specification) of the intention and the context. To commence discourse about architecture one must establish a lexicon: a personal vocabulary that specifically illuminates one's position and interpretation. Architecture has a long history in need of reversibility. This begins with a definition.

Fundamentally, architecture is everything. It is a systemic approach to a creative process. Its product and media is anchored around space, but the halo of disciplines and methods surrounding this encompasses everything. This fundamental premise opens the parameters of consideration and opportunity for the discipline. All aspects are important and relevant. At its most essential, the unassailable aspiration of architecture is *artful simplicity*. Simplicity can only emerge out of holistic and complex thinking. Broad understanding, inclusion, and fervent iterative production provide the path to integrative simplicity. The artist endows it all with philosophical resonance and meaning.

Architecture is innately associated with shelter. As a fundamentally human need, it is as essential as food. Shelter is consumable, functioning with critical responsibility. It relates to our body and its needs relative to the realities of the natural world. Architecture, like love, elevates building from the functional to the aspirational, moving from the dogmatically definable to the ephemeral and spiritual. This is the point of translation into an art. Here the roots of the relationship with shelter are questioned and elaborated upon.

ARCHITECTURAL SELF

The delineation of an individual's relationship to Architecture establishes an intrinsically personal identity defining a methodology for how one can proceed as a designer. As an author in a creative endeavor there must be an underlying spirit that drives the work and the sensibilities one pursues. This establishes a mission and a line of inquiry. Architecture must begin with the aspiration to trans-

hydra
simultaneous multiplicity

the primitive hut
Marc-Antoine Laugier

form. As architecture defines the world in which we live through its encompassing physical presence, we must challenge it to lead humanity. The opportunity to advance the discipline as a critical step cannot become overwrought with novelty nor can it become indulgent with self-sensibility. Novelty is a pitfall of singularity. It represents heightened engagement with a singular facet as opposed to a comprehensive whole. The danger of the celebration of any singular working method is that it limits the diversification of the conversation and thus reduces the Darwinian opportunities for architecture to respond with multifaceted intelligence. Design must find a medium without losing autonomy.

COMPLEXITY OF CONTEXT

Architecture is everything all at once. As a creative undertaking it is an art and a science and a service. By its very nature it necessitates engagement with broader constraints. Physics, budgets, codes, clients, sites, programs, et cetera, all establish parameters and relationships. Connected to the lineage of history while emergent from place, need, and opportunity; architecture is necessarily affected by myriad forces. Like the hydra, architecture has multiple heads and must respond to numerous constraints considerations simultaneously coalescing into a single body. Architecture must establish responsive forward movement of what humanity is, can be, and should be.

Now, more than ever, our contemporary cultural context is challenged by substantive issues of globalism, technology, energy, natural resources, and cultural and sociological diversity all relative to the scale and sustainability of mankind's practices. This context has bred an intertwined and combinatory complexity. Issues of political governance, economics, and cultural relativism are each individually complex and when commingled as a collective organism, become impossible to affect without a total engagement. The diversification and proliferation of information and knowledge has produced an intellectualism founded in a specificity of localized depth that prohibits the possibility of interconnected breadth. The Renaissance Man is dead. The full spectrum understanding and comprehensive thinking that allowed inter-associations and provided a synthetic combination of art, the natural sciences, philosophy, and religion is no more. Finite knowledge is no more. The new emergence is a multi-disciplinary collaboration that employs team methodologies to combine the diverse talents of varied disciplines to privilege the collective and preclude the assertion of the individual. The architect has a responsibility between. Their voice must not be drowned out for the sake of the collective as the amalgamation needs choreography. This hybridized method of operation allows for a persistence of traditionalist attitudes of the romantic individualist and the associative opportunities of intuition. Intuition provides from within oneself something that is greater than the sum of the parts (the individuated bodies of knowledge that one holds in reserve and the ability to assemble them with a conscious hint of where things are going balanced by a deeper internal subconscious reflex). Standing on the shoulders of experience the ideal manifestation of intuition provides for the illumination of the authorial self. The reflex with intention offers the collaborative a leader.

The Noble Means of Architecture

THEMATIC INGREDIENTS

The topical themes that are touchstone consider-ations of an architectural project (and determine the primary components of most academic curricula) include: organizational and effectual logics; historical traditions and precedents; performative technolo-gies; materials and methods of construction; and the necessary legalities and service responsibilities surrounding practice. Each of these has subset considerations and opportunities for engagement with myriad considerations that must be evaluated in hierarchy and dominance. The following examines them individually.

ORGANIZATIONAL AND EFFECTUAL LOGICS

Design at its base is a systemic approach to mak-ing. It is a methodology applied to intent providing a process by which to create. Through the history of architecture different systems have emerged. Some of these systems are based in referential rules to establish order and prescriptive ratios to construct proportions [Classicism]; while some techniques use methodologically based tools to create responsive or data driven form; while some use social contexts to engage systemic solutions; and others use tectonic logics of material systems to establish a design language. In any scenario the rationale of the method provides the structure for the evolution of the design. An initial intention must be rigorously pursued to result in a well-crafted and self-resolving object. The object itself must bridge to inform the perception and evaluation of the viewer. The reading of a resulting affinity is always relative to the viewer's own sense of self and their preferences that emerge from the aggregated sum of their life experiences and associated judgments on these experiences. An object can be simultaneously dubbed fundamentally off-base in the premise of its application or exquisitely calibrated. This is where the philosophical association of aesthetics and the personal intellectual structures of one's experience and emotive response of what one "likes" governs the perception. The rigor of essential design should transcend such conditions of style or preference. Essential design should provide from premise until execution a self-justification through its talent and cleverness.

To accomplish this rigor requires a deep and embed-ded understanding of rational principles of systemic order along with the emotive characteristics of ex-perience. From the spiritual effectual capabilities of space, light, and material to the organizational logics of plan typologies, to more general principles of sym-metry, hierarchy, and proportion;[16] an understanding of the traditions and techniques of architecture is essential. Through their mastery and their collective deployment the designer can synthetically create and extend the lineage of architecture.

HISTORICAL TRADITIONS AND PRECEDENTS

A deep understanding of historical precedent, their originating rationalities and effectual outcomes is critical to fuel the foundations of a creative process. To advance design, it must be emergent from, in reference to, and thus a part of history. Working the

blowerless air conditioning system
functional form

Tauba Auerbach
50/50 VI
effectual field

FA-18 going transonic
the invisbile visible

"wet edge" of the creative process, a referential leg-acy is critical to establish the rationality of a method. To insert into the conversation one must engage it. Any reading of a creative endeavor is relative to its context, and thus an awareness of this context is essential to design within it.

If we look at history as both a palette and an im-mersive condition that we can selectively reference and engage, we must require an anachronism and detachment from the rationale from which it origi-nated. Form as a lexicon has a rationale. Style only exists if you remove the content of association from the intent. A driving premise is what something does as a foregrounded rationale for its being. The mass and diversity of culture introduces whimsy and simulacrum as a more dominant condition. The artifice of the form is easily overridden but scrutiny of its rationale must remain.

PERFORMATIVE TECHNOLOGIES

Performative technologies are those design conditions that require functional responses at their origins. Temperature, energy efficiency, structural stability, sound, light, et cetera, are all pragmatic demands that must be answered. Rooted in technical responses, these functionalist answers must be integrated and synthetically engaged as design opportunities. The larger process requires a holistic understanding of both: (1) the principles to establish the design sensibility, followed by (2) the detailed technical execution. Architecture is perpetually creating a "new product;" a custom one-off. As a result each undertaking, though rooted in traditions and systems of experience, must begin with answering the most fundamental of questions of building firmness.[17]

Each of these performative technologies emerges from specific contextual constraints responsive to natural systems and ecological forces. Their technical responses and mechanical systems have evolved as elaborately detailed and repetitively deployed tradi-tions. These products must be understood relative to their originating forces that facilitate their being. This synthetic integration provides the performative with an essential core sensibility. Understanding the forces that drive both the natural and human-made world is a fundamental point of departure for any designer. Many forces lack visual manifestation despite their significant physical and environmental effect. Psychological space, social space, political space, economic space, and even much of the natural world, exists at diverse micro or macro scales that render them seemingly invisible. These systems, though not overt, remain critically relevant. When an aircraft moves through air it creates a series of pressure waves in front and behind it. As the aircraft reaches the speed of sound (761 mph at sea level)[18] these waves are forced together, compressing and aggregating into a single shock wave. A sonic boom is the associated sound at this threshold replicating an explosion. The moment of occurrence realizes a transformative threshold where speed traverses the responsive boundary of sound and converts from one systemic operation and mechanism into another. The invisible becomes visible.

Architecture must confront, address, and reside in the overtness of such opportunity. These moments are celebrations of the synthetic combinatory mode that allows for a cross connection of elements. Here the re-appropriation[19] allows and facilitates a recombination of perception and understanding relative to the traditions of our known world. It is only through the challenge of these functional boundaries that one can release the sensibilities and standardized logics to find innovation.

MATERIALS: MADE, ASSEMBLED, CONSTRUCTED

Materials are the matter by which a thing is made. Its presence is as equal as the designer in dictating performance and form. This assertion establishes a critical interface and collaborative responsibility. Understanding of the fundamental capabilities of the material itself as well as its associative tools, crafts, and traditions of construction (both as a root material and as product) is a critical point of a design's departure. How something is made, fabricated, assembled, and constructed is critical to its realization and integrity. This assertion of material dominance is true of the painter, the sculptor, and the architect equally.

LEGALITIES OF AND SERVICES OF PRACTICE

Practice is a term that engages the professional mode of architecture. The contemporary definition of practice positions architecture as a service based profession responding to client based need. In this narrative, a design problem is formulated and brought to the architect with differing amounts of opportunity and constraint. This positions the project and its diverse constituents as critical components. The continuity of the architect's work, personal vein of inquiry and thematic interests evolve relative to opportunity shifting the trajectory of thinking. They must jog, absorb, and respond to the varied callings and opportunities afforded. This, by its very nature, establishes the work not as a self-motivated trajectory but rather an evolutionary process: a design technique that is challenged and nurtured by the happenstance of opportunity and the diversity of conditional need.

This erratic origin to the project itself is further complicated by the architect's moral responsibility. When given the opportunity of a project, the architect becomes servant to the multiple masters of: client, city, and the social continuity of society as a whole while maintaining an extension of their personal art and approach. This moral imperative between the "self" and the "collective constituencies" must be reconciled and mediated through the resulting object. The composition manifests all of these influences.

Fountain
Marcel Duchamp
the making of meaning

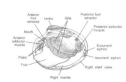

anatomy of a clam
responsive form

PRECEDENT
Thresholds and Transitions

The enormity of this responsibility, particularly when challenged by the elongated time line of a project and the multiplicity of localized decisions that must occur to provide for the collective resolution, exemplifies the complexity of practice.

The following five sections describe five significant thresholds in architectural thinking. Each project introduces a significant new sensibility that resonates as a touchstone principle critical to contemporary design thinking. An examination of a representative precedent allows for an unpacking of their origins to provide insight into a methodology of design thinking: *New Essentialism*. It supplies precision without prescription and defines an arena of formal investigation through a methodological basis.

The ability to produce design pragmatism (alongside the blurred sensibilities of combinatorial influences of cultural and artistic practice) requires the experiential to be privileged. Through material manipulation, rooted in conceptual, effectual, and geometric dominance of form; the approach implies a new opportunity for architecture. Joining a discourse that is broad in nature and responsive to the larger cultural construct beyond just the well-trodden historical precedents of our own discipline, *New Essentialism* provides an opportunity to insert and intertwine our thinking with the realities of the world. This multi-faceted approach of integrative innovation and creative synthesis provides the opportunity for architecture to transcend disciplinary relevance to offer a cohesive and referential integration of the collective consciousness of our time, place and era.

Each of the following five themes illuminates critical transitions in the historical evolution of our discipline. These analytical case studies are coupled with five clustered and generative investigations into future practice. The analytical historical precedents: (1) begin with the privileging of formal systems and their engagement of geometric and rational yet abstract systems to create architectural experience through the promenade; (2) they move into an integrative relationship of form with material introducing atmosphere, phenomenology, and perception as modes of engaging spatial and formal constructs through experience; (3) they integrate performative functionalism of structure as a generative technology that demands overt expressionism of the tectonic logic rendering the intrinsic physical forces previously subordinated; (4) the hyper-engagement of geometric systems as overarching logics that provide rule sets and specific formal languages for organizational tactics (integrating synthetically the urban gesture of the elemental façade to organize and gather subordinate spaces within a single cohesive composition); (5) and ultimately an engagement with the fabrication techniques and material properties emergent from the innovation of transparency and the serial production of the industrialized assembly line to create an architecture rooted in parts, assembly systems and construction techniques transforming architecture into a deeper performative relationship emergent from materials.

Each of these critical thresholds and historical evolutions identify primary themes that underpin the contemporary architectural inquiry. They are critical touchstones of design thinking representing discrete ways of understanding both the overarching conceptual opportunities of their themes as well as more compartmentalized and individuated regulatory constructs that imply techniques and traditions for the detailed articulation of form.

In response to these thresholds and precedents, there are similarly five families of design inquiry that interrogate processes through design propositions. (1) Beginning with the single-family domestic house as a typology, the *20 propositions for suburban living* is a deep investigation of the ubiquitous American condition providing an opportunity to look at domesticity through the diverse lenses and cultural forces that influence and evolve its thinking in contemporary society. (2) The *[X]perience Mechanisms* and *spaceframes* focus on the primal opportunities surrounding experience and perception in architecture. Engaging a series of architectural fragments and domestic rituals as an opportunity for the cultivation of discrete phenomenologically based curated experiences, these prototypes suggest both the formal opportunities of everyday moments as well as a re-conceptualization of architecture's ultimate responsibility. These culminate in a production of momentary experiential relationships that begin to create environments into which the viewer must enter and perceive. (3) *Intensity Frames* is a series of iterative systems founded in diverse expressions of aggregated structural forces that are overtly celebrated as visual compositions through variable rule-based systems derivative of their primal geometric relationships. (4) Through the *Tower House* (a conventional residential renovation addition project) there is a deep inquiry of architecture through a ubiquitous condition. Modifying a single-family postwar house with a modest budget and conventional program, the project develops a series of spatial details and material conditions that allow the architecture to be both expressive and responsive to the traditions, pragmatics, legalities, constraints, and functionalities of the building type. (5) Engaging material's role in perception, a series of installations (*Light Frames, Density Frames*, and *Furlined*) create fully immersive environmental conditions founded in a relationship of materials in space to engage light and experience. This combination of affects is governed by principles and formal types that emerge from structural logics rooted in the material systems. Iterative in nature, the series of investigations suggest a broader inquiry of material to experience.

collective figuration

Collectively these five chapters offer a diverse array of methodological approaches to varied principles that confront contemporary practice. Their approach and methodology suggest tactics beyond their specific design solutions providing a broader sensibility about where architecture and a *New Essentialism* of thinking must reside.

These investigations address architecture to provide opportunities to reconsider the legacy of the discipline and to confront the realities and responsibilities of what it must become. Integrating multi-dimensional thinking (to offer sophisticated answers to complex problems) with the formal, effectual, and compositionally spatial disciplinary roots of architecture, provides a mechanism for the discipline's enlightenment of the human spirit. We must exceed the functional. We must over exert the pragmatic. We must over respond to the performative. We cannot lose sight of our broader mission and the humanity of the person based nature of architecture for any distractive tool, method, or morphology. We must assert a *New Essentialism* for our discipline. We must confront the growing responsibility of our thinking. Only through this aspirational methodology can we endow humanity with the creative opportunities of the built environment.

36

THRESHOLDS AND PROPOSITIONS:

Precedents and generative inquiries

RE-VISIONING

TYPOLOGY

MEANING
Function, Materiality, and Aesthetics

"The significance of the work is in its effort, not its intentions." [20]

- Richard Serra

Architecture is not a portable object. It is not a work that can be relocated. It is a work that deals with environmental components of given places. It emerges from a specific need, at a specific time, in a specific place. Its scale, size, position, and experience are determined by the place. Through its addition, it restructures (both conceptually and perceptually) the organization of the place. Architecture is not an object to be singular but rather demands to be synthetic with its context. The historical concepts of formal hierarchy and order and their effectual associated separation (similar to placing sculpture on a pedestal to establish a break between the object and the viewer) announces significance but similarly removes the object from continuity. The erasure of these introduces a synthetic behavioral space in which the viewer interacts with the architecture in its context.[21] Through place one can find meaning.

ARCHITECTURE AND ITS CONTEXT

Space is the sum of successive perceptions of place. The viewer becomes the subject. One's identity as a person is closely connected with the experience of space through place.

MAKING

The process of making something is as critical an interest and importance as the result. Architecture must adopt the elemental concepts of material and process, mass and weight, scale and experience, and site and context. By engaging physical materiality, (even the cheap and easily available) architecture can reject the traditions of hierarchy. Intrinsically, there must be concern to avoid the engagement of the surface and the ornament of material over the effect. In Richard Serra's list of verbs:

"to roll, to crease, to fold, to bend, to twist, et cetera," he *"was very involved with the physical activity of making. ... It struck (him) that instead of thinking about what a sculpture is going to be and how you're going to do it compositionally, what if you just enacted those verbs in relation to a material, and didn't worry about the result? So (he) started tearing and cutting and folding lead."* [22]

This premise offers an architectural translation. The use of industrial materials is long standing and fundamental to the making of buildings but the requirement of transcendence is their translation to an architectural New Essentialism. The action of material process provides translation through its

double negative
Michael Heizer
the making of place

Larry Poons studio
residuals of process

fundamental association with making. This indulgence in the physicality and the lack of association that materials can offer provides for abstraction of object. The abstraction of architectural space provides something different still. Emergent from material composition, it can position the spectator in a different relationship to their perception delivering aspects of human experience that figuration and referential formalism cannot. Its exploratory indulgence is essential.

In Rosalind E. Krauss' 1986 essay for MOMA on Richard Serra, she applies Maurice Merleau-Ponty's phenomenological characterizations of perception to understand his work. In her view Serra is "strip[ping] the work of art of all possible illusionism," creating "a field force that's being generated, so that the space is discerned physically rather than optically," and establishing chiasma, "a relationship of crossing and exchange" that marks the "mutual interaction of seer and seen."[23] This view is reiterated in the 1998 Dia catalogue essay by Mark Taylor where he argues that Serra's art, unlike that of Robert Irwin, Larry Bell, James Turrell, and Bruce Nauman, is "not opting for opticality as its content. It has more to do with a field force that's being generated."[24] Further, Taylor extends Krauss's conclusion by stating: "By creating space that is in motion, Serra folds temporality into spatiality."[25] Architecture must do the same.

MEANING
[AND THE COMPONENTS OF MEANING]

To mean is to be.[26] The ability to embody content into an inanimate object is the basis of creative culture. The prescriptive nature of an object's original designed intention and its actual interpretation and reception are disparate issues. Born of an individual through the thoughts, actions, and intentions of the designer, the life of an object truly begins through the interpretation of its being.

The object's designer and their design process are the initial choreography of the meaning of an object. Identity is instilled in the object through its form and performance. The form thus conveys what any object wants to say. The performance determines its utility.

The language of architecture is a formal one. The architect thus must master his or her relationship with form. However, form as a destination in itself is not possible as function (at the base instigating level for existence or at the professional level of life, safety, and welfare) will and must intrinsically exist to be architecture. As a result, the justification of architecture based solely on form is not possible. Form must always be countered by its performance and its experience. The essence of the architecture is in this simultaneity. The ideal architecture must synthesize diverse areas of knowledge. It is only through their confluence that architecture can exist. It is through the complexity of issues, their harmonious unification and synthetic convergence that beauty emerges. Architecture is found in this confluence. The juncture must first however rest on elemental understanding. These touchstones are driving authorities in the process: function, material, experience, beauty, nature, and context.

FUNCTION

An object's function positions its use. The task that is set out for the object to accomplish determines an essential responsibility. It must work. The rubric of evaluation is broad. The idea that an object can exist without function is perhaps impossible. Sculpture can be challenged as an object without function, but sculpture assumes the function of confrontation, interpretation, and inspiration; each with deep burdens of responsibility and aesthetic function. Any function can be the instigation of any object. Function is not singular. Function is not solely instilled upon its point of creation (a rock can be a round tool, a sharp edge for cutting, a blunt face for hammering, yet the creation of the rock never assumed such responsibilities).

MATERIAL

Material is essential to form. Material has intrinsic qualities of performance, manufacturing processes, and formal capabilities. Thus the associative qualities of any object are distinctly intertwined with the material and its tools and processes of production. What something is made of and how something is made determines the characteristics of its presence. Matter, method, tool, and the systemic logics of their interface emerge as critical touchstones of how something is made. These processes govern the product.

Materiality is subject to constant critical reassessment and expansion. It is no longer the simplicity of nineteenth-century materialisms (such as Gottfried Semper's theory of material change)[27] solely rooted in truth to materials. Phenomenological engagement with experience, embodiment, and affect, generate a critical shift to the material qualities, the thingness, and the atmospheric nature of its engagement. Ecology, sustainability, energy, and ethics have introduced a performative moralism. Fundamentally the specific role and meaning of materials verses the implications of form or idea offer an architecture that operates through the material rather than solely the conceptual.

In "Spiritual Materiality," Klaus Ottman asserts that the 1939 American critic Clement Greenberg's essay "Avant-Garde and Kitsch" can be considered a modern descendant of Gottfried Semper's materialism.[28] Semper defined art by the parameters of material and technique. Greenberg extends this to include the "pure preoccupation with the invention and arrangement of spaces, surfaces, shapes, colors, et cetera, to the exclusion of whatever is not necessarily implicated in those factors."[29] This extension implicates the material through the process to engage the ancillary effectual conditions. Further, the French structuralist Roland Barthes suggests that "instead of a mechanical-materialistic formalism, an object's materiality as theoretical act as it is this structuralist activity that defines the object. Establishing the constraints and condition of physicality, the material comes with a regimented rule system and encircling logic within which it must function."[30] As materiality provides physicality it "makes something appear which remained invisible, or if one prefers, unintelligible, in the natural object."[31] Materials thus exist [1] relative to their purity, [2] relative to their larger systems and affectual readings, and [3] relative to

exploded engine
the articulation of the part
to assembly

Homage to the Square
Josef Albers

Homage to the Square
Josef Albers
essential optical
effectualism

the constructed processes intrinsic to their being. This tripartite combinatory consideration has a primal essentialism in design thinking that attributes meaning to materials themselves. Material demands that the viewer share responsibility with its being. Through its engagement there is participation with the authorial creator to facilitate the object. American visual artist Roni Horn illustrates this by establishing in the viewer's responsibility stating: "I address the bodily and not just the mental/non-physical being. The viewer must take responsibility for being there, otherwise there is nothing there."[32] This is a critical assertion of a mind to body to material integration.

PRIMITIVISM – ESSENTIALISM – [X]PERIENCE

The ideal of primitivism comes from a quest for essentiality. It is a bluntness that in its crude and basic nature allows for a multi-dimensional starkness. Complexity breeds an ornamental quality of the non-essential. Adornment, decoration, and embellishment distract through their additive nature to supplement inadequacies in the original object itself. The lack of essentialism to ornament is what defines it as an extraneous and additive enhancement. The object of origin (the thing to which ornament is being applied) demands an intrinsic sense of being. The innate beauty of things is core to the essence.

BEAUTY

To define beauty one must establish a datum. This can be defined through numerous methods: adoption, breeding, evolutionary, referential, or methodologically established. Beauty's greatest potency comes through a shared sensibility or transference of thinking from the individual to a collective. Though beauty is not absolute or fixed, and remains relative to emotive thought and interpretation, categoricals can be determined. Newness is often confused with beauty, as differentiation is a desired stimulant to the known. The duration of this qualifier is critical and leads to issues of impermanence and temporal relevance. Beauty is an evaluative tool, not a generative one and thus relative to design process it has value and presence only in the feedback loop. Beauty must emerge from the systemic logic of the inception. Formal ugliness may be beautiful if rigorously generated. The conceptual rule and the rigor of its execution are of paramount consideration.

NATURE AND ARCHITECTURE

To build is to make a mark in and on the landscape. This act of violation is an operation into an already perfect system every architect must consider. No matter how seemingly forsaken or inhospitable a geographic condition, the natural and physical contexts are a crucial frame of operation. The truest mark on the landscape is one which adds for the better to the condition. Simulation of nature is a poor replication. Contradiction in geometry and prismatic contrast (that which nature cannot provide as a poetic frame for itself) is where architecture can respond with originality and authenticity. The ability of the datum to impose regularity upon the organic creates a harmonic foil. The logic within itself allows for subset irregularity to occur as moments of oscillation within and against this sensibility. The two together create a dynamic scenario with a complementary dialogue. Design as the manifestation of an idea must emerge from an additive benefit. It cannot be a distraction from that which we have come to forget but a connection to it.

The city is an organic entity that deserves equitable consideration. The city has an ecology with vastly different systemic logics from the natural world. It lacks poetry and essentialism. Survival as the essential driver of the natural world has bred efficiency and authenticity of essentialism through evolution. Man's diffused focus and inefficiencies embodied in the city are at the root of all global problems. War, energy, waste, hierarchy; these are all things that natural systems have readily dealt with and found harmonic balances that not only mediate the situation but optimize the rationale for their existence. Architecture must aspire for this optimized simplicity.

Nature is the fundamental. It provides the primal meta-systems (wind, water, temperature, et cetera) that architecture must address and compliment. Every part of architecture must engage this condition. A window must have a dialogue between inside and out; a door must have a relationship with the body; et cetera. Architecture must compose these interfaces.

There are three primary conditions. Nature as a pre-existing super-structural condition is on one side. Technology as an artificial and created systemic construct of our own rationale and scientific condition is on the other side. Humans are the middle condition as a part of both but consistently oscillating between and across each as a hybrid.

Prosthetics of technology through information and collective connectivity have grown as synthetic appendages to our biological selves. The automobile, the laptop, the Internet, the smart phone, the Fit Bit, the Google Glass, these all become elements of liberation and simultaneously natural degradation. The synthetic linkage of body to mind to information creates a new problematized context to which architecture must respond. The discipline is no longer simply the performative requirements of safety from the environment but a new responsibility to build on the social and to directly relate to our spiritual interface with technology.

Technology as a construction of humans has a predicated systemic logic. This is created and thus readily derivable in the things that we make. The natural world can equally be mapped into systemic rules that balance how operational systems govern relative relationships. The understanding of these systems provides for opportunity to engage and control them. An upstream relationship with these control points creates a mechanism by which the designer can find their authority and affect the outcome.

Critical to this is our current condition. Human scale and multiplicity has reached a tipping point. Our footprint on this world has become bold and is to the point of damaging the reflexive systems of the natural world. We have arrived at a point of destabilization. Set upon the precipice of an irreparable edge, we must consider our actions immediately and retroactively relative to this pending crisis. Architecture stands on the front lines of this conversation. It must respond. It is the new nature.

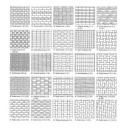

masonry patterns
type and variant

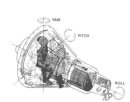

Mercury spacecraft control
anthropomorphic
determinism

CONTEXTUALISM AND PLACE[33]

The role of nature is critically founded upon the specifics of place. If we honor that every locality (both human-made and natural) has a genius loci,[34] then the response to operating within such a condition is the foundation of architecture. Permanence and the specificity of the locality are the conversation a building joins. The filtered attitude of what the additive making process imposes onto the context is a legible condition of being.

Context must be expanded beyond physical constraints to include: histories, economies, legalities, materials, geologies, ethnicities, cultures, and programs as multifaceted readings of place. These conditions (only some of which are visually manifested) are the arena for design operation and response.

Critical Regionalism:[35] the collective sensibility of a contextual approach across a localized area establishes a sensibility of region. Culture, climate, legalities, and even conversational schools of thought create a specificity of design operation linked to place. In the ever expanding homogeneity of globalism, the locality of a region has begun to wane. This individualism must be identified as an essential subset of architectural thinking. During modernism, critical regionalism took the overarching principles of approach and applied them relative to the local condition, need, and community. This operation was a powerful premise offered by Kenneth Frampton in that it provided a conversation with the "meta" intent and the driving influence of a "singular" architecture at a very specific time within humankind's evolution, but then allows for the authorial relativism of the specifics of place, culture, and tradition. Vision of newness and the continuity of the vernacular remain in simultaneous autonomy and a potent intertwined conversation. This approach offers solutions to humanity while maintaining the specificity of local iterative variant.[36]

Vernacular: the vernacular of a place emerges from the traditions and evolutions of locality. Methods of building, forms of growth, cultural affinities are all manifest in the built environment. These forms become a specific disciplinary language that a project must speak to and act within. They hold insights into efficiency and emerge from a simpler condition: one of loose occupation, frank material responses, and instinctual technological engagement. Through these the vernacular provides an essentialism that relates to body, culture, and geography with admirable intensity and precision. These affinities must have a place of honor for design.

The New Condition of the Average: global economic production, a vast network of relatively efficient physical transportation, and the ubiquitous and simultaneous dispensation of information has collectively created a meta-blanket of connectivity. This amalgamation has created a new mode of association with place. The traditional boundaries of "who" and "where" are dissolving. Though one physically exists within a specific context, our virtual interconnection allows for massive cross-pollination on a continual basis. The place of here is no more. As a result there is a new conditional average. In the United States this is most clearly manifest through serial typologies. The most ubiquitous and daily

Meaning: Function, Materiality and Aesthetics

interface of architecture is at the scale of the house. The American manifestation is a specific ideality of residential living: suburbanism.

"When I was in China I learned the character called 'Chung,' which means 'the middle.' The Chinese have a quotation, 'The middle of everything is the best.' We don't have any sense of this middle ground anymore because we're either racing forward too quickly or reacting backward too quickly, thus making extremes meet. And then there's no movement in the circle; the goals become the same."[37]

- **Mark Tobey**
The Artist's Voice

The middle is the average. It is the ubiquitous. It is the field and the point of greatest influence and opportunity for architecture. Engagement with it strikes at the body of the built environment. Here is architecture's greatest opportunity.

The average is a condition that does not truly exist but rather describes the "'middle" of the population in their needs and their perceptions. The intersection occurs in the belly, the heart, a centric locale, defining the place of the everyday. Not concerned with the fringe or the exception but looking squarely at the rule, the essence of the place and the culture of the body and its grouping. The built environment in service of this condition are currently unadorned and ill-considered objects. The advancement of society and social norms accelerates daily yet architecture lags dramatically behind. Emerging cultural and technological paradigms remain trapped in a cultural milieu, as anachronistic collages emergent from the rules, social conventions, technologies, and biases of past eras of production.

The artifacts of the average are the ones that impact daily life. The solution for change is not one of style or form, but rather an intellectual polemic: a belief mechanism that drives the production, consumption, and use of the middle. The insertion of intent provide opportunity for the multi-pluralism of the diversity of intention. The form of function is no longer enough. The aesthetic is not enough. Objects must emerge from and convey a method. The deeper ethics that drive and govern the object holds the potential for making.

The middle landscape is the foothold for architecture. Its gaping lack of design consideration and the untapped scale of its potential demonstrate how the social capacity of architecture remains unused. The impact of the built world is immeasurable, yet the percentage of the built world that is designed with a conceptual consciousness (not to mention the larger polemical determination capable of validation and subscription) remains overwhelmed by the constructed but ill-considered landscape.

WHAT MATTER(S): THE DIVERSITY OF IMPORTANCE

The broad nature and perpetual indeterminacy of the question, "what matters?" requires a continued evaluation and calibration by every architect (and ultimately every individual) to come to terms with how they live their lives. The essential and idealized nature

Michael Heizer
North, East, South, West
Dia Beacon
presence of absence

Donald Judd
chairs
type and variant

of the profession is gone (if it even ever existed). The discrepancy between education and the actualities of critical practice are vast (perhaps strategically) and only growing resulting in a frustration on both parts and complicating the bridge between. The result is a massive disconnect between what architects value and see as opportunity; what society as a whole recognizes in terms of architecture's value; and what the practice is willing to deliver. Architecture has left the hands of the architect and now is placed firmly in the realm of client requiring a visionary request to allow for its provision. The result is a removal of the authority of the architect.

The design of the world has vast impact on how we use and exist in our surroundings and how we interact as a social system. Space is perhaps the most unpredictable and massive opportunity and moment of true conviction that we have as a culture. The loss of its importance (or quite simply the dormant nature of its being) quarantines it into the obscure and holds us small.

The emergence of new methods for framing the practice of architecture through the diversification of methodologies and the deployment of designers into all aspects of society and culture are the opportunity for revolution. A confluence of social, political, economic, and spatial typologies (a return to the Jeffersonian insertion of architecture as a fundamental at the foundation of freedom and democracy); a technological revolution that provides opportunity for the architect to synthesize with craftsman (providing a directness of fabrication and design that unifies construction); and the proactive development of the architect to define the project and facilitate it without the limitation of a client based authorial premise (the investment based model allowing forward movement of the profession to occur pre service as opposed to post service). These models do not eliminate or even erode the current methods of practice but rather serve as diversified methodologies that allow for a speed of adaptability and a deployment of design on a multiplicity of fronts. The complementary nature of a multi-pronged attack allows for the advancement of the position of design in culture.

To establish a path forward, one must be rooted in solutionism. To accomplish this there needs to be some critical touchstones to the premise.

The idea of making is a conceptual and literal model.

There must be a working knowledge of technology that facilitates refinement.

There must be foundational rooting in abstract making.

There must be underpinning in conceptual modeling and graphic capability of thought.

Architecture must emerge from precedent.

Architecture must address site and context.

Architecture must engage the vernacular.

None of these must reference form but must analytically recognize conceptual underpinnings.

Architecture must fabricate a place, emergent from program to orchestrate event.

Architecture must be evaluated in terms of use and phenomenological experience.

Architecture must deal with form relative to the environment.

Architecture must deal with form relative to program.

Architecture must deal with form relative to materials and tectonics.

Architecture must look towards how we fabricate.

THE ULTRAMODERN

The aspiration for architecture to be an extension of the built landscape must be founded in an understanding of the needs, forms, and functions to which contemporary culture subscribes. Architecture is responsive to: the formal, effectual, emotional, and material; and the qualitative nature of space; all in subscription to a higher meaning. As opposed to simply housing culture, architecture is a product of culture and a leader of culture, thus one must begin to understand these cultural foundations that drive its rationale.

Culture refers to ambient society in all aspects of its demeanor, from the machinery to the economics, from the fashion and music to the art and literature that define it. Integrating the popular with the intellectual, culture is all things simultaneously. Culture is an all-encompassing umbrella of activity and environment. The assignment of hierarchy to culture, or to try to order, negate, or elevate certain aspects is futile. Culture is a multivalent field of non-determinism. Information defines a culture. It is the simultaneity of all events, activities, and components. Architecture must respond to this multiplicity.

Traditionally, architecture has been conceptualized and dominantly discussed as form. The roots of architecture are grounded in the proportional two-dimensional rationale of the classical system. This rule based system established in Greek and Roman society, evolved in systemic rigor through the Renaissance, was geometrically expanded in complexity through the Baroque and ultimately exploded in the post-enlightenment era of the modern technological revolution, all the while remaining a self-referential formal system. With the advent of industrialization, the simultaneous introduction of mass-production, a massive population boom, and the introduction of mechanization and technologically based solutions in all aspects of daily life, the context of architecture changed. There emerged a new sensibility highlighted by modernist sensibilities that shifted the focus to space over order. The ambition of architecture was expanded to include the social (the Marseille Block by Le Corbusier), the conceptual (the Barcelona Pavilion by Mies Van der Rohe), and the form based experiential (the Usonian House by Frank Lloyd Wright). These expansionist considerations shifted architectural thinking to now bridge the traditions of an architecture dependent primarily upon a formal order and structure, to an architecture responsive to culture. We still operate in the wake of this paradigm and the dichotomy of these approaches.

This insertion of a cultural attitude demands a broader definition of the responsibilities of the discipline than simply "form follows function."[38] It requires a responsive mechanism that is less descriptive and more interpretive. Though program may remain a viable point of conceptual departure, it is not simply the functional necessities of architectural pragmatism, but rather the associative social and cultural implications and opportunities that must be mined. Typologies must be investigated for their underpinning qualities avoiding the limitations of tradition. Space must be the informing element. Architecture thus must move beyond, expanding conceptual premise to be proactive in shattering the

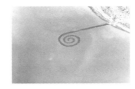

Spiral Jetty
Robert Smithson
place and being

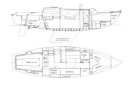

36-foot Cascade
layout to use

traditional subscription to linear sequence, singularity of use, material conventionalism, and even the fundamentals of economic norms. Investment must focus on the social and intellectual premise for the cultural valuation of architectural form. Form remains a critical component. It is the tangible figure that establishes spatial poetics and the emotive qualities of experience. These suggest a greater quality and responsibility to the built artifact.

The result must be founded in liberation, engaging in the complexities and uncertainties. Buildings must stem from a cultural response and the overlay of the architectural intellect, depiction, description, and maintenance. Architecture thus becomes and subscribes to these multiple realms of opportunity.

TERRAIN

Architecture cannot be only the revolutionary. It needs to be the everyday. Currently architecture is rarefied, something few experience, held for discrete moments within an otherwise bland and ill-considered built environment. Even in well-developed communities and cultural cities, we are immersed in bleak landscapes of ignored and unconsidered buildings. The majority needs simple exposure to architecture. Architecture must enter into the system. It must emerge from this infrastructure. It must be ubiquitous.

This requires a reconsideration of the architect's mission. Extremity and innovation cannot be the solely privileged vantage. Clarity of intent and rigor of execution must be the focus. This necessitates a higher level of reading to architecture with sophistication beyond the "different." Skill and craft of technique must establish new touchstones. Newness alone is a detriment.

The territory of operation must be the everyday. The suburban is the landscape in which I was born and now live. Los Angeles and Houston are the hyper exaggeration of the suburban on the edge of "full." Rooted in the American Dream, manifest destiny, and the homestead as an isolated land based ownership system, the horizontal city is both at a point of fruition and crisis. This landscape begins with the house. Residential typologies sociologically describe what it means to dwell locally relative to the evolving trends of collective culture and technology. In the United States the most ubiquitous building block is the single family detached residence. The house as the fundamental architectural composition is a critical point of departure. In it we must augment with a look toward phenomenology, toward form, toward qualities of light, space and material, with each positioned within the spectrum and realities of economy. The solution must come from a place where architecture is gleaned, founded, and orchestrated into and out of the common palette. The product must be a formalization of a culture; a definer of how we live. These subdivisions are component compositions that work as fragments in the larger city. They are the pieces that fill the matrix of urbanity and define the sprawl of the modern megalopolis. The part represents the whole.

To generate architecture that is of its time (now) means that it is ultimately extinguishable and destined to become irrelevant. There need to be moments of extreme contemporary articulation but also a reference to the timelessness of our seemingly static biology (including both the mutability of the products that are included within our routines and the base natural physicality of how we live). The specific must become commutable to permit a uniqueness of formal composition relative a more general condition. A resonance of qualities and traditions that surround objects and their formal objectification within the organizational composition allows for architecture to push culture forward by not being simply avant-garde but rather by remaining feasible and achievable. This is a key tether to economy and the current dominance of a capitalist society. The touchstones are choice in need, competition of priority, cyclicality of economy, cultural sharing, and commonality of product availability.

Much of conventional contemporary building vocabulary has no authorial identity but rather is employed as a regressive decision to look towards the past to fabricate identity and allow architecture to be dictated by tradition rather than culture. The relevancy of the reference is however no longer available and thus results in compositionally hollow falsities. A lack of understanding of the language of architecture compounded by cyclical irreverence of meaning and dependency upon simulation has hollowed the conversation. Architecture is not learned as a language and thus is spoken by very few. Operating in anachronistic dialects poisons the discipline. The authenticity of now has been violated.

The systemic tectonic infrastructures we have to choose from: slab on grade, post and beam, gable roof, et cetera; are not morally bankrupt or corrupt, but rather forms that have come through an authentic legacy and tradition of building. The critical concern is how to embody these types with relevance avoiding anachronistic reference. Their current meaning relative to their original intention must be culturally commuted through the object to re-establish them for employment within our contemporary vocabulary. This leaves architecture with the responsibility to defend and redefine what it can bring to society rather than appease it. This establishes a contradictory model to the service role. It requires that it be forward looking as opposed to being solely responsive. It must avoid being simply collagist and growing from the past as opposed to building upon it. The key must be the assimilation of society and culture via architecture.

As a perpetual "one-off," architecture must repeatedly master client, personality, site, culture, geography, economy, et cetera. It cannot be a serial object for anybody anywhere and so it must define itself as a process. We have created a cultural and consumerist infrastructure that demands such a model but the realities of the system and profession cannot provide it. The underpinning misalignment resides in the fact that the desire of the American Dream and the physical autonomy of architecture as a manifestation of this are rooted in individuality. If we look at the single family detached suburban house as the predominate mode of domestic production in North America, and understand that the house is the largest financial investment an individual will have, then the overlay of individual freedom and personal dream means that the qualities of independent individuality cannot be regulated by desire, but rather are dominated by the fiscal infrastructure

Sun Tunnels
Nancy Holt
object to place

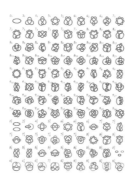

knot theory
systemic logics of ordered
form

that maintains a commutability to the pieces. This tempers the whimsy of personality. The house has to subscribe to the commutable capabilities of the larger system. The system dictates that the house must be "of" a certain quality and these qualities have distinct directions as to the outcome of form, space and experience. This prevents a hyper-tailoring towards an individual and prevents the potential of dispensable and disposable to provide for the house to become an object focused toward multiple people's desires it has to subscribe to a generic medium to maintain commutability through resale.

This generic medium does not imply the lowest common denominator or simply a singular solution homogenizing the entire vocabulary but rather establishes a natural context containing the spectrum of opportunity. This assertion neutralizes fashion and taste as fleeting and provides opportunity for greater touchstones. Function has repeatedly emerged as not enough. There has to be a formal and experiential vocabulary that can rise above this. The traditions of domesticity that make a house in a specific place a home, allow for the translation. This translation must underpin a formal investigation of the domestic type. Architecture emerges from a desire to look at the existing condition, to understand it as commutable, to take on the constraints and conditions of current operation, and from within this system provide opportunities to develop a component within a broader system with a broader series of rules. The product becomes a celebration of inevitabilities, where one loves what one can afford to love and from this generate a composition that can actually be practiced, that can be made, to produce a unique composition that still subscribes to the general principles. This methodology allows for the seriality of a type with a re-interpretive method of domesticity. Challenging the priority of space; the definition and perception of form; the expression of material; the interface of the inhabitant to the object as mediated by the phenomenology of experience; the architecture detaches from features and becomes defined by the contemporary nature of a cultural need. The house becomes a facilitator for event and activity, an enclosure that can house both humans and objects and allows for interface and social interaction of individual to group generating both family and society. The relationships between these networks are facilitated through the activities of simply living. What seems like the mundane is allowed to prosper through the choreography of the situation. That situation is one that is orchestrated through a series of organizational concepts:

MATERIAL TECHNOLOGY

Materiality as the means by which we make is a critical consideration. That which humans can do is different from that which a human typically does. Culture has evolved a class system of material application. Commonality has secured certain inalienable rights through pervasiveness. Technique, code, tradition, and experience determine the way in which we build and result in the forms and organizations typically possible. Technological expressionism of both the tool and technique in collaboration with the physical nature of material things determines processes. Governance of these actualities provide for reconsideration and immateriality. They provide an inroad to reconsidered realization.

PROGRAMMATIC SIMULTANEITY

The singular functional allocation of a space is no more. Functional articulation occurs through the apparatus and configuration of occupation. These specifics allow for the body to do certain things. Biological needs of: eat, bathe, sleep, et cetera, provide for primal goals but technology and its synthesis and ubiquitous portability has blurred any singularity. The body no longer goes to the object. The experience comes to the body.

FORMAL EXPRESSIONISM

Form is like flavor, there are many and they must work in a collective compliment. Some are liked universally, others disliked universally. Diversity is needed to provide a range of thinking to establish relativism: contrast against which form can be read. Form must be derived from the rigors of process. A rule set logic establishes the foundations of both generation and evaluation. These systems of thinking are governors of form.

PHENOMENOLOGICAL SEQUENCE - SPATIAL LAYERING

The experiential is the critical touchstone of architectural aspiration. Everything is an experience. Some are good, some are bad, most are unrecognizable. Full spectrum relativism is important as equity of experiential hierarchy renders everything bland. If brushing one's teeth has the same pomp and circumstance as getting married the significance of either is skewed.

Hereabout
Clement Meadmore
material to form

perspective machine
Albrecht Durer, 1525
constucted ways of seeing

Ritual and serial actions forge moments of remembrance and perspective. These balance and temper our actions. These traditions are the experiences that endow architecture with opportunity. They serially form the social contracts with the world around us. Our scale, dimension, weight, and physical characteristics alongside our humanity, emotion, and active moral codes determine our engagement. The emotive qualities of architecture to engage these remains an essential touchstone.

SPATIAL CONFIGURATION: POETICS OF LIGHT, SPACE, AND FORM

Organization and juxtaposition provide and highlight relativisms. These can complement or shock convention. Space orchestrates the sequence of experiential movement through the choreography of scale, light, and even the "feel" of a condition to provide compositional opportunity for better living. They suggest a greater potential for the synthesis of space and action, intellect and form, body and mind through the denial of any dialectical juxtaposition in favor of defining culture as a combinatory proposition of simultaneity, visual and formal complexity, and architectonic liberation from the marginalization and formal perception that currently dictates its evaluation and development. The subject here is not a replacement but rather a total re-conceptualization of the architectural premise presenting the profession, the product, and the public with buildings that make sense within our culture, our environment of daily activities, and our ways and processes of making, living, remembering, thinking, and advancing. They become a total embodiment of cultural meaning through their process.

CULTURAL CONTEXT
The Time and Place of Operation

"There is simply no real separation line, only an intellectual one, between the object and its time environment. They are completely interlocking: nothing can exist in the world independent of all the other things in the world."[39]

- **Robert Irwin**,
Seeing is Forgetting the Name of the Thing One Sees

- Space is of a culture, in a place, at a time.

- All that we know and understand is relative to our experience.

- Things that are taken for granted can only be recognized when interrogated.[40]

impossible triangle
geometry and percpetion

ARCHITECTURE AND SITE

The premise that a site has a genius loci[41] or spirit is a significant premise for architecture. Its resonance is only increasing as globalism expands with relentless homogeneity and architects engage work farther and farther afield from their localities. This unique nomadic condition of the designer requires a greater responsibility to engage and educate themselves on the specific understanding of place. The sensibility of a place can be read at three broad levels: (1) the natural systems and their legacy of an evolutionary place (this includes the geological evolution, the current ecosystems, and the environmental seasons, constraints, and microcosms that define the pragmatics of being specifically somewhere); (2) the historical evolution of a place through its physical and cultural sensibilities demonstrate a chronology and evolution of events, people, and their physical manifestations to define a place; and (3) the actual current state a site is operating in with the specific details of the context alongside the cultural conditions that are precise to the locality in a specific time and place. These are the physical and cultural backdrops into which an architect is operating and adding. In the collective of these three readings, a total picture of a place emerges. The opportunity to respond to this personality and sense of being is an essential point of departure.

PLACE

Places have specificity. They have orientations, climates, histories, and cultures. Places have neighbors and occupants. The idea of what a place "is," is multifaceted. An experience and understanding of each aspect must be engaged as a critical undertaking in the design process. Architecture is a response that comes through the internalization of place coupled with a positional attitude. Functional requirements, material selections, structural systems, site forms and alignments, climatic responses, all emerge from the context and the history of a place to determine form. Place is the ultimate beginning.

Thai Meterological Department
Weather Chart
July 25th, 2013
conditional localities

CONTEXT

Context is the specificity of the adjacent. It is the relative language of a place: the zoning, the functions, the materials, the scales, the setbacks, and the dimensions. These specifics have emerged over time from tradition and history. It provides the detailed specificity in which a project will operate. Context can provide suggestive relativisms including: programmatic functions, dimensional cues, volumetric and formal cues, material palettes, details of articulation, and performative expressions. Each provides cues and opportunities to engage. To add to a place is to join and thus become a part of a place. Understanding a context, knowing its references, and having a relationship with these conditions is essential. They redefine the place making the addition integrated and now determinate of the locale.

Context can exist independent of a singular physical and finite site. A chair has a conditional context. A building as a more static object should be of even greater association with a context. The response to these localities and sensibilities provides an indicator and responsibility of what it means to be in a locale.

The emerging dominance of globalism is innately problematic to the contextual. To understand the detail, climate, culture, et cetera of a locality takes a sensitivity and submersion to be fluent in the diverse dialects connected distinctly to a project's place. The process of making architecture intrinsically pushes a detachment from site. Teams of designers who work remotely from the site; associate architects that implement the legalities and oversee the execution; a creative making that happens at a distance facilitate a detachment that handicaps the relationship to context. The contemporary architect that provides landmark building in a personal style in diverse locales undermines the power of a place. This model easily lacks the innate sensibility for the architecture to truly understand and accompany place.

A relationship to place is cultivated with attention over time. Architecture must validate this relationship. Though design must be in subscription to higher concepts, principles, and ideals (often formally and conceptually abstract); these must also respond to the locale. This dialogue is what sets architecture as a compositional art apart from the detached nature of painting or sculpture. Architecture operates in the immersed spatial condition. It thus maintains connectivity to its surrounds and demands an associated response.

VERNACULAR

The vernacular of a place expands beyond the immediacy of the local site and context and instead refers to the broader region and its trends, traditions, and historical developments. A vernacular language can develop specific building typologies (dogtrot or shotgun houses of the American southeast) or material systems (North Carolina or Texas brick due to geologic conditions) or traditions of elements (such as the screened porch in the south or the mudroom in the north). Each of these formal and functional elements evolves from the conventions of the place. Typically stemming from climate and its associate needs and provisions from the natural environment (through temperature, geology, plantings, weather, et cetera) that architecture has had to respond to over time, in conjunction with the cultural traditions (trades, lifestyles, and technologies, et cetera); the specificity of the responses to these demands has formed localized solutions that have developed associative morphologies. The repetition of these morphologies has established spatial types that through their seriality have ingrained themselves into the identity of place. Charleston is uniquely different from Nantucket.

These histories and traditions establish a relative condition of pragmatism and formal reference that is unique to architecture. These underpinning sensibilities establish the roots of a place. Understanding these specificities of a place and being able to insert into these origins makes any addition a part of the history and legacy. Architecture must extend these through integration, interpretation, and a representation of their intentions and origins with the updates of contemporary culture and technology. Place, identity, and the iconography of locality emerge from these trends. Architecture must work itself into this understanding.

TYPE

Type emerges from context and vernacular but is typically specific to a building function. The programmatic usage of a space as a classification system provides a precise functional and formal response. The functional needs combine with the traditions and legacies of a place. The locality provides specific iterative types. The details, operations, and configurations of a specific functional type emerge from, and are determined by, the hybridization of the place with the function. Type provides a lineage within which function evolves.

AMERICANISM AND THE LATE 20TH CENTURY

Consideration of where the action and implementation of architecture is to occur requires an engagement of the individual's role within the natural and human-made geography: the regional city. American democracy and capitalism preference the individuated object building. This renders the city never fully "present" as a fabric. It remains a loose weave of open aggregation lacking the density to establish continuity. Hyper-articulation of the object endorsing iconic form with individuated recognition has furthered this divide. Zoning has mandated parceled plots of land requiring independence and self-sufficiency denying the ability for an urban building to dominantly exist in the American landscape. This individuated form coupled with interchangeability has favored the disposable fragment. There is no greater picture; only the localized individuality of the moment. There is no essentialism or permanence. The object must now assume this responsibility.

The American fabric is suburban. As the American condition, it should not be demonized or lamented, but rather accepted as a contextual fact. Though there are intrinsic benefits and drawbacks to this condition, this is the cultural and physical and spatial milieu in which we operate. The suburban is not any one entity's singular creation, but as architects it is now our responsibility. There is fascination in its culture

millstone types
type: form to performative effect

and perception; its popularity and dominance in the American dream. Its lack of design leaves it outside. It must be engaged through growth. Growth cannot follow its current trajectory but rather subscribe to a metabolic growth: a replacing growth that is both constructing and taking apart. Like a body constantly rejuvenating itself, the tissue and organs grow and die simultaneously. It is through this metabolism that we can find a threshold into this conversation, a glimmer of entry and by entering the designer can suddenly steer.

TO BE AN AMERICAN ARCHITECT

The role of nationality in a global economy may seem irrelevant, but somehow remains a fundamental point of origin. We are one in the biological foundations of our perception. Perception is the basis for action either to maintain or change; it is a critical point of departure. Culture, tradition, and associative rituals of living remain connected to the specifics of place and nationality. It is the commingling connection of these two that moves between form and experience.

Space is always present, architects simply shape it. Through objects and the processes of their making, there emerges an ability to convey intention through a language that establishes form. Newness is not an adequate driver as it is self-extinguishing. Newness does however provide a method of evolution. It establishes a perpetual motion that is intrinsically self-denying. It requires consistent seeds of dissatisfaction with what we have done. It guarantees that we can never truly arrive at a destination. This endows dominance to the process. It also generates an intrinsic disposability of architecture. Permanence is an unachievable condition. There is no timeless building. Even civic structures and cultural landmarks have inconsequential life spans when compared to geologic or cosmic time. Change requires their destruction for something new. This is the hyper-exaggerated in the American condition. A new country with vibrant evolutionary processes ingrained in its origins, it has produced a cultural fabric that has no ability to fill-in or grow upon itself. The result is never a palimpsest, but the erasure and the blank slate of the American grid; the block that serves as plinth or canvas; the white frame waiting for something new. Space has become a commodity and amenity linked to the cyclical change of fashion and technology. It lacks self-justification.

It is time for change.

AMERICAN SPACE: OUR SUBURBAN

The nationality of space and the collective culture of origin establish a vantage of engagement and perception. The United States is a country of individuals, grouped together in an agreement of equality. Our collective web of social, political, and economic interconnectivity keeps us consistently in motion but similarly steady in terms of an internal Darwinism. We are built on growth, change, and evolution. Mass-production, mass-media, and the associative mass-appeal facilitated by these are the touchstones of the American way. The collective consciousness of American "likeness" (the things that we share, know, buy, and care about as a group) thread through our individual religious, racial, and cultural diversity to establish interconnectivity through our consumption. We buy the things we like and this shared communality provides for and feeds contemporary culture. In 1999 marketing analyst Laurie Volk of Zimmerman/Volk Associates[42] estimated that in that year, one particular design accounted for as much as thirty percent of all new single family detached housing throughout the country. This homogeneity pervades and defines an American space.

The contemporary American built landscape has evolved as a manifestation of our culture. Throughout history the economics, beliefs, geographies, and technologies of the time have assembled to define the constructed environment. The close dissection and understanding of each of these components provides a clear understanding of the resulting built forms and the mechanisms that produced them.

The diversity of density (from the urban medieval town tightly gathered for security, commerce, and interdependence to the rural dispersion of isolated and independent compounds) has evolved a spectrum of spatial types providing a complete gradient of density. The most recent (and growingly dominant condition) has been the middle; an American type of spatial occupation: the suburban.

The suburban condition has been almost universally condemned as ecologically unsound, ergonomically inconvenient, and aesthetically unattractive. Though these descriptions are accurate, the suburban condition is also a pure spatial manifestation of the overlay of democracy, capitalism, and American agrarian foundation facilitated by geography.

The foundational premise of democracy is the inalienable right of freedom assigned to each and every individual. The right to free thought, speech, and action provides for the flexibility and beliefs of each and every citizen to not only be held, but also defended without fear of persecution. The result is a celebration of difference. The synthesis of cultures, religions, and beliefs establishes the most diverse sociological condition ever created by humans. Its foundation in individuality and independence facilitate the extension of these beliefs into the constructed environment. The formulation of a spatial patchwork of diverse and individually articulated pieces, each associatively connected through a communal circulation infrastructure, defines the methodical parceling of the space and the associated diversity of its occupation and use.

Ian Strange
reinterpretation of the known

Ikea dishwasher tub assembly
part to whole

Capitalism similarly triumphs the simultaneous independence and interdependence of the individual. The relationship of finance to a methodological free trade initiative requires self-sustenance. Individual ability is traded in a single interconnected marketplace. The diversity of each offering is balanced with the associated need and bartered at a relative valuation. As a result the action and offering to the group is valued collectively but governed individually. The ability to make money is dependent upon self-sufficiency in terms of participation, but requires interdependence for the transference and valuation of goods. The individual is thus simultaneously governed only by oneself yet remains inescapably bound to society and the group as a whole. The part and whole are equally essential.

The landscape geography of the new world was rich and untouched and included vast regions of diverse climates, topographies, and ecosystems. The massive scale and abundance of land represented opportunity. Throughout the settling of the new continent, from the development of the eastern seaboard to the manifest destiny of westward expansion, the geographic spreading of place and location presented the individual potential for self-sufficiency ingrained in the pioneering spirit of uniquely "American" values. This presented a new method of spatial development: the singular and independent parceled allotment as the primary spatial building block. Caught between the density of the European city and the loose isolation of the farm or villa, the suburban condition emerged.

At the turn of the twentieth century, the nation faced an exploding population and an emerging technological revolution. The division of labor necessary to accommodate the needs of the assembly line developed a class system and flooded the market with mass-produced affordable products. Workers grew in specialization as trade based crafts were compartmentalized into partial and staged fragments collectively involved in the production of increasingly complex merchandise. The associated technological advancements focused on the production of mechanisms of convenience. The washing machine, dishwasher, air conditioner, and automobile (amongst others) emerged to make menial tasks simpler, faster, and more hygienic. The result was the production of a space governed by speed. The resulting effect was twofold: a spatial collapse (extending the totality of everything into individuated but simultaneous parts) and the production of leisure.

The automobile emerged as an essential facilitator translating the speed and mode of perception of space collapsing both time and distance. The extension of the individual's sphere of influence expanded the boundaries of daily activity and instigated an urban dependence upon the infrastructure of travel. The car extended our isolation by encapsulating our movement while transforming the traditional continuity of community into episodic moments. Satellite destinations dispersed the dense continuity of the "urban" into auto accessible nodes connected by rivers of circulation. Highways, parkways, toll-roads, and streets transformed how and when social interaction occurred. As the distances between places expanded, layered rings of new infrastructure emerged to expand the system and reach farther and farther. The result was sprawl: a cyclical reproduction of the same built landscape, layered upon itself in homogeneous and repeating waves.

The navigation of such a cyclical landscape relied upon a folding signage and brand as the primary governors of path and destination. The transformation from an associated neighborhood of connected and continuous diversity to a landscape of distinct nodal moments, isolated and specific in content eroded the experience of chance. Brand names and product identity provided consistent and predictable experiences. The result however was the transformation of everyplace into the same place.

Brands associate their identity with specific spatial types in order to reinforce their image, yet each type subscribes to shared principles essential to their survival in suburban space: visibility and convenience. These formally translate as image (signage) and location (parking). Each subscribe to the singular goal of enticing patronage and consumption. Within these generic universals, distinct suburban commercial spatial types can be codified as follows:

Island architecture is a spatial type referring to the freestanding store founded in convenience, typically selling products that are low cost and high speed (the fast food restaurant or gas station are quintessential examples). Island architecture is typically ringed by vehicular circulation and parking for ease of access and speed of engagement. It dominantly serves the vehicle even providing drive-thru opportunities for "on-the-go" service and commerce.

The strip mall refers to a conglomeration of stores that service cyclical needs organized in a linear configuration. Hugging major circulation routes, the strip mall is set behind a blanket of parking. Independent and localized stores[43] mix with brand name chains (typically stores that carry broad ranges of products) to create shopping hubs. Their grouping provides for diverse offerings not strong enough a draw to maintain independent "island" status, but when gathered together provide for mixed variety of commercial types within a single commercial location.

The big box emerged from mass-production and standardization that led to an explosion in the number of products available. Dimensionally responding to the number of products while overlaying availability (through "in-stock" quantities), convenience (size of lots, aisles, and selection), and economy (lowest price) the big box employs a modified warehouse typology. The synthesis of storage and display, hygiene and self-service, and diverse types of product offerings gather all the offerings of the traditional main street into the single collective of the mega-store and super-center. The efficiency of this building type and the streamlined nature of their amenities make them a disposable typology lacking connection with the touchstones of architectural experience.

The mall is the final and perhaps least suburban commercial type as it locally simulates the pedestrian density of traditional urbanism. Relying upon an extracted "main street" that is hermetically sealed and conveniently enveloped with parking, the mall relies upon anchor stores with brand name draw linked by lesser feeder stores. Gathering around an interior pedestrian arcade, piped in music and artificial climates create a sensory environment of sanitized

Jeffersonian grid of agriculture
geometry versus locality in the democratic grid

connectivity. The dramatic density of the mall overly contrasts the looseness of the suburban spatial type. Despite its exterior scale and configuration, the interior holds vestiges of an urban center linked with mixed-use diversity extending its daily life-cycle and use beyond the singularity of the commercial type.

These elemental commercial typologies each define the components of the suburban fabric as a terrain for engagement. They are each facilitated by the single family detached suburban house: the feeder of the spatial type and the economic engine for consumption.

AMERICAN SPACE: LAND AND THE SUBURBAN

The suburban is a uniquely American creation. Founded in the agrarian foundations of the United States, this connection to the land as a productive and self-sufficient landscape in combination with a democratic political system and a capitalist economic system, establish the suburban as the ideal spatial typology intertwined with the origins of our nationality. Thomas Jefferson's mapping[44] of the United States as a democratic grid established a uniformity of division based on the rationale of an equal grid. This standardized segmentation systematized the variation of topography, landscape, and nature. The regimental order of the blanketing modular system overarched and equalized the variation of locality and rationalized the wildness of the natural condition.

This geometric subdivision allied itself with the ideal of land ownership new to the native context (previously land was not owned and the migratory sense of temporal occupation was rooted in a partnership with the natural ecology). The dominance of individualism and autonomy is at the root of the American dream. The homestead as the building block of westward expansion was facilitated by the promissory support of 40-acre plots[45] available if people would settle, farm, and populate the land.

Self-sufficiency, economic prosperity, and the homestead all emerged from the geometry of the uniform regularization of the landscape. Early on, land was associated with rights. The individual only had the right to vote if a landowner.[46] This associated a connection of place with power and political representation. Manifest destiny and the intertwining of the American dream with the opportunity for engaging an individuated existence, established the single family house at the root of the suburban. Densities increasing over time, the introduction of the automobile, building and planning codes all emerged to reinforce and exacerbate this condition. Problematic or pure, the suburban is the American standard.

The detached single family house is the foundational building block of this system. Serving as the spatial generator and primary unit; it embodies all the principles of suburban spatial planning. It is the master premise that the remainder of the landscape serves.

THE NEW NATURAL

These typologies have facilitated a spatial evolution that has defined a new natural emergent from our cultural norms. The formula of spatial understanding, development, and growth subscribes to societal preference rather than a land ethos. The economic infrastructure overrides the legacy of the landscape denaturing its raw presence and removing any direct dependence on the ecological. This shifts the focus and attention to the increased diversity of an occupant's mind and body.

Nature is no longer in our everyday existence. The dependence upon a formalization of the event of nature occurs through our conscious need to visit it as a destination. The "McMansion" architecturally separates the site from the building; and the indoor from outdoor. The reliance upon REI[47] as a mediator to the "adventure" of experience without any fear of danger (getting lost, being hurt, drowning, falling, starving, et cetera) sanitizes our ecosystem. The connection to nature is only maintained as a reminder of our link within the larger system of plant and animal life; of the terrain and topography of an enormity of scale. Nature's preservation and experience (in both a pure and bastardized state) offers an intellectual and spiritual connection to an era of dependence and interaction with it. It is a reminder of our own mortality, complexity, and biological fragility. In a landscape governed by sprawl the natural exists as the infill converging and humanizing the vast in-between that exists in side yards and medians. It is the "was."

The infrastructure of the denatured landscape presents a new nature: one led by the expansion of knowledge and the representation of its ideals. Its interpretation suggests a new world: one that we create and interpret. It is a vague infrastructure that allows for the hierarchy of the activity through event to break the homogeneity of the whole.

Your House
Olafur Eliasson
constructed space

Cosmic Thing
Damian Ortega
part to whole

SUBURBANISM AND EVENT AS SPECTACLE

The following episodes represent the terrain in which we currently operate. Beginning with the placelessness of the suburban condition, the contemporary built landscape grapples with identity and meaning through the context in which we now operate.

This new locale bred an iconography and language but also shifted the conversation of architecture to focus on the spectacle as a monument to create the extremity of the event to define a place. Together form, place, and event define the emergent parameters for architectural consideration.

[1] SUBURBAN PLACELESSNESS
AND IDENTITY

"Tyler Durden:
Do you know what a duvet is?

Narrator:
Comforter.

Tyler Durden:
It's a blanket, just a blanket. Why do guys like you and I know what a duvet is? Is this essential to our survival in the hunter-gather sense of the word? No. What are we then?

Narrator:
You know ... consumers.

Tyler Durden:
Right we are consumers. We are a by-product of a lifestyle obsession. Murder, crime, poverty, these things don't concern me, what concerns me are celebrity magazines, television with 500 channels, some guy's name on my underwear, Rogaine, Viagra, Allestra ...

Narrator:
Martha Stewart.

Tyler Durden:
Fuck Martha Stewart. Martha's polishing the brass on the Titanic. It is all going down man. So fuck off, with your sofa unit and stream green stripe patterns. I say never be complete. I say stop being perfect. I say let's evolve, chips fall where they may. That's me. I could be wrong. Maybe it's a terrible tragedy.

Narrator:
No, it's just stuff.

Tyler Durden:
Well you did lose a lot of versatile solutions for modern living."⁴⁸

- *Fight Club*

"*Unlike James Watts's steam engine, for example, the body concentrates order. It continuously self-repairs. Every five-days you get a new stomach lining. You get a new liver every two months. Your skin replaces itself every six weeks. Every year, ninety-eight percent of the atoms of your body are replaced. This non-stop chemical replacement, metabolism, is a sure sign of life. The 'machine' demands continual input of chemical energy and materials (food).*"⁴⁹

- **What is life?**

Submerged into the homogeneity of a relentless lack of differentiation, the sameness forces a transition of "way-finding" from the physical references of formalized space to the abstracted language of Google Maps. Graphics and linguistic alternatives usurp the potential for intrigue or understanding based upon visual references. The megalopolis is no longer understood through the oculus of the automobile window, but along the colored graphic of the map.

The identity of the American dream (or at least the narrow perception contemporary society holds as the American dream) imbibes the suburban landscape with an awkward likeness of bastardized remnants of irrelevant traditions. The formalization of these nostalgic artifacts results in the production of a disjunctive caricature of a bygone precedent repeated overtly and irreverently in American neighborhoods.

The introduction of industrialization and the accompanying assembly line capabilities that allowed for the serial production of commercialized products began the descent. The separation and resulting specialization of labor necessary for the segmental assembly line production based upon efficiency and speed induced a compartmentalization of individual knowledge. As the parameters of information now expand beyond any singular capacity, their re-connectivity becomes impossible. Diversification entangles with the inherent eradication of relevance by only allowing a "little" understanding of the myriad of topical issues in contemporary society positioning the individual shallowly in any one focus. The result becomes a hyper-articulation of a singular ability. The individual must now have a precise personal infrastructure of knowledge to maintain oneself in an ever-expanding sphere of informational occupations. This in combination with an ever-fluctuating economy, influenced by social and political transitions, repeatedly shifts its stability and organization. To maintain relevance in the expanded web of a global economy, a nomadic culture is demanded. Work is no longer related to the land or the traditions of the homestead. Any associated maintenance of a continuously owned and occupied space is defunct. The individual must define place as a relevant location to being. The old sayings: "home is where you hang your hat," or "home is where the heart is," suggest an associative relevance being a spatial condition in conjunction with the object of reference interchanging a coat rack with the emotional bonds of relationship. The dissolution of the legacy of individual heritage of space demands an architecturalization that must allow for everyone and no one. The diversity of individuality is dumbed down. A two party political system; a television season of thirteen weekly episodes that spans a calendar year of fifty-two weeks; a marketplace that relies upon a standardization of experience (as typified by McDonald's, Wal-Mart and Home Depot to represent the same space and product arrangement regardless of place, space, or locality) have resulted in the blanding of culture.

As machines increase the boundaries of capably occupiable space,⁵⁰ the individual has expanded their sphere of finite space. The homestead represented a life of predictable experiences shared by generations as survival consumed the majority of daily activity. With an explosion of this model, the individual detaches the self from place and turns to infrastructure to predict experience. The landscape of sameness emerges to provide a predetermination of components that allow for a safe, clear, and communicable existence that simultaneously eliminates any chance of either surprise or responsibility.

The foundations of our contemporary nomadic culture demand that place remain only briefly outlined for static ownership.⁵¹ The constant fluctuation foils the traditional presence of the homestead that allowed for a single family to cultivate and maintain a multi-generational heritage of specific association with place. The increased movement of man, though permitting broader geographic visual experience, has demanded homogeneity to the landscape as a whole. The commutability forces change to occur upon all of our surroundings simultaneously. The sphere of knowledge must remain the same despite the increase in the boundaries of physical perception. The known experience is demanded to ease the complex lifestyles through predictable presence eliminating the diversity of place. The home must become predictable. It extends the serial mentality of standardized production. It subscribes to a singular rational understanding to be a commodity. The identity of place is instead deferred to the monument. The locality becomes about the hierarchical symbol that is identifiable as a representative logo of place. The Space Needle, the Statue of Liberty, the St. Louis Arch, the Guggenheim at Bilbao, et cetera, all become emblematic exaggerations of fantastic distinctness necessary to define where you are. The language and geography that used to determine lifestyle and attitude are leveled by the ever-expanding global sprawl and blanketing ubiquitous information uniformly available via mobile and web based technologies. The in-between becomes the sameness necessary to allow for the consistent jumping of temporal presence. The contemporary nomadic lifestyle generates placelessness.

The identity of locale thus must become formulaic to respond to market claims. The Garlinghouse Company produces a text that offers yearly the plans and specifications that define "contemporary architecture." In Design #92515 entitled "Space Efficient Styling" they provide a collage of features that represent the fashions of the current marketplace:

"The elegant styling of this very space efficient plan features the charm and elegance of brick and stucco. As you enter the foyer, you find the spacious dining room to your right and to the rear of the foyer is a very large den. The dining room has eleven-foot ceilings and Palladian windows. A large country kitchen is located to the rear of the dining area and features built-in double ovens, cook top, and vent hood, double sink and disposal, as well as a dishwasher and desk. The breakfast bar opens into the large breakfast room. The den is entered from this area and features ten-foot ceilings and a brick fireplace with two sets of double French doors that open onto the patio area. The bedrooms are designed to split the master bedroom away from the other two. From the den there is a very short hall that leads to two smaller bedrooms, both with walk-in closets. The master bedroom features a ten-foot trey ceiling and large walk-in closet. The master bath has double vanities, linen closet, whirlpool tub, separate shower and private toilet compartment."[52]

People demand standardization as the leveling of rules establish quantifiable features that can be compared and hierarchically arranged. As a result, lifestyle must be communicable and equally referential to a social scale that follows an evolution of status.[53] The home is striated by gradients of floor area and amenity. From the starter 1,500-square-foot entry level house, expanding to the distended obesity of the 5,000 to 6,000-square-foot McMansion, the spectrum of types subscribe to a consistent and comparable language of features. That which once used to bear a permanence and solidity, has become temporary. As a disposable commodity the market disallows the capability to maintain a continuity of place. The house, as the penultimate product, subscribes to the same infrastructure of sameness to allow for transferability rather than a specific. Architecture becomes transferable merchandise

and the relationship of place to presence is further subordinated. The detachment from the responsive specificity of location with the detail of varied functional needs and user preference establishes a blanket relationship.

The innate nomadic nature of the individual is provided for by the reactionary relationship accelerating the speed of participation, interaction, and consumption. Events now occur in a matter of seconds but with an increasing frequency. The course of duration is diminished and the saturation is hyper-extended. Consistency is deemed un-desirable as commercial consumption requires a cycle of self-replacement. The waves of release and replacement provide a false variety. The system carefully maintains an over identity of sameness that permits a continuum of relevance, of cultural understanding and "way-finding" amidst the seemingly ever-expanding vastness of pop information.[54] The necessity to locate the "self" and define quantifiable conveniences and experiences that can be leaned upon for cultural confidence and support, establish a referential shell of "favorites." Favorite experiences, tastes, smells, songs, movies, et cetera, each define the characteristics of personal identity. In their quantifiable repetition they demand a re-visitation to establish and maintain their prominence and relevance. When coupled with our increased scale of movement, seriality facilitates the sameness of experience despite the difference of time and place. This condition creates a stylized present. The iconic elements that arise out of historical practicality slowly deform and deteriorate as sequential bastardizations remove the presence of their original intentions and convictions formulating a detached and unmistakably postmodern present. As a symbol, these elements reduce themselves to superficial entities that limit their relevance and necessity. The categorical scrutiny of these elements allows for an understanding of their origin, their rationale for perpetuation, and the contemporary employment of their symbolism. The following represent a highlight of a selection of contemporary single-family suburban residential features.

TRADEMARK NEIGHBORHOOD

The naming of place fabricates an idealized identity; an isolated and seemingly distinct condition that remains generically appreciable. The Sablechases, Greenbriers, and Foxcrofts relentlessly stake their claims while attempting to provide a unique identity to their neighborhood grouping. The cartoonish application of an identity of generic specificity contributes to the false production of a community group consciousness. Their identities, regardless of nomenclature, are like the Coca-Cola can: representative of the dependably quintessential sameness. The identity of place is caricatured to embrace the symbols of a past founded in relevance and associativity, but now serving as a nomenclature feature to maintain consistent property values through place based brand.

STREET NUMBER

The acceleration of technology and knowledge has collapsed space, expanding the scale and speed of our experience. The perception of the suburban street (confronted with the serial thresholds of the automated garage door) requires reliance upon street numbers to provide precision of place. The standardized segmentation of an organic landscape into regularized parcels establishes location in a non-hierarchical referential system. The Jeffersonian democratic grid equalizes the field by uniformly carving it into geometrically identical pieces despite terrain, potential, adjacency, or climate implying anonymity to the expansive system. Occupation has been zoned and uniformly compartmentalized.

GABLE

Emerging in its traditional form as a practical geometric configuration for shedding water, the gable roof has assumed an iconic status of formal reference. Challenged by material evolution and associated construction technologies, the increase in scale has liberated the form and possibility of the roof. The expanding size of the roof plane has transformed the necessity and role of the eave. Their edges are no longer extensions of the sub-structural systems but have instead become an appliqué to the elevation to provide a false density to contradict and subdivide the enormity of scale. Each eave suggests a now superficial interior subdivision employing a traditional architectural massing tool that related a distinction of form to a division of space. The surface becomes a decorated box with exterior detailing irreverent to the interior workings. Their multiplicity establishes a reciprocal relationship between gable quantity and market price. More is more. The association of a historical form to an extraneous function denies the real, translating it to a symbol.

COLUMN

The classical column (despite its historical formalism) detaches itself from its originating structural responsibility. It has transformed from a solid into a hollow shell formed from molded plastic units.[55] Their applied status masks the disparate system of their interior function. The hollow shells of the Ronald McDonald mannequin and the plastic replicas of Greek gods and classical constructs at Caesar's Palace, Las Vegas[56] find muted resonance on the front porches of the suburban domestic realm. It no longer carries its performative association. The contemporary column enforces a referential style allowing a three-dimensionality to compositionally appear and provide a detached historical reference.

APPLIED MULLIONS

The distance of visual inspection established by the organization and scale of the street and yard, accentuates the dominance of the elevational surface as image consumed from a specific scale, distance, and vantage. A passing glance from the distant vista and all seems appropriate. Closer inspection reveals the artificiality of the system. Historically, the mullion existed to aggregate the limited scale of glass production capabilities. The panes were arrayed to create larger fields of transparency. Contemporary technologies allow for larger production, but the desire of the associative image remains. For functional purposes of both making larger pieces of glass and providing a single unbroken surface for cleaning, the superstructure of the mullion and mutton necessary to support the panes of glass have been engulfed and incorporated internally into the artificial vacuum-sealed and gas injected interior of

the multi-pane window. The result is an inversion of authenticity through the streamlined re-presentation.[57] The accompanying visual thinness of their physical presence is representative of the applied conceptual illusion. The desire to maintain the past while embracing the present results in an artificial hybrid in which neither system benefits. The blurred vision provides a referential statement about the associative legacy of an unemployed construction system, while the innovation allows for faster production of energy efficient and durable constructs. The desire for the honesty of cultural currency is irrelevant as the placelessness doesn't allow for an understanding or confidence in our current condition, but rather relies upon the historic safety of an experience and a form that had reference, identity, and predetermination. The subscription to image provides the maintenance of marketability, commutability, and thus mobility.

SHUTTER

The American shutter emerges from the traditions of America's colonial foundations. In a pre-industrial era when screens and climate control were not yet conceived, shutters were employed to protect and insulate fragile window apertures providing insulation, security, enclosure, and privacy. Their utility demanded operability. The contemporary shutter is a mere symbol of its previous calling. It has become a hollow vacuum-molded plastic shell,[58] single faced and statically fixed to the frontal surface image of the building. As a visual tool, their purpose is as a comforting remnant that references an architectural style by flanking apertures to provide depth and relief (regardless of how shallow) subdividing the vast quantities of vinyl siding and veneer brick.

LAWN

The front yard is employed as a pre-amble. It is not a physical place of occupation, but a visual one. The green carpet, toiled upon and relentlessly labored over as a controlled natural, provides a symbol of leisure time dispensed upon the perfection of an isolated coiffure. The front lawn becomes for show, the side yards for utility and the back yard for occasional recreation.[59] The encircling field is an amenity emergent from historical type but divorced from need. It remains critical to type, urban presence, and spatial aggregation.

PLASTIC ROCKS

Plastic rock speakers synthesize familiarity through artificial means. Represented as a necessity of modern existence in the Atlanta Street of Dreams Home Showcase,[60] they demonstrate the desire to simulate something that is fundamentally natural to maintain familiarity despite the technological innovation and expanded perceptual experience of their concealed function. Music, emitting from the molded plastic rock, extends the simulacra and hybridity through their cross-pollination.

GARAGE[61]

Despite the traditional language employed by the architecture of historicist reference, necessity confronts, contradicts, and demands the presence of a storage facility for the automobile. The car folds infrastructure into the domestic sphere. The scale

Corb stack

and enormity of the driveway extends the street into the house. The direct insertion results in a violation of the pedestrian realm. The garage merges into the body of the house as a gaping hole that opens to engulf not just the body, but the entire extension of our mechanically mobilized existence. The formal incorporation occurs through the parasitic adhesion of a lean-to shed tacked disjunctively on the front or a cored out void taken directly from the mass. The incorporation of the garage represents the suburban's relationship with the automobile: denied necessity. As *the* most substantial accessory (second only to the house itself in both physical and economic scale) the automobile becomes a combination of our financial means and personal desires. The car is fetishized. Its prominent location on the facade illustrates the superiority of standardized subscription over architectural and individual capability. It is readily obtainable, referentially decipherable of labeled status, and innately nomadic. The automobile is dominant in the suburban.

FEATURES

The house and its subsidiary spaces have become functional checklists of amenities. Subscribing to the realtor's listing as a generative recipe, features, and statistics replace space, form, and experience. The standard homogeneous gypsum board spaces are articulated with features including: cove lighting, distended moldings, and plastic doors, that simulate and recreate traditional details of building in artificial materials as applied ornament. Kitchen islands, garden tubs, and walk-in closets adorn the numerous bedrooms (3/2, 4/4.5, 5/5, et cetera) that establish validity based upon their frequency rather than necessity. The design exists where quantity trumps quality. More means "sale-ability" and thus consistency of liquidity facilitating the nomadic mobility of the middle class.

ENTRY, FOYER, STAIR

To compensate for the enormity and dominance of the automobile's presence (requiring the garage and garage door) the entry, foyer, and stair become overtly scaled and stylized. The transition, movement, and display of bodily motion through entry become entrenched in the traditions of a collaged vision of applied artificiality. The sweeping stair references the southern mansions that Scarlet O'Hare swept down during her jubilant entrances.[62] With the automobile's insertion, the necessity for a pedestrian entrance has been usurped. Its presence is obsolete. The front door is the garage door. The employment of this exuberant space only finds relevance during the infrequent social gatherings that draw the semi-public visitor through this orchestrated portal. The stage set reveals its edges as the polished marble abruptly transitions into wall-to-wall carpeting. The formality of the frontal experiential artifice bulges briefly inward as an interior spatial condition.

GAME ROOM / HOME THEATER

The game room and/or home theater provides the infrastructure for entertainment and escape to the resident. The experiential constructs of the visually produced world provide a diversion from bland and undefined average life. Abandoning the city to import experience, these entertainment spaces provide an artificial access. Gaming allows a confrontation of ability permitting simulated engagement though artificial insertion of control and dominance. The home theater creates the optimal experience for the immersion into the lives and stories of others as a passive viewer. The removal of any social interaction that may have occurred during a traditional interlude to a conventional theater or experience is internalized to the home. The social interface is minimized as real experience is supplemented by virtual and visual experience. Media serially presents images of beauty, love, knowledge, and even debonair attitude. Their incredulousness is their forte. The formula is predictable. The "happy ending" allows for a greater existence than we could ever hope to achieve in our own right. The result is the destructive second-class consideration of our real presence. That which we *are*, can never be as good as that which is cinematically *projectable*.

To create within this placeless context requires an architecture that no longer focuses on the structuring of a physical formalization *for* living, but rather subscribes to a process *of* living. Society has dramatically evolved with technological innovations and social advancements. The decision for difference reflects in the subscription to a personal identity. The contemporary model of existence is the selection of a product set that relates to a lifestyle. The subscription determines not only what we wear and what we eat, but how we live and think. The distinct and stereotypical models that Hollywood represents as diagrammatic condensations are dispensed in an articulate and enormously strategic marketing machine of succulently suggestive and desirably emulative models. The resulting projected images provide guidance for society. Products are marketed by association allowing an ever-fluctuating model of seasonal dispensation. The totality supports our disposable world. Product, lifestyle and place all succumb to the lack of necessity for attachment. Contemporary culture (dominated formally by the serial suburbia of the middle landscape) remains adrift, peripheralized by the vagueness of our bland presence. The individual sets no bounds. The individual has no bounds. The relationship of the individual to the societal group relates with the same structure as the democratic system. The direction, competency and success of the whole are uniquely dependent upon the ability of the individual. The lack of boundary and understanding, in combination with the indeterminate social presence of a *cultural* place, prevent the completion of the individual resulting in the perpetuation of an inappropriate model of presence. Change must emerge from a connectivity to "self" so place and identity can be defined from within.

"Advertising has us chasing cars and clothes, working jobs we hate so we can buy shit we don't need. We are the middle children of history man, no purpose or place. We have no great war, no great depression. Our great war is the spiritual war; our great depression is our lives. We've all been raised on television to believe that one day we'd all be millionaires, and movie gods, rock stars, but we won't, we are slowly learning that fact and are very, very pissed off."[63]

- *Fight Club*

[2] EVENT AND THE SPECTACLE AS MONUMENT

As a result of the aforementioned "sameness," differentiation in the contemporary suburban landscape has been formed by spectacle. The industrial revolution introduced the assembly line. Mass production dominated the new consumer culture through an efficiency of seriality. Commerce and consumption governed all else. The automobile emerged as the quintessential product of the new system changing the scale and organization of the fabric of American suburbanism drastically over the following century. Its speed collapsed the scale of distance. Its elaborate infrastructure provided the means to comfortably traverse the vastness of the open continent. The capturing of the open frontier of westward expansion and manifest destiny internalized the American dream. Sameness traversed the singular typology of the suburban landscape. The distinction of individuality became articulated by the spectacle intertwining the attraction with identity.

As urban edges flood into a growing periphery, the individuality of the American town quickly corrupts, changing and dissipating under the infiltration of chain stores and homogenized ideals. Tradition is replaced by fad, as authenticity is lost to fashion.[64]

The products of consumer culture cyclically reproduce themselves erasing their predecessors. The continuity of a spectacle becomes iconic to define place by the uniqueness of event. These moments of extremity establish the fundamental references for urbanism. Their influence on the survival and definition of the American "place" provide an insight into the sociological foundations of local culture.

The historical role of the monument has shifted to allow the commodified event to govern identity. The contemporary monument is one of amusement or amazement rather than commemoration or history. The monument no longer maps a singular point in the historical progression but relies upon event as an extended experience of interaction. Leisure and entertainment invade contemplation to facilitate participation with the event physically rather than cognitively. The artifact of event has been replaced by the event itself.

The monument is the foundational spark of identity of place. The spectacle serves as the lifeblood of our interactive society. Disneyland, California; Marfa, Texas; The Rocket Garden, Florida; Dollywood, Tennessee; Spaceport USA; SeaWorld, Orlando; and Rock City, Georgia (amongst others);[65] serve as landmark attractions.

The monument is formed by the uniqueness of its identity and differentiation amidst the sameness of its context and contemporary culture. They gain prominence through their extremity. The ability to be recognized justifies their presence. It is essential to classify, identify, and articulate the contemporary constructed identity manifested in the spectacle. The premise of contemporary urbanism lies in the cultural occupation of its fabric. The extremity of our culture has generated a de-sensitivity. The spectacle is the solution.

SPECTACLE

Contemporary global economics have permitted the birth of the safe. Job safety, financial safety, and methods of standardized production have created predictability. Standardized fashions,[66] networks,[67] store environments,[68] and fast food chains,[69] (amongst any and everything else) have defined a homogeneous blanket applied regardless of geographic, ethnic, cultural, religious, racial, sexual, and political boundaries. The homogeneous banal where the suburban strip is the city center on American terms are for anyone and of everyone. They remain concurrently alike establishing the potential to remove a core sample from any strip, or any block, or any neighborhood, and the condition, brands and forms will be congruent. As a result, this fabrication of an "anywhere" condition through the sameness of convenience and association removes the potential for fear, confusion, or discovery. One is never too far from the safe womb of McDonald's, Starbucks, and the Gap.

The urban result is a cyclical repetition. The fabric becomes a collection of combinations: each unique to the demographics and densities of *a* specific place, while never deviating from the iconic forms and formulas perfected by globalized economics. The ordinary becomes the norm. Awkward attempts at differentiation, contextualism, and identity simply overlay upon the homogeneity of the existing infrastructure forcing the focus of contemporary urbanism to shift in response. The object and the fabric that once defined the city's organization and spatial, formal, and cultural differentiation (the Baroque city plan[70] or the democratic grid[71]) has transformed and repositioned their dominance to the *event*.

Event urbanism evolved through the development of districting: the compartmentalization of the city as subsets based upon programmatic categories defining the conglomeration of business, ethnicities, and religions. From the garment district in New York City, to the museum district in Houston,[72] Disney's "Main Street" USA, to the Latin Quarter in Paris; area and identity are defined by the event of inhabitation. The process is governed by homogenization. Chinatown exists in New York City, San Francisco, and Los Angeles alike. As a result, the banality of sameness engulfs again the form and sense of spatial definition and uniqueness of identity.

Event, when challenging homogeneity, overcomes through the hyper-expression of extremity. The fantasy and extremity of disbelief is tapped. Their curiosity makes The Space Needle or the Las Vegas Strip iconic places for pilgrimage. These representative examples each present a different implementation of the spectacle as monument.

THE MONUMENT OF THE SNOW GLOBE

The Saint Louis Arch, the Golden Gate Bridge, the Chinese Theater (as representative iconic landmarks found in snow globes[73]) capture the object architectures that create the identity elements that define local place. The object is validated through its extremity. That which is irreproducible, forbearing, and identifiable employs spectacle to define place. American urbanism is not recognized by the fabric of the city or the history of a place because it lacks both.

It relies upon the monument, the spectacular objects, to describe the identity of place. This presents an important shift in the foundations of urbanism uniquely represented in the fabric of American architecture: the role of form based object building. Form, as a commercialized tool of capitalist production, presents the opportunity for corporate or product identity. American urbanism has founded itself upon presentations of iconic structures that value an exceptional ideal moment as opposed to the everyday fabric. The result is a quarantine of considered valuation. The spectacle becomes the dominant facilitating reason. These flagship icons (housing a variety of programmatic functions) assume the urban responsibilities of the monument in traditional historic city fabric. Rather than demarcating military conquest, political accomplishment or cultural prowess,[74] the icon becomes a product of spectacle. Identity becomes a marketing ploy. The object architecture deploys extremity (typically height, material, form, et cetera) defining an extremity of urban association that erodes the continuity of circumstantial wonder for the domination of logo type moments. The object defines the contemporary American urban fabric by standing apart from it.

This model of formal differentiation denies any continuity in the urban fabric by its neglecting the in-between of the normative condition. The result is a deferral to the serial language of suburban placelessness. McDonalds employs architecture of brand identity providing for convenience through standardization of recognition. Seriality reinforces its potency. The combination creates a visual vocabulary fabricated to compete for attention. The spectacle of being seen, recognized, and indulged is the formula for contemporary business. Architecture employs it to define its connection to urbanism. Competition by subscribing to an extremity of vocabulary, cancels out its effectiveness and premise. Economics minimizes the investment and the default becomes the sign. It is no coincidence that Walt Disney Corporation as the quintessential fabricator of event based spectacle has fabricated the city itself. Celebration[75] (the planned community funded and fabricated by Disney Corporation) serves as an artificial example so hygienic in its conception and execution the extremity becomes the draw. Celebration is a caricature of a town. Suggesting a synthesized typology of the ideal small town with the suburban, it generates a fabricated stage set as an urban proposition. The totality of the assembled effect is only possible through the domination of activity (program) curation and control of style and oversight of every aspect of the constructed landscape. Setbacks, styles, color, lighting, nomenclature, stop signs, police force, commerce, et cetera are all carefully governed[76] by the Disney Corporation. The singular master as an all controlling entity provides comprehensive control. The extremity of the production creates a surreal landscape that more closely approximates the idealized stage sets of television families like "Leave It to Beaver" and "My Three Sons"[77] than the diversity of personality and unpredictability of life typical of a collaged urban fabric. This control and streamlining of chance, diversity, and happenstance is the spectacle itself. Urbanism joins with the extremity of the theme park.

The spectacle is the accomplishment of the projected ideal. The quality of the constructed environment develops the collective object as an encompassing and singular fabric based event.

Las Vegas[78] similarly developed an artifice of escape through experience to heighten and fabricate spectacle as a business model. The production of a landscape so artificial to the typical social and physical environment that it could be fabricated in the middle of a desert generated a city founded on extremity. The premise, evolution, and specificity are governed by the same principles: economics. What works is celebrated and rewarded, what doesn't is quickly removed. Experimentation advances and accelerates the cycle of indulgence (i.e. how long things are tested through deployment before being replaced or upgraded). Economic Darwinism, in its purest form, is the central principle responsible for the landscape of Las Vegas.

The Volcano at the Mirage[79] is a case study fabrication of circumstance. The average time it takes for a parking attendant to take your ticket, locate your car, and return to the port cochere is seven minutes. During this time, the patron is un-entertained resulting in a "down time." The horror vaccui that attaches spectacle to every event establishes the need to fill this time. The Mirage Hotel fabricated a full-scale volcano adjacent to the parking lot and directly visible from the attendant stand that erupts on a periodic cycle. The spectacle of the event makes the necessary wait an opportunity to entertain.[80]

Culture has increased the extremity of spectacle in all aspects of its fabric: fast food keeps building higher and bigger signs; movies take on more far-fetched and fantastic themes; greater violence becomes more evident as video games get a higher and higher level of extreme reality. The result is a general desensitization. The spectacle breeds extremity. The result is the fantastic becoming the norm.

The competitive attitudes of capitalist production are brought into every aspect of society and fabricate a dependence upon the newness of an idea. The extremity of the caricature becomes the formula for success. The next spectacle has to outdo the previous. The result is a self-destructive cycle that escalates the stakes to an unobtainable level. For the method to work, the relative level of intensity has to be established for the spectacle to step above the common. The collective subscription cancels out the effectiveness of any one application.

The ramifications of such a reading of the urban fabric allows for an inversion of the system. The potential for collaborative planning, spatial diversity, and the fabrication of an architecture of the banal provide opportunity for a revaluation of the entire system. The collective attention to the urban fabric demands an associative understanding of building program and identity to provide for a consistency of the fabric as a whole. The responsibility for the individual component to benefit the whole has proven foundations in game theory and socialism.[81] The resulting method provides for a collaborative success mechanism that allows for a lesser extremity shifting the responsibility of identity from one iconic element to the responsibility of the fabric as a collective whole.

[3] REPRODUCTION, AUTHENTICITY, AND PLACE

"Carbon copy cat cloned

Researchers in Texas are the first to successfully clone a do-mestic cat. Although the two-month-old kitten is just another addition to the growing list of successfully cloned animals, her birth may mark the beginning of a pet-cloning era.

The carbon copy kitten called 'Cc:' appears healthy and energetic, although she is completely unlike her tabby surrogate mother.

Mark Westhusin and colleagues at Texas A&M University, College Station, created Cc: by transplanting DNA from a female three-colored (tortoiseshell or calico) cat into an egg cell whose nucleus had been removed. They then implanted this embryo into the surrogate tabby.

Cc:'s coat color suggests that she is a clone. A genetic match between Cc: and the donor mother confirms this, the re-searchers say.

She does not, however, look identical to her DNA donor. The pattern on cats' coats is only partly genetically determined - it also depends on other factors during development.

Out of 87 implanted cloned embryos, Cc: is the only one to survive - comparable to the success rate in sheep, mice, cows, goats and pigs. If these odds can be shortened and Cc: remains in good health the possibility of pet cloning and concomitant ethical problems, could be just a whisker away."[82]

- Tom Clarke
"Pet cloning could be just a whisker away"

We love a "copycat."

Reproduction is ambient in contemporary culture. The serial production of limited types reliant upon simulated reference, define a falsity that has become true. The premise of this de-evolution is founded in the advancement of technology and science. The architectural legacy of the development of "the reproduction" is intertwined with the development of tectonics. The association of the definition of a form with the methods of material production and construction has systematically assumed respon-sibility for form relative to culture and era.

The relationship of tectonics to form is evident in the foundations of building craft. From the Parthenon (reproducing the rafter tails of the heavy timber roof in the stone entablature) through the Palazzo Medici-Riccardi (where Michelozzo di Bartolommeo employs the classical order as veneered surface reproducing the structural lines in a vocabulary of classical identity) reference to tectonics is used to create ornamental detail. The methods result in an architecture that generates form out of referential reproduction. The method denies authenticity through an artificial application that generates iconography as a surficial veil founded in the reproduction of another rationality. The origin, though founded in function and traditions of craft, is reproduced and employed as a culturally loaded referential artifact. The fractured character of the resulting anachronism divorces the form from its originating rationale leaving only the reference. The process turns the artificial into the actual and culture consumes authenticity as the real.

The quintessential contemporary example is found in the fantasy and disbelief of the exaggerated ar-tificiality of the landscapes of Disneyland and Las Vegas. These complete environments, fabricated to provide escape and wonder, are designed to fissure the inhabitant from conventional and familiar archi-tectonic forms in favor of idealized forms. The result is the production of fantasy and amusement. This total extremity permits its method of reproduction to become its authenticity.

These environments in all of their specifics (from the forms, the themes, the hyper-oxygenated air, to the costumed employees, et cetera) synthesize to formulate an artificial real. The thematic repro-duction of past cultures becomes the premise for the fabricated wonderment of today. Three distinct typologies emerge relative to the themed identities that establish the premise for the fabrication of the artificial: era, place, and event. Through these types, the fabrication itself becomes genuine by transposing the reproduction into a produced contemporary reality.

ERA

The first classification of the themed reproduction relies upon the historical, collapsing an entire era (exaggerated in its depiction of culture synthesizing its references and iconic monuments) into a singular themed complex. Exemplary casino's subscribing to this order of identity and place-making include Caesar's Palace (based upon a hybrid of the Roman Forum, Nero's Palace and collection of Roman and Greek references), the Luxor (a reproduction of the pyramids at Cheops), and Excalibur (a castle founded on the legends and traditions surrounding the Medi-eval Era). Their collective premise, though themed differently, is formulaically identical. The thematic eras instigate the specific forms, spaces and events to create an extreme identity emergent from refer-ence. The reproductions of the visual references of the era are overlaid with contemporary methods of fabrication and a drastically differential programmatic premise to interlace fantasy and artificiality. Plastic columns, glass pyramids, spray painted sphinxes, and fiberglass heavy timber wedding chapels artifi-cially re-present the formal markers of the historical through contemporary techniques. The representation as an anachronistic reference achieves its success through this fanciful juxtaposition. Getting married in Sherwood Forest, shopping in the Roman Forum, and checking in to your hotel room while standing on a barge in a ten-foot-wide Nile make the extremity of the reproduction so different it produces an entirely new condition. The artificial now becomes more real than the detached historical premise.

PLACE

The second classification relies upon an idealized and artificial reproduction of phenomenological highlights from a diversity of geographical locations, synthesized, hybridized, and sanitized into a singular complex of collapsed spaces and events themed for identity. The Venetian, the Paris, and New York, New York™ subscribe to this urban reproduction. Employing existing places (held as iconic places in their own right) the simulation recreates myriad experiences within a locality in a simultaneous fabrication. One moves into the Venetian's recreation of the Doge's Place (physically edging the Piazza San Marco in

Venice) and its interior reveals the Piazza San Marco. The inversion of the space reproduces the spatial sequences; lining the iconic shell with and iconic space that is lined with an iconic shell. The inverted paradox of the reproduction synthesizes place into a simultaneous understanding of a re-articulated object with simultaneous time-space correlations. The collaged facades of New York, New York™ employ the same curtain wall systems as the buildings themselves, applying the skins of Mies van der Rohe's Seagram Building, Skidmore Owings & Merrill's Lever House, and Caesar Pelli's Battery Park Development. The effect is a quilt of the New York Skyline encircled with a roller coaster subway. The synthetic nature of the collage creates a new real out of the referential sense of place.

EVENT

The third and final type relies upon the spectacle of event as a premise for the thematic engagement. The Mirage, Circus Circus, and the Hard Rock refer to extreme conditions of permanent temporality; the event made institution. The collection of these thematic premises relies again upon the extremity of their fabrication. This extremity of their reproduction makes them more than the events they mimic. The Hard Rock Cafe, as a tribute to the musical performance, performs as the house dedicated to the performance, while housing the exact performance that instigated it. The collection of the event, as the event, within the event, reproduces the theme in a cyclical self-re-definition. The reproduction produces a new unique and thus self-identifiable entity.

POSTMODERN

The premise of postmodernism is founded in referential simulation. Denied visual formal content through the streamlined and abstract machine forms of modern architecture, postmodern architecture turned to history to instill meaning. The forms, previously descendant from cultural, vernacular material construction, and historical tradition were resurrected and applied. Their reproduction removed the originating justification from the forms, applying them in a culture devoid of understanding. The result was the production of empty symbols that hollowed out architectural meaning. Through reproduction the iteration lost the meaning of attachment to the original.

This formal reproduction is met with an experiential and typological reproduction through the single family house. Providing the same opportunity of ownership requires serial production to ensure commutability. The reproduction emerges from the governing economics of the consumer marketplace. The formulaic model, when overlaid with the horizontal geography of the United States and its capitalist growth based economy, results in the growth of the homogeneous suburban. The reproductive formula of the house (as a base urban module) establishes its governing cultural and market construct. The result is a predictable landscape of seriality.

The mentality of a serial product finds its efficiency in the repetition and standardization of the assembly line. The contemporary marketplace requires a collective subscription to standardization providing predictable and shared experience. The reproduc-

ible requires a reduction of overhead and variety to optimize cost resulting in a homogeneous form determined to maximize appeal. The global landscape is consumed by the seriality of this reproduction. The average is propagated. Despite the scientific and cultural capabilities possible, contemporary production has marginalized the opportunity for individuality and originality.

Reproduction employs artificialities in the process making them "real." Their identity is detached and removed from the originating reference through cultural erosion that the resultant has arrived as a distinct element deserving of its own identity. The product allows the false to become true establishing the basis for the next simulation: a simulated simulation of multiple recursive reproductive generations.

The result is a reinvention that the reproduction allows a reinterpretation. The association is no longer relevant as the layered levels of removal relieve the responsibility for any connection. The reproduction results in a reproduced "new." The role of the copy now provides a better "new." The Darwinism of the evolution that allows for a "survival of the fittest" is short circuited. The applied systems through their re-appropriation requires their transition and that transition produces change. The reproduction through the circumstantial re-habitation becomes an opportunity for celebration and discovery.

The cat has been copied.

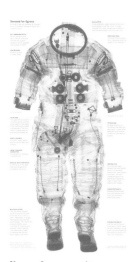

X-ray of a spacesuit use and occupation

[4] OCCUPATION ARCHITECTURE

The presence we bring to space through occupation defines an architecture where the way in which we use and personalize a space speaks about the spatial and formal rituals of architecture's future. In a society governed by standardization, the mass production of the assembly line narrowly defines the product set available for purchase, ownership, and self-definition. The result is the fabrication of a matrix. Discrete in its content and options available, individual personality determines the collaged accumulation of the personal choices one makes. The collection of products becomes the physical manifestation of serial choices. The conglomerate association through accumulation defines occupation. *Personality is exhibited by that which is bought.*

Architectural componential construction has similarly arrived at a pre-determined destination. Building products have reached a level of tectonic sophistication that no longer permits the individual to insert oneself into an originating role in the process. Products, systems, and parts determine what architecture can be. Design is their collagist assembly. Contemporary architecture is defined by the specification: a catalogue choice from a product set. This product set thus determines social structure. Distinction occurs in the subtleties of assembly. Individuality emerges from the collaged consumption. The architecture of occupation reveals the specific methods of living. Economy and standardization have sterilized space. It is the collection that defines the uniqueness of place and individuality.

A forensic dissection of possessions catalogs their associations and reveals identity. The object and the activity become the facilitator for identity. The individual is expressed, molded, and ultimately articulated through the occupation of presence.

OCCUPATION

Architecture, governed by systemic practicalities is banal. The generic homogeneity of its standardization is represented by its common forms and experiences alike. The current sameness of space (as defined by the traditional aspects of both building and space making) standardizes the framework for occupancy. The definition of architectural event emerges from activities of "spatial occupation." The contemporary definition of individual identity emerges out of the occupation of space. Habitation becomes the facilitator for opportunity through event. This occupation occurs in two primary modes: the static and the passive. These realms bridge both the animate activity and inanimate form to collectively engulf both realms.

EVENT

Interaction defines architectural occupation. Presence (passive and active, with inanimate and animate objects) generates experiences that define living. The presence is an active element that influences the activities around them. The result is a series of instigators that affect, dictate, and govern the adjacent activity. The result is a matrix of influential elements, from programmatic adjacencies, to material choices, to furniture arrangements, each facilitating the event in generation, happening, and resonance.

The role of spontaneity of event is in fact orchestrated by the adjacency of formal elements. Two chairs arranged for an intimate conversation or a snow globe from Miami to spark discourse about shopping in the Art Deco district, each represent the power of the inanimate to influence the animate. The object as possession maintains the presence of the reasoning for purchase. Cost, use, color, whim, et cetera, each remain as determinants of the mindset of purchase. The combination of a series of these decisions develops a collective collage of reasoning, preference, geography; chance and fiscal position combine to define personality. The result is the opportunity for interface as representative of the cognitive or physical reaction. These boundaries create a perimeter of circumstance establishing the edges of understanding, exposure, and perception.

BODY

The body as a physical presence serves as the instigator of occupancy. Architectural form, furniture, and objects of occupation each react, respond, and relate to the body. As the biological point of departure defining scale, use, and reasoning, the static form must engage its constraints. When set into motion, the movement of the body demands a re-allocation of use based upon the spontaneity of consideration. The primary animator of space, the reactionary consideration is established based upon the five perceptive senses that allow for the ingestion of the information to define experience. The combination of multiple bodies establishes the relationship between individuals. The emotional and physical bond of contact, feeling, and expression are determined based upon the physical layering of socially acceptable levels of exposure, touch, and revelation. The collection determines the experience.

STYLE

Style is temporal with innate fluctuations of appeal. By definition it is perpetually in flux. Style as fashion applies to all aspects of life. Its valuation is inherently determined by the subjectivity of preference. The following represent moments for articulated shifts for action and reaction.

Paint: The thinness of applied surficial pigmentation permits an encompassing colored veil. The temporality, ease, and abundance of the product and its accessible process allow the opportunity for a frequency of renewal or change. The cosmetic nature of paint allows a variety of perceptual personalities assignable to the same static space. The media provides an infrastructural transitional ability for newness of occupation. The identity of mood is established by the resurfacing with color and its theory and perception.

Furniture: The layered population of architecture with furniture facilitates the interface of our physical form across a variety of required physical situations (from sitting to sleeping to dining, et cetera) determining the subdivision of spatial articulation. Furniture facilitates event effecting both space and interaction. Active bodily engagement establishes the primary point of interaction. Their specifics determine opportunity as they provide the specific choreography of physical occupation. The space, object, and event ebb and flow together as intertwined facilitators of experience. As previously mentioned, the framework for categorization is established by the impact of ownership history, culture, and era. The innate character of the inanimate is determined by the triangulation of these points. The power of formal suggestion and the traditional association that each hold, determines the way in which an object is employed. The role of the inanimate's animation is determined by a culturally shared collective perception of stylistic association, functional use, and compositional arrangement. A chair is rarely placed atop a table for seating. Rules of biology, practicality, and etiquette all suggest otherwise, however the view from atop one dining room table is in fact quite splendid. The result of tradition is a homogenization of consideration and experience.[83]

Collections: The role of collections similarly associates the history of object with the identity of ownership. The collection provides an object lineage establishing a relative continuity within which one can place themselves. The role of the physical catalog of type attempts to capture history (both prior to perception and autobiographical alike) documenting event and experiences to self through nostalgia. The collection of objects associates with the continuity of experience with the moment of purpose (time, place, position, and reason) equally established through the presence of object. The combined effect of the collection is the objectification of purpose. The result is marking in a formal way the experiences of life and the associated meaning of presence as defined by the collected actions of experience through consumption. The collection focuses the intention, highlighting the action, and representing the perseverance of presence defining contemporary survival through the adjacency of comparative contrast.

Still Image: The immediate preservation of the experienced event is preserved in the collected and displayed still image. As a photographic or manual production, the image has the power to capture. The collected events of experience are captured and gathered in a direct way. The image provides a personalized historical documentary of events, people, places, and ultimately experience. The simultaneity of collected and displayed imagery collapses time and highlights selective moments. Their presence provides a return or new interaction by transposing the moment. The emotion and action of the moment remains active through its interface.

Artificial Imported Environments: To compliment and accelerate event, the addition of atmosphere can establish mood through audio and visual productions of projected environments (music, web, television, movies, et cetera). The speed and diversity can broadly influence experience. Their presence creates an atmosphere that impacts the interaction of occupation. (Audible Mood): Music creates mood and influences adjacent activities. Level, intensity, rhythm, and genre each assist in the definition of place. The temporality of presence through the short duration of a song facilitates cyclical differentiated types of occupation. Circumstance orchestrates the occupant. (Projected Image): The desire for an escape from the practical realities of everyday circumstance results in a demand for the artificial imagery of movies and television to inflate to become a dimension of occupation. Through the visual simulacra we travel to distant places. Reality becomes one version as the ethereal world of projected dreams and fantasies expand perceptual realms. The television (TV) as the contemporary point of information control and dispensation is responsible for the cyclical disappearance of boundaries. Normal (typical) and artificial actions breed in its passive glow. The mechanism allows for the two-dimensional projected "reality" of fantasy to collapse time, space, and information. The projected escapism of the virtual experience temporarily transports the mind to cognitively re-adjust our method of occupation.

The value of the architecturalization of occupancy is the diverse role of the inhabitant who infinitely changes the presence of place. Space is immutable but similarly transmutable allowing for the ebb and flow of perception along all lines of duration relative to the details of the moment. The mind and heart, emotion and cognition, each respond and react to the presence of the contextual environment differently. The inanimate forms of one's surroundings impose their presence on its activities. The stage generates the scene as the actors are influenced by the surrounds that determine their presence.

We each are a product of the actions and things that surround us. The result is the accumulation of experience that we bring to the next situation to deal with the action and things that will take us to the next situation and so on. The realization is that at each moment and each situation we re-define ourselves based upon the previous experiences and the adjacencies of context. Color, form, light, sound, and image each invade our territories to confront our sensibilities and demand our attention. The result is the occupation of our space to allow the determination of our presence. The "self" is stitched into the "other" through the unique circumstances of the physical locale. The result is the architecturalization of occupation and the orchestration of its resultant. Architecture moves beyond the static form of its completed construction and instead presents itself in the incomplete cycle of its use. The collection of identities and experiences, associative representations and recollections, each stitch into the active and passive to present instigators and systems for the methods of presence. The architecture emerges through the occupation.

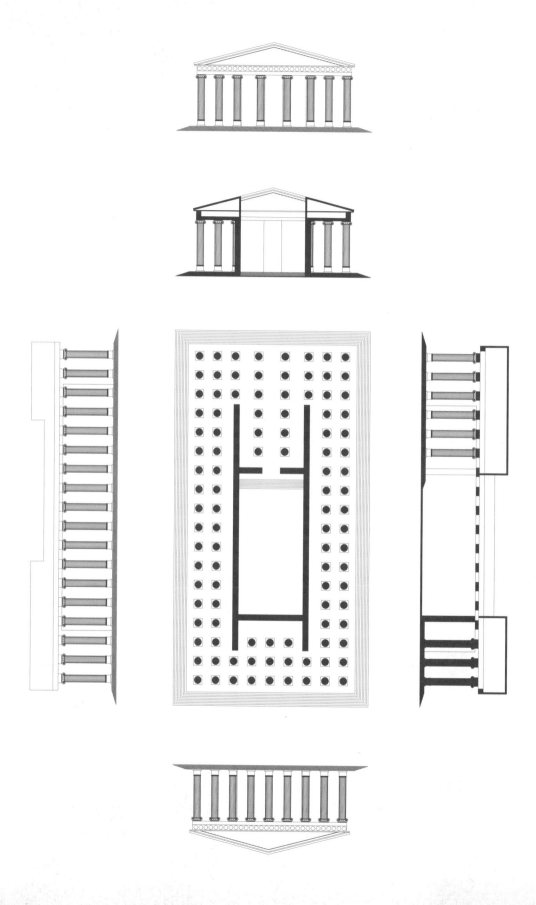

TEMPLE OF ARTEMIS

SYSTEMATIZED LOGIC + ABSTRACT GEOMETRY

Plan

The dominance of the geometry of the regularized gridded field privileges the abstract system produced by self-similar elements repeated in a multivalent field. The regimental purity produces an abstract array: detached from reference to natural systems and ordered into an abstract perfection of repeated sameness. This manifest geometry shifts spatial conception to strive for idyllic and encompassing environments regulated by order. The compositional regularity requires the occupation through activity, movement, and localized hierarchy to exist relative to the body and the perception of self.

THRESHOLD 1
Systematized Logic and Abstract Geometry

TEMPLE OF ARTEMIS

The Greek Temple of Artemis[84] in Ephesus was initially built during the Bronze Age and then destroyed by a flood during the 7th century BCE. Reconstruction began around 550 BCE, under the Cretan architect Chersiphron and his son Metagenes. This version of the Temple of Artemis at Ephesus was the first temple to be made entirely of marble and one of the largest Greek temples ever built measuring 377 feet long and 180 feet wide.[85] Pliny describes the temple with 127 columns, each sixty feet high. Thirty-six of these columns were decorated by carvings in relief.[86] Vitruvius describes it as dipteral octastyle: comprised of two rows of columns encircling the perimeter temple with eight across on the front and rear façades.[87] A central cella housed the goddess's cult image.

The tripartite construction of the temple (base, column field, and roof) is reiterated through the tripartite articulation of the individual column's base, shaft and capital. With layered levels of detail in the upper and lower portions of each system, the middle generates exaggerated verticality to draw the eye and establish an abstract and geometrically rationalized field system. The cella located at the rear of the composition is differentiated through the simple boundary of its planar wall system that redirects the axis to the vertical: emphasizing the axis mundi of the spiritual connection through the open yet framed sky space.

The componential construction of the system, rendered in a homogeneous material, is locally made formally distinct through the segmental resolution of each element. Each part of the compositional and tectonic system is articulated by individuated and rational pieces based upon their compositional function, tectonic role, and inter-legibility of ornament and form.

The Greek temple is a deeply ordered object. Visually dominated by the primary field of encircling columns, the composition is made through systemic, discrete pieces rhythmically assembled. The experience of the temple is defined by an axial sequence. This primary processional establishes a layered hierarchy through the multi-directional and homogeneous columnar field. The Temple of Artemis exaggerates the effect of the columnar field through its double layer of perimeter columns. This perimeter encircling ambulatory creates flanking pathways that impress a multiplicity to the plan beyond the central axis. Though two-dimensionally organized, the arrayed repetitive lattice of the column field is three-dimensionally perceived through its stacking in depth. The result is an optical offset that allows for the focal cone of perspectival perception to create a shifted visual position through the recession of object layers. Accentuated by light (banded by the open closed nature of the alternating columns) each layer is activated with varied and recessional tonal gradients.

The combined offset establishes palimpsest depth through the optical perception of the layers.

The path of approach moves the viewer on and off axis to allow the perception of the three-dimensional form when off (by accentuating the oblique) and the ordered directional hierarchy emphasizing the totality of the organizing system when on. The sectional progression amplifies this experience by developing critical thresholds through vertical shifts along the path. The elevated siting allows for the exaggeration of the height positioning the approach from below. The plinth is a series of ascending steps separating the form from the ground plane, objectifying the figure, and providing dominance and detachment over the surrounding landscape. This disconnection emphasizes the abstract nature of the arrayed column field. The repetitive multivalent banding of the column field creates an environment defined by the regularity of the geometry. The equality of the hierarchy of the gridded field establishes an equality to the localized yet encompassing surroundings that requires a centering on the body in order to map oneself in the abstract space. The delegation of presence relative to the equality of the uniform surroundings eliminates the specificity of context and creates an immersive and disconnecting environment. Privileging geometry and proportion of the system based in abstract continuity, the role of the body is foregrounded through its contrasting nature. Like the 100 untitled works in mill aluminum by Donald Judd,[88] the repeating elements aggregate to establish an engulfing field that allows for the systemic blanketing of body within a larger geometrically derived context. This shift from an organic and differentiated environment to the regularized and homogeneously articulated array allows for the preferential establishment of an abstract systemization. Derived from hyper-articulated and elemental components, the collective establishes a perceptually encompassing whole in the abstract grid. Governed by the array of geometric rationalities, the emphatic system establishes the perceptual plane as the dominate condition: intellectually constructed and optically mapped into a cohesive environment. The Temple of Artemis represents several significant conceptual thresholds for architecture:

THE DEVELOPMENT OF THE ABSTRACT MULTIVALENT FIELD

Through serial repetition, the column field introduced a geometrically regularized abstract space. Immersive to the body and thus unable to be fully perceived from within, the creation of this intangible field introduced the role of geometry and regularity of order to create a reductive environment. The abstract removal facilitated a centering on the body as the foreign object to the abstract system requiring a reflective sense of self as the relative perceptual frame by which it should be read. This privileging of the body in space is a primary touchstone of architecture that allows for buildings to aspire to emotive and effectual ambitions beyond simply functional necessities.

THE INTRODUCTION OF THE HEROIC

The use of hierarchy to subordinate the normalcy of the anthropomorphic dimension creates a heroic scale. The massive overwhelming of the anthropomorphic dimension creates a monumentality that announces significance, introduces awe, and creates an elevating nature to the space through scale. The use of scale as a primary compositional element is made monumental by detaching the experience

from the everyday, announcing the significance and power of the place and its experience, creating an "other" worldly plane to the architecture.

THE DEVELOPMENT OF SEQUENTIAL EXPERIENCE: A CHOREOGRAPHED PATH

The articulation of sequence with variation and transition along a path introduced the architectural promenade. The engagement of perceptive experiences that evolve over time with critical thresholds, moments of hierarchy and ceremony to orchestrate an experience as the purpose of the architecture displaces the reading of the object as a compositional and formal element and instead privileges the experiential sequence as a generative event. The perceptual engagement with the totality of the sensorial spectrum to evoke a ritualized and curated effect transitioned the fundamental opportunity for architecture to move beyond form alone to engage experience.

HOMOGENEITY OF MATERIAL WITH FORMAL EXPRESSIONISM OF TECTONIC LOGIC

Made from a consistent material palette, the articulation of the pieces through their localized form and referential detailing generated a visual vocabulary to establish an expressive language. Founded in a rule based sensibility, the geometry, order, and hierarchy of the pieces create a collective language of architecture that allows for a reading of the parts and their referential combination into a collective composition governed by an overall system. The establishment of a rule system and organizational logic for architecture to follow with a prescriptive sensibility established the premise of the architectural discipline, the commutability of the reading and the subscription to a collectively shared ideal.

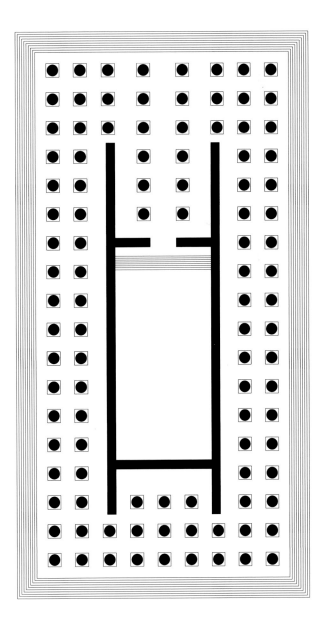

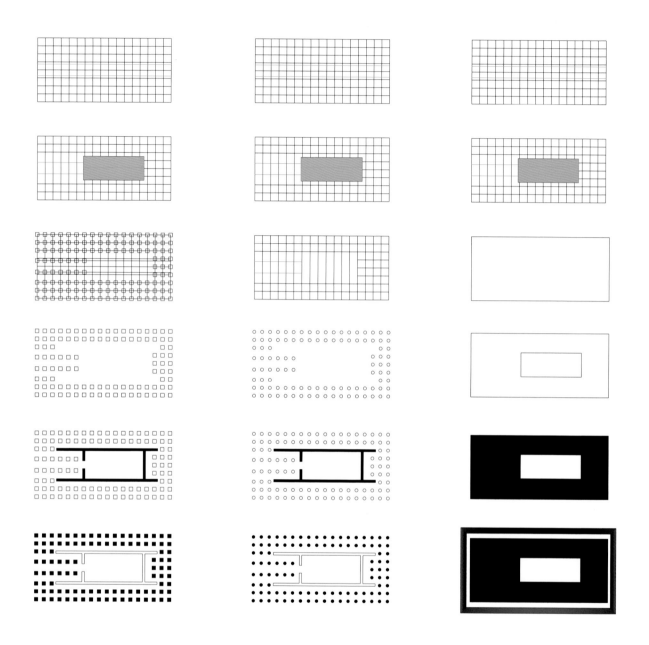

Planametric Figuration

The fundamental organizational system of the Temple of Artemis is the grid field. Establishing the base system for all other elements, the square grid is an equal, multivalent field. Irregularities in the system are introduced to create a shifted offset for wider central entry axes (one from each direction). The central cella sets within the field extending past the grid crossings in all directions. The shifted position allows the cella to read independently from the field as a discrete object set within the larger system. The columns sit at the nodal crossing points of the grid. As a three-dimensional extension of the two-dimen-

sional logic, the resulting hypostyle field furthers the dominance of the geometric order through their repetitive deployment. The density and equality of the resulting pattern creates a balanced oscillation between positive and negative. Both present as object and absent as space, the two intertwine with balanced ambiguity lacking dominance between the experience and object equally privileging each through the emphatic rationality of the geometry.

Elemental Constructs

The overall massing of the Temple of Artemis highlights its segmental and tripartite systemic formulation. The base as an elevating plinth detaches the composition from the ground and establishes a hierarchical and "other worldly" plane that creates a separation through ascension providing dominance to the independence of the geometric order.

The column field extends the nodal crossings of the grid vertically to create a blanketing extrusion of abstract geometry. The roof creates a cap that frames a void over the cella for vertical extension (an implied axis mundi) through its ocular aperture.

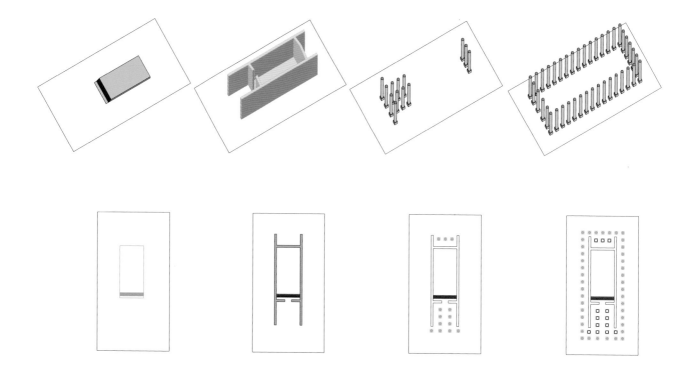

Sequential Components

Working from the center outward, each of the elemental systems of the Temple of Artemis allow for individual expression of sequential experiential layers. The central cella is marked by an elevated plane that ascends to provide hierarchy to the position. Encircling this platform are bounding walls that turn the eye upward to create a vertical axis to the sky. Nested within these walls are columnar clusters that extend the field on one end while separating it to create a central aisle on the other. Encircling this are two rings of columns. Equally spaced, they create edge corridors through their doubling while still emphasizing and privileging the central axis. Lastly is the perimeter stairs that equally ascend in all directions to produce an elevating plinth that objectifies the whole. The roof covers the columnar field, gathering the individual elements into a connected system while bending the axis vertically to frame the sky through its massive aperture. The collective elements create a sequential experience of moments along a ceremonial path.

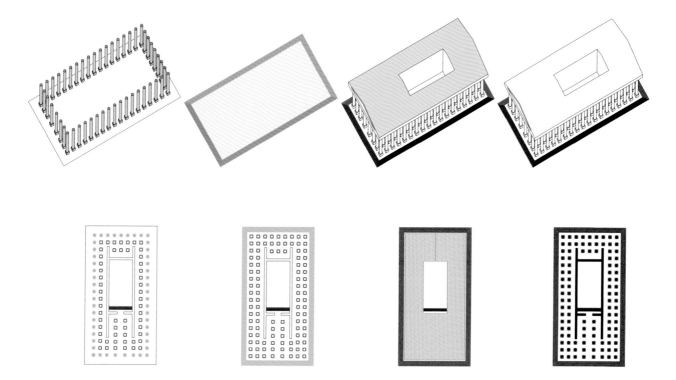

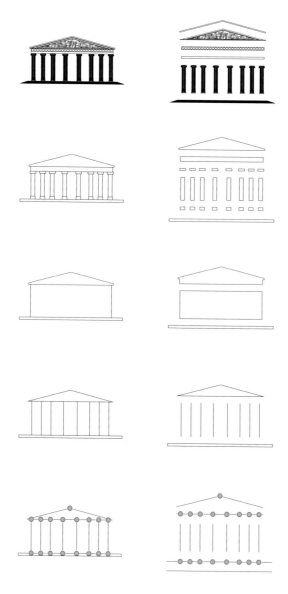

Facade Elemental Composition

Analysis of the elevational components of the Temple of Artemis illustrates the building's striation into a three part composition. Formally represented by (1) line, (2) rectangle, and (3) triangle, these three elements extend their platonic geometries into their individuated articulation. The base is a series of terraced and stacking rectangles forming an ascending four sided pyramid that offsets in the X axis. The central columnar field is an array of extruded points (each capped in a base and a capital) that extend upward along the Z axis. The roof is a triangle pulled the length of the building in the Y axis.

These elements assume the associated structural functions of foundation/plinth, column, and trussed roofing spanning and capping the field.

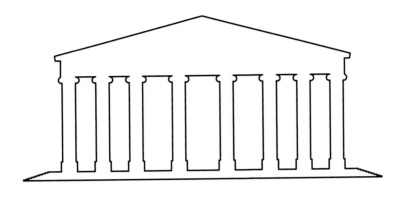

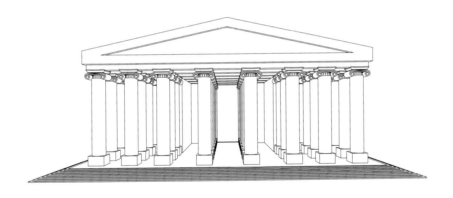

Projective vs. Perspectival

The flat projective facade of the Temple of Artemis reveals the regular meter of the columns organized by a central axial void to create a hierarchical pathway. This alignment creates the main circulation path leading through the column field towards the cella. This widened gap, exaggerated through a perspectival reading, provides an accentuation of the layers and an exaggerated revelation of the receding increment. The perspectival perception of the arrayed column field generates a layered progression of the optical recessive field. The visual offset of the aligned field (read through the layered grid) exaggerates the depth through the revelation of the anterior rows. The narrowing increment of the column spacing toward the outside edges (in combination with the extended stacking of the oblique and peripheral view) allows an accelerated perception of the recessional field. The density of the system accumulates to exaggerate the layering and depth of field.

20 PROPOSITIONS FOR SUBURBAN LIVING

20 PROPOSITIONS
FOR SUBURBAN LIVING
20 Single-Family Housing Prototypes

These projects are propositions for introducing ultra-modern single-family housing into the current suburban landscape. To demonstrate the multiplicity of formal solutions possible from a set of governing design principles, a series of twenty houses have been developed. These are not proposals for a singular design solution but a comprehensive method. Six of the twenty are articulated in greater detail to provide in-depth exploration and representative detailing.

The houses employ: phasability; material and spatial modularity; prefabrication; efficient and experiential spatial planning; readily available and sustainable materials with minimal modification; programmatic zoning; and connection of interior and exterior; to maintain affordability, update the current conception of the "house," and increase the quality of the space, experience, and formal composition by introducing architecture to the ubiquitous developer led building typology. These proposals selectively re-present aspects of the current suburban domestic condition while beginning an evolution to a new way of living. They are proposals to make the ordinary extraordinary.

The inquiry is organized in four parts: the first [1] textually depicting the conceptual framework, establishing the need and premise of the proposal; the second [2] illustrating the conceptual framework behind the design solutions, the third [3] documenting 6 houses in depth; and the fourth [4] briefly cataloging the remaining 14 designs.

SUBURBAN

Architecture must exist in the everyday. The current suburban landscape is a bleak vision of an ignored composition. Working within the existing infrastructure these propositions work to bring change and generate architecture as a fabrication of culture that demands a re-presentation of the formal considerations, material considerations, economic considerations, and technological considerations of the everyday. This vision must position itself within the suburban landscape in which we live, asking the question: "how do we live"?

The component compositions as fragments in the larger city become the pieces that fill the matrix of urbanity and drive the sprawl of the modern megalopolis. The site within the pattern becomes the seminal grain, the premise of terrain and occupation. The 60-foot by 120-foot lot is the beginning. Overlaid upon this physical condition is the cultural heritage of the domestic realm. The redefinition of domesticity, sociological associations, phenomenological experiences, formal fabrications, and the effectual qualities of light, space, and material, positioned within the realities of economy generates the opportunity

for the reinsertion of architecture into the suburban house. Their organization determines how we think about the making of place and the idea of building the realm of possibilities for contemporary living.

The infrastructures we have to choose from: slab on grade, balloon framing, gable roofs, et cetera are not corrupt ideas, but rather forms and techniques that have come through a legacy and tradition of building. Their meaning and original intention culturally commuted through the object has been lost and must be evolved to be employed in our current vocabulary. The transposition of identity (applying history to acquire a referential formalism that mimics tradition rather than responding to culture) removes relevancy. The result is falsity founded in simulation. To shift to a generative cultural method rather than an associative reference implies client, personality, site, culture, geography, economy, et cetera, must be addressed as influential and instigating mechanisms.

The single family detached suburban house is the predominate mode of domestic production in North America. The house has become the largest individual financial investment. Despite the American Dream associating individual freedom with homeownership, the formal and functional qualities of the home are tightly regulated by a fiscal infrastructure that demands economic commutability. The house has to subscribe to the "sellable" capabilities of the larger market system. The system dictates that the house must be of a certain quality and these qualities have distinct mandates dictating the form, space, and experience of the home. The system thus innately denies any tailoring towards an individual as it must remain, at least potentially, dispensable, disposable, and exchangeable. The system however does not require the generic medium to which we currently subscribe. The potential exists for a move away from the homogenized domestic vocabulary through a holistic view of the housing market. Fashion remains fleeting, function is inadequate, the synthesis of the cultural and technological condition relative to the making of the domestic realm is ignored and thus the parameter for formal determination cannot be definitely found in economics only generally suggested.

The greatest current housing supply and demand in the United States occurs in the suburbs. The single-family house is the American dream and the standard to which the majority aspires. Currently these landscapes are devoid of architecture. They are dominated by speculative builders that subscribe to a singular model of development regardless of family size, geographic location, material quality, or formal meaning. The house has eroded all synchronized sense of practicality and iconography of home. The result is a bleak and pervasive landscape studded with the conventionally bland. These propositions assume the responsibility of providing for new ways of living within this framework. The celebration of the processes that determine the house provide for its reconfiguration.

HORIZONTAL PRODUCTION AND
SUBURBAN SERIALITY

The horizontal production of American space is led by the suburban single-family detached home. The serial, isolated, individual allotments of owned space (house) define individuality in a society and economy dominated by the standardization of mass production. Legislative codes combined with market demands and nomadic ownership prevents the maintenance of the tradition of the homestead. Professions, detached from the cultivation of the land, have transitioned the role of the landscape as an active entity employed for sustenance, to a banal backdrop of cataloged class structure. The positioning of the yard (lawn) and its ornamentation against the standardized and representative false fronts of suburban imagery illustrates the contemporary condition.

Disposable income, market forces, and cultural extremes have established personal identity as the collection of accumulated possessions. These objects manifest individuality in a tangible form. Architecture enters as a cultural mediator in this landscape. Blanketed by the serial desires and methods of production, the system produces a repetitive homogeneity to the contemporary domestic type. It has become a backdrop, removed from individual vision or local consideration. Assimilated by an artificial but culturally symbolic language, the haze of the background (suburbanity) focuses uniqueness on the foreground (collection of possessions). The shells are the same with only the aggregated content curation defining the difference.

Sub-urbanism is a loose fill. Traversed by rivers of asphalt, negotiated through rear view mirrors, and experienced with radio soundtracks, the landscape becomes insular. Occupied by automobiles, the suburban is an arena dominated by the speed and dimension of mechanized mobility. The experiential cone of vision is cropped and reconfigured. The physical cage of extended social space engulfs the dimension of the seated group. The scale and character must adjust to this transition. The operation of the machine detaches the individual from the sequential experience of detail or individuality denying the necessity for these elements to exist. Curb appeal claims the borderland.

The landscape pays homage to the infrastructure and ultimately the participation in social discourse. Democracy is represented only in its ideality. The orchestration of the field subscribes to a nostalgic legacy of history, form, symbol, necessity, and scale. Identity and thus individuality of ownership emerges only out of occupation.

Architects serving only the adventurous individual and the economically privileged have ignored the contemporary domestic realm too long. The result is an ever growing landscape that consumes more of our time and space than any other building type and more investment than any other economic forum, yet less design.

The 20 propositions are a projection upon a historical and pictorial dissection of the contemporary condition emerging from a post-World War II neighborhood to the contemporary suburban development. The attitudes and operative considerations that emerge from this architectural orchestration provides for the collective underpinnings of the serial landscape and their opportunities for engagement.

THE HOUSE

The house is *the* essential possession. It represents an inner world of personal space, leisure, and repose. It is the most intimate of spaces as a nest and a dwelling. The importance of the home is paramount to our human existence. Identity relative to the appearance of this structure becomes intertwined with our individual personality, taste, and circumstance. It represents us through not just the forms of what we live in but the configuration and nuance of the spaces themselves. The home represents freedom, individuality, and the partitioning of a world that belongs to the individual. It demands architectural consideration.

The current American domestic landscape is the suburb. The loose density of the single-family suburban home is defined by a freestanding structure (shelter) and encircling land of individual ownership. The house is the most significant space one interacts with on a recurring daily basis. A homeowner spends more time in their dwelling than in any other building. The importance of its organization, material, and form demands attention and consideration.

program house

The house is an investment as well as a practical and functional object. The house is thus governed by both the individual and the group. Though the specific homeowner owns and controls the configuration and appearance of their home, the market economy dictates resale and value. This bifurcated balance of location relative to amenities, size relative to features, and taste relative to fashion define the assessment of value.

The definition of family has diversified its configurations. The provision of a quality of architecture and contemporary domestic consideration (social and technological) while remaining competitive with standard market influences, presents an opportunity for a shift in the real estate development market to generate an entirely new definition of home. Simultaneously upgrading the prefabricated home, the modular home, the mobile home, and the "kit" or cookie cutter development plan book models with quality of space and orchestration of performance and perception (while firmly maintaining their underpinning economic parameters) these houses offer a path forward within the system.

The potential for the home emerges from the proposition of a reassessment of how we live through a cultural update of the domestic type and the presentation of a diversity of methods of development. This restructuring within the current planning and market structure proposes alternative solutions.

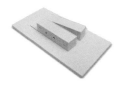

gradient house

This investigation is demonstrated with the production of multiple houses to demonstrate a process over solutionism. Methods of construction, materiality, programmatic arrangement, and spatial configuration are variably addressed across each of the prototypes highlighting the potential for their formal, physical, and experiential impact on the architecture. The practicality of the seemingly impractical is the strength of these propositions.

porch house

Each house is organized along a different conceptualization of living. Individual needs such as scale, finance, function, and form are all varied to provide a diversity of types. They are seen as a collection of solutions. Each responding to aspects and needs, suggestions and negotiations, these houses are intended to disperse to infill existing neighborhoods or aggregate to form new ones. Their context is contemporary culture and their motivation is the production of affordable residential architecture that provides—through the single family detached house—new ways of looking at an underdeveloped yet dominant building type.

The contemporary landscape is suburban.

The "common" landscape of suburbia is the architectural frontier. American architecture with its suburban condition and the associated trends and traditions of sprawl is founded on the basic building block of the single-family detached house. The American Dream of home ownership propagates loose development that spawns the expanding ringing sprawl of downtown centers. Arterial development lined with commercial strip centers and big box commercial stores, provide waves of serial brand names extending a uniformity. The house as a ubiquitous program has become a facilitator and commodity evolving as a hybridized generic image of living. Individuality has been sacrificed for iconography.

The current single-family house subscribes to a model that addresses bank loan guidelines but denies the contemporary cultural condition. The forms, organization, and styles (though commonplace) are anachronistic and divorced from their original intention. Technological booms demand an associated evolutionary ingestion into the home with formal, functional, and programmatic response. The parameters of domesticity have been changed. The house needs to respond. The focus on this type, via intent rather than nostalgia, will provide meaning through cultural evolution as reconsiderations of the single-family home.

The following propositions present opportunities for the conventional and average condition. They are considered iterations emergent from the standard economic, programmatic, and functional requirements accelerated to illustrate the potential to find architecture in the "ordinary." By focusing on both the contemporary use and lifestyle along with the governing infrastructures of finance, development, and construction that shape the house; these prototypes establish a method of design that privileges contemporary culture as the foundation for specific and viable solutions for changing our constructed landscape. These prototype houses *"build what we are."*

tube house

This architectural investigation emerges from a desire to look at the existing condition, operate within its constraints and conditions, and find within this system the opportunity to provide architecture. The product, as a celebration of inevitabilities, relies upon a love of what one can afford to love and from that the generation of a composition that can be practiced, that can be fabricated, and that can be integrated and synthesized to allow for the individual and unique composition while still subscribing to the general principles. This allows for the serial investigation of a type (the detached single-family residence) not as a formal play but rather a re-interpretive method of

how one lives, the priority of spaces, the definition of form, the expression of material, the relationship of space, the association of the inhabitant with the object, and the innate phenomenology of these experiences.

The architecture of this investigation comes into play with the art, wonder, and beauty of each moment celebrated to its full potentials, while still subscribing to a fundamental premise: single family house on a 60-foot by 120-foot lot with a three bedroom and two and a half bath program. The intent is for these actualities of living to be impacted by their space. The architecture, rather than becoming hinged upon simple features, becomes hinged upon the synthesis of the experience with the contemporary nature of a cultural need. The house is a facilitator for event, for activity, it is an enclosure that contains both human and objects, allowing for an interface and social interaction. The relationships between its innate networks are facilitated through the activities of simply living. The mundane and "the given" are allowed to prosper through the choreography of the situation.

PRINCIPLES OF COMPARATIVE ANALYSIS

The production of a new model for suburban living that reconsiders the possibilities of its inception demands a comparative analysis of the existing condition. Primary principles include: surface area, program, typology, service and served, public and private, day and night, indoor and outdoor, phasing and mutability, material and modularity, experience, and cost. Each of these elements becomes topical methods for re-approaching contemporary living. The following principles represent the foundational investigation of these topics providing an artifactual background to the premise of each proposition.

20 Propositions For Suburban Living

Surface area:

Each proposition adopts the standard 60-foot-wide by 120-foot-deep site with associated and conforming setbacks. Basing its proportional size on comparable 1,800-square-foot homes, the propositions look at the quality and perceived size of space as opposed to simple square footage. Increased costs for material upgrades and transparency are offset by reduced square footages of interior spaces to produce more efficient footprints with greater functional and effectual consideration. The focus is on the quality of space over the quantity of space.

Program:

The proposition's engage the standard house program of three bedrooms with two and a half bathrooms. They re-conceive the contemporary use of spaces to allow for an organizational re-zoning of the house. They engage a less compartmentalized and monolithic conception of functions in favor of varied spatial types that facilitate efficiency and celebrate function through occupation to create a ceremony to use. Ganging and privileging, typically aerosolized, and utilitarian spaces allow for pragmatic elements to breed efficiency and compositionally express typically subordinated functions of the house.

constellation house

Typology:

The propositions emerge from diverse historical typologies (dogtrot, shotgun, et cetera) but shed the traditions of their referential forms in favor of their hierarchical and conceptual principles. Reconsidering organization and overall spatial planning through broad formal operations, the propositions re-investigate and reinterpret traditional spatial and formal models.

enclosure house

Material + Modularity:

The propositions use off the shelf whole module material construction. Each house is carefully constructed on a full 4-foot by 8-foot material module to reduce modifications and labor. Apertures are located at seams and conventional details and building techniques of common materials are favored for efficiency. Reconsideration of traditions of finish and exaggerated efficiency of fabrication are both foregrounded. The potential for factory built prefabrication is accommodated to provide the option of production efficiency, cost savings, speed and ease of construction, and sequential phasability based upon a responsive approach to programmatic expansion over time.

Cost:

The propositions work within the same bank guidelines and target market based price points of the existing suburban housing stock. Affordability is achieved through a reduction of square footage, use of common off-the-shelf materials in whole dimensions to reduce waste, extensive use of modular construction, and potential factory built prefabrication.

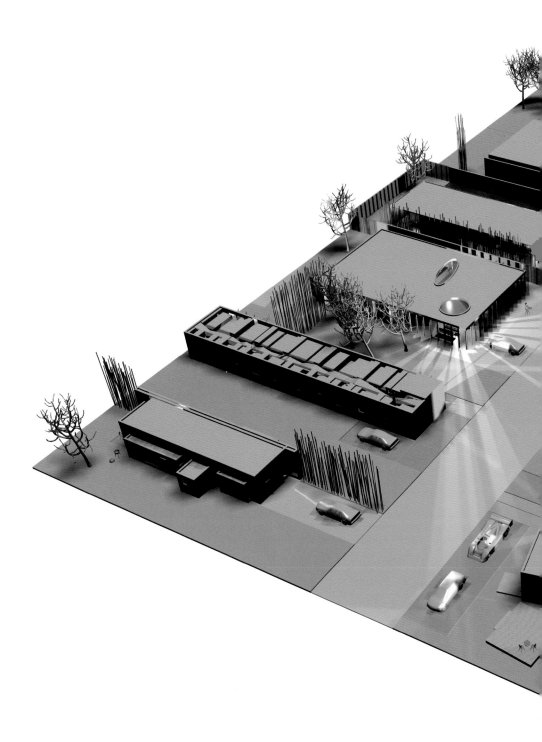

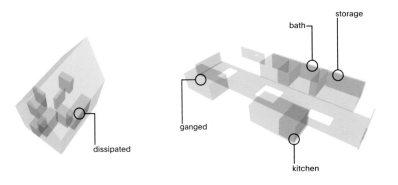

Service/Served

The typical home dissipates service functions such as storage, utility, bath, and kitchen facilities. As a spatial type their organization bleeds throughout the house generating awkward juxtapositions and limited segmental usage. They are everywhere and nowhere.

The propositions gang service functions to provide for clear articulation and ordering of these spaces. This provides for a separation of service and served while streamlining their needs and efficiencies through their grouped association.

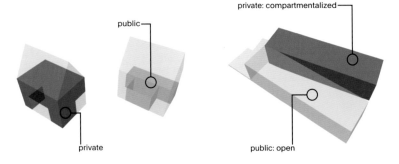

Public/Private

The typical house is singular in form relying upon the articulation of space as public or private to be determined by furniture and name. Traditionally the upper level is held for sleeping (potentially with a ground floor master suite). The public spaces fill in the remainder of the house. The result is spaces that do not reflect the character of their use and have awkward juxtapositions and inefficiencies.

By zoning the public and private and articulating their boundaries through formal expression, the propositions allow for a greater spatial articulation, formality, and diversity within a smaller square footage.

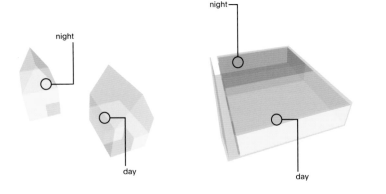

Day/Night

Similar to the public and private separations, the day to night delineations in the conventional home are typically sectional inhibiting the cross-usage of these spaces across the 24-hour cycle. The result is the need for more space to serve the singularly articulated functions.

The propositions attempt to blur the singular functionality of any one space. Employing zones rather than rooms, the single story free plans allow for an efficiency through a multiplicity of functional interpretations.

20 Propositions For Suburban Living

Indoor/Outdoor

The bounded forms of the typical house deny connectivity between interior spaces and the adjacent landscape. The separation requires a formal decision to move from one zone to the other establishing each as destination experiences. The yard and lawn demand a great deal of time and maintenance and receive minimal use (physical or visual) due to this lack of spatial connectivity.

The spatial connectivity of the propositions provides for a fluid movement between inside and out connecting and expanding the efficient interior spaces both visually and physically with the exterior. Any increased costs to accomplish this transparent and operable connectivity are balanced by a reduction in square footage relying upon the perceived spatial expansion to maintain a quality of spatial scale.

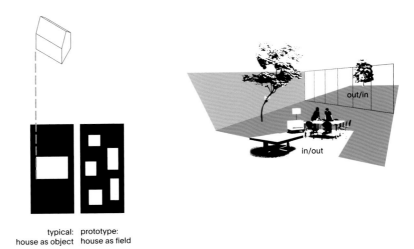

typical: house as object   prototype: house as field

out/in

in/out

Phasing [1+2+3]

The static conception of the typical home requires the construction of the entire structure and all of its amenities in one burst. As a result the threshold for home ownership is increased and the market requires a nomadic attitude requiring one to move to a larger house for expansion. This nomadism further emphasizes the house as a translatable commodity and prevents the traditions of the homestead and associative sense of place and community. The singularity of the composition does not provide for the natural expansion and contraction that occur across the life of a home and its occupants.

The propositions are based in the idea of mutability: the allowance for the expansion and contraction of the house based upon changing needs over time. The composition, established through an efficiency of modularity and sequence, provides for the segmental construction of the home. The evolution allows investment in place despite changing requirements.

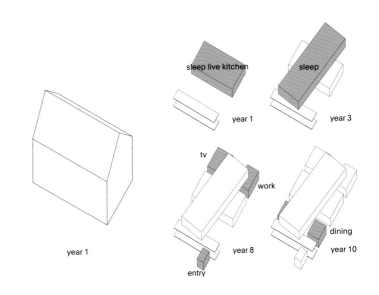

sleep live kitchen

sleep

year 1

year 3

tv

work

dining

year 8

year 10

entry

year 1

Experience/Quality

The typical suburban home subscribes to features rather than architecture to fabricate "quality." Identifiable, realtor based checklists have replaced space, light, and form. The feature as opposed to experience, determines commodifyable worth.

Subscribing to a compositional connectivity, the propositions rely upon a return to form and space to orchestrate the experience of architecture. Each house subscribes to varied formats of spatial organization and intention, yet rely upon the composition to develop the quality of perception and experience to ennoble everyday activities.

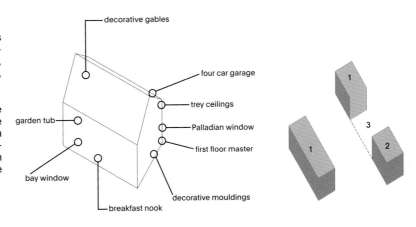

decorative gables

four car garage

trey ceilings

garden tub

Palladian window

first floor master

bay window

decorative mouldings

breakfast nook

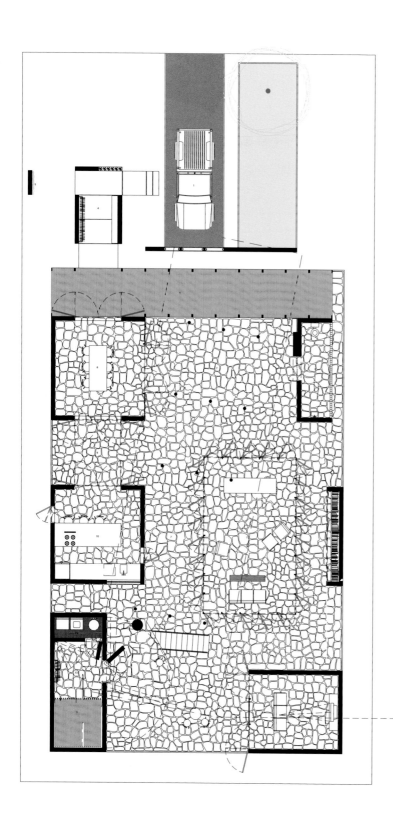

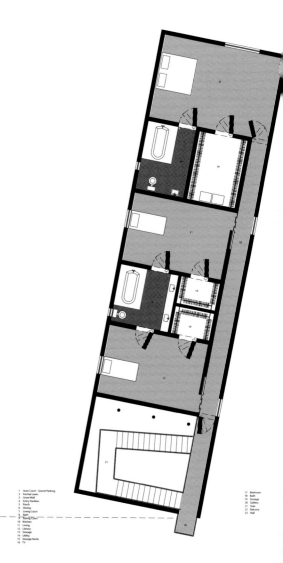

1   Auto Court - Gravel Parking
2   Formal Lawn
3   Grow Wall
4   Entry Pavilion
5   Porch
6   Dining
7   Living Court
8   Bath
9   Eating Court
10 Kitchen
11 Living
12 Library
13 Storage
14 Utility
15 Storage Racks
16 TV

17 Bedroom
18 Bath
19 Storage
20 Gallery
21 Stair
22 Balcony
23 Hall

[HOUSE 01]

The Program House relies upon three primary guiding principles: [1] the articulation of form based upon programmatic function; [2] the collection of these articulated programs as a campus of pavilions connected by an indoor-outdoor utility plinth; and [3] the ability to optionally prefabricate and phase these programmatic elements over time.

Zoned in section into public and private functions, each program is articulated in distinct pavilions. Their collection sets the individual pavilions in dialogue through an interstitial space that bridges and blurs the boundaries and compartmentalization of each program defining the house as a collective campus of interior and exterior spaces.

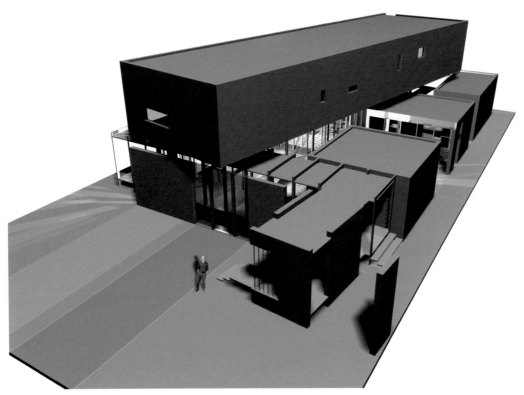

aerial view from street

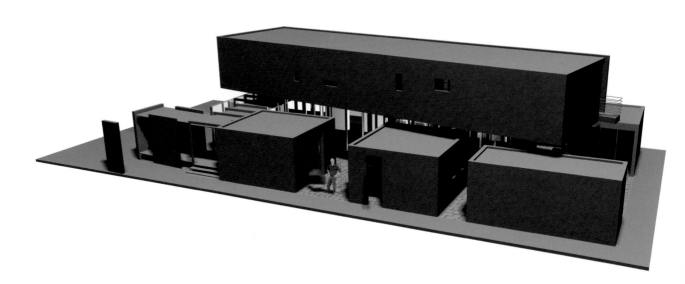

side view

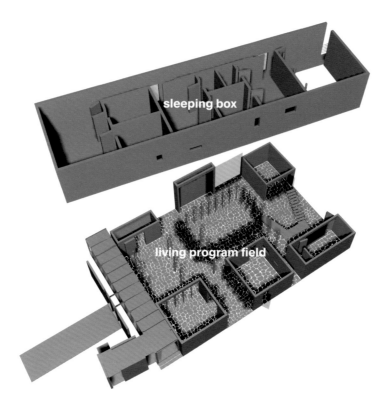

sleeping box

living program field

axonometric

view from porch

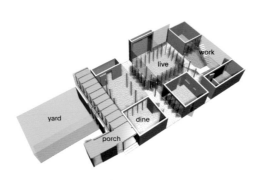

Program

The functions of the Program House are aerosolized and individuated in discrete pavilions. Activities occur in specifically tailored spaces. Set in a field upon a connective plinth, the spaces are mediated by interstitial exterior rooms formed between pavilions.

Day / Night + Public / Private

The day to night and public to private zoning of the Program House is governed by the section. An elevated sleeping box rotates off the geometry of the lower pavilions and adjusts to align with an ornamental tree in the front yard. The hovering box shields the lower spaces as a canopy and ceiling accessed by a covered exterior stair that folds down from the upper volume. The regularized structural column grid of the rotated upper volume skewers the lower geometry of the living plinth subdividing and orchestrating the spaces.

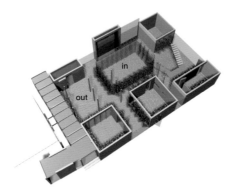

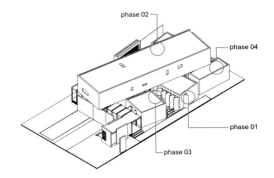

Interior / Exterior

The lower level of the Program House consists of a series of phasable pavilions linked by exterior spaces. The articulation of each independent form relative to its functional requirements allows for specific and ceremonial engagement and customization based upon need. The exterior connective zones allow for the flexible expansion of each volume providing interconnectivity of spaces and programs with the whole of the site.

Plinth + Field

The connective plinth of the Program House contains the shared services and utilities of the house. Feeding and gathering the pavilions it serves as a collective pedestal for the individually articulated pavilions. The plinth and its infrastructural services readily provide for phased expansion to be built over time as needed and afforded.

longitudinal section

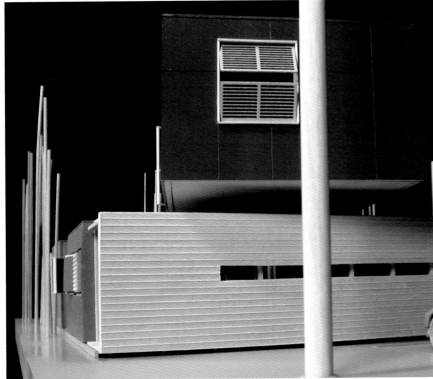
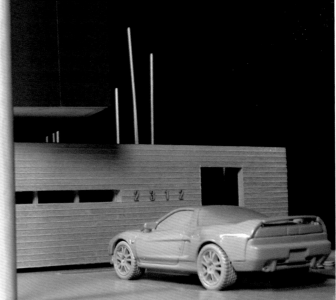

view from street

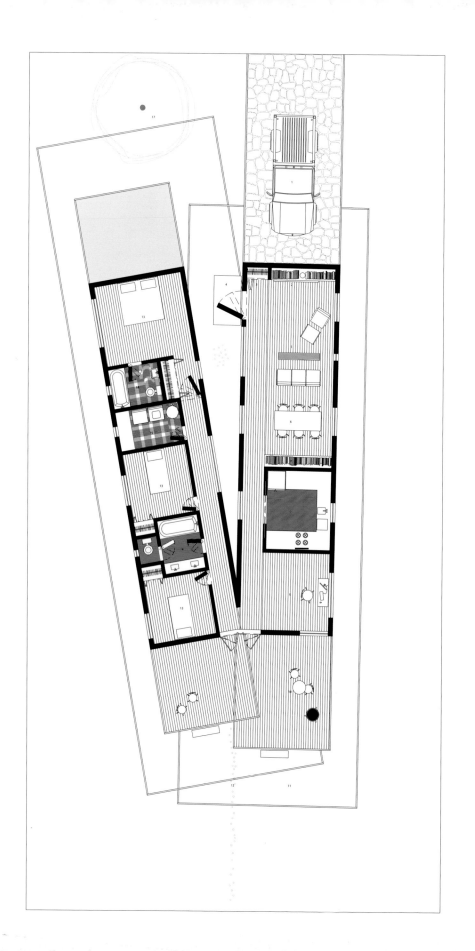

1   Auto Court - Gravel Parking
2   Fireplace
3   Coat Closet
4   Entry
5   Living
6   Dining
7   Library
8   Kitchen
9   Work
10 Porch
11 Gravel Plinth
12 Bamboo Plane
13 Sleeping
14 Bath
15 Utility
16 Formal Lawn
17 Ornamental Tree

GRADIENT HOUSE

[HOUSE 06]

The Gradient House zones programs into public and private functions each individually contained in two identically dimensioned bars. Pivoting at their intersection, the forms rotate out of alignment. The shifted geometries allow for the two bars to gently touch and create a diversity of bracketed and residual spaces across the site. The floor plates extend past each of the figures to create a superimposed rear porch. Each of the forms inscribes their geometries in the landscape with concentric gravel footprints that serve as splash plates for their oscillating shed roofs. The simple and efficient forms use material modularity to define both their dimensions (as a module of the flatbed tractor trailer allowing factory built prefabrication) and govern the location and size of apertures.

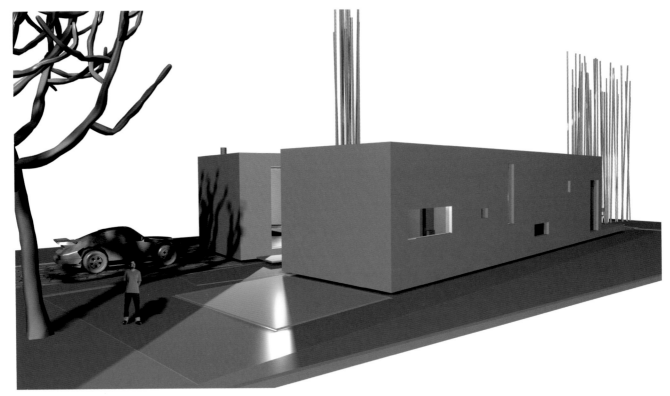

view from street

converging geometries

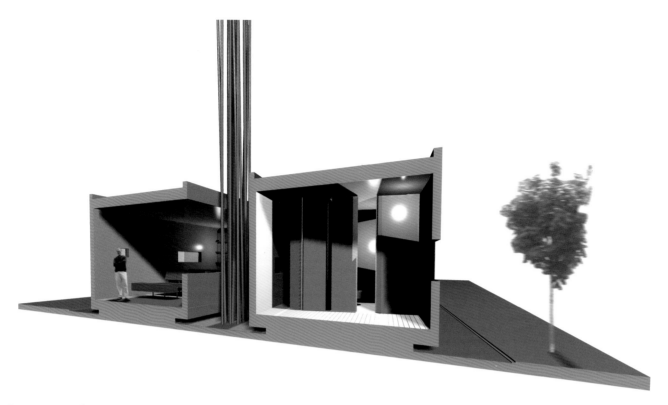

transverse section

back porch

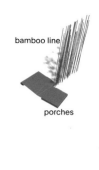

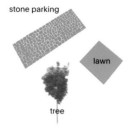

Public / Private

The Gradient House is defined by two identically dimensioned modular bars set in dialog with rotational geometries and zoned programming. The gradient of differential activity from public to private and day to night allows the pieces to balance and foil one another functionally and compositionally.

Landscape Elements

Four primary elements extend the "kissing" geometries of the Gradient House: [1] the back porches overlap and step down into the garden; [2] the vertical compaction resonates in a line of bamboo extending into the landscape; [3] the front trajectory of the public bar is extended to the street with a stone pad for vehicular parking; and [4] the private bar is extended by a formal objectified lawn, scribed in the gravel pad and balanced by a single tree. The remainder of the site is left as an indigenous and naturally raw landscape.

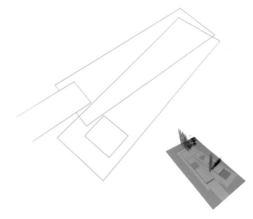

Open / Closed

Though identical in exterior scale and proportion, the two bars of the Gradient House subscribe to different interior spatial types: a free plan for the living space and a compartmentalized cellular space for the sleeping spaces. Associatively zoned as public and private, day and night, open and closed, each realm identifies itself in contrasting relativity to the other. The diversity of spatial types expands the complexity and dynamism of the efficient forms.

Geometry

In the Gradient House offset geometric outlines score themselves in the landscape and create a steel edge encasing a gravel pad for roof drainage. The remaining yard is left as indigenous vegetation. The echo of the house resonating into the landscape emphasizes and extends the geometric shift of the primary forms.

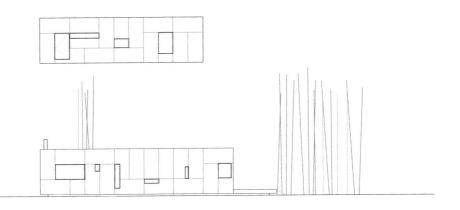

side elevation

modular construction

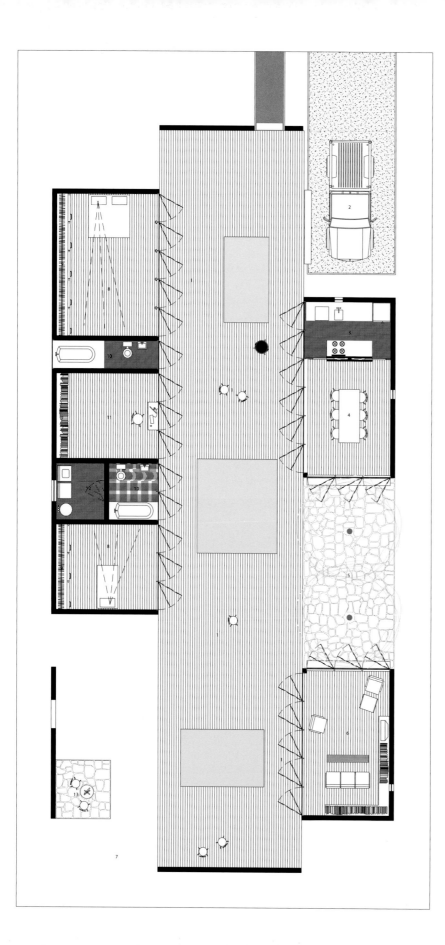

1   Porch
2   Auto Court - Gravel Parking
3   Kitchen
4   Dining
5   Flagstone Patio
6   Living
7   Lawn [Indigenous Material]
8   Sleeping
9   Storage Wall
10 Bath
11 Work
12 Utility
13 Fire Pit

PORCH
HOUSE

[HOUSE 08]

The Porch House organizes the landscape and daily activities of the house around a central porch. Despite the small, surrounded, and confined lot an exterior room is carved out and defined by using the building, segregated into multiple pavilions by programmatic function, to encircle an exterior porch. The central stage becomes room and corridor that one consistently traverses opening the house to the site and expanding the scale and perception of square footage. The table is a porch no longer relating to the street that is now contaminated by the scale, speed, sound, and dehumanization of the vehicle. The porch is redefined as an internalized and

The perimeter of the Porch House is created by: [1] programmatic pavilions (sequentially addable and modular to the tractor trailer); [2] a series of bracketing site walls; and [3] the car when parked. The house itself becomes the shielding frame that protects and privatizes the internal courtyard space from the surrounding context.

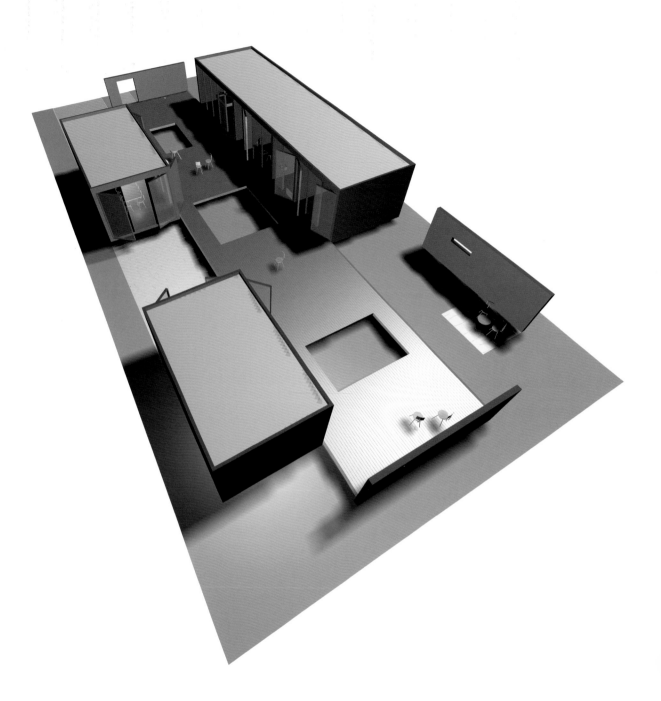

The pavilions of the house open with transparent faces and operable edges towards the lush interior. Selective punched openings penetrate the panelized exterior shell.

The pavilions of the Porch House are subdivided into three distinct programmatic zones: eating (preparation and consumption) and living on one side, and sleeping/bathing on the other; zoning the edges into public and private. The programs depend upon allostasis (the ability to maintain stability through change) to celebrate the environment and the landscape as an active participant with daily events. Action occurs out of context.

Affordability in the Porch House is achieved through a reduction of size, modular construction, use of common materials, potential prefabrication, and individuation of programs into discrete pavilions providing the responsive ability of sequential expansion based on need.

longitudinal section through private pavilion

view across porch from living pavilion

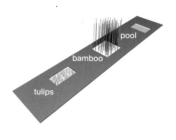

Public / Private

Individually articulated program boxes of the Porch House arrange on either side of the central porch to zonally separate the house into private and public realms.

Cultivated Plug-ins

The central porch of the Porch House is perforated with a series of openings housing diverse natural materials of varied scales. Rock, bamboo, water, productive gardens, and ornamental plantings supply dimension, sound, color, and texture to the porch and adjacent pavilions alike.

Perimeter

A visual perimeter frame is created to bracket and privatize the central exterior room of the Porch House. The pavilions are joined by shielding garden walls, plantings, and the parked automobile to gather defensively around the porch to provide a protective perimeter.

Expanded Field

The Porch House pavilions are dimensioned on a whole material module of the opaque outer skin (punctured only for select views and always along a material module) and a transparent and operable inner face. The small pavilions expand and bracket the broader room of the inner table and its framed landscape.

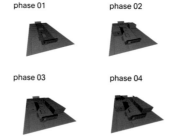

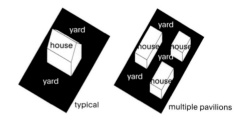

Object to Field

The Porch House turns the typical house inside out. Placing the porch as a void at the heart of the house, it becomes an outdoor room ringed by pavilions and garden walls that embrace and shield the central space.

Phasing

The segmented formal composition of the Porch House provides an opportunity for phasing relative to need. The house as a campus of diverse pavilions allows the pavilions to become discrete phasable pieces. Dimensioned as a module of the highway (permitting factory-built prefabrication) and individuated by the functions of the program; the pavilions allow for independent and sequential construction and installation.

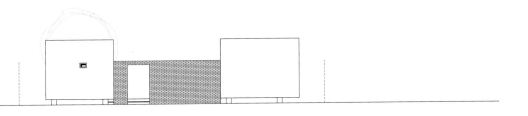

street elevation

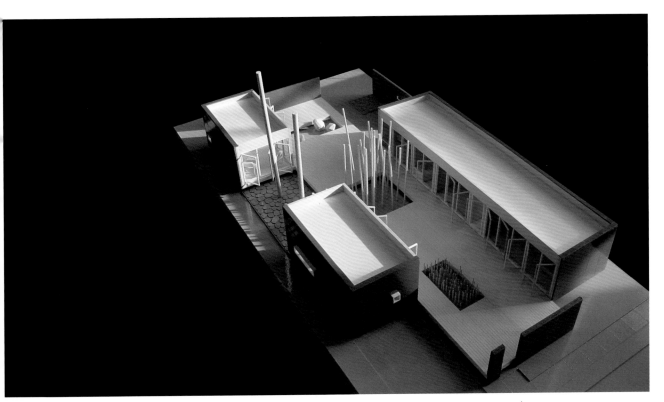

pavilion field

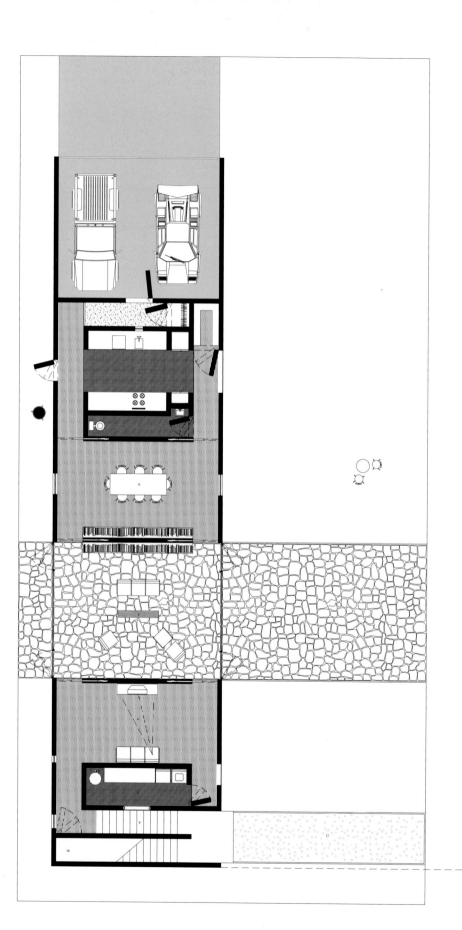

1 Garage
2 Entry
3 Utility
4 TV
5 Living
6 Dining
7 Kitchen
8 Bath
9 Stair
10 Storage
11 Bamboo - Vertical Lawn
12 Bedroom

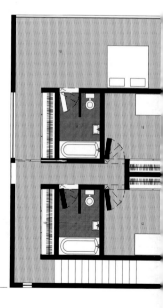

TUBE HOUSE

[HOUSE 19]

Sequentially staging: garage, entry, kitchen, dining, living, TV, laundry, stair, closet, bath, and bedroom; the organization is based on the repetitive sequential routine of a 24 hour daily cycle of domestic activity. The section is activated by the subdivision of public/ day (down) and private/night (up) allowing for the second story programs to be reclusive, with a greater openness and direct connection to the landscape on the lower level. The house is constructed on a four-foot material module and clad in horizontal width of the footprint provides the opportunity for double density on a single site reducing the land costs and allowing for additional budget allocation to additional square footage.

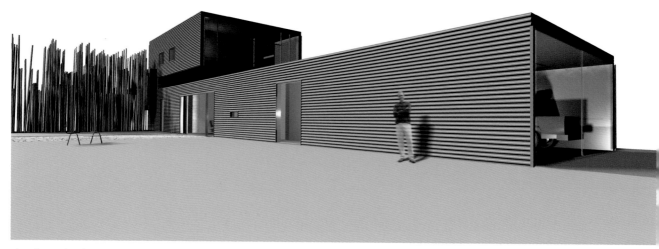

view from street

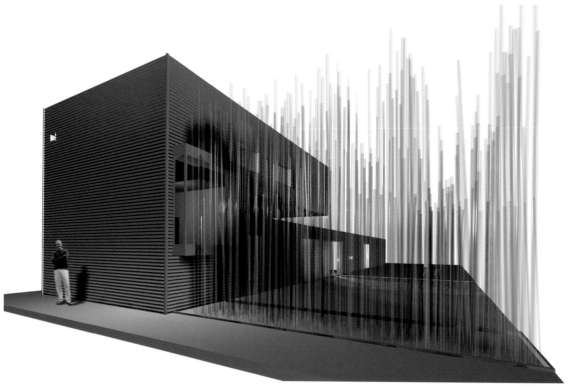

view from back

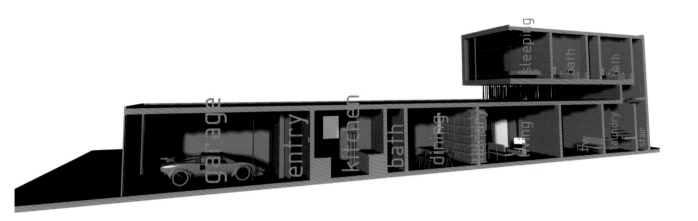

longitudinal program section

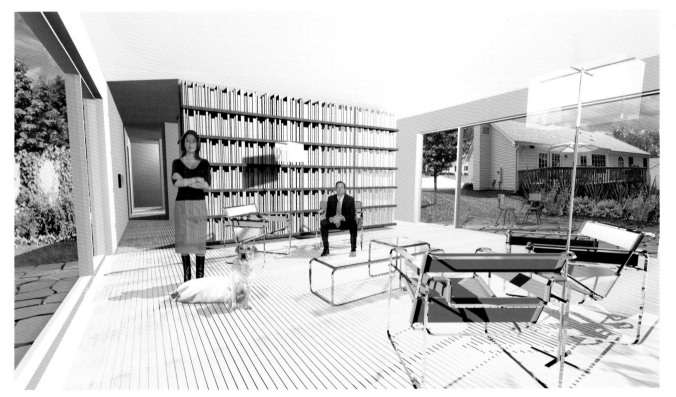

view from living room

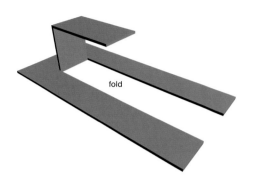

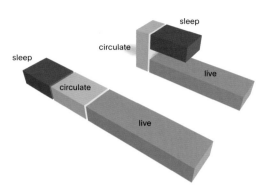

Fold

The Tube House forms from the folding of a linearly arranged, chronologically organized program along the break from day to night. The folded form becomes the cul-de-sac of daily activity, cyclically engaging the inhabitant and their routine.

Zoning

The folding action of the Tube House breaks the bar into three zones: [1] a lower living bar striated with daily activities; [2] a middle vertical circulation zone that allows you to briefly emerge from the constraints of the tubular volume to announce a cyclical threshold; and [3] a sleeping bar, elevated for privacy and security.

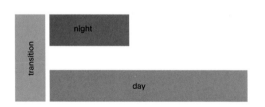

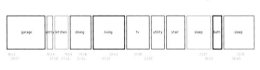

Day / Night

The diurnal cycle of domestic activities is openly exaggerated in the form of the Tube House. The connectivity of the two generates a vertical directional threshold subdividing between the sectionally defined zones of day and night.

Program

The arrangement of program in the Tube House accumulates activities along a daily time loop moving from the most public to the most private functions. Each space, sequenced by adjacency, is migrated through twice daily: once arriving and receding into the house and once advancing and departing the house. The result is a gradual linear occupation of the entire folding form over the 24 hour cycle.

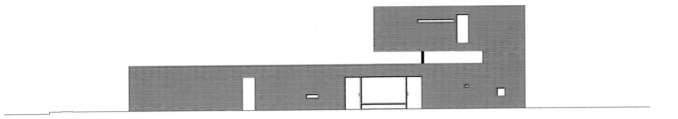

side elevation

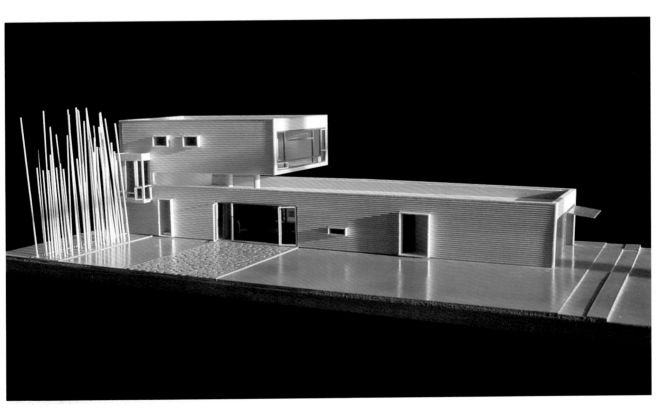

view from side yard

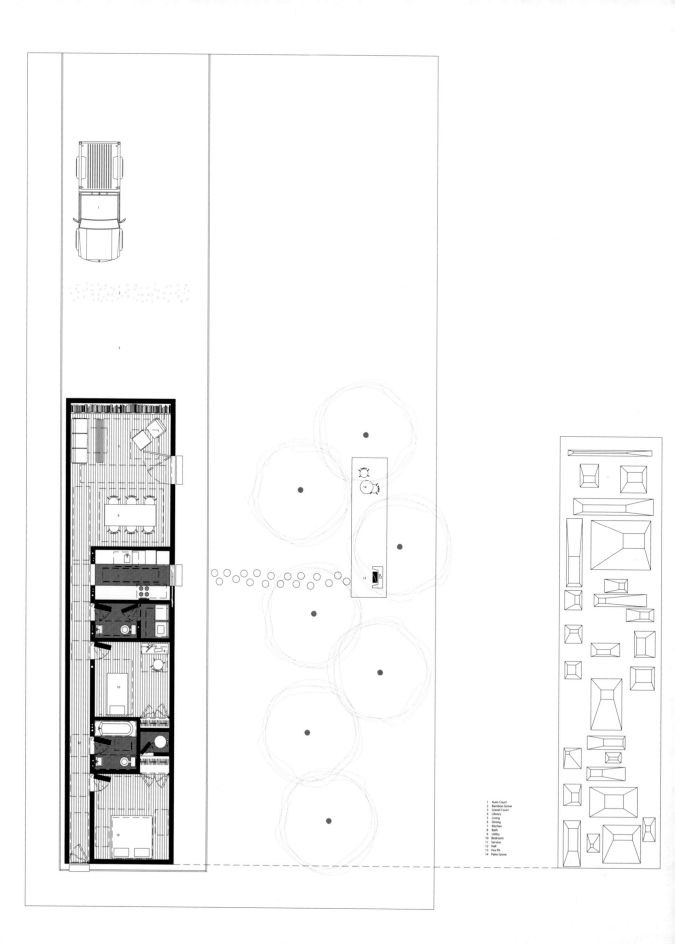

1   Auto Court
2   Bamboo Grove
3   Gravel Court
4   Library
5   Living
6   Dining
7   Kitchen
8   Bath
9   Utility
10 Bedroom
11 Service
12 Hall
13 Fire Pit
14 Patio Grove

CONSTELLATION HOUSE

[HOUSE 34]

The Constellation House shifts the traditional responsibility of the wall aperture to the roof. The result is an internal world articulated by large roof funnels that draw you through the house with their projecting light. The perimeter is only perforated with select shuttered portals for physical entry. The modular panelized box relies upon its figurative roof for its formal exterior articulation and internal spatial articulation. The dimension and quality of the aperture correlates with the associated space below and the activity it illuminates. The movement between the shafts of light draws the activity and inhabitant through the house defining function and experience simultaneously. The house is activated based on the sun's path. Changing functional zones as highlighted and activated by light based on time and associated function are created through the orientation of the projecting aperture.

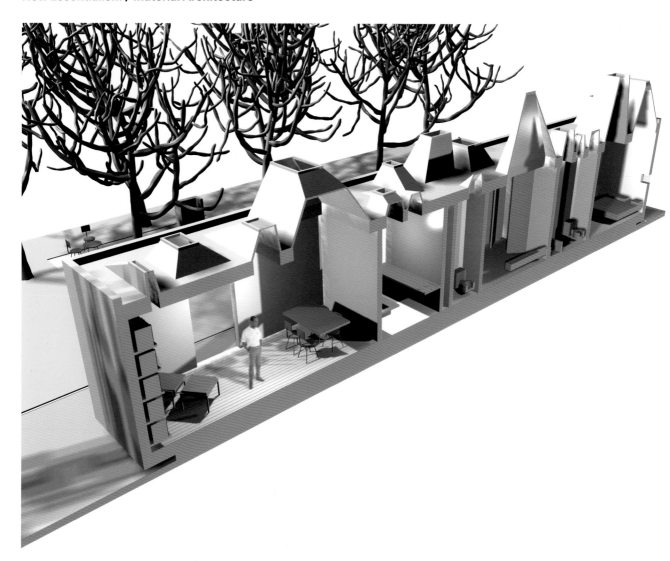

longitudinal section

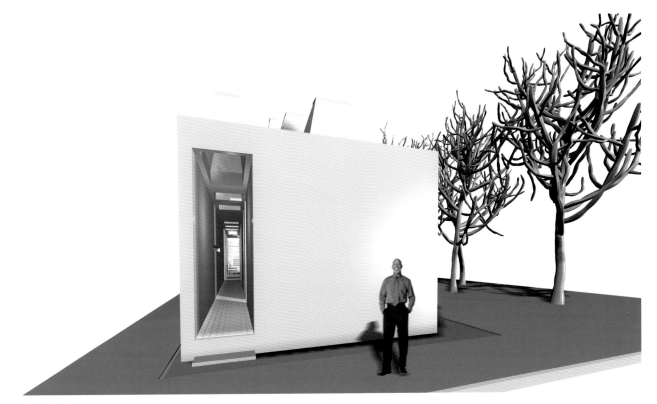

view from back

living room looking down hallway

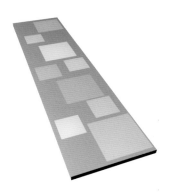

Light

Light is the experience in the Constellation House. Varying intensities and focal points carve subdividing spaces out of the simple rectangular box by projecting light through the articulated roof. The density, scale, position, and intensity are determined by the relationship of light activating diverse functions sequentially within daily rituals.

Open Roof / Closed Sides

The perimeter of the Constellation House is largely opaque with shutterable apertures to defer to the roof to provide curated light to articulate the spaces. The roofscape is highly choreographed to generate the qualities and subdivisions of the space below. The result is a simple spatial container with minimal rooms that are effectually orchestrated by the roof apertures.

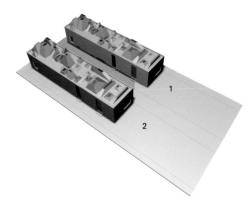

Zoning

A single, large, public space feeds compartmentalized, private, service spaces accessed by a single loaded corridor in the Constellation House. Spatial qualities and internal implied subdivisions are articulated by changing light projections choreographed through the funnels of the roofscape. The house reconfigures its internal spatial conditions based upon the time of day and its activation by light.

Double Density

The narrow efficiency of the plan of the Constellation House combined with the vertical visual orientation allows for a double density to the traditional 60-foot by 120-foot site. This allows for significant reduction in land cost (able to be reapplied to the complexity of the roofscape) and increased density.

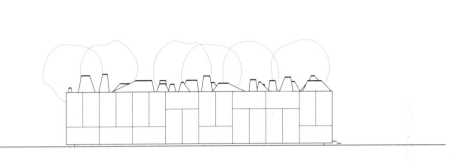

side elevation

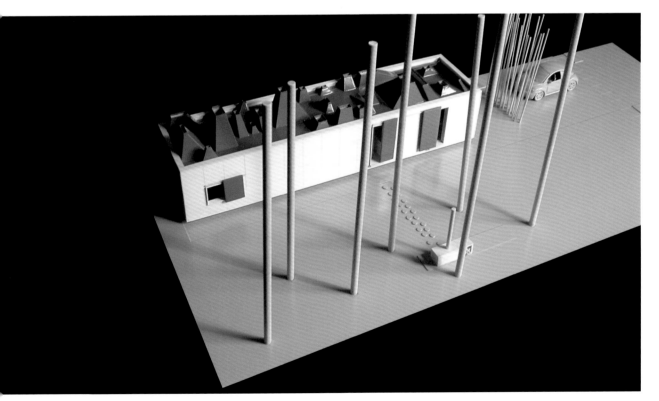

view from side yard

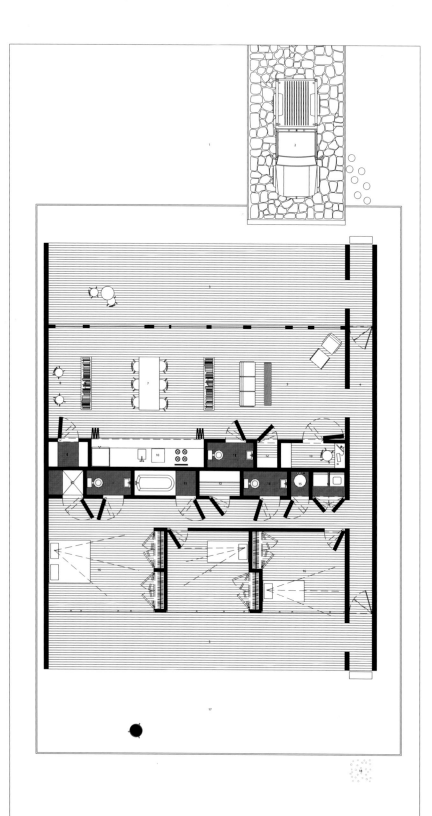

1   Lawn
2   Auto Court
3   Porch
4   Hall
5   Living
6   Library
7   Dining
8   Sitting
9   Pantry
10 Kitchen
11 Bath
12 Storage
13 Work
14 Laundry
15 Utility
16 Bedroom
17 Gravel Field
18 Bamboo Grove

ENCLOSURE HOUSE

[HOUSE 37]

The Enclosure House uses a single folding wrapper (clad in standing seam metal) to establish its form. Recessed lateral walls provide covered porches both to the front street and backyard. The front wall creates a public face with functionally and compositionally choreographed punched openings cropping and framing its context. The back elevation is a transparent, operable facade, recessed for privacy and sun shading and incrementally studded with colored metal panels for storage. A central core houses the service components of the house bifurcating the house into public and private, and day and night realms. The metal shell simplifies the construction and maintenance required while establishing the iconography of the structure.

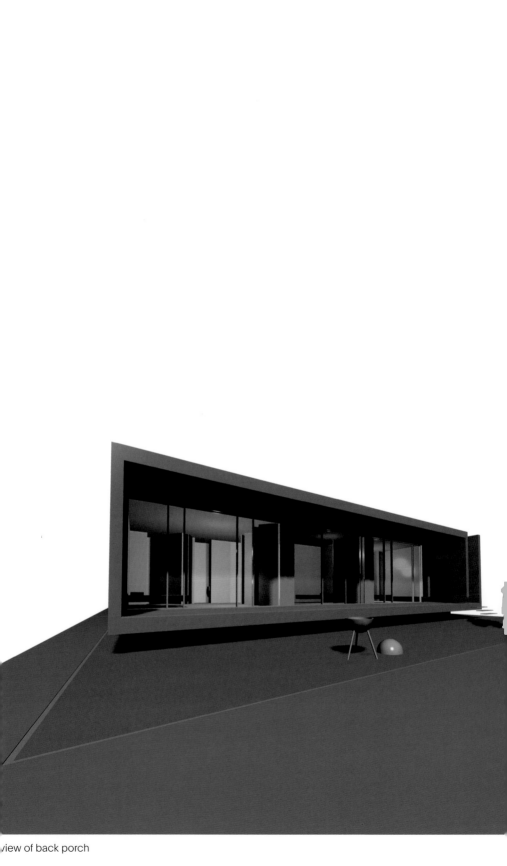

view of back porch

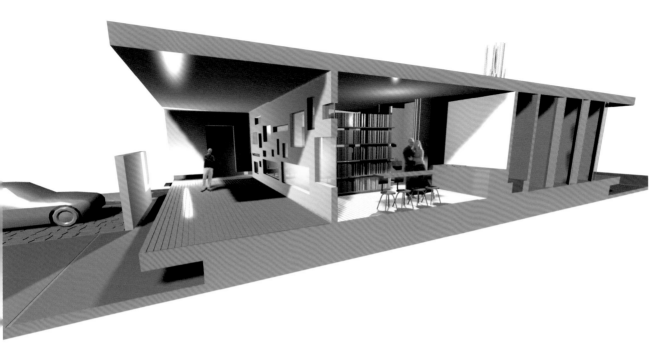

longitudinal section

view across living

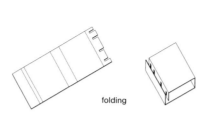

folding

glazing

shell

punched

Wrapper

The wrapper of the Enclosure House is formulated by a single continuous plane that folds to encircle the volume of the house. The continuous surface devoid of perforations provides modularity and efficiency to the application of the standing seam metal. The result is a low maintenance and durable matchbox-like shield.

Front / Back

The Enclosure House is primarily defined by the single opaque wrapper that folds to define the house. The remaining end conditions are tailored with articulated inserts to express the functional activities of their anterior spaces.

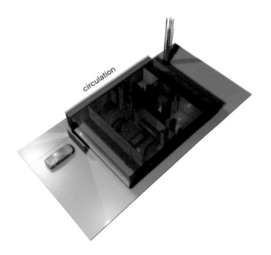

circulation

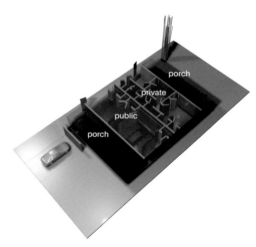

porch

private

public

porch

Circulation

The circulation of the Enclosure House is a single corridor feeding six layered zones: [1] front public porch; [2] public space (living / dining); [3] public service (kitchen / half-bath / utility); [4] private service (baths / storage); [5] private space (bedrooms); and [6] back private porch. Moving from indoors to out, the side circulation spine links the various pieces by providing penetrations through the edges of the folding wrapper formally separating and celebrating the thresholds between them.

Zoning

A central lateral service spine separates the Enclosure House into two zones of public (front) and private (back). Each face of the service bar opens onto the adjacent spaces housing the utilitarian functional necessities of the house and emphasizing rituals of occupation. The public front has an open floor plan subdivided by furniture configuration while the rear private is segmentally compartmentalized into three bedrooms.

back elevation

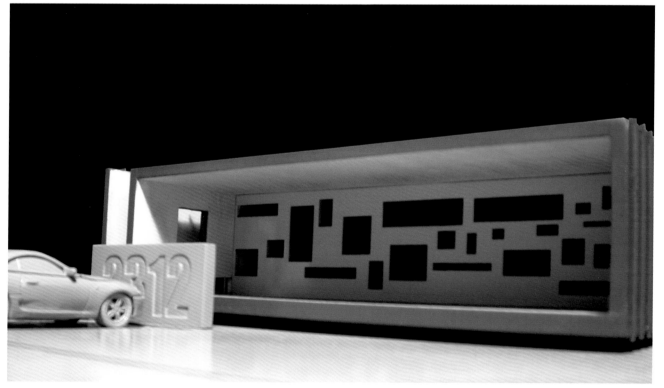

view of front porch

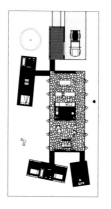

Radial House [House 03]

The Radial House extends articulated individual private programs emanating from a central transparent public living space. Each of the radiating pavilions develops an independent form emerging out of its function and context (both compositional and contextual). The collective composition creates a multi-figured campus in the landscape. The segmentation of the elements provides for programmatic and scalar flexibility while allowing for phasable and sequential construction. The house is able to expand and contract with the homeowner's need. The house form diffuses into the landscape allowing one figure to be read from another allowing the house to act as a neighbor to itself.

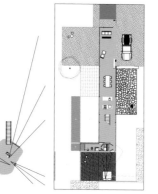
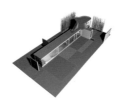

Bar House [House 05]

The Bar House consolidates the programmatic functions of the house into a single line. With transparent operable glass walls, the bar house relies upon the landscape to generate barriers that shield and privatize spaces along its length. Each zone of the house relates to alternating exterior sides of the bar forming defined landscape rooms based upon the articulation of the ground plane. The free plan of the living spaces open and extend onto a gravel field; dining opens onto an exterior patio; bathing evolves and slips into a pool; the sleeping space opens to a private sleeping porch. The rigid rectangularity of the lower bar is balanced by a curvilinear and organic form housing an elevated and reclusive opaque workspace.

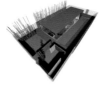

Innards House [House 09]

The Innards House is an operable transparent box with a tri-axial undulating wood paneled core. This central opaque mass houses the functional service requirements of the house with their associated served spaces clustered around the perimeter. The boundary of the site is edged with a translucent glow wall that simultaneously shields and bounds the site while generating an artificial illuminated horizon. The space between the house and perimeter wall becomes a zone of liminal spaces: influenced by the adjacent condition and use of the core yet conceptually mutable in terms of a single boundary or function.

Bi-Fur House [House 10]

The Bi-Fur House axially divides the house and site into two equal zones. The front zone is public while the back zone is private. The public zone is a single space clad in operable and transparent glass doors. It houses three internal mobile units that collaborate with mobile furniture for adaptive configuration and subdivision of the interior. The roof has three large oculus openings that provide an organic subdivision of the regimented rectangular shell. The private zone is spatially compartmentalized with thickened storage walls bounding intimate sleeping rooms and utilitarian compartments. Carved and funneling openings allow light into the rooms while targeting and framing precisely composed views.

20 Propositions For Suburban Living

Layer House [House 11]

The Layer House striates its program into parallel bands of function alternating between transparency and opacity. The gravel yard of the parking zone penetrates through a plane of bamboo to reveal the entry. Moving through a thick storage and display wall, the adjacent transparent corridor serves as a gallery. A band of bedrooms is separated by internal light wells. The living room is a transparent band smeared along the back of the primary figure, opening onto the backyard and punctured by three pavilions functionally zoned: library, dining, and utility. The yard continues the layered banding with contrasting grasses.

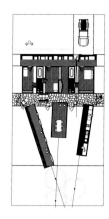

Laminate House [House 12]

The Laminate House layers two zones on either side of a central orthogonal service wall. Zoned with public functions on one side and private functions on the other, the spaces are respectively collective and individual. The collective edge is bound by an undulating ferro-concrete shell wall. Its figure is determined by internal spatial needs while responding to preserve existing trees on the exterior. Its surfaces operate independently of one another to locally negotiate and mediate adjacent needs. The private volumetric shapes are organically defined by the motions of the activities contained within. The living spaces happen in the residual zone between the laminates.

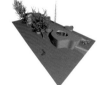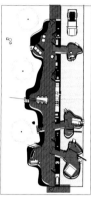

Topo House [House 13]

The Topo House shifts the responsibility of spatial subdivision from the wall to the roof. The house is longitudinally subdivided into three bands: service wall, circulation corridor, and living spaces. Three reciprocal undulating roof bands generate topographic ceilings that respond to the programmatic transitions below. The locally responsive ceiling provides sectional variation in response to the functional need and effectual quality of each space. Their individuated orchestration allows for localized specificity and collective choreography. The misregistration of the parallel bands is glazed to provide lateral light through the clerestory separations.

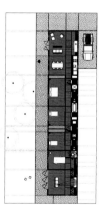

Courtyard House [House 15]

The Courtyard House maximizes the allowable volume of the zoning setbacks as a two-story mass, coring out internal courtyards to provide light, introduce exterior landscape spaces, and subdivide the interior. Penetrating vertically and horizontally, the removals dissolve the primary figure creating a porous plan, section, and elevation. Each interior space is accompanied by a reciprocal exterior space. The house is programmatically zoned with the lower level containing the public activities and the upper level serving as a private retreat. The voids in the volume provide inner yards and elevated overlooks permitting large transparent walls to edge intimate spaces without sacrificing privacy.

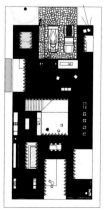

123

Organ House [House 16]

The Organ House centrifugally arrays a series of organic bulges off a central, square, free plan, living space. Geometrically untouched on the interior by the distensions, spatial zones are articulated by the large apertures on the roof. A series of frame windows perforate the remaining perimeter wall. The exterior is dominated by the organic forms of the curvilinear surfaces. Each bulge is determined by the scale and motion of the internal activities. The articulated shapes allow for tailored spaces that provide efficient individuated rooms. Defined by light and silhouetted against the rectilinear backdrop of the house core, the bulges as sensuous forms remain efficiently responsive to their functional necessities.

Boxes House [House 31]

The Boxes House is organized by an oscillation between opaque service bands and transparent served bands. Paired and balanced programs of closed and open associate service functions with their served spaces. Each zone elongates to extend laterally across the entire width of the house. Kitchen and pantry associate with dining. Powder room, archival storage, and utility closet associate with the work space. The library wall and entertainment equipment associate with the living space. The bathroom and closet associate with sleeping spaces. The zones alternate between: [1] open and closed; [2] outward expanding and inward focused; and [3] transparent operable wall and opaque fixed mass.

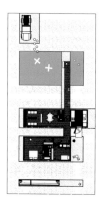

Orchard House [House 38]

The Orchard House emerges from the field density of a grove of trees. The repetition of the ordered bosque provides a collective, figured field. Threading into the regularity of their gridded planting, the house generates interior and exterior rooms through an interwoven presence. Viewed externally as a mass, the only variation is a car sized void with stepping stones disappearing through an edge. The path draws the visitor into a formal lawn with an encircling perimeter boundary of trees. An oversized elevated walkway wicks you from the lawn, back into the grove, skewering first the public living pavilion and ultimately the private sleeping box. A storage and service shed is located at the back of the site.

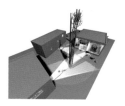

Pavilions House [House 39]

The Pavilions House clusters four distinct forms around a circular patio. Programmatically subdivided into living, sleeping, working, and porch, the four orthogonal figures organize themselves along individual axes relating to the contextual landscape and the adjacent pavilions. Each pavilion opens onto the central patio mediated by an intermediate deck. The dissolution of the house into multiple discrete elements allows for a cyclical engagement with the yard and expands the experiential and spatial sequence of the otherwise efficient components.

01

05

09

02

06

10

03

07

11

04

08

12

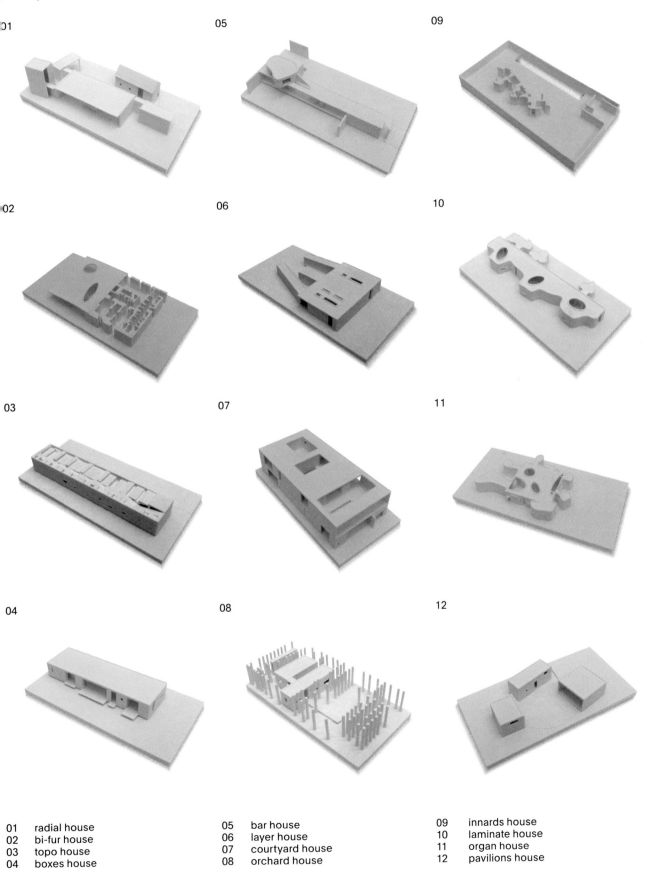

01	radial house	05	bar house	09	innards house
02	bi-fur house	06	layer house	10	laminate house
03	topo house	07	courtyard house	11	organ house
04	boxes house	08	orchard house	12	pavilions house

EXPERIENCE

EXPERIENCE

EXPERIENCE AS ARTIFACT

Experience is architecture. The vision and methodology for making experience is established through careful planning and discrete and evocative representational models. The building as an artifact is the physical manifestation of the spatial condition. The experience of the space is the architecture. The composition, the cinematic quality, the tectonic expression, the emotive feeling of light and sound and temperature; these combine to define an elusive yet quintessential element.

The harnessing of experience in architecture occurs through four primary modalities: (1) the physical presence of the object itself; (2) the ritual and ceremony of event and action (formal or informal) that the architecture creates; (3) the engagement and orchestration of perception through the biological systems of sensorial experience; and (4) the commutability and repetition through a shared cultural engagement. Each of these themes provides insights into the perceptual quality of experience as architecture.

THEME 1 — PHYSICAL PRESENCE AND THE OBJECT

The physicality of an object demands scrutiny of its specifics. Specific materials, specific size and dimension, specific form, specific position and placement; these characteristics each endow the object with defining attributes that make it both precise and unique. The relative evaluation of these specific characteristics allows for moments of design decision to serve as touch points for operation.

Form is something to be read and as a legible figure, something to be evaluated. The physical is tangible and finite and explicit. Its precision is its authenticity. The reading of a physical object is dictated by the relativity of our bodies. Our physical presence in space and the perceptive tools of our sensorial bodies establish the parameters by which we can understand our environment and ultimately ourselves. The relativism of the two (the internal and the external) establishes the mind to body dialectic representative of the object's reading as interpreted through cognitive perception. The slippage between these two points is mediated by a tertiary liminal realm of the emotive and sensorial perception of space and object through experience. Here the sensorial nature of effectual compositional environments creates an affect based experience. The body is submerged into its environment and moves through this spatial condition to interface, perceive, and generate an experience.

The specifics of physically being are the compositional legacy of architecture. Legibility of system, organizational rules, orders, hierarchy, axis, sequence, geometry and proportion, et cetera; each provide logics of control of compositional form. The detachment from regularized systemic rules during modernity allowed for abstraction to remove the articulation of applied surface and referential

Arrest 1
Bridget Riley, 1965
patterned effect

formalism (of both parts and the whole) to focus on the nature of the surface itself: the material and the tectonic actualities relative to form. Composition is determined and evaluated by alternate means. Form tells a different story through its articulation. The physical is read for its essence. The quality of being becomes the language of meaning.

THEME 2 — RITUAL AND CEREMONY

Poetry is a ceremony. Actions of daily life are undertaken with repetitive motion and in their familiarity we rarely stop to recognize their presence or significance. Each event through its staged sequential steps creates a formalized ceremony. The repetition of events and sequences establishes them as rituals. The ability to read the regularity of the experience through the stages of a ritualized ceremony establishes a rhythm of repetition and resonance beyond the event itself. As a serial act, the learned quality of the repeated event provides a life beyond the moment and independent of the action itself. The engagement of the ceremony as a design opportunity allows for the development of the experience as a constructed element. Developing the narrative of a perceptive sequence through a specific environment engages the foundations of space and form as compositional entities connected to ceremony. The development of architectural ritual is the development of experience.

The functional programs that have developed typologies in architecture are derived from their rituals of use. As building types, room types, or spatial types, serial actions such as bathing, eating, or sleeping are met with reciprocal spatial and functional types of: bathroom, dining room, and bedroom. The spatial manifestation of a functional action provides the ritual with legibility in the associative form. Engagement with the ritual to unpack its steps and sensibilities and expand these into larger design articulations and opportunities provides for a foregrounding of the experiential through a choreographed sequence.

THEME 3 — PERCEPTION

"The Process of a Compounded Abstraction"

"Irwin defines perception as the individual's originary, direct interface with the phenomenally given. We are speaking here of the overbrimming synesthesia of undifferentiated sensations – they are not even defined yet as sounds versus colors, and so forth – they exist as the plenum of experience. With the next stage, conception, the individual (who now, for the first time, arises as a being differentiated from his surroundings, a cogito, an 'I') through the operations of his mind isolates zones of focus: this splash, that tree, that horizon, this car, and so forth; and yet, at this stage, though isolated, these zones remain unnamed. Naming comes at the next stage, form, where that isolated zone of focus, that tree, now becomes 'that tree.'

With naming, and myriad parallel operations, it now becomes possible for the first time for individuals to communicate with each other; community comes into being. At the next stage, formful, these named things begin to be deployed through relational patterns: day and night, hot and cool, loud and soft, and so forth. At the next stage, formal, these patterns in turn begin to be reified, to become standardized into the more efficient deployments of social usage: clock time, calendars, color wheels, temperature readings, and so forth. At the final stage, formalized, it is these standardized measures that begin to dictate our behavior, a behavior that has now become

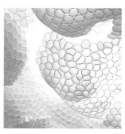

Styrofoam Cup Sculpture
Tara Donovan
aggregated effect

utterly estranged from direct perceptual experience. Thus, for example, we shuttle ourselves through a world of nine-to-five jobs, daylight saving time, thermostatic controls, and so forth.

'This process of compounding abstraction is not so much a temporal progression as a phenomenological one. At any given moment, for any given individual, all six phases are operating simultaneously, and yet earlier phases exist prior to the later ones in the sense that they ground them, they constitute the source out of which the more compound stages emerge. In this sense, perception is originary, the foundation of everything. And yet, like the bottommost stratum at an archeological dig, perception is the hardest to reach."[89]

Robert Irwin
Seeing is Forgetting the Name of the Thing One Sees

'New York Projections, this Whitney Museum project, is intended to act out (in on-site installations), illustrate (in aerial photographs of New York), and develop the argumentation (in the catalog essay) for perception as the essential subject of art. Assuming that context is not only the bond of knowledge, but the basis of perception/conception, this exhibition has been developed contextually. By holding the most essential contextual thread (those elements taken from perception and used in 'art,' i.e., line, shape, and color, et cetera) and removing in turn each of the additional contextual threads (imagery, permanence, method, painting, sculpture, et cetera) which have come to be thought of as usual in the recognition of what is art, we arrive at the essential subject of art. In effect, this is accomplished by a principal change in the relationship of the indicator (object of art) and what is indicated (subject of art), form their acting as one in the art object to their being on in the aesthetic perception of the individual observer.'"[90]

Robert Irwin
Whitney Show 1977

Perception is the means by which we experience the world around us. Perception is not always real, though it is based in the real. Perception is an extension of an environment or space met by an extension of our bodies and their innate systems. It does not belong to either but bridges between the two. As a discrete entity to itself, perception requires facilitation on both the part of the individual and the elements that it is engaging with. Music, art, food, weather, architecture, et cetera; they are all connected to us through perception. At their best they generate an experience that is unique, even new, and intentionally enlightening to our emotive sensibilities. This engagement with emotion as a perceptual marker, to create something that makes us feel and respond (positively or negatively) is an essential goal. It goes beyond the middle ground of the dulled and seemingly generic condition and results in a differentiation that provides a sensorial response that triggers in our personal selves a feeling.

There are two processes to perception: (1) the processing of the sensory input converting the raw data acquired by our senses into information (light or shape converting into objects) through transduction,[91] and (2) the processing of this information that tethers the initial information to the individual's personal experiences (knowledge) and its associated expectations creating the perception.[92] These two processes both occur as complex functions of our biological nervous system, but remain outside of our cognitive conscious awareness. As a result design operation in the perceptual realm offers opportunity to engage sensory information and the innovative potential of the experience (as a detachment from previously experienced or known conditions) and its engagement of the variable readings based upon diverse frameworks of understanding engaging our varied environment.

The perceptive actions[93] through the rules of our bodies can be engaged proactively. To design the effectual requires the compositional establishment of a mood in a sensorial environment. Abstraction offers a reductive and destabilizing condition. Through the foiled disassociation with the natural world, the overt reliance upon the rigor and systemization of geometry, and the focused and intended application of color and form and material; abstraction facilitates a clarity that permits the focused attention to another sensibility. The further reduction to a minimalist environment forces the focus onto the few remaining elemental expressions. Architecture as a facilitator of space through light and material generates a condition in which events and experience can occur. Architecture is not the event itself but rather a facilitator providing and allowing the event. As a silent hand it orchestrates an experience that permits the environment to resonate with ourselves and temporarily capture the vitality and essentialism of our world and our being within the moment at a specific place.

Jackson Pollock in studio
process to pattern

Perception begins through the internalization of experience. Using our senses, the five physical elements of sight, sound, smell, touch, and taste are complimented by the cognitive complexities of associated memories, instinctual biological cues, learning, expectation, and personalized evaluative opinion based in previous experience. These engage with the complexities of personality, mood, and the diverse components of the human condition to form our perception relative to the input of information and its processing. These five senses each extend their detail as adaptations:

"— Depth perception consists of processing over half a dozen visual cues, each of which is based on a regularity of the physical world. Vision evolved to respond to the narrow range of electromagnetic energy that is plentiful and that does not pass through objects.
— Sound waves provide useful information about the sources of and distances to objects, with larger animals making and hearing lower-frequency sounds and smaller animals making and hearing higher-frequency sounds.
— Taste and smell respond to chemicals in the environment that were significant for fitness in the environment of evolutionary adaptedness.
— The sense of touch is actually many senses, including pressure, heat, cold, tickle, and pain."

"An important adaptation for senses is range shifting, by which the organism becomes temporarily more or less sensitive to sensation (for example, one's eyes automatically adjust to dim or bright ambient light). Sensory abilities of different organisms often coevolve, as is the case with the hearing of echolocating bats and that of the moths that have evolved to respond to the sounds that the bats make."[94]

-Steven J. C. Gaulin and
Donald H. McBurney
Evolutionary Psychology

Each of these perceptual mechanisms, though not exactly perceived by everyone the same way, will be collectively perceived with similarity. These moments of perceptual community are design opportunities for the compositional generation of architecture. Through the experience we can find the method of engagement.

Criollo
Edgar Orlaineta, 2005
hybridized modification

Vision, as our primary sense for experiencing architecture, provides various perceptual methods including constancy[95] (color and shape, roughness, sound, et cetera); grouping[96] (which establishes relativisms based upon patterns and associated objects); and contrast[97] (which emerges from contextual relativism). Each of these biologically determined perceptual techniques offers compositional cues for tactics for proactive design operation. Fundamental to perception's operation is the requisite need for attention: the focused awareness of the event, action, condition of being, et cetera. This critical factor is something that is ever subsiding as information through digital technology competes with the actuality of contextual physicality for a focused moment of presence at any one time. Attention brings an essential root concentration: a mindfulness of being and a larger sense to the moment that bridges to the emotive part of our self and allows for the mind through the body to connect to the emotional nature of the heart. The power of this conductive experience is the root language of all creative inquiries. Architecture through its scale and enveloping nature has an authority and presence unmatched by other media. Space is our vehicle.

THEME 4 — COMMUTABILITY THROUGH CULTURAL ENGAGEMENT

Critical to object, ritual, and perception is the commutability of a repeatable and thus shared experience. It is this condition that provides the connectivity to allow for a cultural presence and consequence of being. The connection to culture implies both a larger connectivity to the diverse media, strains and informational transactions that unite, connect, and define human history, while also facilitating the bridging vantage from which we understand and relate. It is from this context that we establish our perception. From this communality we find the shared humanity that provides for the collective production and experience of an effect. This connectivity occurs both internally and externally. The internal connectivity allows for a sensorial engagement with those touchstones facilitated by the visceral reading of the perceptual connected to our emotive and inner primal essential selves. The external connectivity occurs through the shared communality of the iteratively felt experience. The communal nature of the individualized moment of experience collectively felt through shared knowledge allows the moment to iterate its effect. The shared nature of this individual event places the effectual quality into a collective realm. Here it is iterated and examined and made more extensive through a life of its own independence. This experience becomes autonomous as an artifact that provides another life; a reading through memory, discussion, and evolution of its retelling.

ALLEGORY
EVENT
EMBEDDED
STRUCTURE
ORDERED
LANDSCAPE
RECOLLECTIONS
NARRATIVE
CHANGING
SIGN
MEANING
SITUATION
INHABITANT
ADAPTED
INTERWOVEN
FABRIC
INCORPORATION
EVENT
PLACE
HAPPENINGS
LEVEL
ORDINARY
UNIVERSAL
BALANCE
LIMIT
BOUNDARY
BANAL
MEMORY
COLLECTION CHAOS
SERIES
READABLE
ELEMENTS
RULES
ANALYSIS
VERNACULAR
TOPOGRAPHY
RITUAL PARTICIPATION
ACCIDENTAL
CONTINGENT
ORDER OF THINGS

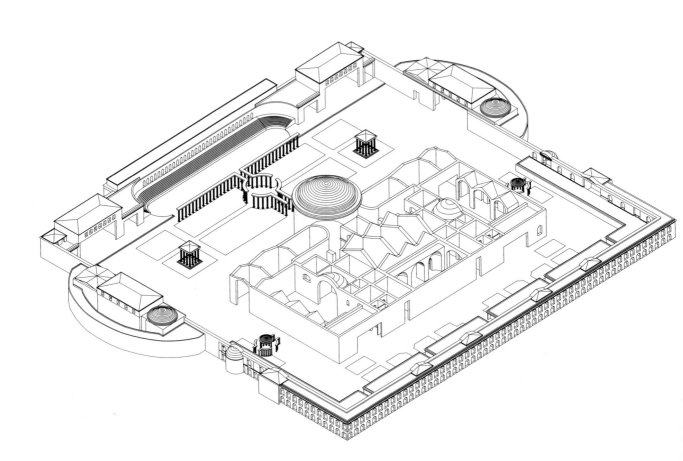

BATHS OF CARACALLA

EXPERIENCE + MATERIAL + FORM

Axonometric

The axonometric of the Baths of Caracalla illustrates how the plan based forms of the rooms increase in complexity as they deploy varied techniques to structurally span their individuated enclosures. Including trussed pitches, domes, vaults, and post and lintel beams, each of these techniques add to the sectional variety of the planametrically formed chambers. The diversity creates a varied hierarchy within the mat building that extends the plan figuration into sectional volumes that are articulated by their individuated roof forms.

THRESHOLD 2
Experience, Material, and Form

THE BATHS OF CARACALLA

The Baths of Caracalla were built by Emperor Caracalla in Rome in 217 AD as a piece of political propaganda. Serving as both a monument to himself and a resource for the people, the baths were free and open to the public serving Romans from every social class. The complex of buildings was a comprehensive campus with diverse programs including: a public library (located in exedra on the east and west sides of the bath complex with two separate and equal sized rooms: one for Greek language texts and one for Latin language texts),[98] two palestras (gymnasiums), and shops located along the north wall of the complex. Providing these popular services in a lavish environment created a sense of public unity and greatly improved public opinion of Caracalla.[99]

The design of the bath complex was created by Septimius Severus including both the bathing facilities proper as well as the hypocaust (the infrastructural plumbing and heating system to treat the water) and a dedicated aqueduct (the Marcian Aqueduct) to supply the facility.[100] To accommodate the necessary lower level for these massive functional needs, the bath was elevated 20 feet. The bathing facilities themselves consisted of a central frigidarium (cold room) measuring 183 feet by 79 feet under three groin vaults 108 feet high; a double pool tepidarium (medium temperature); and a caldarium (hot room) 115 feet in diameter. The north end of the bath building contained a natatio (swimming pool); a roofless yet bounded space with overhead bronze mirrors mounted to direct sunlight into the pool area.[101]

The forms of the Baths of Caracalla are founded in gravitationally derived platonic geometries. As a framing mat building, the massing of the complex reads as a singular figure subdivided by a series of pure geometric subtractions. The complex is an array of discrete rooms: each individually articulated yet aggregated into a collective field. The formal expression of each of the figures is axial and centralized. They are individually expressed through curvilinear transitional surfaces that allow the sculptural and effectual to become synthetically conceived with the structural necessities and constraints. Built of unreinforced masonry, the structural forces are resolved through compressive shapes. Vaults, domes, and arches distribute the loads through the segmental masonry forms. The details and ornament emerge from a celebration of the sub-structural hierarchy (set-up to reduce weight) as exaggerated forms of the performative logic. This structural expression through both the overall form to establish the spatial articulation and the localized details celebrated through further ornamental expressional elements (column, coffer, rib, et cetera) creates a performatively expressive formal field.

The collective composition of the series of individuated spaces provided for effectual emphasis to emerge from the transitions from relative conditions. The changing hierarchy of scale; the relative position along a sequence; the body's relationship to the larger geometric shape and order; the changing use of light; the graduated orchestration of temperature and the atmospheric conditions stemming from the sensibilities of each ritual action relative to the ceremonial chamber and environmental condition of water; each provided a localized experience within the relativism of the complex whole. The use of juxtaposing experiences to heighten and inter-relate introduced the role of perception based in sequence as an evolutionary chronology of architectural experience. These varied atmospheres relative to the platonic forms of their structurally performative environments, perceived through light, sequence, and relative scale, engaged a relativist basis of perception to provide the contrasting sensibility to experience the architecture. This required the segmental architectural promenade to engage atmospheres of experience within a choreographed spectrum.

The Baths of Caracalla represents several significant conceptual thresholds for architecture:

USE OF GRAVITATIONAL MASS AND MATERIAL BASED FORMS

A limited ability to isolate and predict the forces within a structure in combination with the use of masonry as the primary material palette, positioned compressive forces as the dominant consideration to resolve the structural system. Gravitational forms governed by the articulation of the forces are one and the same with the geometric figuration of the form. Once the scale and the dimension of the traditional post and lintel were overextended, forms emerged from the necessities of the material. The arch emerged from the load transfer; the vault from the short span; and the dome from the spanning surface of a roof enclosure. The result was a performatively honest collection of form based spaces that integrated the functionality of their structural mass with the effectuality of their interior space. Relying upon poche (or in-between mass in the thickness of the wall) there is solidity and scale intrinsic to the construction technique. This continuity prevents any void or cavity within the wall creating simultaneity of structure and skin. The architecture is pure, being both structure and enclosure in the same system.

THE PURITY OF VARIED GEOMETRIES GATHERED IN COLLECTIVE FIELD

A series of diverse geometries and scales are aggregated into the larger collective field of the bath complex. As localized and discrete forms, the rooms individuate within themselves. Their collective juxtaposition, aggregation, and field based organization into an organized whole provides for a continuous fabric. This collective individuation creates a relativism of perception and experience where the form does not become about any one figure, but rather engages the transition between the numerous figures, scales, and temperatures to create the experience. The collective is aggregated within a jewel box of individually expressive elements, stitched and ultimately unified through their connective array. This preference of the system of the whole over the individuation of the part allowed for the introduction of a collective denial of a formal legibility of the building and instead creates an internalized, space-based experience to the whole.

THE DISPERSION OF THE OBJECT INTO A FIELD OF SOLID AND VOID

The scale of the complex prevents it from being read as an object. Visually engaging the full field of the focal cone, it becomes a spatial array which one must map and understand from within. The formally and tectonically connective body of the mat building provides a singularity to the composition allowing for spaces to directly exist within (both interior and exterior to the building) while remaining connected to the larger body. This complexity of condition requires a referential sequential experience of interiority to better understand and segmentally unpack the complex. As a series of collected rooms, the building becomes more than any one figure residing in the sequence of spaces. The experience happens out of the relativism of the multiplicity of forms and atmospheres. Movement through the rooms and across transitions of scale and spatial quality creates juxtaposing moments. Memory stitches the experiences to one another. The registration of the field is made through the immersive qualities of moments within it accumulated through the navigation of the whole. This shift from the reading of a building as an object (like a figured monument in a singular and complete way) is transitioned to a sequential relativism within a field of spaces. Fragments must unfold over time and be fully perceptually engaged by physical sensorial engagement creating a new reading and opportunity for architecture.

HIERARCHY OF INDIVIDUATED SPACE OF THE CHAMBER WITHIN THE COLLECTIVE COMPOSITION

The room as an autonomous island within the collective composition establishes the body as the primary context to read the local (a specific and discrete form) relative to the collective field through perception. The experience within a space is mediated by the juxtaposition of experiences afforded by the adjacent spaces. Hot is felt as hot, but only relative to understanding cold. Big relates to small, open to closed, et cetera. This introduction of a relativism of referential reading grounds the perceptive spectrum to understand the details of a specific place in relation to the overall constraints within a system. The experience is thus not that of any single condition but rather the juxtaposing moments as one mediates multiple spaces. This shifts architecture away from the specificity of the object privileging the space itself. Once spatially engaged, the singularity of a space's form is further discounted as the relativism of the experience as it transitions across diverse spaces dominates the reading of the collective field over the individuated moment.

PHYSICAL ENGAGEMENT OF BODILY EXPERIENCE

The reading of architecture has moved away from the object focused fully on the interiority of the space itself. This shift to space moves the figure to become the absence not the presence. The governance of architecture is translated into the perception of the body's relativism to its environment as opposed to the reading of the object as a physical form. In the Baths of Caracalla, the use of perception is expanded to include sensorial perceptions that are typically not foregrounded in architecture: temperature, wetness, touch, sound, smell; these join with light and scale to truly engage the full atmospheric spectrum. The architecture becomes an orchestration of experiences. The reading of the body against its environment shifts the terrain of architectural consideration away from functional protections of shelter (which was dedicated to enclosure, protection, and some legibility of meaning in its ornament but only formally expressed) into a fully immersed idea of a space, volume, and comprehensive experience within which the viewer is submerged.

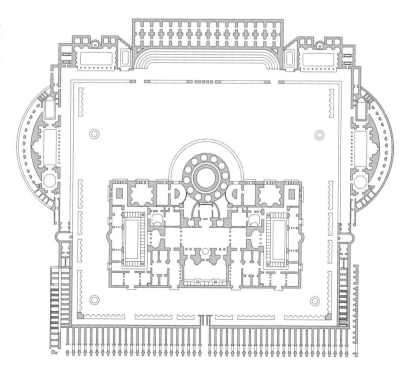

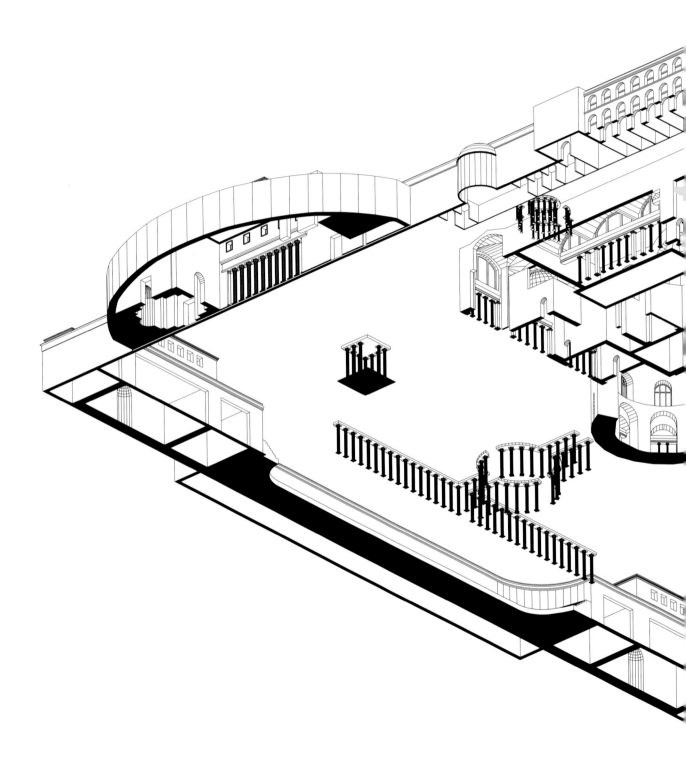

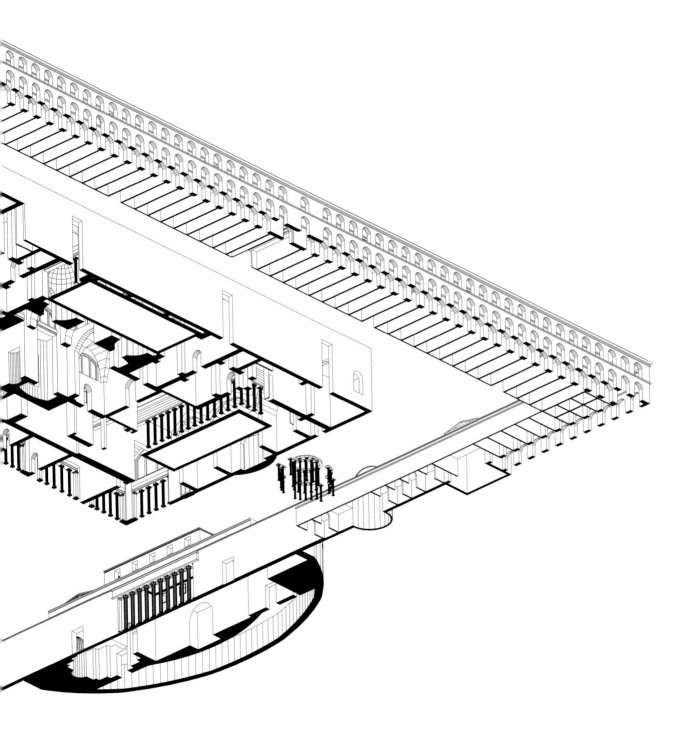

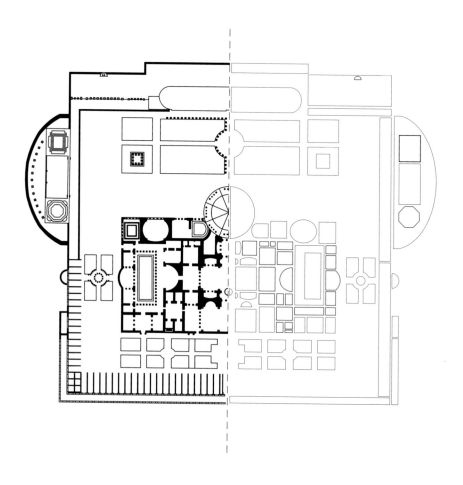

Plan

The plan of the Baths of Caracalla illustrates the unique field based nature of the mat building. As a collection of diverse and discrete functional and spatial experiences, the legibility of the building complex as an object is undermined by its massive scale. Encircled with a perimeter wall that brackets the building from its surroundings, the inner figure of the building within the courtyard further prevents it from being read from a distance as a form. The building's organization, though axially symmetrical, is never read through an overarching understanding of the collective field, but rather is experienced from within the body. Sequence over time is the only facilitating method for understanding the complex. Movement through the field of chambers (each internally whole in figure and juxtaposing to one another) the sequence creates an aggregated whole.

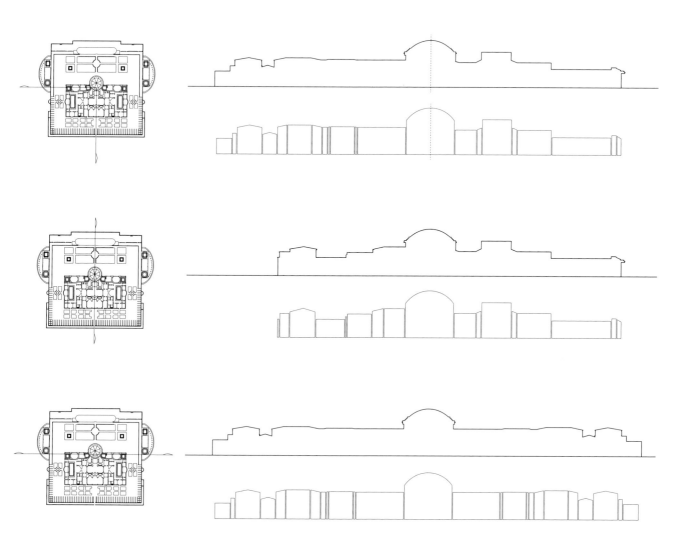

Isolated Sections: Path to Sequence

These sections show the evolutionary quality of the sectional space along select sequential paths through the building. Bending with functional organizational logics and transitioning hierarchies of sequence, the incremental nature of the diverse volumes are celebrated through their relative juxtaposition.

Expansion and contraction as the body moves from one pure volume to the next creates a chain of relativistic spaces. The collective is navigated over time through memory requiring the assemblage of moments into an experiential narrative of the whole.

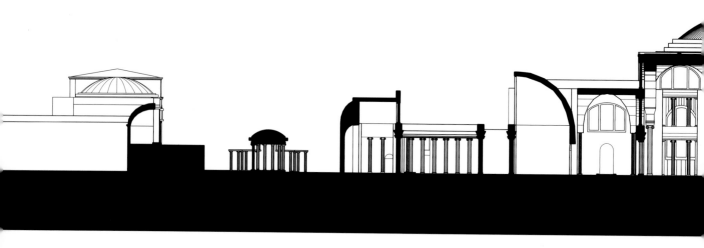

Section

The section of the Baths of Caracalla reveals the aggregation of a diversity of spatial types. Located in tight adjacency, the movement from one figure to the next is synchronized with the movement from room to room and program to program. The orchestration through the varied figures of adjoining spaces allows for a contrasting juxtaposition of scales and forms. The dynamism of the experience is manifest through the associative aggregations.

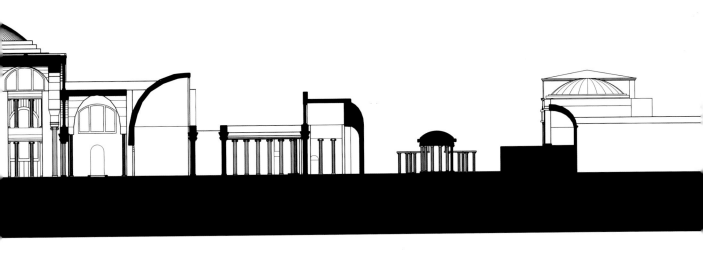

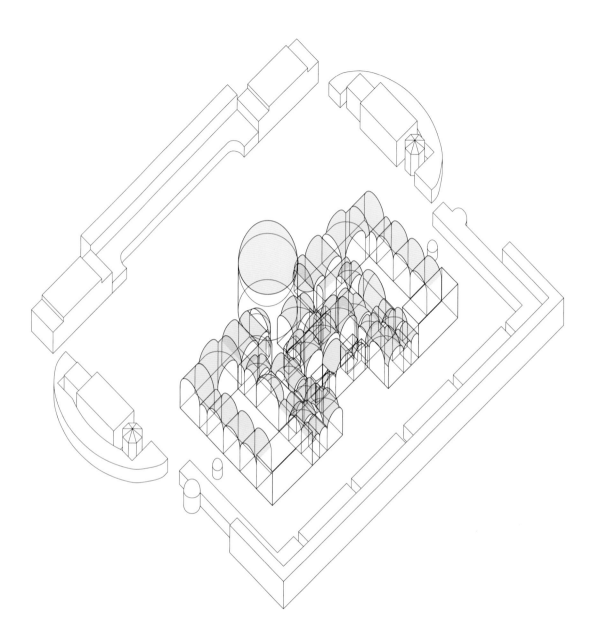

Shells

The use of masonry as the primary material allowed for the articulation to be concentrated in the formal expression of its compressive structural systems. The solid fill of the wall creates poche where the significant mass of wall as an infill rivals the presence and dimension of the remaining spaces. The figure ground carves and interlocks the void with the solid fill of the poche to create a balanced equivalency. The figuration has an economy as enclosure and form are simultaneously determined by structure. The mass of the material system is responsible for both simultaneously.

The figuration is generated by gravitational spaces that create pure shell based systems with vaulting forms to resolve the compressive forces.

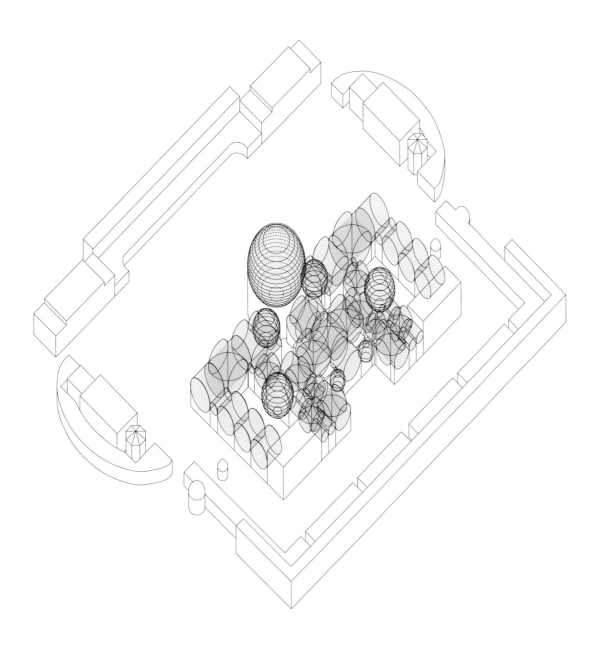

Geometry

Extending the forms of the structural shells, each of the surface based spanning systems implies subordinate platonic geometries. The mapping of their total shapes illustrates the collective field of diverse forms aggregated through their juxtaposition and gathered into a singular mat form. Cylinders and spheres establish the primary vaults and domes of the spaces.

The purity of the compression requires full formal resolution so the midpoint (equator) of each figure is the contact point for the vertical walls to ensure the thrust lines are resolved into fully vertical force lines.

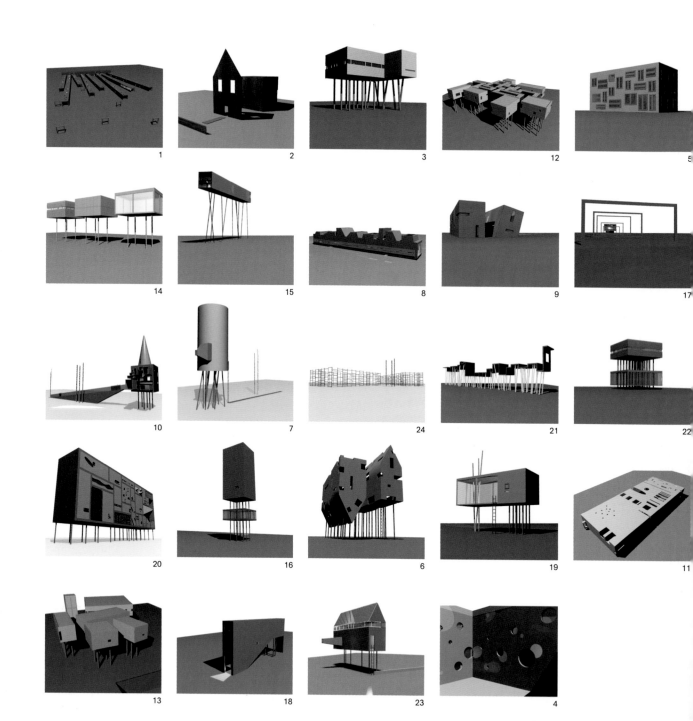

[X]PERIENCE MECHANISMS

[X]PERIENCE MECHANISMS
James River, Virginia

Architecture has moved away from experience. As the current discourse turns to the technologies of visualization, digital manufacturing, new materiality, and issues of form and surface there is little conversation about space.[102] The [X]perience mechanisms project focuses on the orchestration of experience as a formal generator. By using fundamental and archetypal architectural elements as the point of departure, these twenty-four pavilions scattered across a single landscape provide an opportunity to investigate architectural experience as a mediator in the perception of space.

Architecture has the ability to affect people through the space they inhabit. Space determines their perceptual and emotive experience. An architecture that is focused solely on experience allows for the occupant to become self-aware of the immediacies of one's body and its relationship to its context. Walter Pichler's 1967 TV helmet as a portable living room established a controlled experiential boundary to facilitate a solitary engagement of an isolated viewer with their perceptual abilities. Rene Magritte in his paintings *The Human Condition* and *The Listening Room,* offers a depiction of perception as a composed yet artificial re-framing of the natural condition, or the opportunity for the engagement of architecture (in this case through scale) to influence the drama of space through experience. These pavilions are architectural facilitators of such a reconsideration.

CONTEXT OF EXPERIENCE

The premise of experience as function positions architecture in the terrain of art. As David Hockney states: "you have to make the optical experiments to see it."[103] The [X]perience mechanisms sit between painting, building, and sculpture. Founded in this legacy, their premise is not an abandonment of architecture, but rather an investigation of the essentialism of the ubiquitous components of every architectural composition that are so often taken for granted and as a result deployed callously. These moments become the premise of this investigation. They are a completion of the landscape as the drawn portion of Jan Dibbets' *Saenredam-Zadkine III* finishes the photographed cyclorama of the 360-degree experience.

As constructed objects and performative mechanisms they are about the space they generate and its engagement with the occupant. They use light, color, materiality, sequence, and geometry to immerse viewers into an atmosphere of sensations as the primary palette. To use them is to create an engagement that allows the space to be seen and the role of architectural perception to be interrogated.

TV helmet
Walter Pichler, 1967
bodily experience

G-AWZI HS Trident 3
Joiner
perceptual collage

Saenredam-Zadkine III
Jan Dibbets

To design experience, one must start with perception. The eye does not work like a camera. When we visually engage our environment, we scan a scene, building up our view from those elements to which we give our attention. As we sequentially move through a scene we see objects from many points of view and attend more to those that are important to us. The painter and photographer David Hockney believes that many, perhaps most, or even all orthodox photographs are lifeless, and that ultimately they are less real than good paintings and drawings because: "A photograph fixes a single instant, so there is no sense of movement through time. An entire dimension of experience is lost."[104] The attempt to bridge between the traditions of the still life and the cubist assemblage, between the sculpture that one circumnavigates and focuses upon and the building traversed frequently but rarely focused on, allows for the [X]perience mechanisms to occupy a middle ground. They serve as objects to watch, but also objects to engage. They allow for the collective view, but provide distinct and composed moments. The mechanisms, like cubist paintings, require the assemblage of experience over time through their collective fragmentation of the local landscape within a single pavilion and the collective experience across the diverse pavilions.

As Hockney developed multi-faceted photo-collages (which he calls "joiners") from hundreds of smaller photographic images, the mechanisms produce real time spatial experience of motion over time. The sum total of these fragments is the experience: the collection of idea and effect.

The mechanisms serve as a cataloged collection of rituals and architectural fragments. They are individuated and specifically investigated, but represent a family of ubiquitous and often generic moments. Typically not experientially deployed and instead limited in engagement as simple necessity, or overwhelmed by functional requirements, the experience of these ubiquitous moments is often forgotten. Here they are celebrated. Here the experience is celebrated.

[X]perience Mechanisms

1 - LIGHT FUNNELS
2 - FIGURED SLITS
3 - DENSITY LOUVERS
4 - SLAB STRUCTURES [2]
5 - SUSPENDED PODS
6 - GLASS BOX
7 - FORM PAVILLIONS
8 - RANDOMIZED SLITS
9 - ARTIFICIAL SKY
10 - BEADING STRUCTURE
11 - TOTEM FIELD

SECTIONAL SCHEMMATIC LAYERING

PROGRAM AND FORM

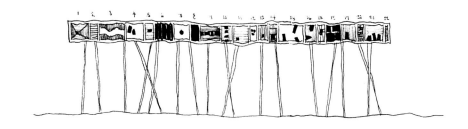

LINEAR VARIANTS - TYPE INFILL

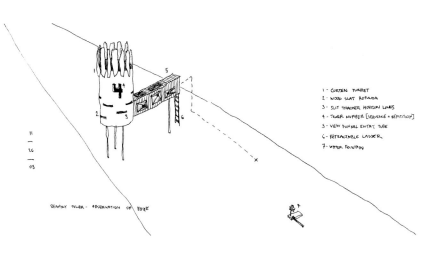

1 - CORTEN TURRET
2 - WOOD SLAT ROTUNDA
3 - SLIT TRACKER HORIZON LINES
4 - TOWER NUMBER [SEQUENCE + REPETITION]
5 - VIEW FUNNEL ENTRY TUBE
6 - RETRACTABLE LADDER
7 - WATER FOUNTAIN

SENTRY TOWER - OBSERVATION OF EDGE

ORGANIZATION

Organization: This investigation of experience is organized at two scales: one at the production of the site based architectural fragment ([X]perience mechanisms); the second in the production of the ritual (spaceframes). The [X]perience mechanisms are comprised of twenty-four individual moments of a fragmented landscape examined through drawings and models. The spaceframes focus on eight daily rituals developed visually and atmospherically through a perceptual engagement of an emotive spatial experience through a full scale two- and three-dimensional integrative installation.

MECHANISMS

The proposition for a boutique hotel in rural Virginia on an untouched 100-acre parcel located on the James River presents a raw site of natural and historical beauty. Diffusing the program into a field of individual pavilions allows for a multiplicity of positions and specific engagements with the site. They watch one another from across the field and through the forest. They are linked by the assemblage of their diverse moments of experience. Through their collective navigation a narration produces experience.

Each mechanism assumes an identity and iconography emergent from: [1] their individual architectural archetype; [2] their engagement with the viewer; [3] their placement relative to the specifics of local landscape; and [4] their relationship to adjacent pavilions. The experience of the landscape is orchestrated simultaneously through the object and the field (the fragment and their collection). The existing site is enhanced by a choreographed experience founded in collected fragments. Moving through the landscape the [X]perience mechanisms serve as facilitators provoking awareness through visual and spatial moments. They allow distinct segments of a fragmented landscape to be seen as a whole. Each pavilion emerges from a single and specific experiential fragment. The experiential inquiries include:

Threshold to Path: How a threshold announces arrival and directs a visitor's trajectory, priming them for their experience and cleansing them from their previous experience to provide a break and an announcement.

Icon Image: How the image of architecture establishes iconography and meaning.

Dialogue Box: The discourse between two forms and their ceremonial activities.

Land Form: The figuration of landscape and the framing mood of spatial immersion.

Shutter Box: The role of repetition and the variable effects of filtering light.

Up Down House: How the identity of form affects perception and directionality of building. How skin defines surface and enclosure, illustrates weight and directionality, and crops an image as a field.

Ocular Rotunda: The focus of a sky eye and the contrasting roles of window for both light and view.

Lighted Corridor: How light affects sequence and the variability of directional light in choreographing mood.

Lean 2: How static form can embody motion.

Four Faces: How surface and form respond to orientation and effect.

View Chamber: How an aperture defines space, curates light, frames a view, provides ventilation, determines occupancy, choreographs activity, becomes a station for seeing.

Corridor Cluster: How collection, sequence, and connectivity produce promenade.

Cluster Group: How individuated aggregation establishes interrelationships.

Three Densities: The variable perceptions of iterative form through the reference of surface and the effects of enclosure.

Icon Tube: The spirituality of a space and the iconography of culturally referential form.

Heavy Light Tower: How the visual weight of a volume effects the compression of space. How a voluminous inward looking space balances against a compact outward looking space.

View Funnel: How a framed view captures, collapses, and composes a landscape.

Stair Viewer: How a stair transitions and frames a vertical motion and arrives at a destination view corridor.

3 Square: How regular structure balances irregular composition; the impact of the tradition of the nine square brought to sectional consideration; the balancing of open against closed.

Rack Collection: The collection and juxtaposition of surfaces and the diversity of skin to affect perception.

Articulated Surface: The elevation of a compositional ground plane and the effect of being on, between, and below a surface.

Weight Stack: The role of weight in perception.

House-Eye: The operation of iconic formal references and the effectual experience of focused vision.

Cage Frames: The frame and its affect on composition.

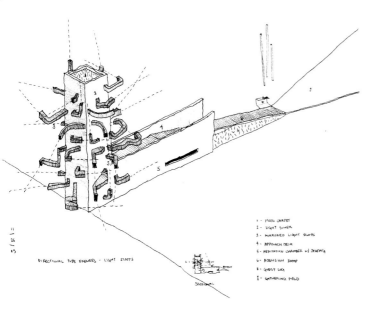

DIRECTIONAL TUBE SPEAKERS · LIGHT SCOOPS

1 - MOSS CARPET
2 - LIGHT TOWER
3 - MIRRORED LIGHT SLOTS
4 - APPROACH DECK
5 - MEDITATION CHAMBER W/ SEATING
6 - ACCENSION RAMP
7 - GUEST LOCK
8 - GATHERING FIELD

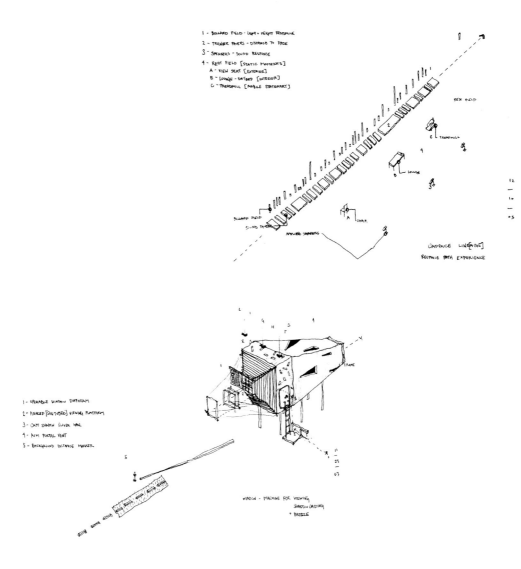

1 - BOLLARD FIELD · LIGHT + HEIGHT RESPONSE
2 - TRIGGER PAVERS · DISTANCE TO PACE
3 - SPEAKERS · SOUND RESPONSE
4 - REST FIELD [STATIC MOMENTS]
    A - VIEW SEAT [EXTERIOR]
    B - LOUNGE · DAYBED [INTERIOR]
    C - TREADMILL [MOBILE STATIONARY]

CADENCE LINKAGE
RESPONSE PATH EXPERIENCE

1 - OPERABLE WINDOW DIAPHRAM
2 - FIGURED [SCULPTURED] VIEWING PLATFORM
3 - CAST SHADOW SLIVER WALL
4 - AIM PORTAL VENT
5 - BACKGROUND DISTANCE MARKER

WINDOW · MACHINE FOR VIEWING
SHADOW CASTING
+ BREEZE

The experience mechanisms have the purpose of creating these compelling experiences by appealing to all senses. Employing form, light, materials, color, sequence, et cetera, the architecture's programmatic concern becomes the perceptual awareness of space.

INDIVIDUAL PAVILIONS

The collection of pavilions scattered in the landscape serve as fragments focusing on the landscape and the perception of space. In the heritage of Donald Judd's Chinati Foundation, Robert Smithson's *Spiral Jetty*, Jenny Holzer's *Sun Tunnels*, Michael Heizer's *Double Negative,* and James Turrell's *Roden Crater*; these works employ architectural mechanisms to mediate between the perceptive capabilities of our bodies and the beauty of the natural environment. As a collection of individual rooms and communal group spaces, each insertion focuses on a specific moment in the landscape and the architecture that heightens and orchestrates its perception.

The proposition for the articulation of distinct experiences in individuated pavilions allows for their specific positioning. Each composition assumes an iconography of individual identity relative to the viewer themselves. The experience is orchestrated through the interface with the object representing and defining a way of seeing and engaging the self and the adjacent terrain. Individually articulated, the delicate pavilions are for watching, residing, entering, and engaging place to understand self. Each dispersed pavilion provides an isolated moment within the larger system. Spatially precise, each mechanism engages a distinct aspect and fundamental component of architecture. The quality of the built environment must be negotiated through these essentials. Fragments of possibility, these mechanisms are [X]perience.

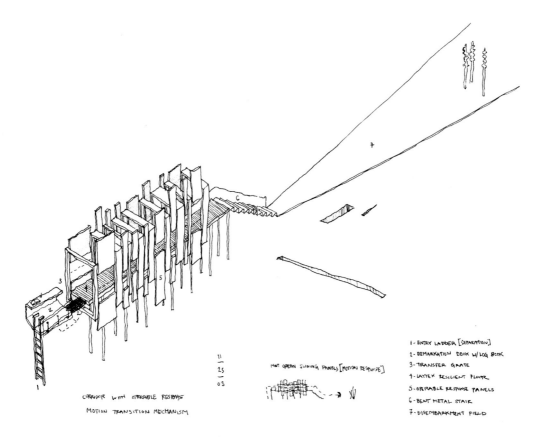

CORRIDOR WITH OPERABLE RESPONSE
MOTION TRANSITION MECHANISM

HOT GREEN SLIDING PANELS [MOTION RESPONSE]

1 - ENTRY LADDER [SEPARATION]
2 - DEMARKATION DECK W/ LOG BOOK
3 - TRANSFER GRATE
4 - LATTEX RESILIENT FLOOR
5 - OPERABLE RESPONSE PANELS
6 - BENT METAL STAIR
7 - DISEMBARKMENT FIELD

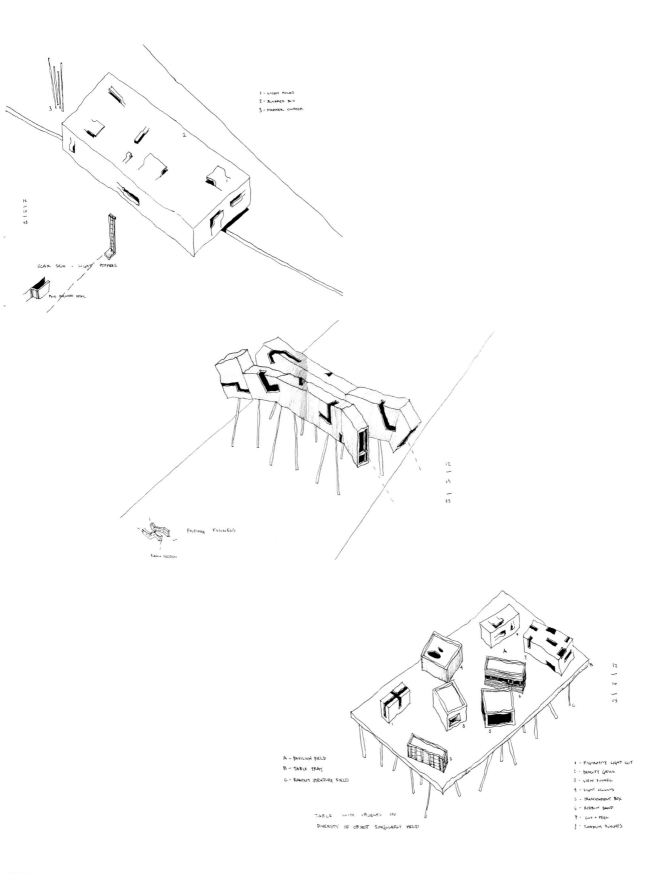

1 – LIGHT FOLDS
2 – BLURRED BOX
3 – MARKER CLUSTER

SCAR SKIN – LIGHT POPPERS

PLAN + SECTION DETAIL

FOLDING FUNNELS

PLAN + SECTION

A – PAVILION FIELD
B – TABLE TRAY
C – RANDOM STRUCTURE FIELD

TABLE WITH OBJECTS ON
DIVERSITY OF OBJECT SINGULARLY HELD

1 – FIGURATIVE LIGHT SLIT
2 – DENSITY GRILL
3 – VIEW FUNNEL
4 – LIGHT OCULUS
5 – TRANSPARENT BOX
6 – RIBBON BAND
7 – CUT + PEEL
8 – RANDOM PUNCHES

153

1 THRESHOLD TO PATH
2 ICON IMAGE
3 PARCEL DIALOGUE
4 LAND FORM
5 SHUTTER BOX
6 UP-DOWN HOUSE
7 OCULAR ROTUNDA
8 LIGHTED CORRIDOR
9 LEAN 2
10 4 FACES
11 VIEW CHAMBER
12 CORRIDOR CLUSTER
13 CLUSTER GROUP
15 ICON TUBE
16 HEAVY LIGHT TOWER
18 STAIR VIEWER CHAMBER
19 3 SQUARE
20 RACK TOWER
21 FOLD SURFACE
22 WEIGHT STACK
24 CAGE FRAMES

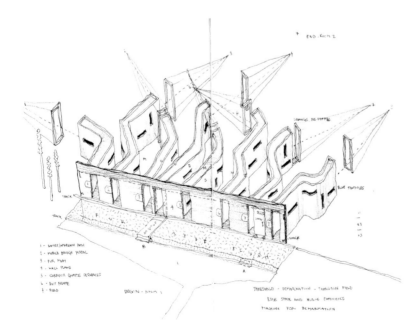

Threshold to Path

Eight linear tendrils accumulate along a single wall plane to offer a threshold to a selection of experiences. Varying in light quality, length, orientation, and outcome; the viewer moves through the threshold to uniquely define their awareness of time, space, and experience relative to moment. One selects an entry and the corridor funnels you to a landscape and [X]perience.

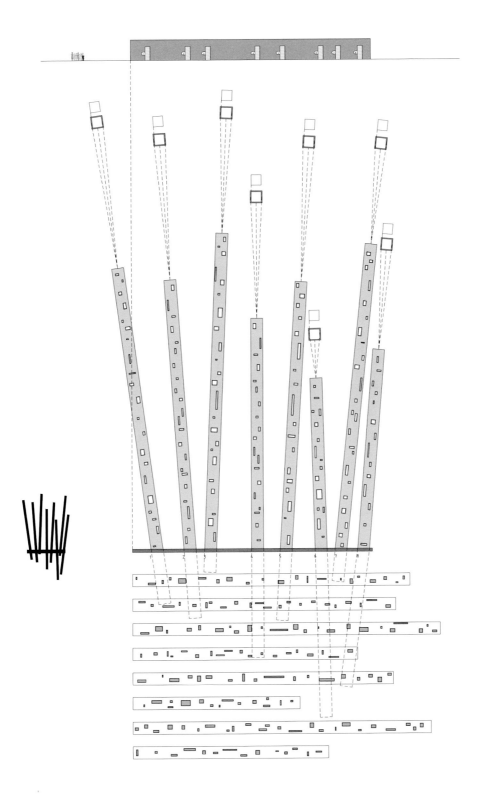

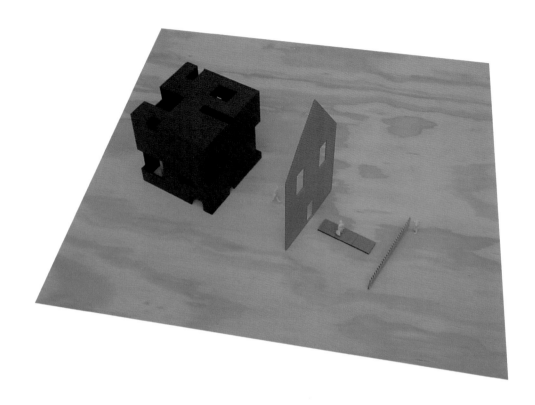

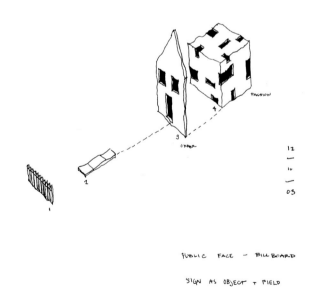

1 - EDGE
2 - SURFACE
3 - PLANE
4 - OBJECT

PUBLIC FACE — BILLBOARD

SIGN AS OBJECT + FIELD

Icon Image

A billboard house form addresses the visitor's axial approach. A perforated cube sets behind. The iconographic figures of fence, yard, and house mask a multivalent, field based enclosure. The juxtaposition of the referential against the abstract positions cultural meaning against physical perception.

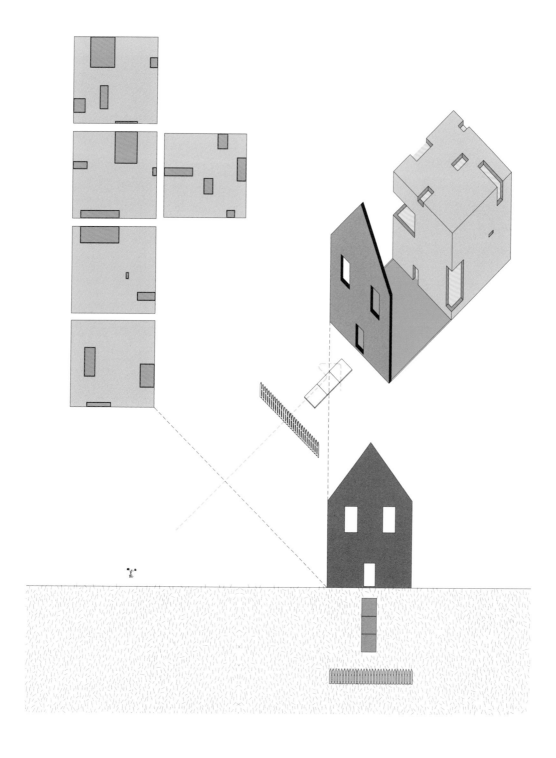

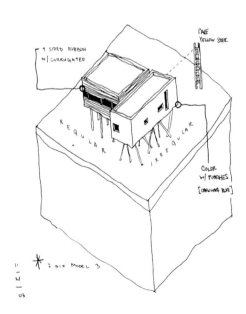

Dialogue Box

A square corrugated metal box with a continuous ribbon of windows on all four faces engages the edge between tree line and clearing.

A contrasting opaque pavilion with irregular structural legs selects specific framed views to stitch into the interior. The two sit in quiet conversation and juxtaposition.

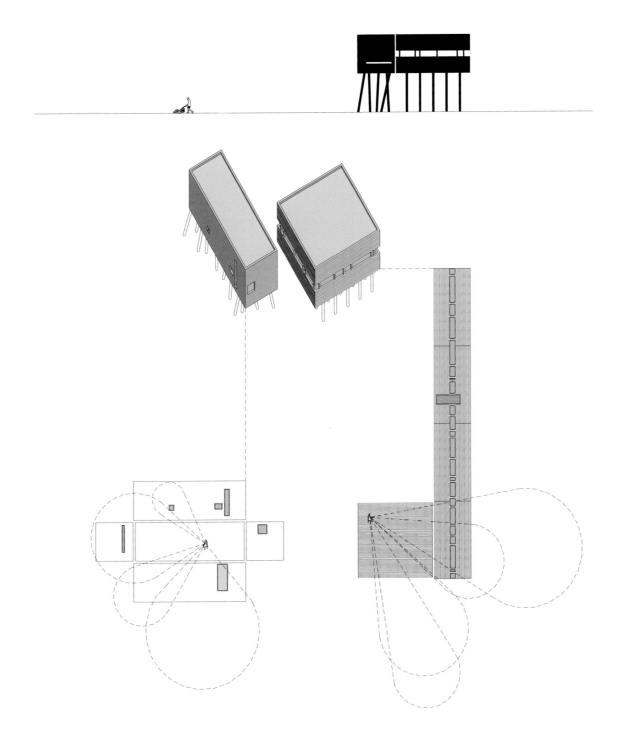

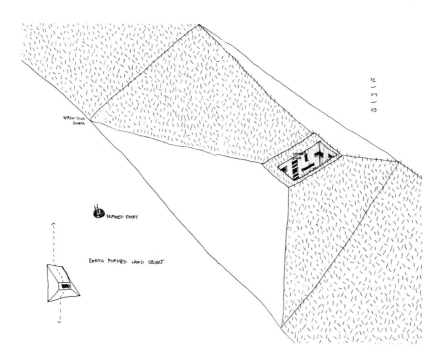

Land Form

A cultivated rise in the topography ascends to a polished stainless steel clad pit. One enters through circular aperture containing a slide that descends through an organic tube.

One arrives in the pit: inorganic and reflective with circular back-lit globes. Music furthers the mood. A ladder provides an exit.

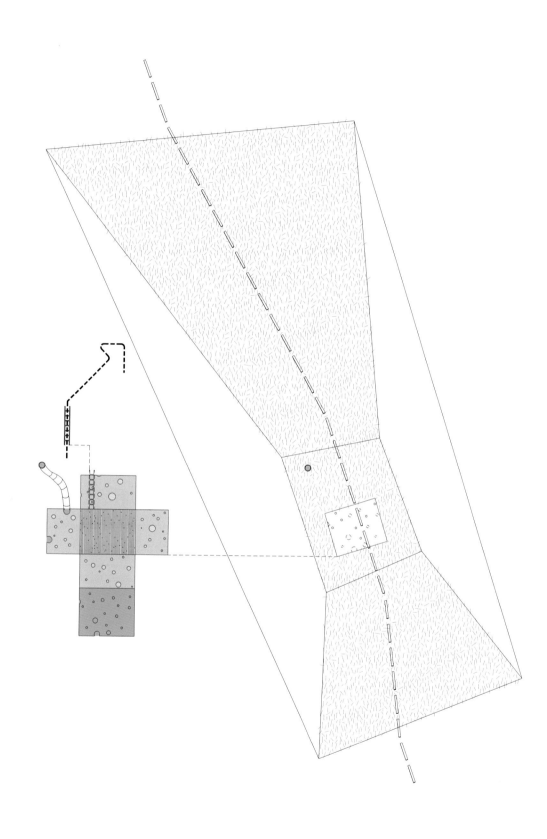

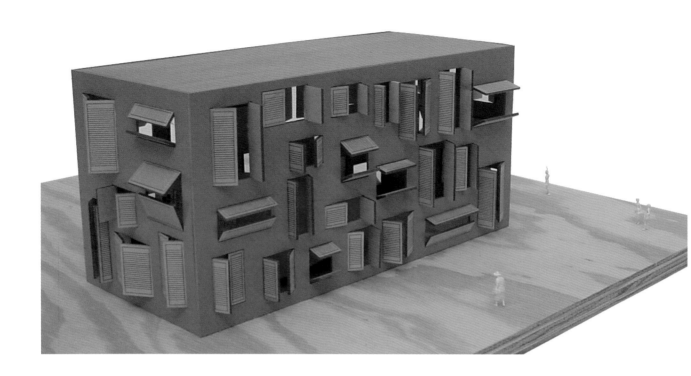

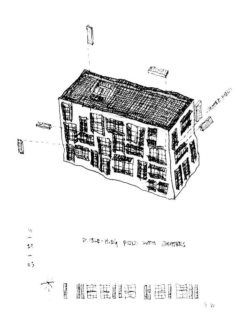

Shutter Box

A series of varying shuttered apertures modulate surface, light, depth, and ventilation. As a field of operable portals, the skin permits a responsive articulation of gradated openness.

The mutable surface, light, shadow, and temperature through air-flow are modulated by the orchestration of pattern.

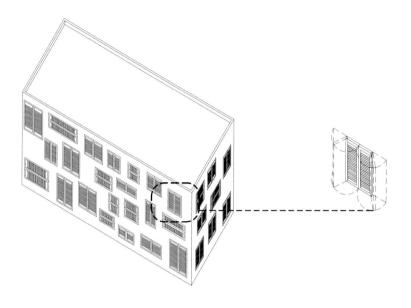

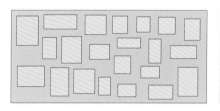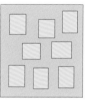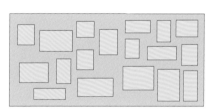

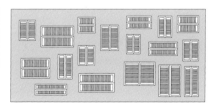

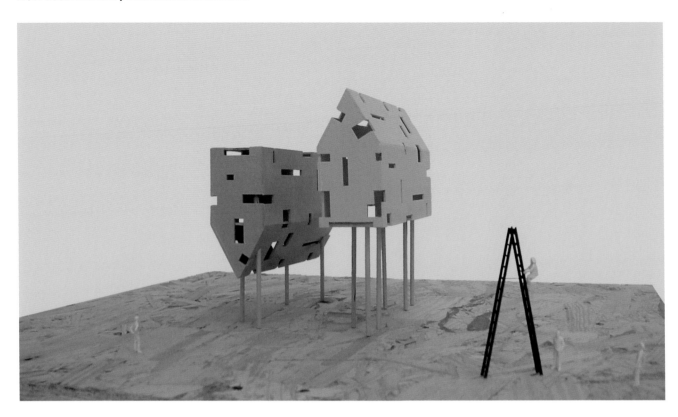

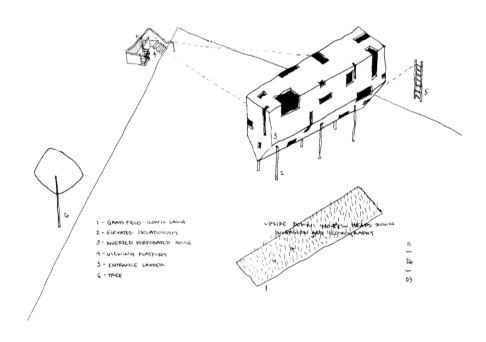

1 – GRASS FIELD - ICONIC LAWN
2 – ELEVATED ISOLATIONISM
3 – INVERTED PERFORATED HOUSE
4 – VIEWING PLATFORM
5 – ENTRANCE LADDER
6 – TREE

UPSIDE DOWN 'HOUSE' HEADS DOWN
INVERSION AND ICONOGRAPHY

11
—
26
—
03

Up Down House

Two iconic images of home perforated with full field apertures are inverted in position relative to one another.

Their form and skin facilitate a redistribution of conventional perception challenging traditions of reference and value.

[X]perience Mechanisms

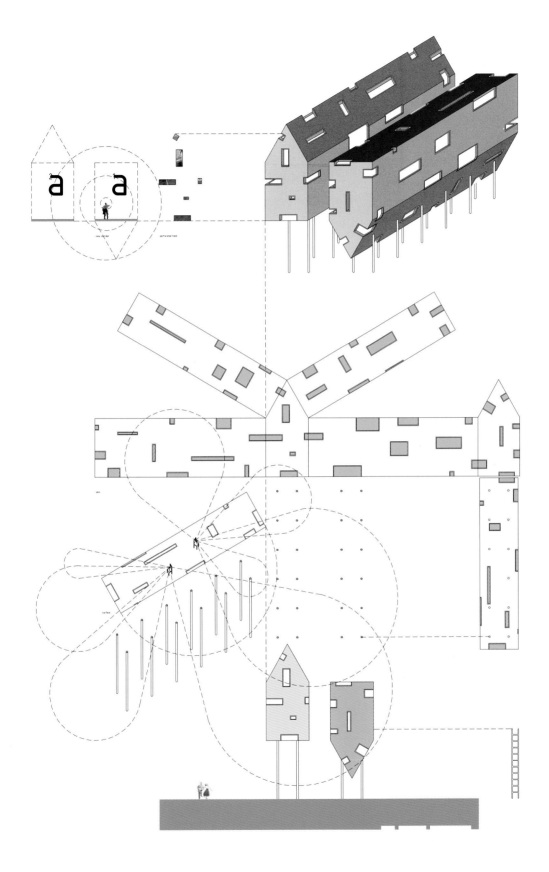

167

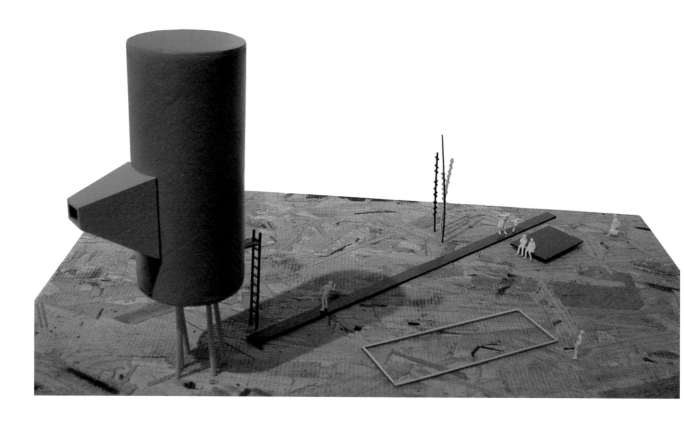

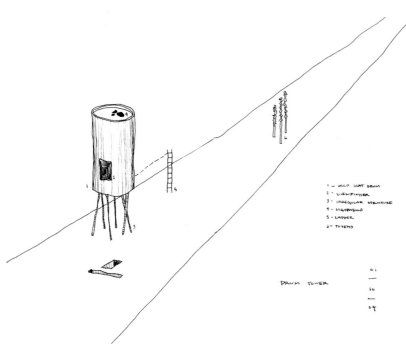

1 - WOOD SLAT DRUM
2 - VIEWFINDER
3 - IRREGULAR STRUCTURE
4 - LIGHTWELLS
5 - LADDER
6 - TOTEMS

DRUM TOWER

Ocular Rotunda

An elevated cylindrical drum receives light through three organic openings in the roof. The gradation of even down-light on the walls provides a flattening to the curvilinear surfaces challenging the relationship of perceived form to actual form. A singular ocular funnel establishes a pictorial and axial view to the James River. Perception and composition sit in dialogue.

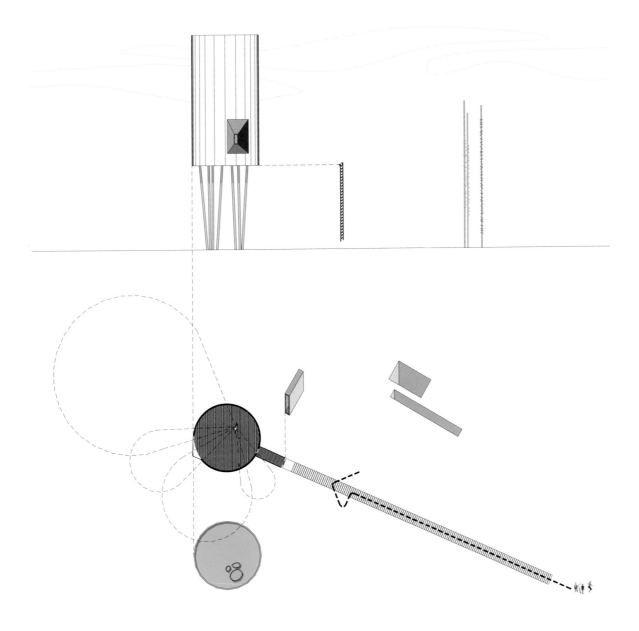

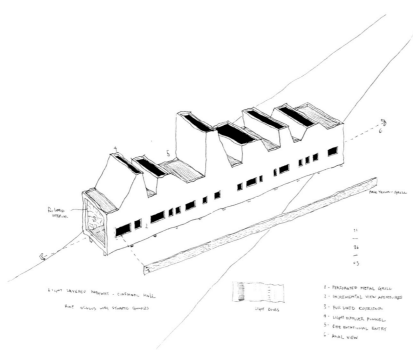

Lighted Corridor

A linear corridor of light is mediated by diverse roof apertures while the alternating horizontal view windows are masked by striped shields.

The linear movement along its path moves through varied light densities and views to re-orchestrate and re-frame the perception of context.

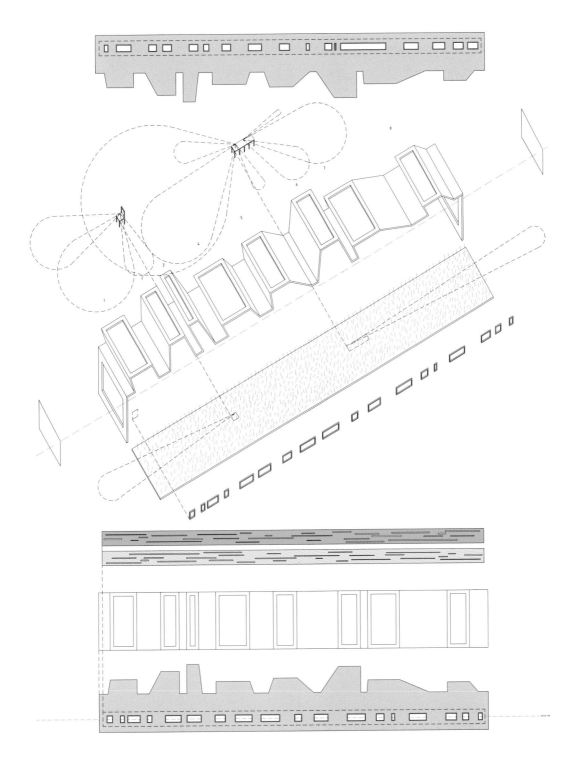

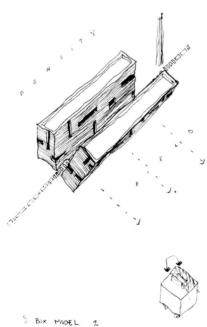

BOX MODEL 2

Lean 2

Two boxes (one level and the other sloping) shift
vertically against each other and the dipping landscape. The datum and shift mark a motion.

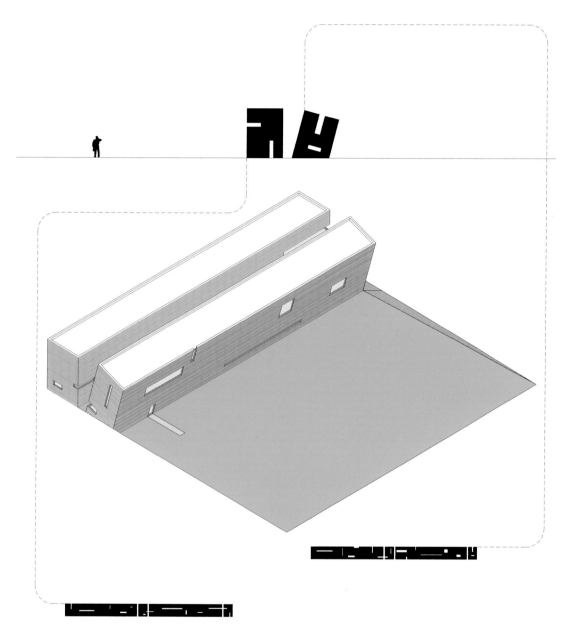

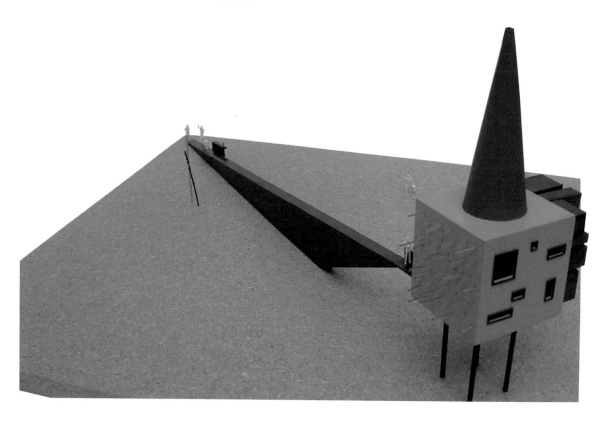

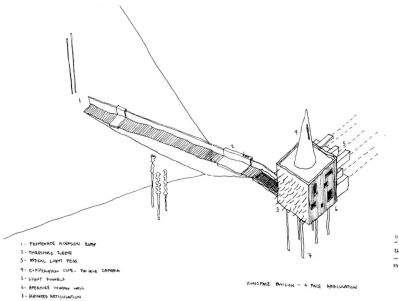

1 - PROMENADE ASCENSION RAMP
2 - THRESHOLD SLEEVE
3 - OPTICAL LIGHT PEGS
4 - CONSTELLATION CORE - PIN HOLE CAMERA
5 - LIGHT FUNNELS
6 - APERTURE WINDOW WALL
7 - ELEVATED ARTICULATION

11
26
—
03

ICONOFACE PAVILION - 4 FACE ARTICULATION

Four Faces

A gently ascending ramp delicately reaches up to an elevated cube. Each of the four faces is varied based upon orientation.

The skin articulation modulates the interior chamber and the experience of the surrounding view.

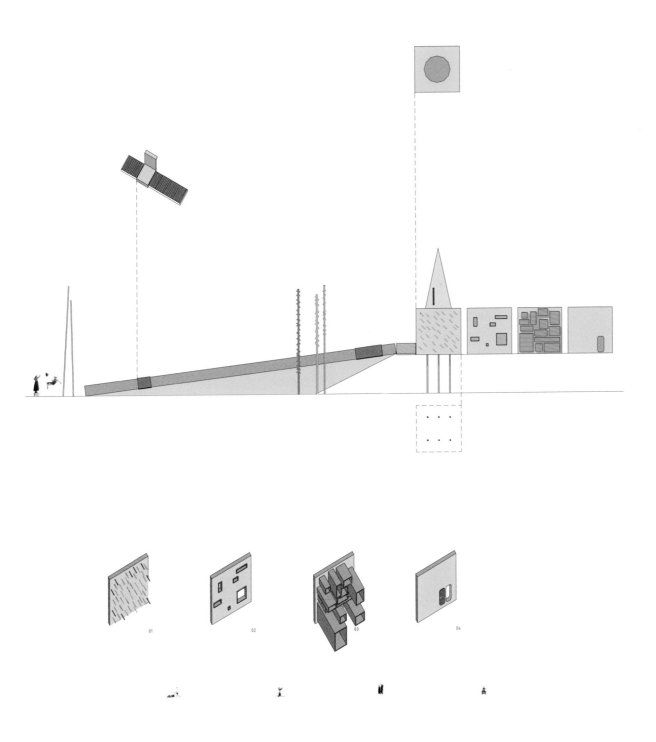

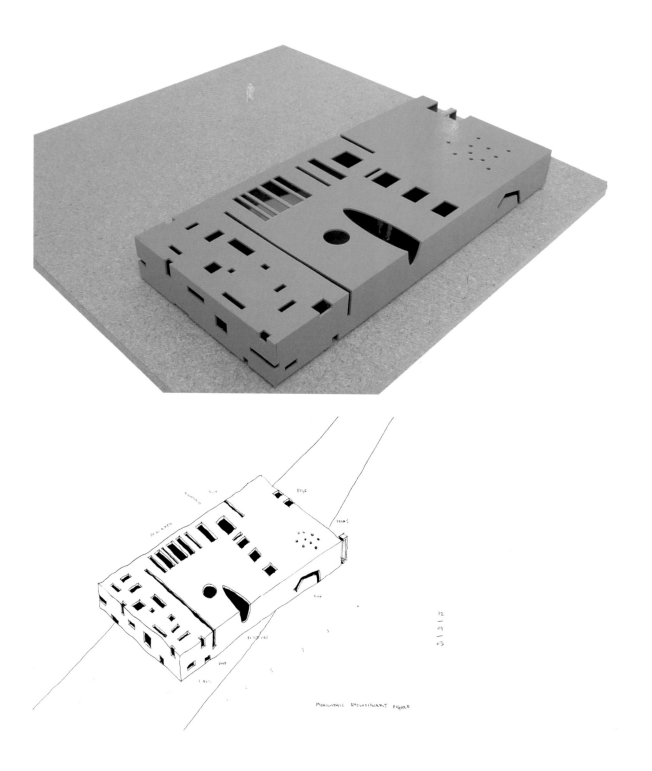

View Chamber

A variably articulated shell surface engages the potential of the aperture. The diversity of opening types in the exterior skin modulate light, view, and ventilation making the chamber an ever changing effectual experience of juxtaposed conditions. The grand hall is flooded with the fragmented images of the surrounding landscape. A secondary interior view chamber serves as a focused vantage for re-perception through a fixed frame.

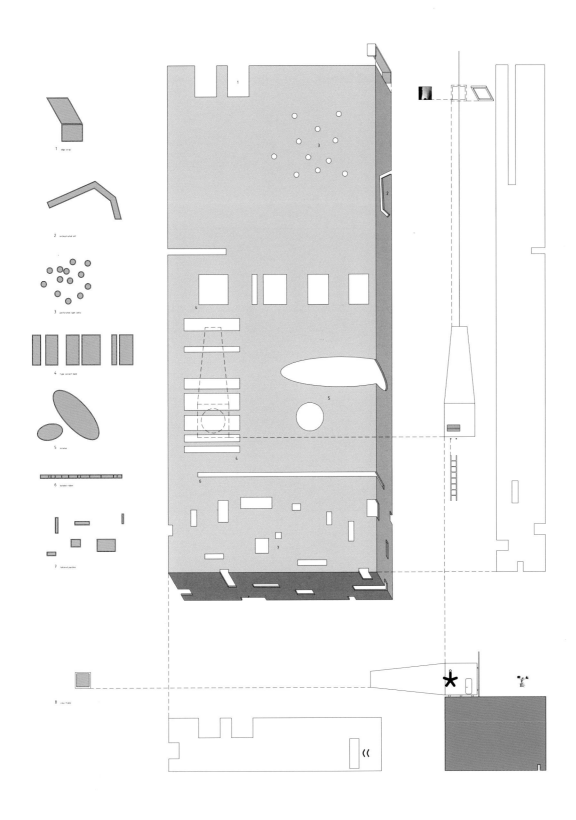

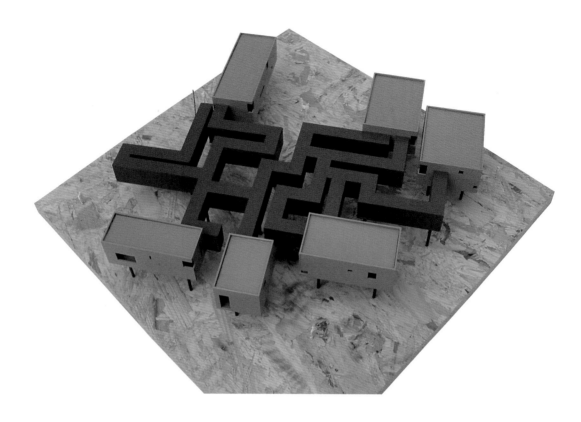

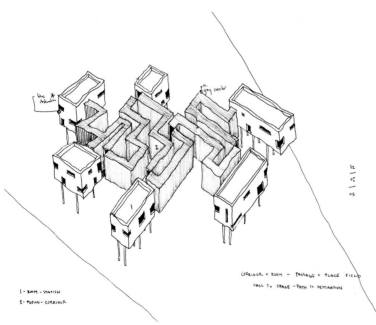

Corridor Cluster

Separate pavilions linked by a meandering pathway objectify the act of motion as an event. Internally lit, the corridors become journeyed sequences connecting the destinations both functionally and effectually.

The arrival at the end pavilions are marked by dis tinct framed windows calibrated to the surrounding landscape, oriented by view.

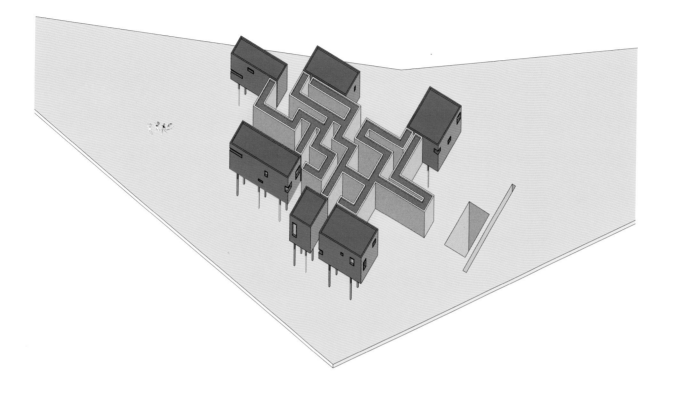

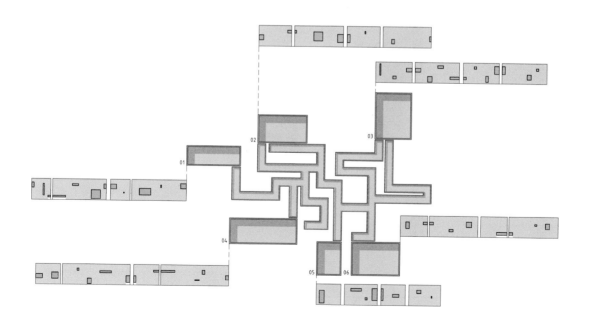

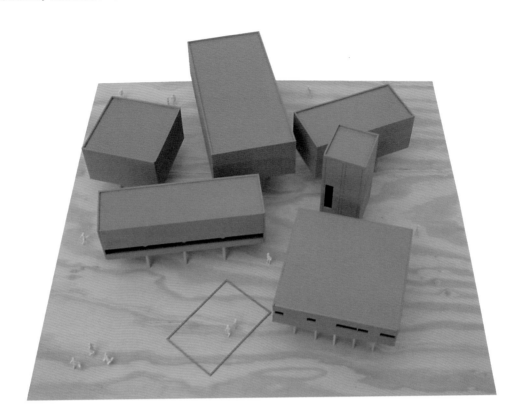

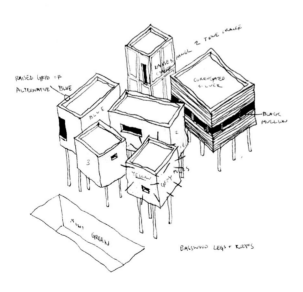

Cluster Group

As a collection of buildings, each pavilion articulates its identity based on the proportions of the space to aperture and material. The relativism of the collection is amplified by their juxtaposition. The seven figures (six elevated and one depressed into the ground) are each for a different day of the week. The experience of the chamber is exaggerated by the separation from one another. One must leave to the exterior, traverse on the ground plane, then re-enter. The singularity of each room within the collection provides the individuated experience. Memory over time engages the collective composition.

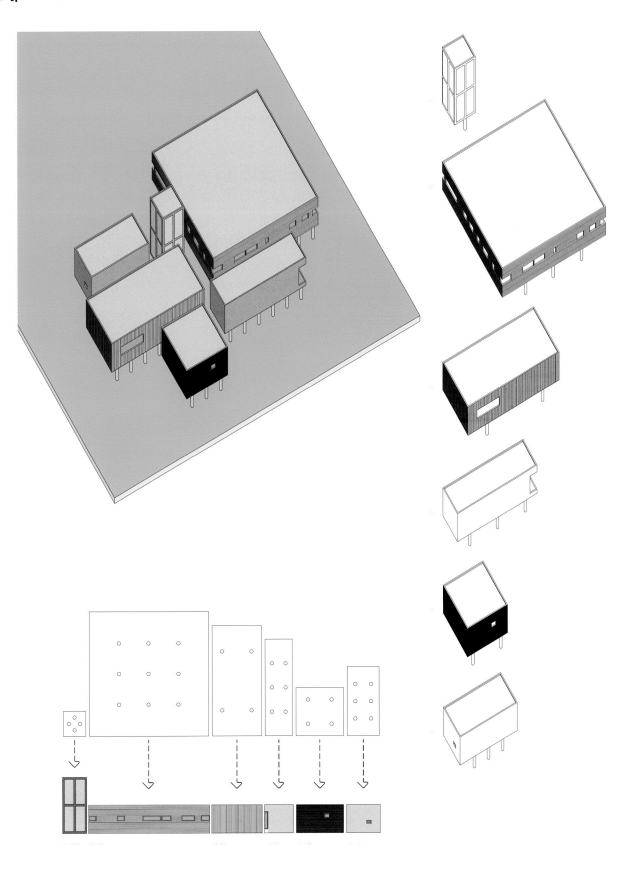

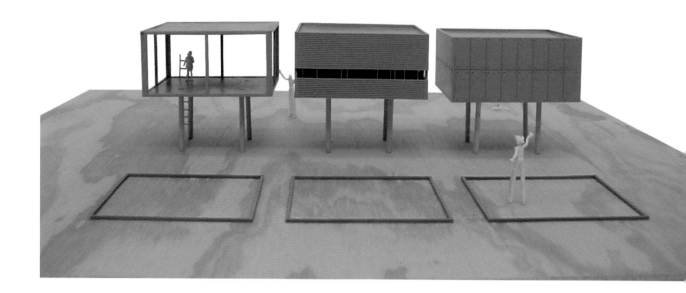

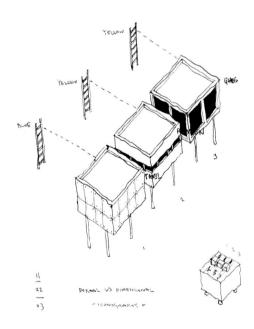

Three Densities

Three dimensionally identical volumes are linearly arranged on a regularized increment. Their identity varies with their materiality: [1] a heavy opaque concrete box, [2] a corrugated metal box with a continuous horizontal ribbon window, and [3] a transparent glass box. Each provide varied levels of environmental publicity, light, and view. Each references iconic modernist palettes: Mies van der Rohe, Le Corbusier, and Louis Kahn.

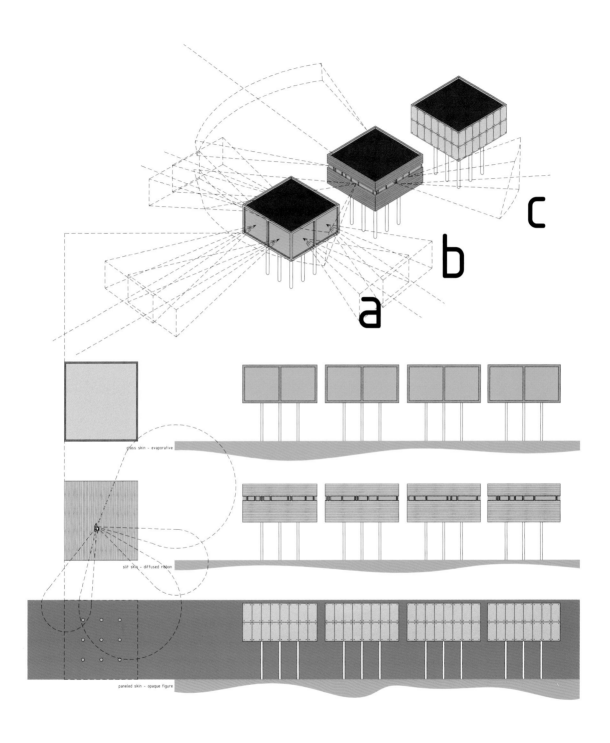

glass skin – evaporative

slit skin – diffused ribbon

paneled skin – opaque figure

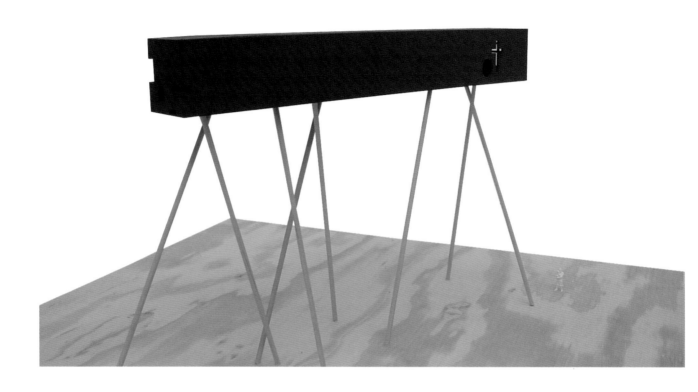

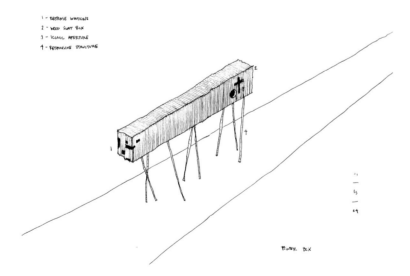

1 - RESPONSIVE WINDOWS
2 - WOOD SLAT BOX
3 - ICONIC APERTURE
4 - RESPONSIVE STRUCTURE

RIVER BOX

Icon Tube

A hovering, wood slat clad tube has a fractured perspective projecting through a break in the trees to reveal the James River.

A lateral cruciform and circle window induce spiritually referential light forms to the chamber.

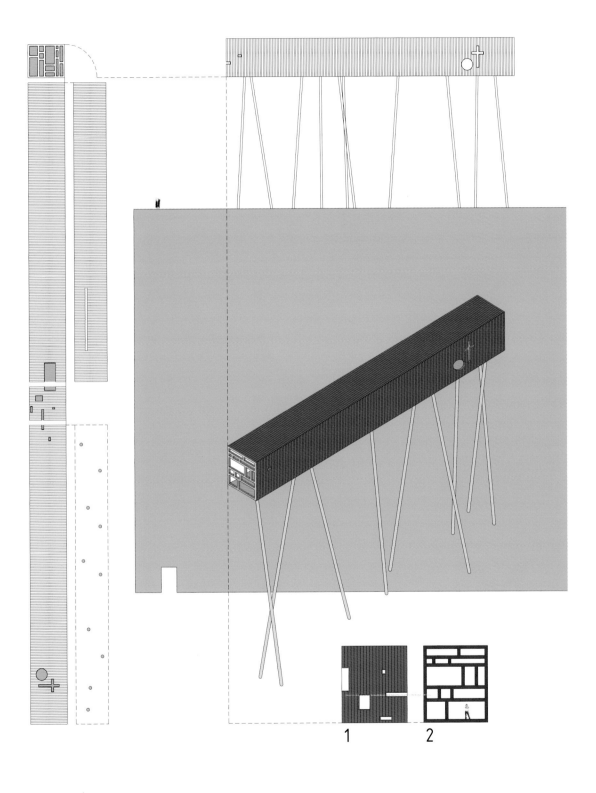

1   2

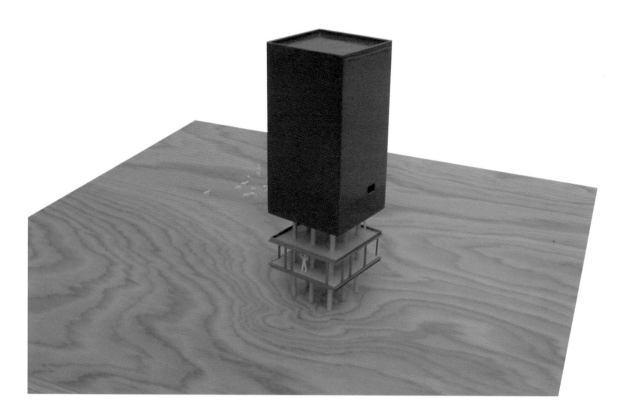

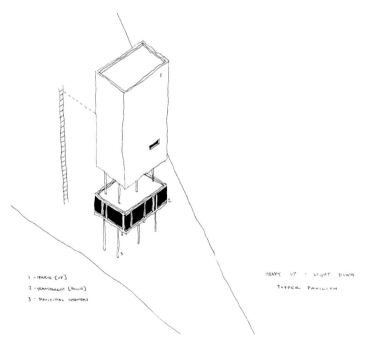

1 - OPAQUE [UP]
2 - TRANSPARENT [DOWN]
3 - STRUCTURAL SKEWERS

HEAVY UP - LIGHT DOWN
TOPPER PAVILION

Heavy Light Tower

An opaque vertical chamber floats on a nine square columnar grid above a transparent horizontal chamber establishing an inverse weight relationship. Dark

Closed contrasts with open. Vertical contrasts with horizontal.

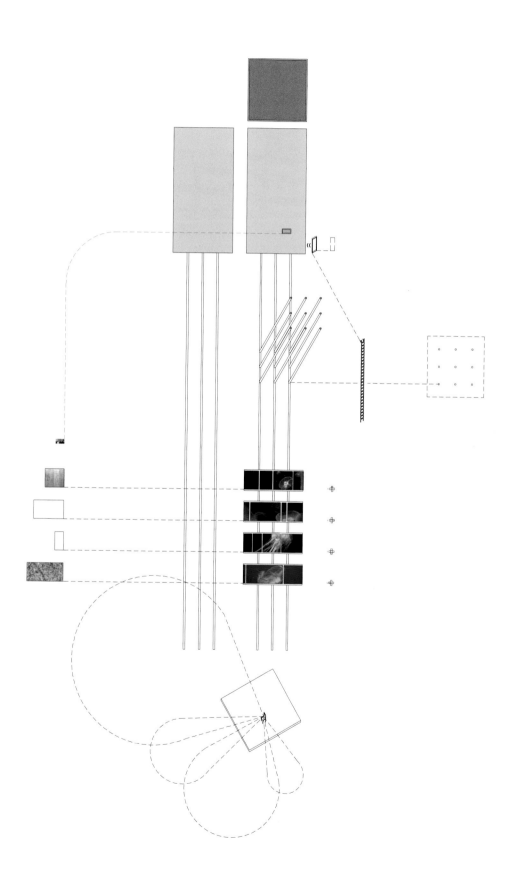

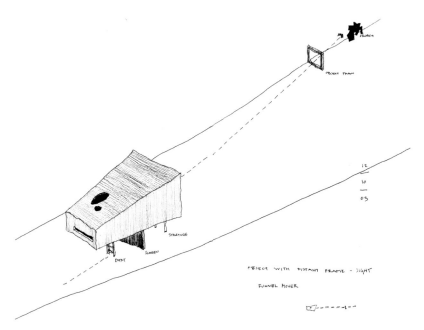

View Funnel

The view funnel creates a focal cone lens to engage the landscape. A single funneling room projects a framed view. A series of receding frames (set into the landscape at a standard increment) diminish in scale as they recede from the viewer. The resulting effect is an accelerated view of the context. The forced perspective marks, measures, and frames the view alley through manipulation of the focal cone.

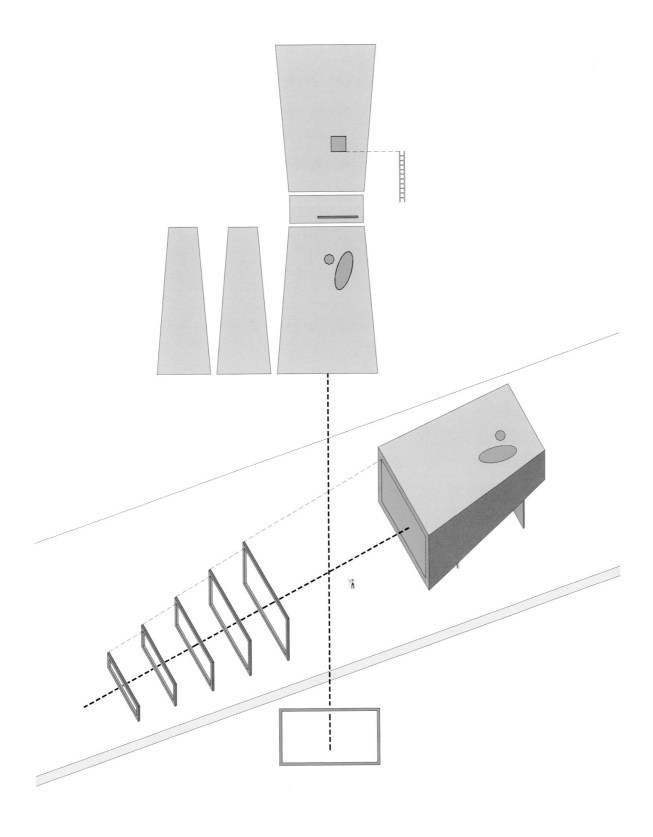

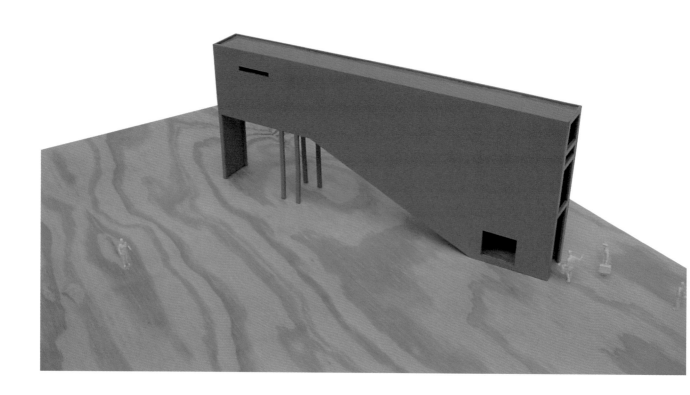

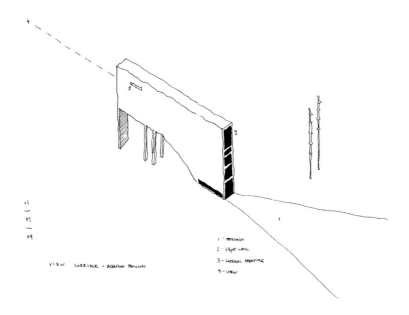

VIEW CORRIDOR - ASCENSION PAVILION

1 - APPROACH
2 - LIGHT WALL
3 - LATERAL APERTURE
4 - VIEW

Stair Viewer

An ascending corridor extends the pedestrian path by elevating it to a framed oculus that overlooks the abandoned alley of a former power line easement.

The seeming infinity of the manicured cut in the forest carries to the horizon. The ascension of the stair allows for the slow emergence of the view.

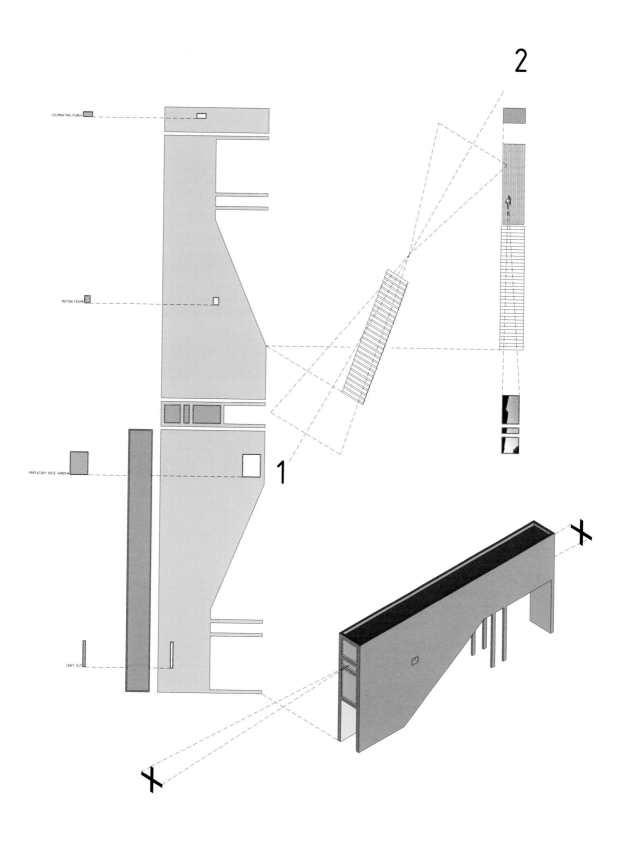

CULMINATING PUNCH

2

MOTION FRAME

1

PREPATORY BASE WINDOW

LIGHT SLIT

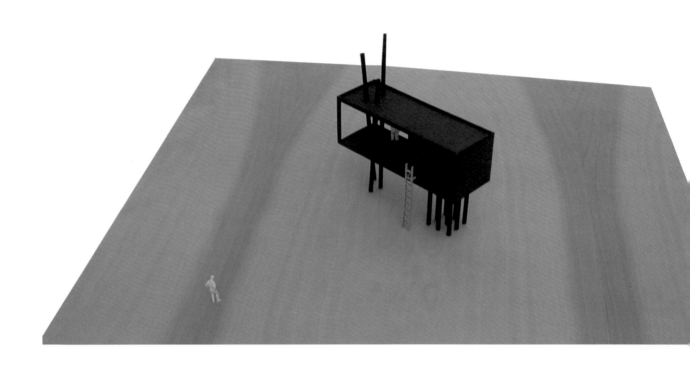

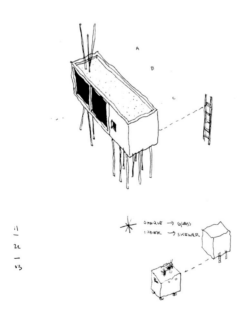

3 Square

Nine cubes define a banded vertical plane of three negative volumes, three positive volumes, and three negative volumes.

Two columnar structures: an ordered nine square and three disordered sculptural pins, elevate the occupiable plane. The form and order of the view box mediates the experience.

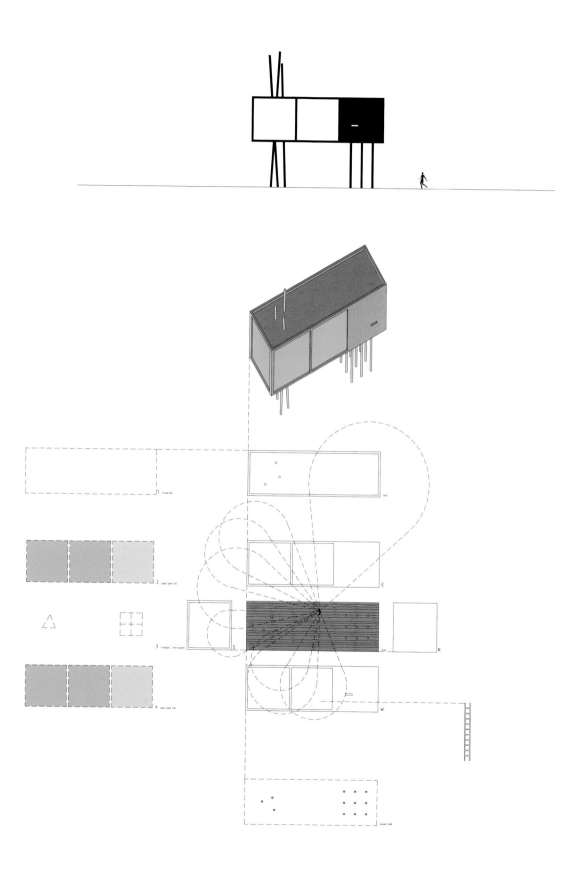

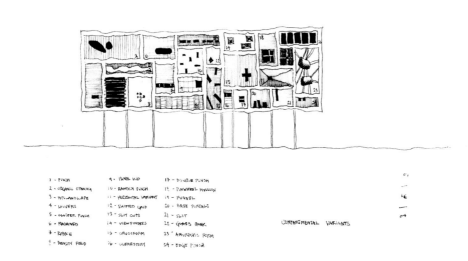

1 - PINCH	9 - PANEL WID	17 - DOUBLE PUNCH		01
2 - ORGANIC OPENING	10 - RANDOM PUNCH	18 - PINWHEEL MULLION		--
3 - TOTEM & SLATE	11 - HORIZONTAL VARIANT	19 - FUNNEL		16
4 - LOUVERS	12 - SHIFTED GRID	20 - BASE PORTALS		--
5 - CLUSTER PUNCH	13 - SLIT CUTS	21 - SLIT		04
6 - MACHINED	14 - VIEWFINDERS	22 - GLASS BANK		
7 - RIBBON	15 - CRUCIFORM	23 - AMORPHOUS FORM	CONTAPTMENTAL VARIANTS	
8 - DENSITY FIELD	16 - CLERESTORY	24 - EDGE PUNCH		

Rack Collection

An elevated collection of rooms are gathered in a framing rack. Each room maintains an individual identity by varying the spatial proportions and skin type.

The same view is mediated by the architectural surface and aperture to heighten the individuality of the experience.

X]perience Mechanisms

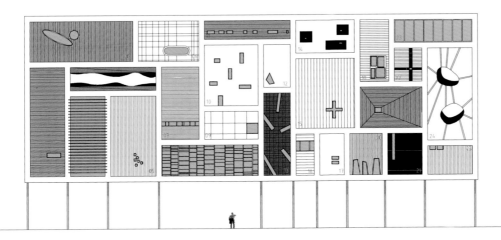

01 – PUNCH
02 – ORGANIC OPENING
03 – TOPOLANDSCAPE
04 – LOUVERS
05 – CLUSTER PUNCH
06 – MACHINED
07 – RIBBON
08 – DENSITY FIELD
09 – PANEL VOID
10 – RANDOM PUNCH
11 – HORIZONTAL VARIANT
12 – SHIFTED GRID
13 – SLIT CUTS
14 – VIEWFINDERS
15 – CRUCIFORM
16 – CLERESTORY
17 – DOUBLE PUNCH
18 – PINWHEEL MULLION
19 – FUNNEL
20 – BASE PORTALS
21 – SLIT
22 – FOCAL
23 – GLASS BANK
24 – AMORPHIC FORM
25 – EDGE PUNCH

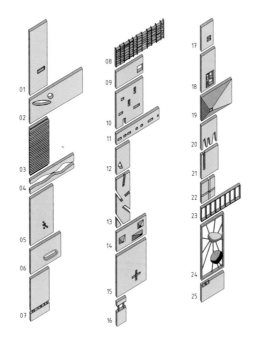

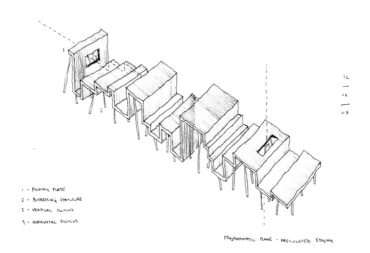

1 - FOLDING PLATE
2 - BUTRESSING STRUCTURE
3 - VERTICAL OCULUS
4 - HORIZONTAL OCULUS

PROGRAMMATIC PLANE - ARTICULATED EDGING

Articulated Surface

A hovering and folding plane serves as an elevated surface for sunbathing. The rigid orthogonal topography structurally dances against the undulating natural topography of the sloping floodplain below.

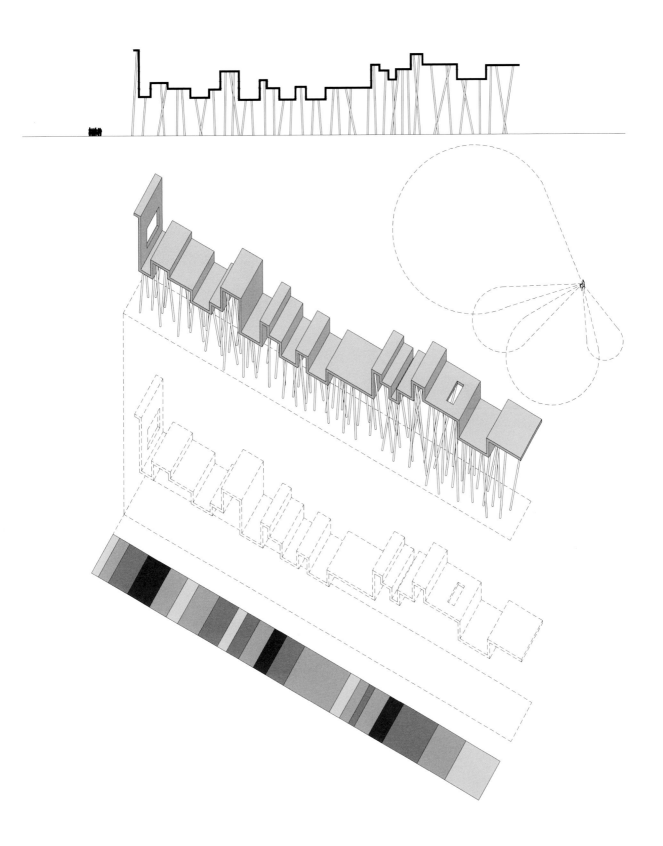

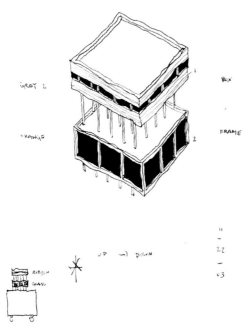

Weight Stack

The weight stack uses the section to deploy a visual weight. The mass of the upper volume atop the delicate frame of the bottom volume sets the two figures in dialogue. The identical dimensions of the positive figures, with half volumes for the negative interstitial figures, establish the vertical rhythm. The hypostyle field of columns connecting the two forms generates the vertical tissue. The weight forms speak in dialogues of open-closed, day-night, down-up.

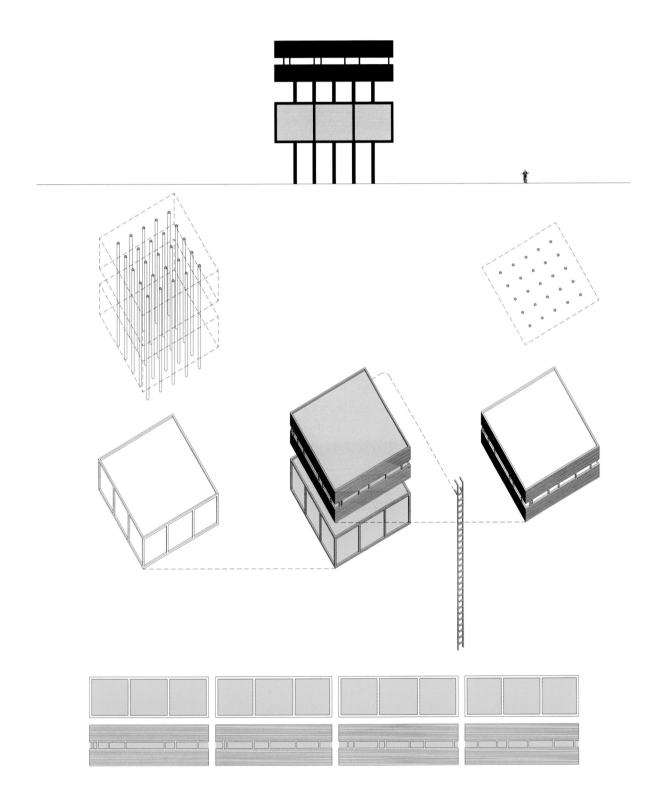

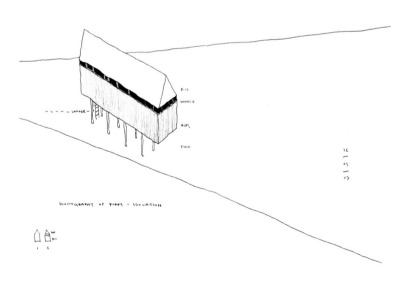

House-Eye

The form of the house is cracked to reveal a continuous ribbon of windows sandwiched between triangle and square. A view funnel directs the attention through a singular framed experience.

The House-Eye stands as a residential watching figure in an ambulatory landscape.

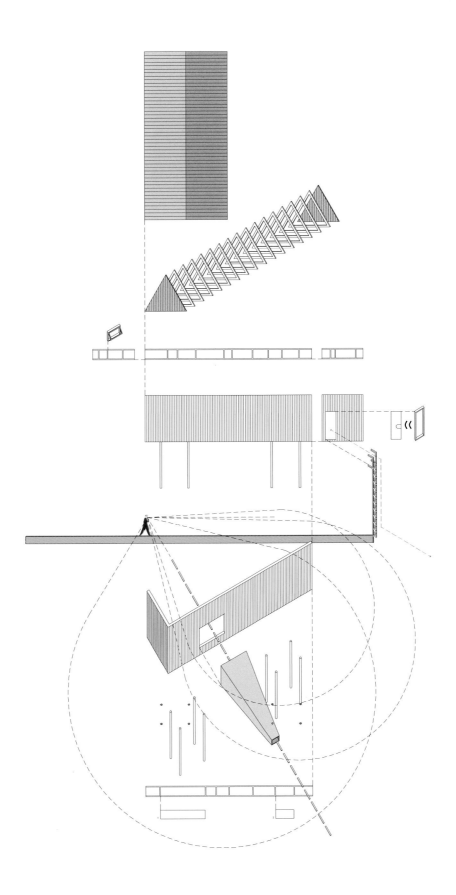

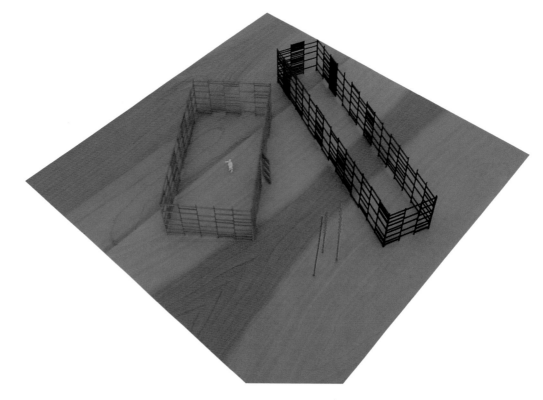

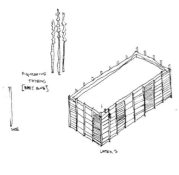

Cage Frames

A standard matrix of columns with harmonically varying frequencies of horizontal infill allow for a collection of visual densities. The porosity of the encircling frame repositions the surrounding landscape.

Three iconic totems mediate the convergence of the rectilinear chambers. The dual density and varied tonality establish a parallel dialogue.

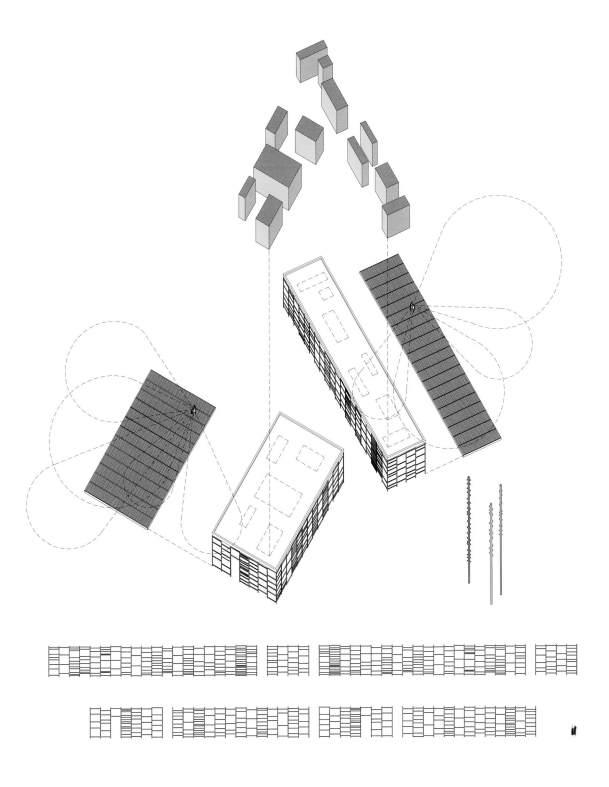

SPACEFRAMES

Each of the eight spaceframes creates an experience. They investigate a fragment of the daily ritual
of domestic life: entry, conversation, work, store,
watch, eat, bathe, and sleep. Exploring the spatial
and phenomenological aspects of these ceremonies
each fabrication is not a representation of experience
but the experience itself. Employing architectural
fragments (hollow core doors, laminated 2×4s,
and door peep-holes) each spaceframe employs a
choreographed view orchestrated by the viewfinder
through a three-dimensional architectural fragment,
arriving at the two-dimensional shallow projected
composition. The sight-line inserts the viewer into
the collective composition stitching the elements
together. Each of the fragments is intended to be
viewed alone and then recombined together through
memory. Exploring the spatial and phenomenological
aspects of these components allows each isolated
piece to precisely articulate its individuated identity.
A process sketchbook accompanies each of the
spaceframes containing conceptual, developmental
and fabrication drawings that aid in the interpolation
of the installation.

8 DOMESTIC FRAGMENTS

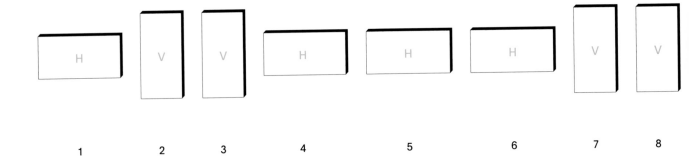

1 2 3 4 5 6 7 8

panel sequence

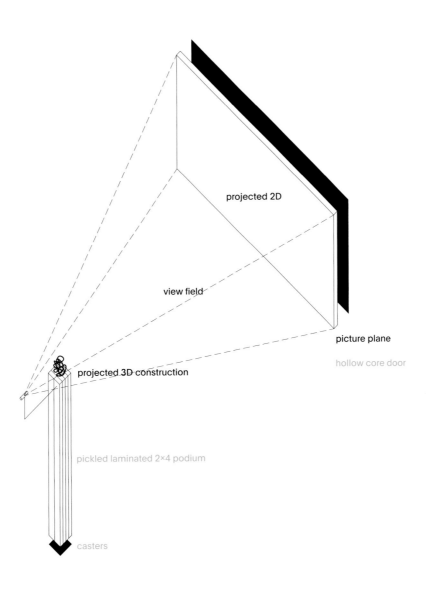

projected 2D

view field

picture plane

hollow core door

projected 3D construction

pickled laminated 2×4 podium

casters

anatomy of a spaceframe

view through entry eye piece

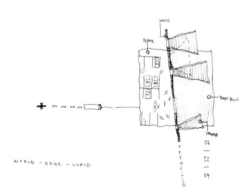

WORLD – EDGE – WORLD

2D panel

construction front

construction back

[ENTRY]

The threshold of the entry spaceframe collapses space from the massive line of the horizon to the microcosmic world of a constructed interior. Entered by a parking field, the view chamber funnels from the collective group to the individual. The figure is used to provide scale and introduce the body as viewer but is abandoned in all other spaceframes requiring distance and dimension to become relative to the composition requiring the viewer to determine scale. Portals through the wall layers the foreground against the background through the framing apertures. The planar voids frame anterior funnel views to reveal fragments of sky, earth, horizon, and all three together.

view through conversation eye piece

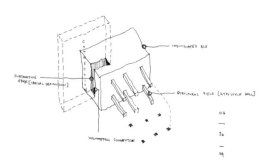

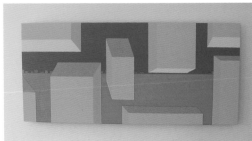

2D panel

3D construction

[CONVERSATION]

The ritual of the conversation spaceframe is foundational to communication and socialization. Grouped interaction begins with the collection. A series of varied volumes create a field of individuated elements. Subtracted volumes (implied by cuts into the larger volumes) suggest a secondary overlapping field: an undertone and interfacing field of voids. The three-dimensional field extends into the two-dimensional field with varied perspective vanishing points. The associated yet varied groupings lead to different conclusions.

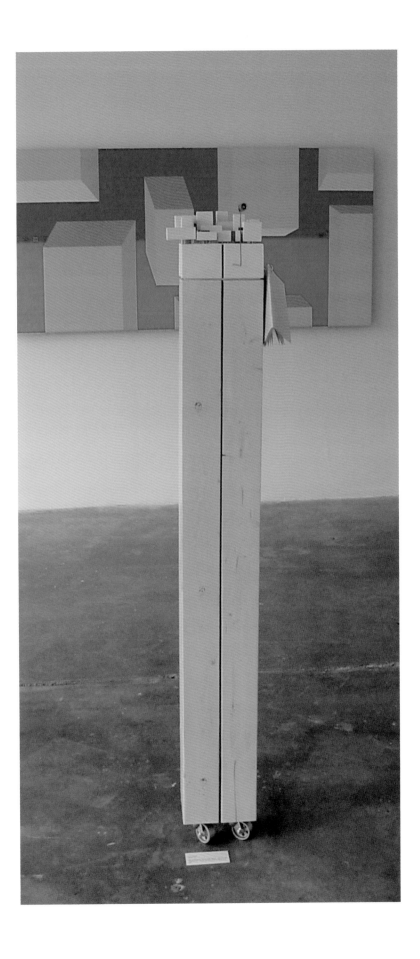

view through store eye piece

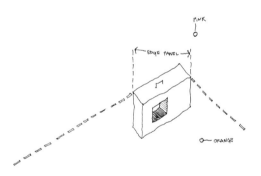

2D panel

3D construction

[STORE]

In the store spaceframe the case as a container suggests something discrete and sacred on its interior. A clustered field of diverse representational suitcases balances a larger case with an internal void. Highlighted from within the field, the larger abstracted case is represented in both two- and three-dimensions. Voids, varying in quantity, suggest an inner removal. The edge of the three-dimensional case defines a resonating edge to the ground plane in the two-dimensional field.

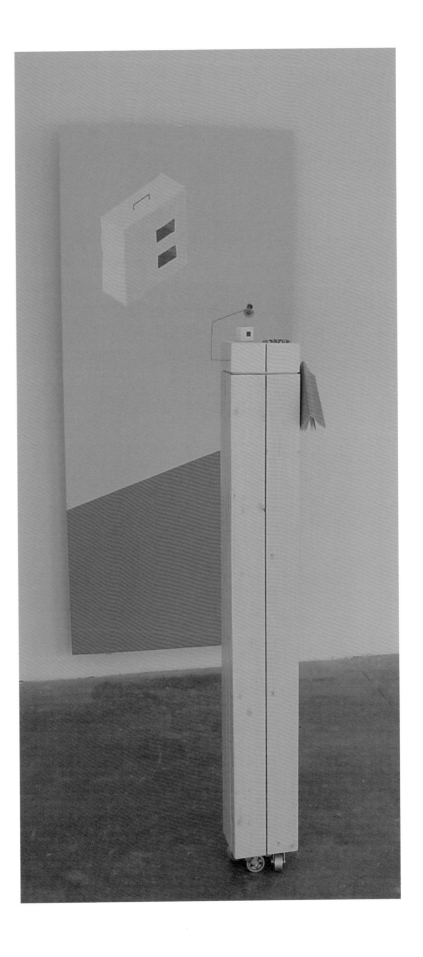

view through work eye piece

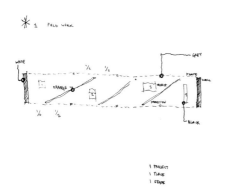

2D panel

construction

[WORK]

The work spaceframe is articulated through the compaction of its surroundings. Two extended, horizontal planes establish an expansive spatial slice. Bulges in their surfaces pinch the sandwiched zone between. Floating vertical walls subdivide and crop the panorama, while a series of layered receding frames establish a foreground, middle ground, and background through their telescoping alignment. A series of framed parallelepipeds oriented to the X, Y, and Z axis correlate to the three chambers and their associated three gradients of gray located on the horizon. Each frame serves as a table: a space for work.

view through watch eye piece

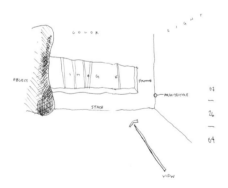

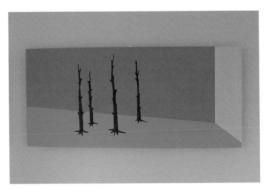

2D panel

3D construction

[WATCH]

The spaceframe focused on watching layers the object in space, with the object in field, upon the object in frame. An elevated box contains an organic form tucked to the left of view. A clerestory window bounces light into the red-orange walled chamber. A parallelogram shaped window frames the projected landscape tightly aligning with the painted two-dimensional back drop. The vertical field aligns with the two-dimensional field hiding, collapsing, and extending its presence. Each of the parts watch and are watched.

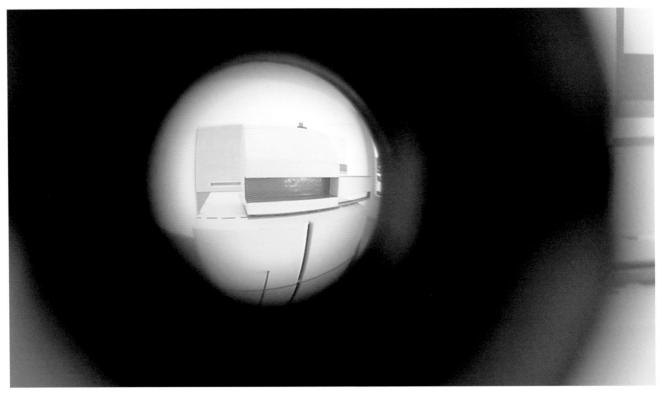

view through eat eye piece

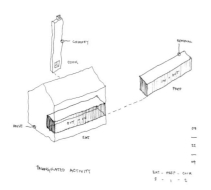

2D panel

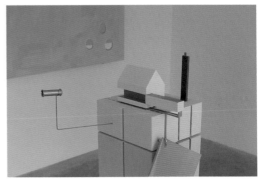

3D construction

[EAT]

The cyclical ritual of the eating spaceframe is a solitary act made social through its shared routine. The archetypal form of the house is cut to allow a slot to slide out of the house. The result is an articulated room outside the form and a corresponding void within the form. An outdoor hearth as cooking pit forms a courtyard. A projected slide out of the house in the opposing direction is held on the picture plane behind. The zones create the tripartite ritual of breakfast, lunch, and dinner.

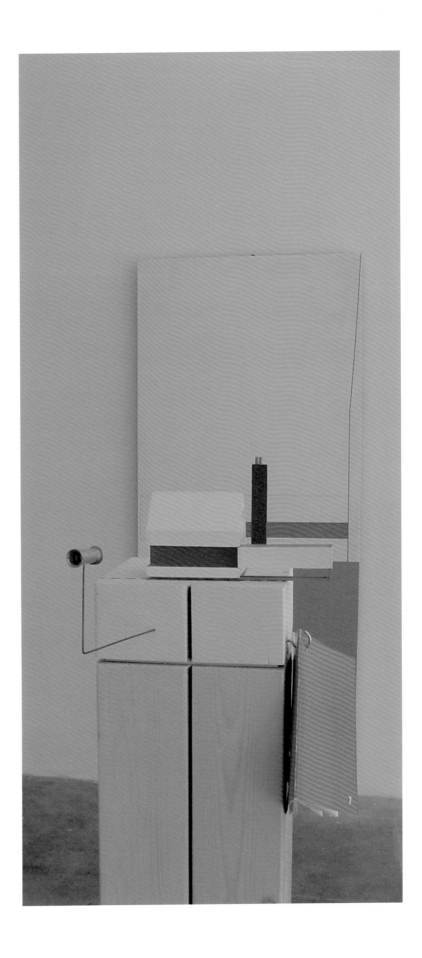

view through sleep eye piece

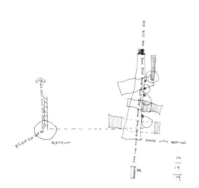

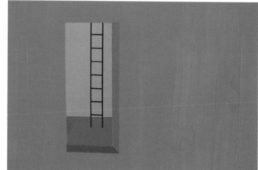

2D panel detail

3D construction

[SLEEP]

The sleep spaceframe takes the typical three-bedroom formula of the single family house and articulates each room as a discrete chamber along a shared path. The unique form of each cell either bridges, sets, or lies upon a funneling corridor. They are each accessed through a ladder located on a neon red-orange circle. A central corridor (with tilted walls to accelerate the perspective) contains a series of openings leading to each of the three room ladders. Framed at the end of the corridor is a fourth projected ladder for ascension to the subconscious accessed during sleep. Three additional picture plane portals suggest a "behind" to the picture plane; an alternative projection representing a diversity of realities or "dream worlds" found through slumber.

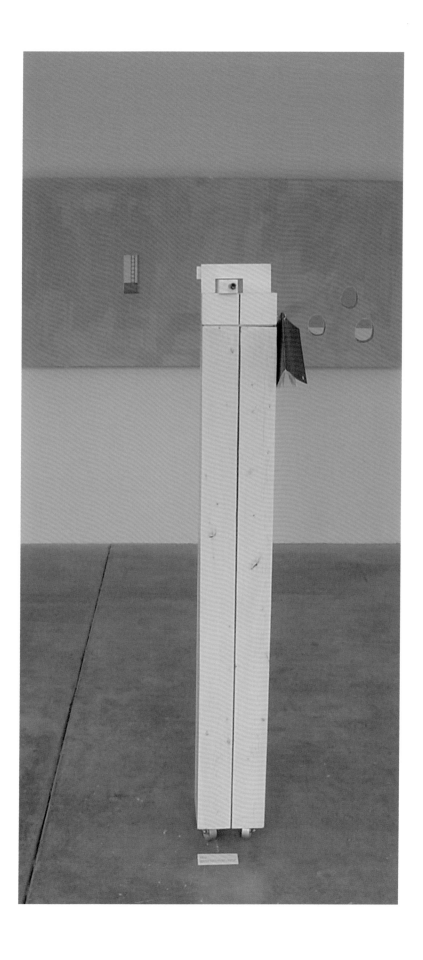

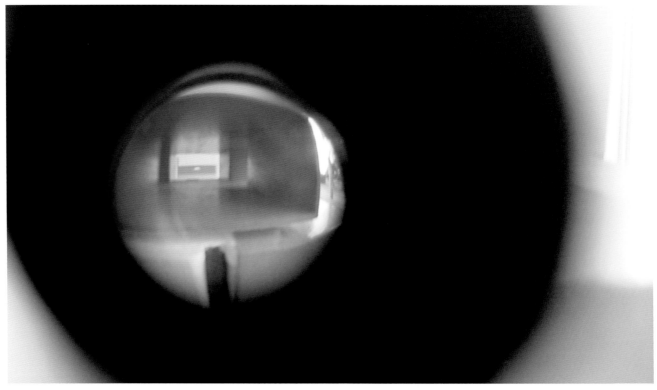

view through bathe eye piece

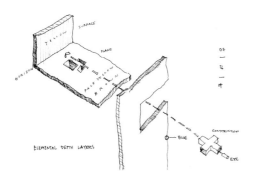

Elemental depth layers

2D panel

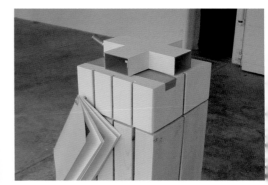

3D construction

[BATHE]

The bathe spaceframe assumes a cruciform shape that provides a four-branched room: [1] one for entry, [2] one for a toilet, [3] one for a sink, and [4] one for a bath. Each opening frames a varied cardinal direction, view, and solar oriented light condition. The curvature of the lens causes the ceiling to present itself as a barrel vault. An outdoor cistern framed by a two-dimensional projected portal aligned with the wall planes, balances the interior plunge pool. Water in and out (relative to the body and viewer) is celebrated.

FORMAL INQUIRIES INTO

MATERIAL
LOGICS

FORMAL INQUIRIES INTO MATERIAL LOGICS

STRUCTURE

The oscillation between structure and architecture establishes the balance between the functional pragmatic resolution of force lines and the organizational and compositional aspirations of design. The two in dialogue offer a resonance that can be combative, subordinated, expressive, or simply incongruous. One driven by the precision of physical need and the requirements of materials, codes, and forces; the other by experiential and compositional aspirations.

Cathedral of Amiens during WW II structural echo

The premise of structure as a discrete and separate relationship to architecture already problematizes their synthetic consideration. The examination as an extractable and independent system (classified as primary, secondary, tertiary structural system as well as materially determinant systems) develops a series of finite typologies with variation and hybrids possible but all still rooted and fundamentally classified by their originating referential family. As types (both formal and material) they can be classified by wall (planar load) system, frame (cage, column and beam) system, and shell (surface) system. In each there is an associated vocabulary of form to materials determined by the physical resolution of static forces in the system. The understanding of these influences in the resolution of a form provides an opportunity for the performative expression of the forces. Revealing these latent but invisible forces presents a language of tectonics and physical responses to environmental circumstances. Their exposure, celebration, understanding, and deployment as an expressive palette provides the opportunity for architectural articulation. Structure alone however, no matter how synthetic, can only provide an elemental component of architecture's system. Enclosure, as a performative skinning providing light, operability, insulation, material durability, roofing (focused on weather and water), surficial interior articulation and housings of mechanical, electrical, plumbing, security, informational systems et cetera. These collective needs as performative families create a series of responsive requirements that buildings must respond to. The adaptive engagement of them (individually and collectively) provides the opportunity for innovative relationships, celebrations, and deployments that permit architectural expression of these most fundamental needs through passive and active systems.

The level of expression of these systems can shift from the hyper-articulated to the subordinate. Their use as a palette of compositional determinism can escalate beyond the functional response to a compositional and experiential opportunity that offers fodder for invention. The synthetic consideration, relative to form and experience of these systemic necessities of environmental response and innovation allows for amenity to collaborate with methodology of

tectonic consideration of form to create architectural composition. The highlighted expression of these base needs presents an essentialism rooted in the pragmatic but addressed with vigorous invention and formal mastery to elicit an experiential resonance to its effectual potential. These essential moments provide a formal and compositional rationale that provides a narrative explanation of systemic logic.

As technology and complexity have grown, architectural systems have become more intricate and articulated. The density of material poche has given way to laminated and framed structures that no longer simply stack material to make a massive wall but now introduced the frame (column and beam) to create a performative precision to the enclosure. Outer cladding is separated from structure which is separated from inner finishing introducing a multi-staged construction technique and defining sub-layers of skills and material mastery. With this new sensibility (division of labor and development of trades) the efficiency of the industrial revolution also provided the technology to mass-produce and to standardize the production and dissemination of parts in new material systems. From specific material evolutions in production (such as the Bessemer furnace, which allowed for the large scale production of steel) the capability of structural loading changed entirely. Shifting from walls and load bearing planes as the basis of architecture into skeletal systems privileged lines and frames. To derive surfaces, wall systems are freely employed as infill or skin not structure. New morphologies emerge permitting radical shifts in the conceptualization of form, space, assembly, and production. The boundaries of built form changed radically through heroic evolutions of material and process.

New technologies have changed the parameters of spatial conceptualization. Advancement in the technology (not just of production but also fabrication) has fostered massive innovation in construction. Buildings and assemblies have increased their sophistication and componental nature. Products have emerged as proprietary developments and evolutions. The industry as a whole has fundamentally integrated the diversity to serve growing populations with innovations at all scales in health, safety, and welfare that advance hygiene and building performance while allowing for new material, programmatic, and formal typologies to emerge.

The acceleration continues to include the emergence of advanced materials and digital process of fabrication (that parallel the digital advancements in computation) shifting the craft of construction from the builder back to the architect by allowing the machine to mediate. The idea of making, based upon tool still reigns but the synthesis between drawing and building has never been closer. Making itself has now become a method to find form. The synthesis of material, process, and representation has never been closer. Playing into the legacy and logic of the role and necessity of tradition, updated and considered relative to localized site and context along with our contemporary cultural condition; the opportunity for performative formal expression presents a rationality of design inquiry and approach.

SYSTEMIC PARTS AND LOGICS
OF OPPORTUNITY

Structure: The expression of the load-bearing systems and how the skeletal systems provide an access of form found responses scaled to the transfer of forces through load configurations and pathways of force collaboration. As quantifiable and specifically predictable constraints, the opportunity to understand the system is locally determinate by the parts and their joints. Fundamentally incorporating horizontal members (beams and plates) that laterally transfer load through span to vertical members (columns and walls) that exert upon transitional joints (foundation systems) that bridge between the natural condition of the found geologic; these rationalized building systems holistically respond. The form, scale, tectonic, and connective method are all determined by the physicality of material as matter and the intrinsic material properties that provide (at the most base level) responsive abilities in tension and compression relative to the modular structural and physical properties of the material to determine shape, profile, and size (length and height) to provide responsive characteristics. The conversation of part to whole, material to local form, and system to building form provides precise revelation of these collaborative sensibilities. A celebration allows for a reading in the final composition that transposes the rational narrative of the performative response into a legible aspect of the architectural experience.

Environmental Control Systems: The responsive need to mitigate climate (temperature and humidity) providing a moderation of the extremities of fluctuation in weather that transition day to day and season to season relative to the specificity of the environment of place. The design response includes both passive and active systemic responses that have associative demands, forms, and requirements. From building orientation to aperture and operability (both local and systemically considered) to comprehensive machinic solutions of forced air, heat pumps, or radiant systems; these technologies become refined solutions demanding full consideration. Dealing with contact, air flow, systems of production, and conveyance of the treated and produced environment allows for a dominance and control of artificially constructed conditioning. This amenity demands a complexity of system, requests an associated efficiency, and tethers to larger systems of energy, cost, and ultimately sustainability in all aspects demanding an ethical and financial commitment to our environment and resources. This (like material harvesting and production and delivery of the one-time impact of the materials for construction) requires an even deeper commitment to an ongoing requirement and reliance upon a daily demand and consumption. The act of engagement remains perpetual.

Light: Like environmental control systems, the technology of the response to light is both passive and active. There is opportunity to use natural daylight and the connective compositions of natural cycles of diurnal movements between earth and sun. Scale, position, orientation, aperture type, et cetera; all provide the types of engagement and highlight the opportunity and compositional potential of natural light. These natural cycles and their transitions are balanced by the artificial and generative composition of light. Incandescent, florescent, LED, et cetera; these are diverse technologies that allow for the produc-

tion of, and thus the compositional deployment of, artificial light. Through contrast and choreography, a careful curation of light provides an access to visual composition of the ephemeral. The combination of the natural and artificial as independent natural, then cohabitational, then independent artificial moments in the cycle of the 24 hour day allows for the integrative dialogue of their compositional, functional, and effectual consideration.

Plumbing: The provision of water and sewage for personal hygiene, cooking and cleaning, irrigation, recreation, and general convenience, allow for a systemic provision on demand of an essential service to our biological selves. Bathing, eating, eliminating waste, these required actions of our bodies require associative responses of localized functions that first provide service (both of the individual and the collective scale that merges with the power of magnitudes) and then follows with experiential (from bath to spa; sustenance to meal; required necessity to ceremonial ritual). These systems are overt in programs of bath and kitchen but latent in systems of plumbing from water supply to waste removal. Networks of infrastructure (internal and external to the building) create a logic of performance that have an opportunity to compositionally engage, express and reveal their presence, function, and necessity.

Information: The evolution of technology relative to Internet systems, information networks, and computational hardware and software as a collective is a relatively new and hyper accelerated amenity. As it grows in presence in daily activity (to include nearly every aspect of our lives) it reduces in physical presence and proposes anonymity of interface in favor of content. Architecture has yet to fully respond to these technological shifts. The capabilities and implications of the smart phone have not been met by the house. Localized responses of linked technologies and user responsive hardware provide an engineered inroad, but the spatial and effectual considerations of information as a responsive system beyond these pragmatics provides a new frontier for architecture to design. This is an entirely emergent aspect of architecture's technological revolution. It must move beyond integration into synthetic assembly.

Joint
tectonic connection as
formal expression

Material: Material is a form of resistance. As a physical object it comes with intrinsic capabilities. How it is handled, where it is found, how it can be worked; these rules establish the parameters by which its manipulation can occur. The intrinsic linking of material and process is inevitable. From the natural or human-made processes that physically make material on the molecular level; through the systems for harvesting, gleaning, and delivering on an industrial scale to provide quantities necessary for architectural application; to the organizing of the material into a tectonic system for implementation; through the regulatory filter of the tools that cut or bend, forge, or extrude affiliated forms, scales dimensions, and quantities; through the tooling and systematizing of the joinery that occurs through the material itself for the typically combinatory systems of material and fastener to derive connection; each of these stages is dependent upon the relationship with the tools and the process permitted by these tools to operate collaboratively. Technology and capability allow for the expansion from the primitive to the sophisticated, but fundamentally the entire system is dependent upon the natural physical properties of the material itself that govern how and what can be done.

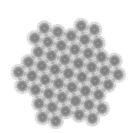

Geometric pattern type and module

Emergent from the material, the basic type and module of construction influences form and thinking. What something is made out of determines its morphological potential. In masonry construction the form emerges from the repetitive yet standardized field of individual units collaborating in field effects to determine overall systems. This same sensibility translates to any material process. A material's physical dimensions, modular properties, and natural features determine their application and ensuing performance and form. The relationship between these properties and design becomes a systemic dialogue where form is limited by material and material is determinate of form. Each physical system implies the potential application of its system to determine form. The predetermination and privileging of either one is simply not possible.

CULTURAL CONSTRUCT
ORAL TRADITION
PLACE HOLDERS
MORAL
LANDSCAPE
POLITICAL SPACE
ECONOMICS
BELIEF STRUCTURE
ZONE
PROJECTION
EXISTING
PRE-EXISTING
CULTURAL FABRIC
OUTSIDE
INSIDE
KIT-OF-PARTS
CULTURE OF PLACE
PASTICHE
BORROWED
EMBEDDED
NATURAL
CRAFT
TECTONIC
MATERIALS
METHOD
BUILDER
TOPOLOGICAL
DIALOGUE
RESULTANT
RECIPROCITY
RESIDUE
COMMON GROUND
RELATIONSHIPS
RECIPROCAL
ORAL STRUCTURE
WRITTEN INTERVENTION
TRADITION
TYPOLOGY
JUXTAPOSITION
MANIPULATION

CHARTRES CATHEDRAL

STRUCTURE + FORM

Axonometric

Chartres Cathedral's formal articulation emerged out of a performative requirement in combination with a limitation of material capability instead of the previously typical compositionally predetermined figure. The formal expression is one of form found necessity. The exoskeletal flying buttresses brace the lateral forces of the increased height and associated wind loads. Tapering to reduce mass and scaffolding off the outer wall of encircling side chapels, the unoccupiable tower elements are driven by structurally performative optimization resolving the column field in a new type.

THRESHOLD 3
Structure and Form

CHARTRES CATHEDRAL

Chartres Cathedral is a medieval Catholic church constructed between 1194 and 1250 in Chartres, France.[105] It demonstrates a high and pure expression of French Gothic architecture largely facilitated by the speed of its construction providing for consistency in its design.

"The plan of the cathedral is cruciform. A two bay narthex at the western end opens into a seven bay nave leading to the crossing, from which wide transepts extend three bays each to north and south. East of the crossing are four rectangular bays terminating in a semicircular apse. The nave and transepts are flanked by single aisles, broadening to a double-aisled ambulatory around the choir and apse. From the ambulatory radiate three deep semi-circular chapels."[106]

Chartres Cathedral's central nave was higher and wider than any previously attempted in France.[107] The vaults stem from the expressive development of the column clad piers[108] which segment in a quadripartite configuration.[109]

"The interior elevation of the nave is banded into three stories with an arcade, a triforium and a clerestory level. By removing the gallery level typical in many early Gothic cathedrals (normally between the arcade and triforium), the glazing of the arcade and clerestory levels was able to expand and be almost equal in height."[110]

The increase in the size of the windows simultaneously reduced the wall. This reduction in the continuity and structural mass of the wall required the external reinforcement of the flying buttresses. These additive exoskeletal elements increased the performative structural wall depth bracing against the substantial lateral thrusts and increase wind loads from the 112-foot-high stone vaults. As a result, the role of the structure became foregrounded as a compositional element.

Chartres Cathedral represents several significant conceptual thresholds for architecture:

EXPRESSION OF STRUCTURE

Chartres Cathedral illustrates the moment where the aspirational formal and effectual qualities of the scale and height of the building confronted natural forces requiring a new role and expressionist presence to the structural system. Wind loads and the increased lateral thrust were now a substantial consideration with the newly achieved heights. The building form responded with the addition of the flying buttresses as an external exoskeleton to laterally brace the wall. This overt expression of the performative requirements created a formal expression of structural forces. The flying buttresses in their repetition and dominant presence in the exterior elevations generated a new revelation of structural form. Previously subordinated into the column which had become a highly figured, stylized, and ornamental element, the flying buttress moved towards total functionalism.

PERFORMATIVELY DEVELOPED FORM

The overall form is rooted in the expression of the force lines. Optimized for the scale and material, the geometry emerges from the expression of the load path. Its honest mapping is a pure expression of the structural forces. This transparent revelation of structural performance in the exaggerated expression of the gravitational form integrates the consideration of a performative sensibility with the architecture.

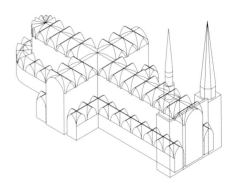

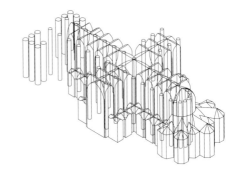

WALL TO FRAME

The dissolution of the surface at Chartres Cathedral translated the planar nature of the load bearing structural wall system into a frame based cage of structural lines and introduced the conversation between frame and infill. The visual legibility of the structural lines (resolved in columns instead of walls) creates an associative formal and expressive figure that opens the plan and dissolves the segmental and partitioned nature of a wall based plan.

ACCENTUATION OF LIGHT AND EFFECT

The exaggerated height of Chartres Cathedral provided for a voluminous space and a large wall surface. Opened through the dissolve of the solid surface, the increased windows provided dramatic stained glass apertures that allow for a choreography and orchestration of light previously unrivaled in size, effect, and monumentality. The dominance of the transparent wall surface introduced the phenomenological opportunities of transparency and light afforded by a glazed infill.

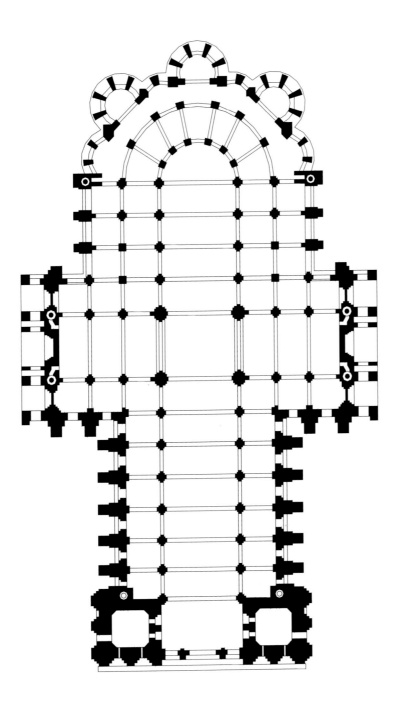

Plan

The plan of Chartres Cathedral reveals the disintegration of the wall as a planar surface into a columnar point based field. The primary cruciform figure of the plan is reiterated in offset layers of side aisles internally (a single offset in the nave and transept and a double offset across the narthex and apse) and exoskeletal buttresses externally. These layers increase the depth of the wall as a structural frame, while reducing the opacity of the wall to allow for the increased scale and frequency of glass apertures. The result in the planametric reading of the building is a field of columnar elements (reminiscent of the Greek Temple) connected in their vaulting but independent in their footprint. Structure as form and ornament dominates the composition.

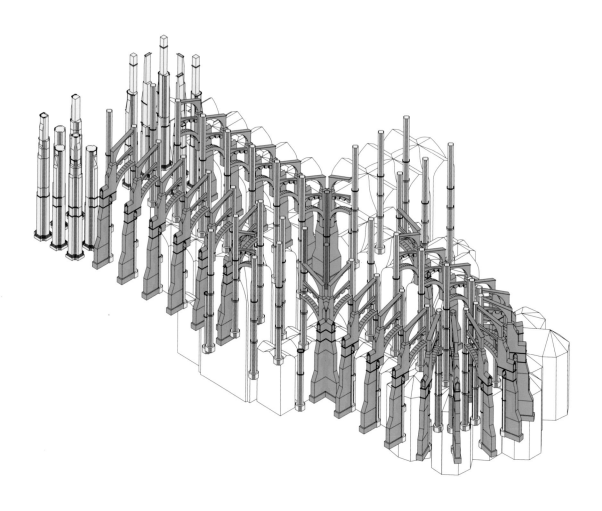

Buttressing

The increased height of the lateral walls of Chartres Cathedral created a reciprocal increase in lateral thrust and wind pressure. As a result the need to brace this surface requires an additive depth to the structure. As an externalized system to privilege the internal experience, the articulated expression is derivative of its functional need. The slender repetition furthers the vertical emphasis and transitions the architectural thinking from a wall based system to an articulated structural frame.

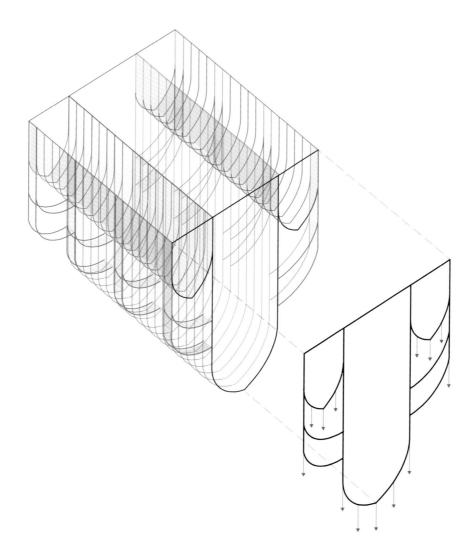

Hanging Chain

The structural optimization of the form of Chartres Cathedral is evident from the hanging chain diagram. Starting from the column points in connection with the ground and spanning the main aisle, the connected line (when inverted) finds its natural gravitational shape. Forming a parabolic arch, the shape is the basis for the Gothic arch. The side chapels flanking the main aisle are extended upward with secondary lean-to bracing members. The collective figure is determined by the regularized efficiency of the structural form.

Shell Surface

The roofing system of Chartres Cathedral is based in a shell surface vaulting. Composed of crossing parabolic figures, the complexity of form emerges out of their overlapping directionality and intersecting geometries. The groin vault (as the result of a criss-crossing intersection of two Gothic barrel vaults) allows for multi-directional spanning supported only in its corners. This aggregation of surface systems into columnar systems allows for a synthetic transition from the opaque plane of roof enclosure to a skeletal columnar system.

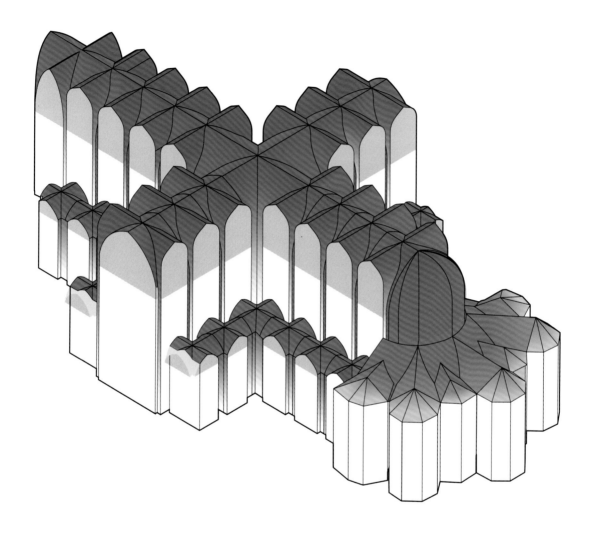

Vaulting

The overlay of the primary figure of the central aisle with the crossing transept of Chartres Cathedral is further subdivided with lateral incremental groin vaults. These provide localized transitions of forces breaking down the scale of the overall form and incrementally lifting the edges to allow for greater height to the stained glass transparency creating increased luminosity through the frame infill. The doubling of the overall scale of crossing with localized subdivision crossings creates a segmental resonating rhythm that repeats across scalar readings.

Load Path Intensity

Tracing the load path intensity through the vaulting into the columnar supports, the pressure lines transition from surface to line. The result is an open field of structural points that allow flexibility and porosity to the plan. The high point of the Gothic vault allows the inverted parabolic form to transition evenly the lateral thrust of the span into axially vertical lines.

This directional resolution into pure compression collaborates with the stone masonry to optimize its material compressive strength. The load diagram of the vault canopy (held by porous but organizing columns) establishes an architectural shift from wall based partitioned space into a columnar field with open flexibility and transparency of infill.

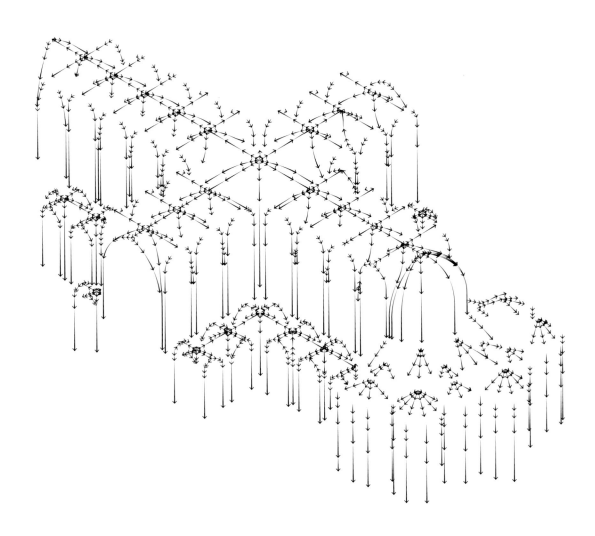

Force Vectors

The force vectors of Chartres Cathedral illustrate the increasing intensity of the gravitational load. The paths trace the edges of the architectural form and synthetically express the resulting composition as a form that is one and the same with the force lines. The translation of this structural system into an architectural form emphasizes the responsive dominance of the performative system as a formal generator. This structural expressionism emerges from a scientific understanding of physical forces and a reductive essentialism to their expression.

INTENSITY FRAMES

5 GRAVITATIONAL FORM FOUND FIGURES

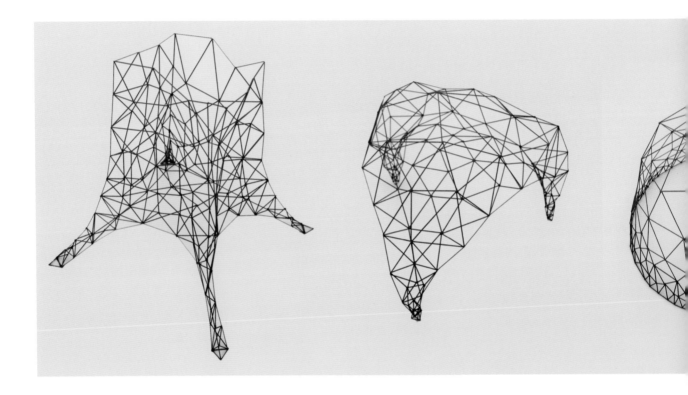

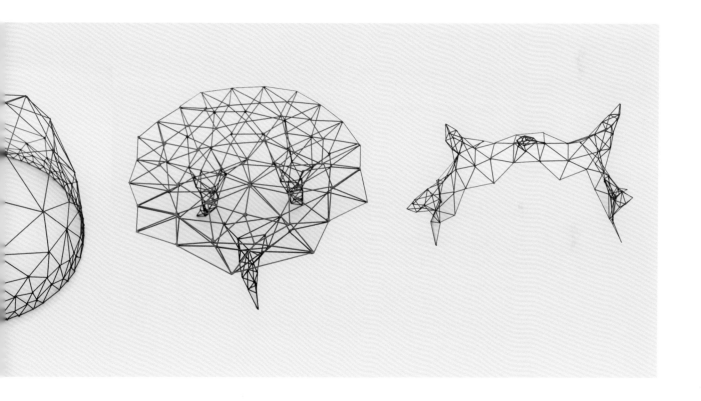

INTENSITY FRAMES
Pacific Design Center
Los Angeles, California

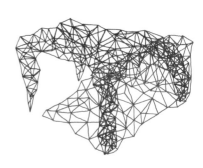

MATERIAL ORIGINS

Architecture is defined by material and process engaged to create space. Governed by the perceptual qualities of experience, the resulting form, function, and effect is dependent upon the user and the systematized sensibilities of how a body engages and relates to the object.

In 1969, as part of an experimental program at LACMA, Robert Irwin and James Turrell outlined a new direction for art, identifying viewer experience as the critical outcome of an artist's creative production and establishing viewers' visual perception of the environment as a principal concern.[111] For Irwin and Turrell, light was the primary medium for investigating these ideas. This project proclaims that material has the same or even greater potential.

The project investigates the potential of built form to be defined and governed by experience and perception while emergent from the systems of material construction logics. Engaging directly the relationship of material and the technological processes that work to transform those materials to generate form, the resulting perceptual and effectual relationships are revealed through the overtness of this expression.

The image is no longer enough. The object is no longer enough. The work must be space. The work must be forces. The work must be experience. The material and technological systems establish a framework allowing the interaction with the community of users to define the specifics of space and place and activity. The object is a collection of decisions manifest in the physicality of the system. Physics of material and system in conversation with the environment become the markers of form.

This project extends a trajectory focused on the relation of iterative triangulation construction and the segmental form of gravitational shapes. The regularity of the system establishes the rule allowing the individuation of form to occur through the series. Each of the five elements is specifically formed to investigate differing gravitational spanning techniques emerging from an identical pre-existing base. A visible network of triangulated geometric relationships (governed by the gravity and material stiffness) are instigated through hybridizations of archetypal architectural forms of dome, plane, cone, and arch. Though individual forms, they are consistent in material, color gradient, and evolutionary density. Collectively they produce a familial conversation.

Fabricated out of piano wire, soldered in graduated modular pieces, and painted in a color gradient chromatically mapping the intensity of structural forces; they are delicate structures. Transitioning from pink to red to purple, the intensity of forces and the density of the members is mimicked in its color. Prefabricated and individually delivered via a standard pick-up truck, the lightweight structures create large volumes through their segmented lines. The gravitational thrust of the faceted figures compliment and brace against the continuous curve of the pre-existing planter pedestal.

Each form is determined through descriptive geometries. As evolutionary synthesized archetypal forms, they have legacy and history embedded in their hybridized forms. The five forms include: [1] a four-arch based walled enclosure joined by an inner dome; [2] a three-legged stacked double dome; [3] a domed shell; [4] a three-columned tabled surface; and [5] a spanning arch with erupting cones.

Each element serves simultaneously as an object and shadow generator. Changing natural illumination of the upper atrium space of the Pacific Design Center creates an ever-changing multiplicity of shadow projections on the sand filled base.

Intensity Frames

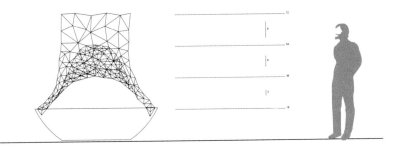

W-01   FOUR ARCH WALLS WITH INNER DOME [OPEN TOP]

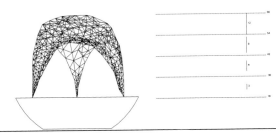

W-02   THREE LEGGED DOUBLE DOME

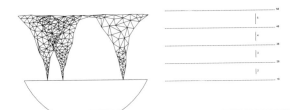

W-03   THREE CONED TABLE SURFACE

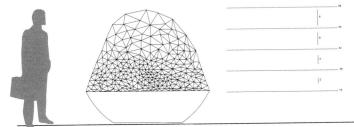

W-04   DENSITY DOME

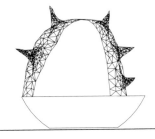

W-05   ARCH WITH DENSITY NODES

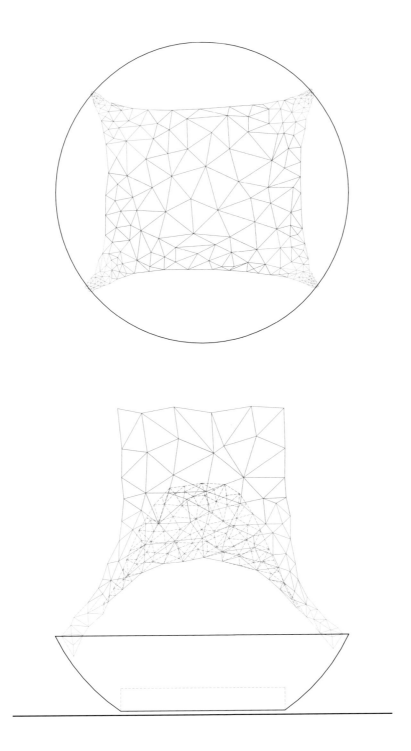

four-arch walls with inner dome

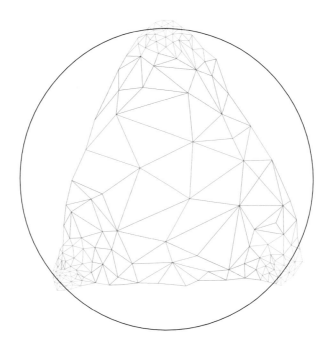

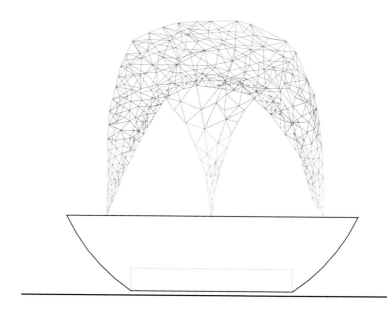

three-legged double dome

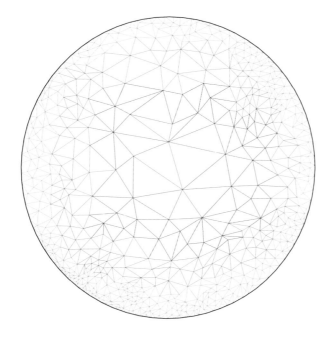

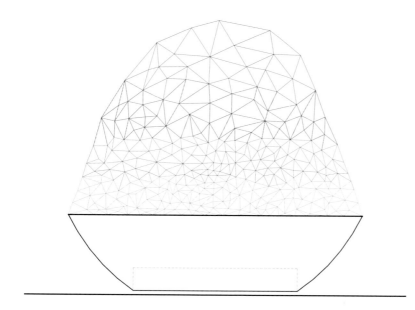

density dome

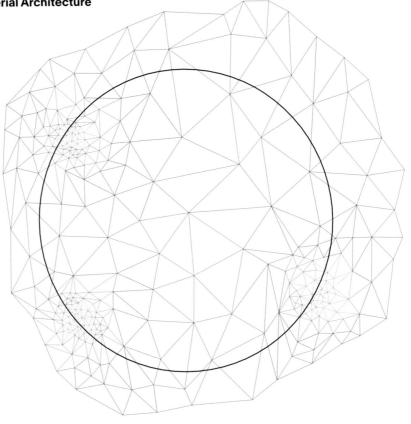

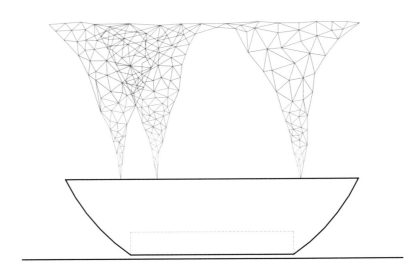

three-coned table surface

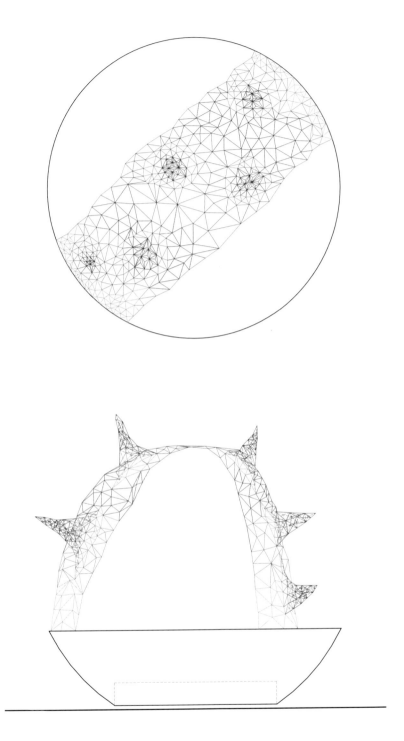

arch with density nodes

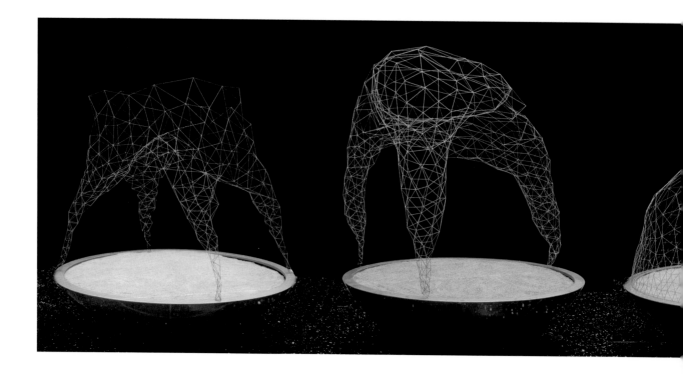

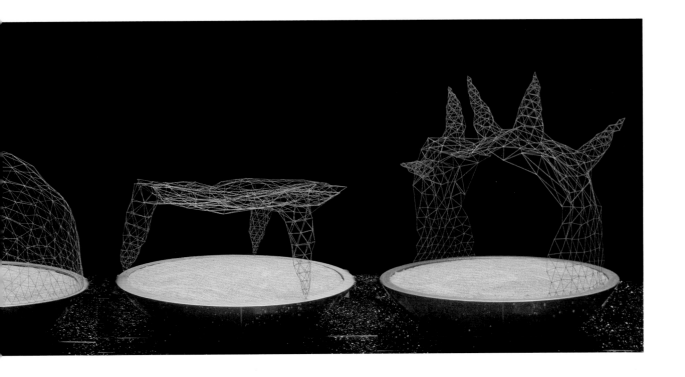

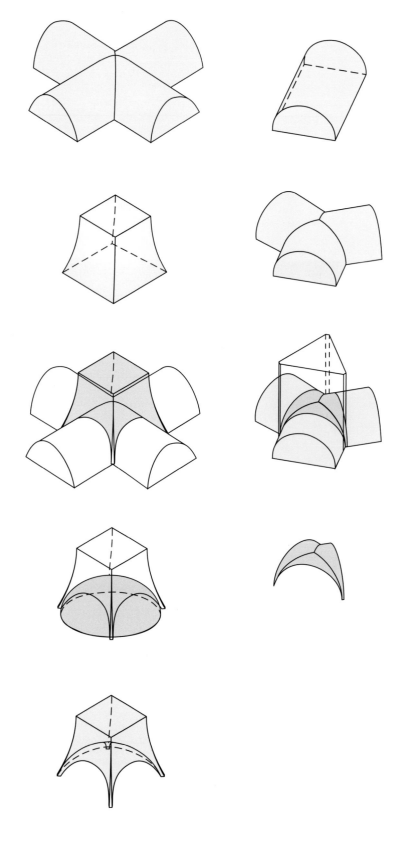

geometric formation

four-arch walls with inner dome

three-legged double dome

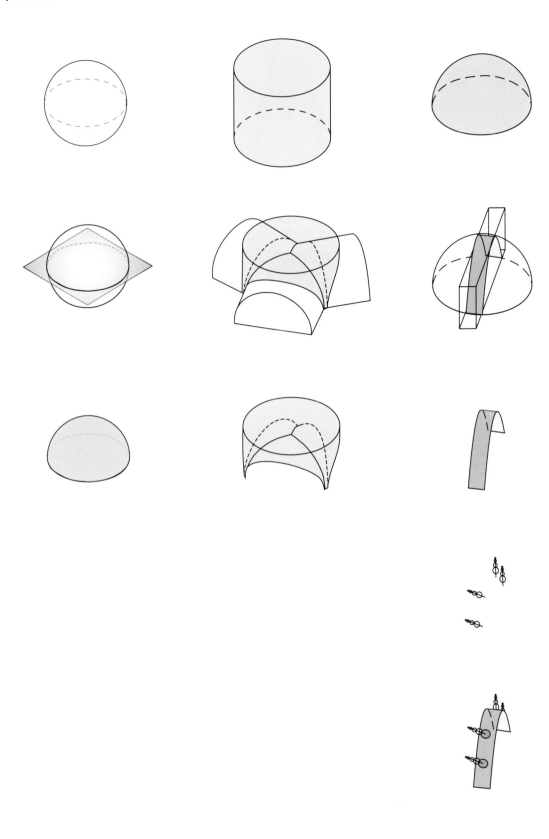

density dome   three-coned table surface   arch with density nodes

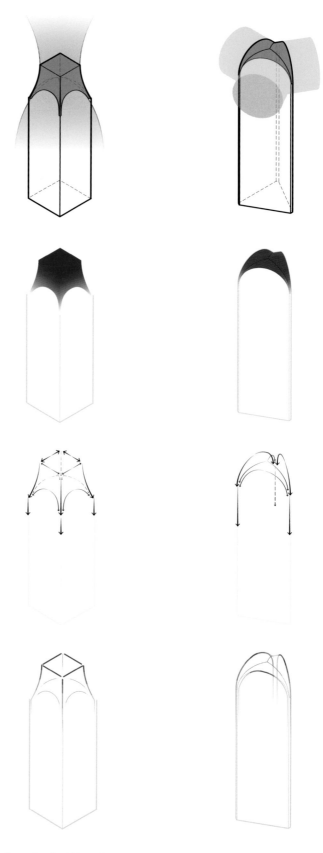

shell force lines

four-arch walls with inner dome

three-legged double dome

density dome   three-coned table surface   arch with density nodes

frame

element

surface

plane

nodes

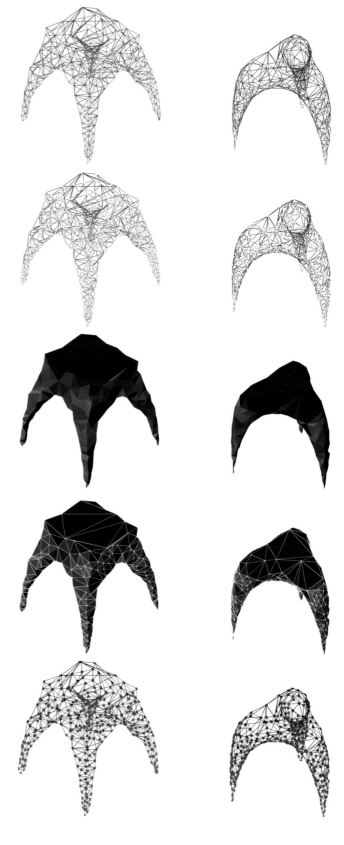

triangulation of surface

four-arch walls with inner dome

three-legged double dome

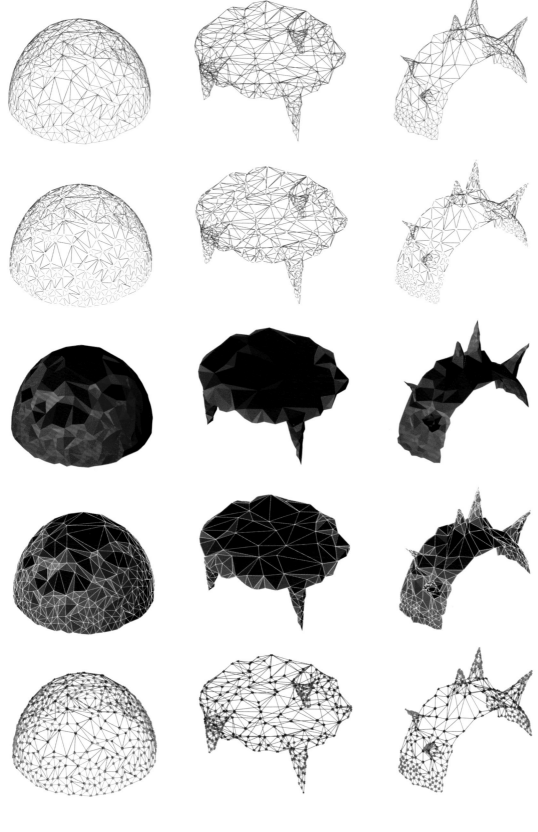

density dome

three-coned table surface

arch with density nodes

CONDITIONAL

APPLICATION

CONDITIONAL APPLICATION
Methods of Engagement

THEME 1 - METHOD OF DESIGN

The production of an architectural project is dependent upon design method. The method establishes a process employed to produce a creative cause and effect relationship. The process is connected deeply to the authorial sensibility as an extension of an architect's identity. This personalization thus breeds a methodology, self-reflexive examination and a collective body of work that provides an individually defining result and commodity.

Though the process and methodology of a design process can be forecasted, the inquiry remains a generative tool. Foundational to its advancement is exploration, risk, and invention. This invention supports innovation through the particular. The process engages discovery. Drawing from one's knowledge and a primal engagement with the totality of one's subconscious allows for the mind, body, and tool to unite synthetically in the making. The design process is simultaneously vague and specific. It is a process of forgetting what you know and rethinking what you believe. It is grounded in method. Through iteration the process must allow for the thought to metamorphose.

The architect as a creative individual has an authority of personality and process. There is a rationale that occurs; a methodical step-by-step justification that goes beyond form into the logic of the whole. The architect has the belief and the means to follow their instinct through approach, study, commitment, and ultimately execution. The personal ideal comes into the overt execution of the end product. To make is to draw oneself into the decision and conclusion.

The design process is a synthetic consideration of simultaneous issues: site, scale, form, rationale, social usage, et cetera. The method comes to the process with convictions: programmatic, formal, organizational, material, et cetera, and/or all of the above. The individual is the point of departure and establishes the hierarchy of priority. Every architect must deal with the same issues, but the order in which they privilege them is unique to the individual. The architect must address and merge their demands to allow for their continuity and coherence.

The specific methods of making are essential to the result. The idea made physical is verified through its process. Made and challenged and remade, it is through this iterative cycle that innovation can occur. The process of making is essential. It is the integration of the intellectual with the craft: the primal definition of architecture. It is the method that determines the outcome.

Tempietto, Bramante 1570
synthetic expression

Temporary pavilion
Aldo van Eyck
disrupted field

THEME 2 - PRACTICE: A VEHICLE AND METHOD

The implementation of architecture is where the transition of the discipline of architecture expands to include all the concerns of professional practice. Professional practice is the core mode within which the execution of architecture occurs. Residing in the traditional role of architect, subordinate to client in a service role, being approached for a project and then developing it under their watchful approval, the constraints and pragmatics dominate the process. As a business, a service, and a condenser of all the practicalities, rules, limitations, and influencing factors that dictate and govern the translation of a concept and intent into a physical actuality, practice is *the* point of translation. Client, program, user, budget, code, material properties, and natural forces insert themselves as governing and dominating forces providing both design constraints and opportunities.

Client: As architecture must rely upon client; then the role of the architect is as a part of a service industry. The architect takes the commission within themselves and serves its localized demands but also tries to do more; to execute work that provides for a larger disciplinary responsibility.

The requirements of the client layout the constraints of a project. They inform a design, directing it to respond to the challenge. Despite trying to answer these, one must never lose sight of the disciplinary calling, responsibility, and that which separates architecture from building. These dual masters must be negotiated to advance.

A project must be constructed within a larger intellectual intent and rubric. The meta-exploration provides a balancing keel and a larger vision against which the localities of the specifics can respond within a larger intent.

Program: The program, as the functional requirements of the building, provides the primary point of departure through the practicalities of use. Modernist traditions implied that functionalism was the deriver of form. Louis Sullivan's "form follows function"[112] established the root sensibility that form identity emergent from the expression of the originating program. Composition, organization, even material expressions were all derivative of this expression. The opportunities for architecture to operate on program, to design and influence its expression and interpretation beyond simple form and into the orchestration of event and interaction can facilitate function emerged through the juxtaposing narratives offered by Rem Koolhaas in his book *Delirious New York*.[113] This social engineering to facilitate the design and re-consider use, placed opportunities for commercialism, social structuring, and the orchestration of the fundamental qualities of life as emergent responsibilities of the architect. Operations on program provide innovative potential. This terrain remains fertile for the spatial, formal, and experiential potentials of architecture. Challenging typologies and traditions of organizational trends allows for iteration and innovation.

User: The user expands beyond the specifics of a particular client broadening to include to the experiences and interfaces of diverse individuals with individual cycles, durations, and interactions across evolving conditions. The engagement with the user is the fundamental touchstone of architecture. Here experience spans from the pragmatic to the spiritual through the effectual. It requires consideration, orchestration, and formal response to facilitate. The user is the root of architecture. It demands prominence in its ambition. It deploys experience.

Budget: Economics persistently rule everything. In a capitalist society, economics establish social classes; determine the type and quantity of our possessions; set daily schedules; govern our food and health choices; and determine our career path. Its domination extends in architecture. Every project is about making new (construction) which intrinsically requires both material and labor (capital). This process is governed by budget. Its capacity influences scale, siting, and even function of an architectural project. Budget even trumps the desire. It establishes boundaries and determines the palettes of materials, construction processes, and form. Economics indelibly influence opportunity. This context requires the architect to ingrain a deep understanding of the construction methods and material capabilities to understand how something can be done and its relative difficulty and investment of time as the basis of cost. Diverse trades offer the specific capability, but the conceptual oversight to understand the implications of cost is paramount to having something realized.

Code: Zoning codes and building codes on the national, state, and local levels are critical influencing factors to architecture. They provide the legal boundaries within which a project can be realized. Zoning establishes building use, size, and even broad formal governance. Building codes, motivated by safety and quality of life establish crucial dimensional limitations, pragmatic organizational requirements, and general constraints that tightly govern the possibilities for architecture. Though a specific lens through which a building must gain authority and perform responsibly, codes are not a destination but a point of departure. Clever consideration, thoughtful integration, and responsive celebration of these inevitabilities provide opportunities to respond. They must become a language of operation, so second nature and integrative to the language of architecture that the meaning can transcend the words.

Material Properties: The physical qualities of matter establish the capabilities of a material. The innate chemical composition, flash point, hardness, elasticity, et cetera each determine a tendency, limitation, and capability. That which we make architecture out of influences what can be made. Spans, durability, workability are all controlled by a material's properties. Architecture must start with the material and its sensibilities to provide for a resonance in the design. Understanding these tendencies and characteristics allows for an authority to engage. Manipulation through collaboration with matter is the root of design. Architecture must begin with materials.

Natural Forces: Natural forces like gravity, wind, and water are the physical context into which architecture is added. These forces, specific to place, establish the realities that architecture must address. Systems, performative responses, and practical limitations emerge from engagement with these conditions.

They place the requirements of stability, durability, and convenience within a precise context. They create the datum and ranges of deviation against which architecture must respond. To be made, architecture must engage these natural forces. They are a critical point of departure and speak to the fundamental responsibilities of architecture. They are rarely exposed, but provide opportunity as the basis of shelter and the originating rationales for architecture's existence and articulation. An overt consideration of their being provides a primal interface with these essential qualities. Architecture emerges from the dialogue of place.

THEME 3 - THE ACADEMY

Architectural education confronts the discipline of architecture by examining the focused dialogues between design and practice. The academy critically establishes the roots of architectural thinking that the discipline will pursue. Introducing history and methodology, the academy instills a process, provides tools, and develops moralities that remain touchstones in facilitating ensuing trajectories. The beginning determines the end.

Architecture currently entertains a close connection of the academy with practice through an intentional overlapping of personnel. Leading practitioners and design thinkers are associated with academic institutions. This connection to teaching represents a critical bridge that endows the academy with an experimental and investigative validity while providing the ever renewing energy, experimentation, and inquiry that feeds and validates a professional office.

Pitch to plane
perception of form to
constructed representation

an assigned program or instigating question. Often coupled with a specific site and functional typological affiliation, the studio project proceeds to develop and evolve a design response emergent from the premise but articulated through the individual vision, method, and effort of the student. Typically originating with precedent analysis and analytical thinking, overall strategies are developed. Refined through iteration and specificity, a design matures and responds with resolution and specificity. Repetitive overlay and palimpsest considerations allow the design to evolve. Decisions are challenged through critical lenses, varied vantages and collective presentation and criticism.

There are many flaws in this system and the sequence itself establishes a specific rhythm of thinking that carries this methodology forward into the profession. It's cyclical and palimpsest consideration with diverse overlays of critical engagement and challenge require positional response through both intellectual intent and pragmatic functionalist resolution. The studio as a forum for creative inquiry intrinsically allows for an investment on the front end of the design process (something disproportionately subordinated in professional practice relinquished to ten or fifteen percent of an overall project) and provides for a communality to the inquiry through the collective collaborative community environment of the studio providing a simultaneous multiplicity of approaches, assertions, and resolutions. The studio presents a diverse spectrum of responses to the same inquiry. This conceptual shotgun blast covers a broad area and allows for an inquiry beyond what an individual designer can endeavor upon.

Experimental topics, experimental methods, focused investigations looking at both parts and wholes; the educational agenda allows for deep and authentic inquiries that can interrogate the potential of the discipline in all regards. The forum does not require the design to resolve fully. They are not actual propositions and so remain insulated from the realities of practice. They offer optimistic hope towards the essence of architecture indulging all of its complexity. This responsibility endows the academy with an authority to lead the discipline by challenging it. It offers a multi-directional expansion of new vantages and opportunities. Examining fabrication, materials, robotics, form, theory, et cetera, each of these topics provides new branches of inquiry and allow for diverse responses to diverse questions. This mode of inquiry drives the discourse of the discipline; fuels the content; and births the future generations of architects to invent, make, and aspire to authenticate their origins.

Tony Smith
systemic figure

LINK
CATALOG
PROXIMITY
SIZE
INTERCONNECTIONS
SPEED OF CHANGE
TRACE
POPULATION
POTENTIAL
MUNDANE
FAMILIAR
RECALL
MAP
WEB OF EVENTS
SCALE
PATTERN
INHABITATION
REFLECTION
MATRIX
PROGRAM
INTERSTITIAL
DISTINCTION
GENERATOR
INTER-CONNECTIONS
ELEMENTS
VISUAL IMAGES
LOGIC
SKIN
FILTER
INTERVENTION
RESOLUTION
CONTESTED SPACE
JOINT
CONNECTION
ROOM
INDIGENOUS CULTURAL FORMS
SHARED SYMBOLIC VEHICLES
CONCLUSION
STORIES

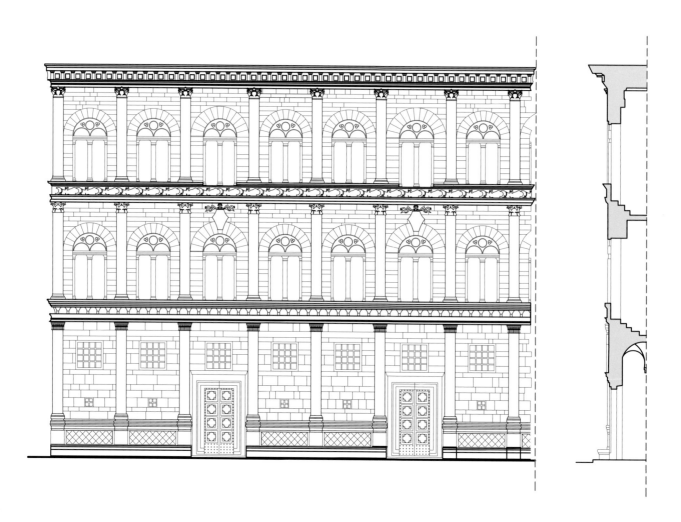

PALAZZO RUCELLAI

VISUAL COMPOSITION + GEOMETRY

The plan of the Palazzo Rucellai reveals the incremental and informal organization that happened over years of episodic construction. As a threshold condition of ad hoc sensibilities meeting regularized and systemically driven logics, the Palazzo Rucellai through its facade organization developed a differential sensibility as to how to treat performative legibility and geometric order. The regularity of the rule as an overarching synthesizer allowed the logic of the geometry to establish a higher systemic order. Its sensibility established a rationalizing system that a collaborating and governing overlay.

THRESHOLD 4
Visual Composition and Geometry

PALAZZO RUCELLAI

Palazzo Rucellai is a Renaissance townhouse in Florence, Italy whose façade was designed by Leon Battista Alberti between 1446 and 1451. The palace was created from a collection of eight smaller buildings acquired over time that were combined to form a single architectural complex arranged around a central courtyard.[114] The external organization required a facade which would unify the diverse elements.

As a regulating façade, the surficial architecture employed pilasters, gradients of apertures, and entablatures in proportional relationships to each other to create a geometric based organizational logic. Using referential elements from ancient Roman architecture, the compositional elements formally reference historical types. Weight and mass are expressed through larger blocks on the ground floor, which heighten the impression of strength and solidity that lighten and refine as the stories ascend. The stone veneer serves as a contrasting background texture juxtaposing with the smooth-faced pilasters and entablatures which divide the facade into three horizontal levels. As the levels ascend, there is increasing ornament and complexity of the order of the pilasters. From austere (Tuscan) to medium (Ionic) to ornate and vegetal (Corinthian) the ascension evolves from massive, sturdy, and geometric to organic and sculpturally expressive. The accentuation of the column synthesizes the performative (formally referencing structure) with the ornamental (through their detail and articulated elements).[115]

The ground floor was programmatically for business[116] and is articulated by two main doorways flanked by stone street benches that run the length of the façade and anchor the base. Using orthogonal geometry in the capitals, apertures, and portals, the rigidity and solidity of form creates a powerful grounding street level. "The second story piano nobile (is the main formal reception floor) and the third story (for the private family and sleeping quarters)"[117] are blanketed in regular "twin-lit, round-arched windows set within arches with highly pronounced voussoirs that span and bridge from pilaster to pilaster"[118] creating a homogenizing middle. The facade culminates in a capping, monumental projecting cornice. The level of refinement increases upward through programs, entablature, and pilaster capitals.

Palazzo Rucellai represents several significant conceptual thresholds for architecture:

SYSTEMIC LOGICS OF GEOMETRY

Palazzo Rucellai introduced a new role for geometry in architecture. Not deployed as a generator of holistic form, but rather as a regulating and organizing surficial system, the geometry is focused on the two-dimensional elevational surface articulated in shallow relief. The project employed a drawn and externally regimented organization system to gather the diverse spaces behind and establish order as primary ambition of the composition. Founded in a rule based language, the articulation of the elements and their regularized deployment rationalizes Classical principles with graduated articulation to provide a comprehensive totality to the organizational logic and ordering hierarchy. The shifting transition of architecture to become compositionally rooted in the two dimensionality of the façade changes the fundamental parameter of architectural design thinking. Removing the spatial occupation as the foundation of perceptual experience, the focus instead shifts to the articulation of the object through a singular frontal façade. The expressive nature of the repetitive field creates an abstraction of tectonic pattern expressed and detailed in its refined articulation despite being a veneer system fully disconnected from the actual load bearing structural system masked behind. The investigation of architecture as a two-dimensional exercise intrinsically privileges the role of drawing in the representation and conceptual thinking. The line as a mark on a planar surface engages composition from a scribed and bas-relief sensibility in the final articulated form. Minimal depth and continuity of material requires the textures and articulation of the surface (through various classical elements) to become the terrain of engagement and occupation. This fundamental shift then privileges the governing techniques of this media: geometry, proportion, and compositional collage. The geometry provides the fundamental systems for ordering the surface. Banding and ultimately griding the surface to denote articulation, these governing logics attempt to visualize through a codification system of positive and negative (closed and open surface) the associative force lines of the gravitational structural lines. With the exaggerated condition of a drawn surface the associative rules of expression emerge from the media based techniques.

PROPORTION, ORDER, AND REPETITION

Using the principles of proportion, repetition, and order to create the hierarchy of the façade, the composition of the Palazzo Rucellai is a highly ordered system. As a project rooted in the systemic logics of its geometry, the composition is governed by organizational rules and hierarchical principles. Drawn into the surface, the material, form, and proportion are all established by the reconciliation of an erratic anterior through a regularized surficial plane. As a true façade, the rule system is established through the drawn lines of the horizontal levels and the vertical rhythmic bays. The ordering system allows the expressive sectional banding of the elevation into the tripartite levels. This three part compositional hierarchy is then echoed through the fenestration, the rustication, and the pilaster column capital style. The order created a geometric rule based system that provided a continuity of composition over the differentiation of anterior form. Homogeneity and ordered seriality with hierarchical layers dominates the visual and conceptual logic. This deference to regimental principles of geometric order privileges the rational to create the composition. Proportion as an imposed relativism rooted in the mathematics of geometric ideals emerges from the two-dimensional drawing. This surficial technique of scale, size, and composition provides guidelines and rules that allow for embedded and quasi-latent rule sets to exist as underlying organizers in the composition. This prescription of a formulated ideal into the compositional logic transitions the methodology of technique of representation into a direct association with the built form. The role of the medium intrinsically joins architecture with the compositional traditions of drawing and painting.

COMPOSITIONAL SKIN: THE BUILDING OF THE DRAWING

The compositional surface articulated through its regimental and blanketing skin, created a new methodology that privileged the façade. The skin assuming the logic for a building shifted the form based sensibility to a shallow and drawn surficial architecture emergent from drawing as a technique. This systemization of planar composition generating architecture allowed for constructed orders, relative internal logics, and compositional organization as a rule based system to introduce a differential reading of architecture through the visual hierarchies, expression of structural forces, and geometric organizational principles of the flat composition. The elevation employs a Neo-Classical compositional language emergent from a finite kit of parts of collaged referential objects. Columns, arches, entablatures, et cetera, each serve as distinct and discrete elements that bring with them their referential legacies providing a prescribed methodology of ordered application. The part itself has intrinsic characteristics that must be compositionally maintained. This subscription to rule establishes a clear formal and compositional role within the larger system. These collective demands become critical determinants of the resulting composition as a collagist surface. An array of field systems that band and stack assembled in relativistic ways to honor their purpose and function while providing the composition. This systemic logic of the Neo-Classical architectural language provides a rationalization of each part in its discrete presence, but also in the part-to-part relationships formulating the overall composition. The two-dimensional characteristic allows for a hyper exaggeration of the architecture in a single surficial picture plane. This shift to a larger appreciation of a rational system, converted architectural thinking from an elemental compositional system to a rule system that is expansive and methodically introduced the compositional perceptual meters of harmonics, proportion, scale, and incremental variation in detail and articulation. Expressive of physical forces, but surficially applied through the flatness of the elevational plane, the composition emerges to formulate a rational narrative of tectonic resolution. The collective governance of geometric composition with systemic performance results in a total harmonic assembly.

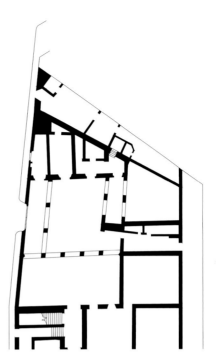

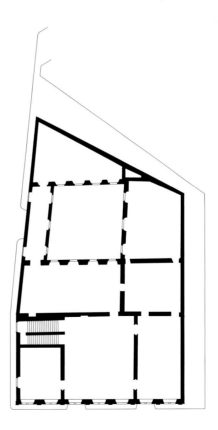

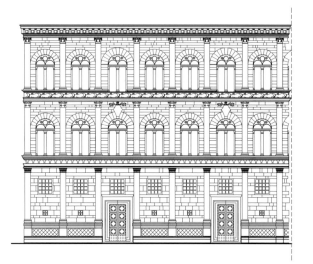

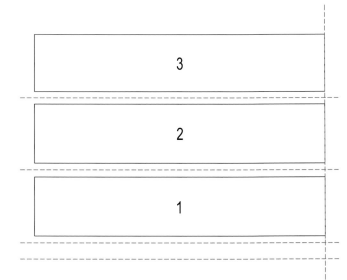

Elevation Systems

Palazzo Rucellai typifies the sensibilities of high Renaissance architecture. Establishing order through systemic geometric based rules, layered with rhythmic proportion, and executed in segmental elements with careful gradients of layered detail; the collective composition regularizes the informal, erratic, and incremental construction of the existing anterior buildings.

The primary organization of the field of the Palazzo Rucellai is in three horizontally striated layers. Stacked, they break the vertical scale into three equal bands set atop an elevating base. These layers then emphasize the programmatic functions and cycles of use for each level. The ground level is the base. It is massive and open to the street at two points. The second level, or piano nobile, housed the main public spaces of the house for the formal aspects of daily living. The third level is for the private functions and sleeping spaces.

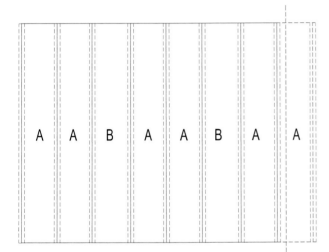

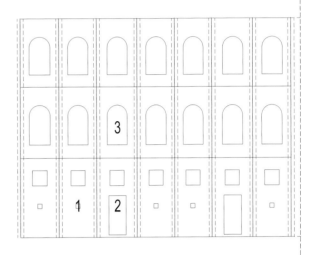

Crossing the three horizontal bands of the Palazzo Rucellai are eight vertical bays set in an alternating rhythm of: A-A-B-A-A-B-A-A. The two entry door bays are set between double bays of repetitive modules. As the site was acquired sequentially over years, the final bays (which would have extended to include another third: B-A-A) though planned, were never completed. The irregular fingered edge was left in preparation and implied anticipation of the final bays that would complete the pattern, resolve the system, and establish both the symmetry and complete rhythm of the overall composition.

The cross weaves of the horizontal layers and vertical bays of the Palazzo Rucellai establish a gridded field. The overlap of these two systems highlights the line of continuity for the vertical forces of the columns and the horizontal entablatures that articulate the floor plates. The remaining field of panels creates an infill wall system. Varied bays with differential wall types include: [1] solid with punched windows, [2] solid with door and punch windows (on the ground level) and [3] a filling arched aperture (on the upper two levels).

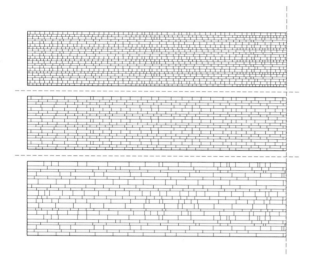

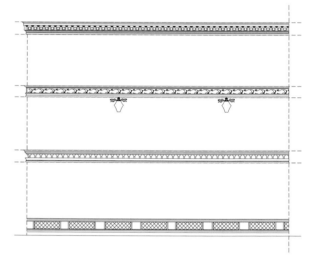

The wall surface of the Palazzo Rucellai itself accentuates its segmental masonry construction through the expression of its ashlar stone. With varied course heights and staggered and irregular head joints, the abstraction of the field across the entire width of the level is accentuated to privilege the collective pattern over the individual block. The scale of the masonry units decreases with the ascension of the levels creating a forced perspective.

The three levels of the Palazzo Rucellai are articulated by their dividing entablatures. As layered expressions of the anterior floor plates, they emphasize the horizontal through their extended presence and ornamental expression. Pulling past the surface of the primary facade plane both laterally and longitudinally, the depth creates a shadow line that further emphasizes the banding. The increasing ornament and detail as the facade ascends furthers the layered hierarchy and refinement of the elevated levels through their articulated seams.

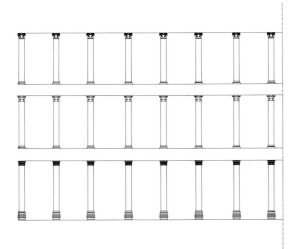

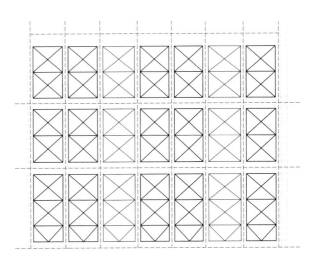

Deploying a field of pilasters (a column subsiding into the surface of the wall plane) the stacked elements collectively illustrate the structural force lines scribed into the surface of the façade of the Palazzo Rucellai. Reinforcing the ascending levels of function of the tripartite organization, the pilasters follow with their articulation and ornament, assuming a similar governing principle. Stacked vertically, the pilasters are regimented in height, type, and increment. Their variation comes in level families through the increasing complexity of their capitals from Tuscan to Ionic to Corinthian.

The geometric bays of the Palazzo Rucellai are further subdivided into two stacked elemental pieces. As a unifying proportion, the repeated unit regularizes the whole through the standardized element. The first level is augmented with an additional half bay (the half is established by the elevating base bench) while the primary three figures each repeat the two bay module. The regimental application of the bay across the facade allows for lateral and vertical regularity. The repetition of the module generates a regularized proportional field that systemically aggregates the whole.

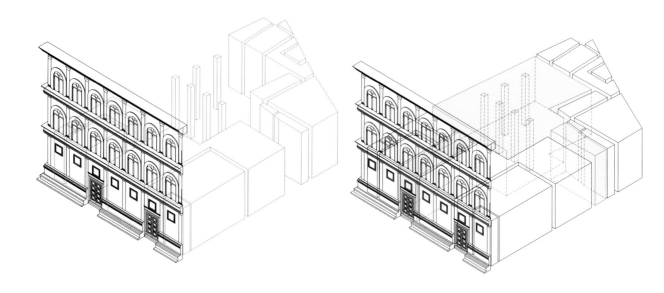

Organizational Surface

The episodic and irregular construction of the anterior spaces of the Palazzo Rucellai is evident in the irregular footprint and ad hoc organization. With an eccentric courtyard encircled by irregular rooms, the new front facade serves as an organizing mask; both regulating and gathering the diverse rear spaces while imposing a new order. The hyper-regularized bay system organizes the disjunctive existing spaces in both plan and section. The result is a blanketing tether that aggregates and regularizes the collective through its dominant regimental rule.

Palazzo Rucellai's asymmetrical and ad hoc anterior spaces of existing rooms and eccentric courtyard represent the varied irregularity of its sequential and individuated construction. The systemic facade based in measure and harmony of Roman elements, orders, and proportional systems, allowed for a gathering of these disparate existing elements to synthetically combine them into a regularized and unified whole. The employment of geometric order through the skin allowed systemic rules and rational application of two-dimensional techniques to govern the composition.

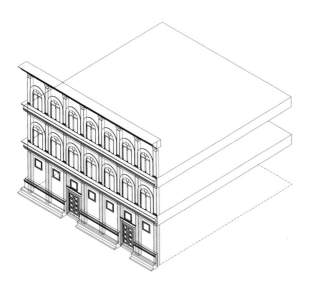
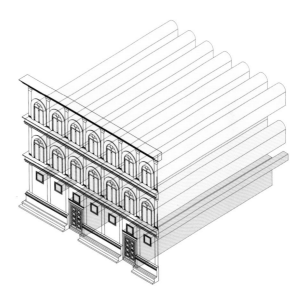

Elemental Constructs

The structural organization of Palazzo Rucellai's façade is rationally arrayed and overtly expressed as a visual language. The planar construction of the primary front facade is dematerialized by the aperture system. These portals waffle the field into a system of openings (with forces transferred by lintels when small or arches when large) that leave only vertical lines (reiterated by the pilasters) and horizontal slabs (reiterated by the entablatures). The collective grid creates the first regularized and rationally modernist expression of physical forces as a grid to line based system of the structural cage.

Each course of the Palazzo Rucellai is dominated by a repetitive aperture element that anchors each bay. These regularized portals establish a rhythmic meter to the diverse spaces and uniformly striate the levels. The regularity of the geometric increment (defined by the aperture system in the thin plane of the façade) resonates through the spatial volumes to create a unifying stitching order. This figurative system is the only legible formal system that carries into the interior and establishes an anterior rule set to unify the diversity of rooms.

TOWER HOUSE

TOWER HOUSE
House 6385

This addition and remodel of a post war house on a modest budget in west Los Angeles is founded in maximizing the minimum. Bracketing the existing house and addition with a series of three towers, they set: [1] in front (flush with the front setback), [2] at the back of the existing house, and [3] at the rear setback. This family of formal elements provide threshold spaces with vertical expansions. Their strategic position allows for minimal and localized surgical interventions on the existing body of the house to expand its spatial layering while providing an articulated contact point for stitching the new with the old. Infilling between the middle and back towers is new square footage for a master bedroom suite and family room.

Clad in cementitious board, the towers serve as spatial expansions. Scooping light and air through their maximized double height space, they allow for vertical and lateral release of the existing efficient but tight spaces. Each tower adopts a different configuration and localized function. [1] The front tower acts as a thermal mass shielding from the harsh and hot southern light while laterally expanding the view corridor to engage the front entry. Its presence boldly announces itself on the street as a shielding, monolithic object. [2] The middle tower edges the back of the existing house transforming the existing master bedroom into a second child's room and providing a contact point for the additional footprint. The function of the tower is split. To the east, a horizontal skylight floods the beginning of the new hallway with natural light beckoning the visitor to the new expansion, while the west side becomes a loft (accessed by a wall mounted ladder leading to a snorkel fort retreat) over the built-in bed/desk and master bath. [3] The rear tower is a double height library with a bookcase spanning the length of the tower wall (floating over the glass wall to the north and folding down at the head of the hallway to form a desk). A wall hung ladder allows for access. A second skylight ends the circulation axis flanking the hall in light.

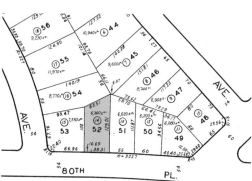

Complementing the towers is a series of three-layered veils of identical, operable, glass walls. Dissolving the back wall of the existing house and dining room and then reiterated in the two walls of the family room, the retractable transparent surfaces allow a literal and visual transition from indoor to out permitting the living and dining of the main house to expand into the newly formed courtyard, carry through the family room and extend into the backyard. The heart of the addition is the void of the newly formed courtyard that spills into both adjacent spaces connecting the architecture to the landscape. This provides for a layered indoor to outdoor living condition essential to Southern California.

The design is a collection of a series of modest interventions each orchestrated to maximize the spatial variety and complexity through their detail. By working within a minimal footprint of 660 square feet (and associated construction costs) the design optimizes experience and effect through the layering and expansion of space.

before

after

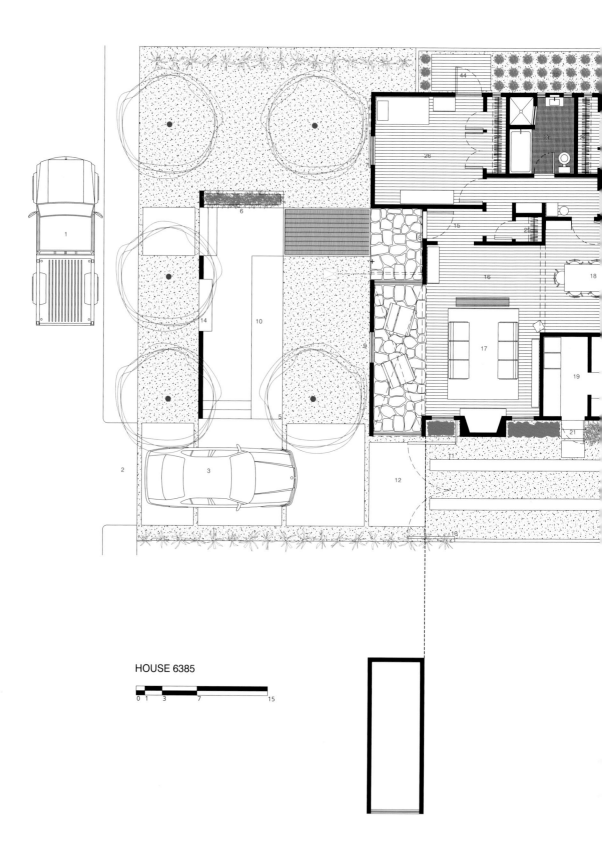

HOUSE 6385

0 1   3   7   15

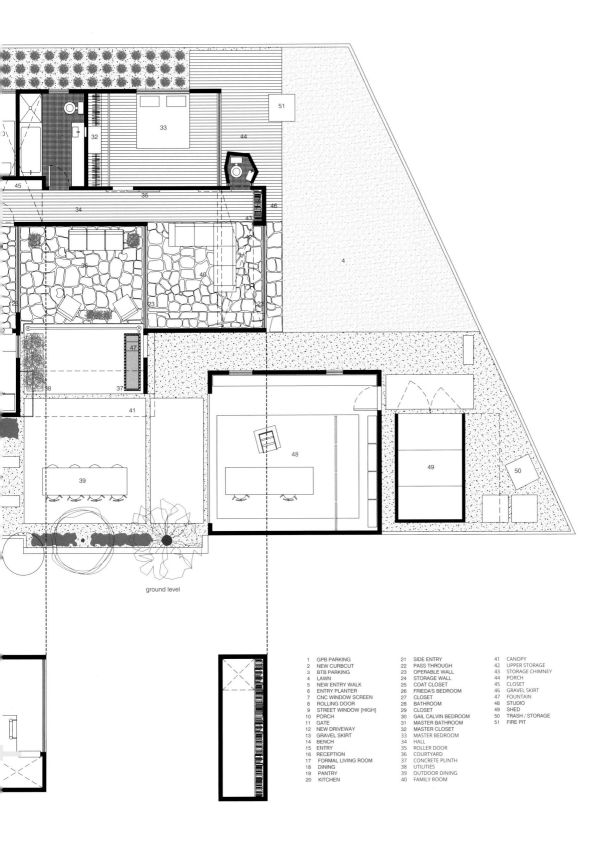

51

33

32

44

45

35

34

46

43

4

36

46

47

23

23

38

37

41

48

39

49

50

50

ground level

1	GPB PARKING	21	SIDE ENTRY	41	CANOPY
2	NEW CURBCUT	22	PASS THROUGH	42	UPPER STORAGE
3	BTB PARKING	23	OPERABLE WALL	43	STORAGE CHIMNEY
4	LAWN	24	STORAGE WALL	44	PORCH
5	NEW ENTRY WALK	25	COAT CLOSET	45	CLOSET
6	ENTRY PLANTER	26	FRIEDA'S BEDROOM	46	GRAVEL SKIRT
7	CNC WINDOW SCREEN	27	CLOSET	47	FOUNTAIN
8	ROLLING DOOR	28	BATHROOM	48	STUDIO
9	STREET WINDOW [HIGH]	29	CLOSET	49	SHED
10	PORCH	30	GAIL CALVIN BEDROOM	50	TRASH / STORAGE
11	GATE	31	MASTER BATHROOM	51	FIRE PIT
12	NEW DRIVEWAY	32	MASTER CLOSET		
13	GRAVEL SKIRT	33	MASTER BEDROOM		
14	BENCH	34	HALL		
15	ENTRY	35	ROLLER DOOR		
16	RECEPTION	36	COURTYARD		
17	FORMAL LIVING ROOM	37	CONCRETE PLINTH		
18	DINING	38	UTILITIES		
19	PANTRY	39	OUTDOOR DINING		
20	KITCHEN	40	FAMILY ROOM		

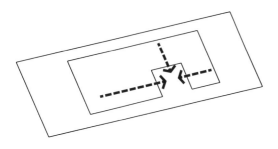

Courtyard

The Southern California climate facilitated the development of a courtyard to create a central exterior room allowing views and uses to span across the layered site. As the heart of the house (bound on three sides and vertically framing the sky) the courtyard space allows for visual and physical layering of the existing and new spaces. Transparent operable lateral walls dissolve the boundary between interior and exterior. The ability to reconfigure the spaces to blend and blur their edges establishes a layered enfilade view through the house. The expansive depth creates programmatic isolation and individuation while allowing the visual borrowing of adjacent spaces to expand each room and zone beyond its own boundaries.

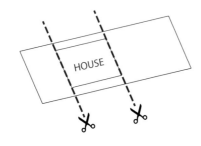

Incisions

As a remodel of an existing 1940s post war home, the budget required maintaining everything original. To optimize the impact and collectively address the house as a whole, the surgical removal of the front and back allowed for a bracketing to establish a new identity while incorporating the economy of the existing. The cuts are then filled with the addition of formally and materially differentiated towers. A third tower anchors the back of the site allowing the addition to span between. The towers serve as totems providing spatial release to the existing spaces through their verticality. Everything existing was painted black to monolithically engage the asphalt roof with the stucco walls. This is further extended into anodized bronze window frames and flooring of black slate that provide texture and detail while retaining a monolithic visual continuity. This singularity emphasizes the contrast of smooth cementitious surface of the towers. By comprehensively engaging the house from front to back, the layered towers allow for a re-reading of the existing through the "all over" addition.

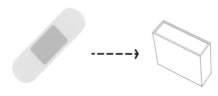

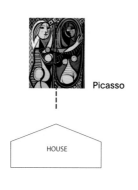

Picasso

Coverage

The front tower covers half of the existing elevation (revealing the existing house on the west side) re-framing the existing with a solemn monolith. Its dominant and contrasting presence asserts the architecture. Serving as a protective wall to the street and the relentless southern exposure, the tower has transparent sides that allow for openness while maintaining privacy. The half mask coverage recaptures the front setback. A grove of Palo Verde trees encompass an elevating (concrete) and bridging (galvanized bar grating) entry plinth (the fourth implied tower).

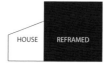

Tower House

Space of Refuge

Designed for a nuclear family of four, each of the three bedrooms is provided with a secondary space of private refuge. Moving [1] over, [2] up, and [3] out; the associative spaces allow for a layering of each of the private spaces with an outward expansion and connection to the exterior. Each private retreat is directly connected to the landscape with an operable transition that provides a blurring of the boundary between outside and in. Using side yard setbacks as secret gardens (south bedroom), tower heights as ladder accessed lofts (middle bedroom), and operable walls and garden porches as extended spaces (master bedroom); these secondary zones allow for an optimization of the site into layered private retreats.

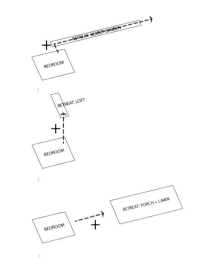

1 + 1 + X + 1 + Y + 1

The addition of the four elements (one low and three high) allows for a layered banding through the depth of the site. [1] The first element is an entry plinth (ramp, stair and planter) creating a detached porch. It slides inside a Palo Verde grove extending the house towards the street, recapturing the front yard, and mediating the transition in scale from public to private. [1] The second element is a vertical tower space extending forward and protecting and identifying the house from the street. A 16' glass wall frames the lateral lengths. [X] The pre-existing house with all lateral walls removed, establishes the front body. [1] The middle tower is the hinge to the addition setting at the back of the existing footprint, expanding and dissolving its boundary. [Y] The addition of the new spaces flanking and encircling a central courtyard provide the expanded zones to the house. [1] The back tower is a double height volume providing for an upper library storage wall while transparent and open to the rear yard at the bottom of the north face. The collective composition layers, expands, and sequences the house.

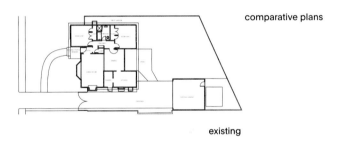

comparative plans

existing

new

Figured Light

Each of the towers engages light through a focal aperture using different orientations based upon position and effect. The front tower opens on the lateral edges to allow for a heroic scale of glass edging walls to laterally project light into the front living room and porch. The rear towers aggregate to bracket the gallery hallway with vertical shafts capped in flush concealed skylights dissolving the ceiling and roof to create Turrell like sky spaces. Located in both the middle and back tower, they wash each end of the hall with light creating a vertical illuminated shaft that draws the viewer through the house. The vertical expansions of space partner with shifting light conditions to allow a cinematically choreographed engagement of sky.

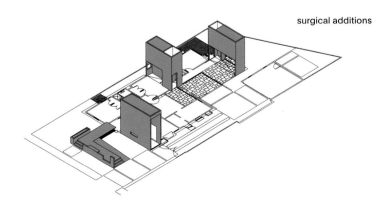

surgical additions

master bedroom deck and polished stainless steel powder room

Landscape

Every part of the site is engaged by the house. Each of the resulting exterior spaces (front, sides, between, back) takes on a room-like quality through its material and configuration. Xeriscaping the yard to restore the indigenous desert was accomplished through compacted decomposed granite that skirts the front and east side of the house. A grove of Palo Verde trees shades the house to the south providing a sculptural and figurative grove. A concrete plinth with carved stairs and ramp is topped with: an under lit floating bench, a formal specimen garden, a rail for collections (to the west), and a rail for changing seasonal decorations (to the south) to create a series of formal gestures to the street.

The central slate courtyard extends the flooring from the dining room addition across the courtyard, through the family room, and into the backyard. A second concrete plinth is set off the courtyard, leading to the detached studio and an outdoor dining room with shade canopy between. The courtyard is passively cooled by a bubbling fountain filled through a channelized trough from a water spigot.

The rear yard is grass spanning from the master deck (which is anchored with a corten fire pit) along a formalized grow wall leading to a firewood storage and potting table that each resolve axial view lines through the house.

Tower House

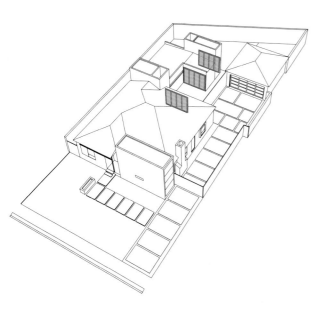

glass retractable walls

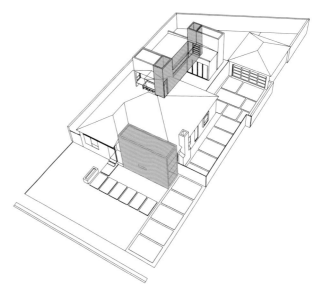

towers

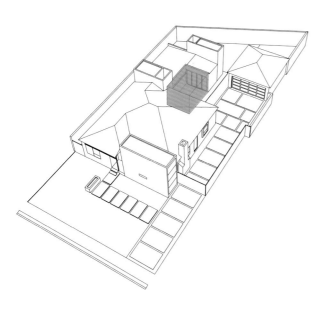

courtyard

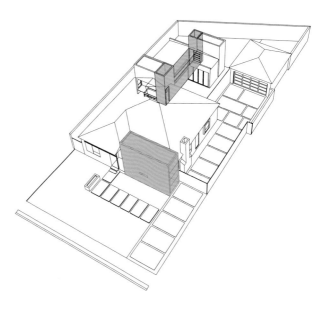

light shaft

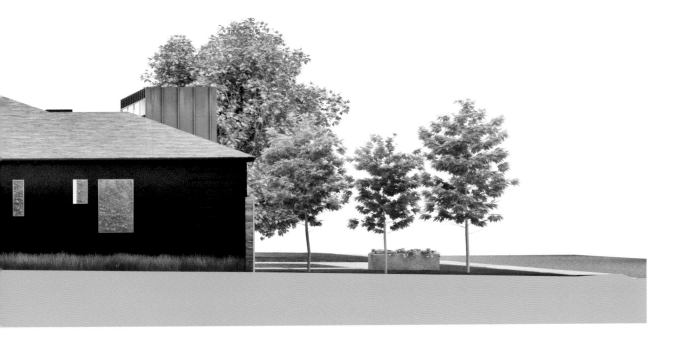

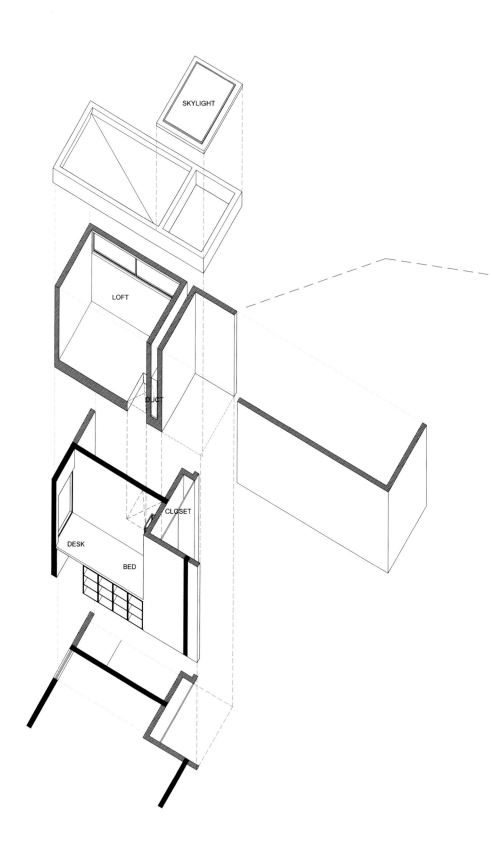

tower loft

Tower House

Expand Along

The front bedroom is expanded through a side door to a secret garden with a diving board porch that hovers above a newly cultivated field of variegated plants. As a private retreat for reading, the isolation of the space is expansive yet hidden.

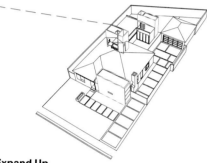

Expand Up

The middle bedroom is expanded upward into a second level of the tower to provide a play loft. Illuminated and ventilated with a ribbon window facing north, the space expands over the adjacent shower and bathtub to provide a reclusive fort. A built-in platform housing desk and bed spans the void below, keeping the room free of furniture.

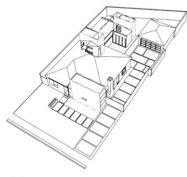

Expand Out

The master suite is edged with a concealing storage wall to the south and a large operable glass wall opening north to the rear yard. The spatial layering expands the room onto a private porch with an outdoor corten fire pit. A polished stainless steel figure engages the porch and bedroom cladding the half bath off the family room.

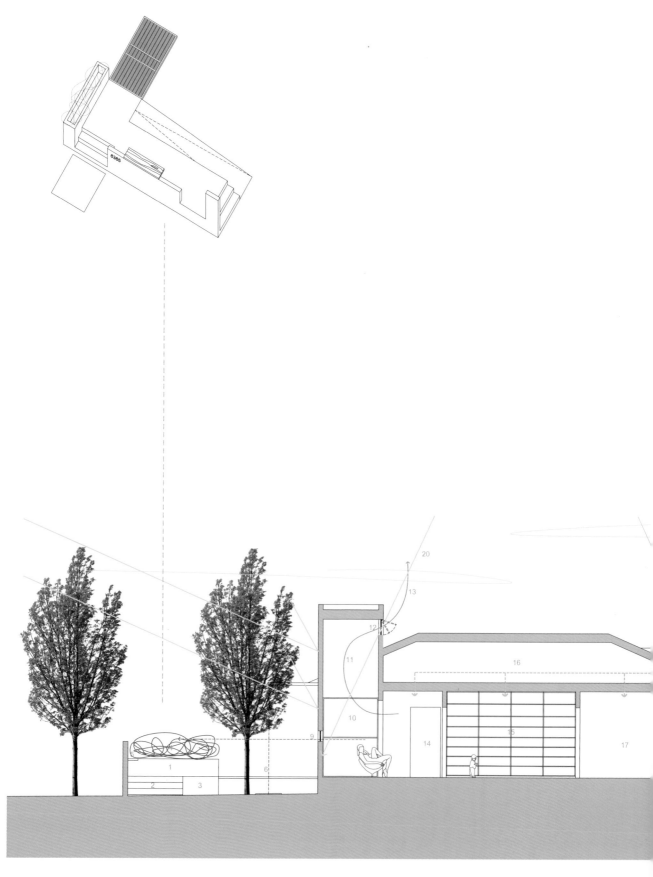

Space and Performance

The spatial, formal, and performative elements of the house all collaborate. The towers serve as double-height light snorkels, ventilation chimneys, and sky chambers. The vegetation is indigenous desert landscape with Palo Verde trees that need little water yet shade the house from direct southern light. The roof water is collected via a series of celebrated scuppers. The courtyard's operable walls allow the full calibration of the house to engage the changing temperature, use, and wind while connecting to the landscape and expanding the enfilade view. Interspersed nodes of work, live, display, and play allow for the house to be a performative machine for living.

1   ENTRY PORCH
2   STAIR
3   RAMP
4   PLANTER
5   BENCH
6   BAR GRATING BRIDGE
7   GUTTER AND DRIP CHAIN TO CISTERN
8   THERMAL WALL
9   OBSERVATION WINDOW
10 ENTRY PORCH WINDOW
11 DOUBLE HEIGHT
12 OPERABLE NORTH FACING CLERESTORY
13 PASSIVE STACK EFFECT
14 THRESHOLD TO PRIVATE WING
15 STORAGE WALL
16 ATTIC WITH MECHANICAL SYSTEM
17 MIDDLE BEDROOM
18 LOFT PUNCH WINDOW
19 OPERABLE SKYLIGHT
20 LIGHT
21 SKYVIEW
22 BATHROOM
23 MASTER BEDROOM
24 GALLERY
25 ROLLING DOOR
26 DESK
27 PORCH
28 YARD

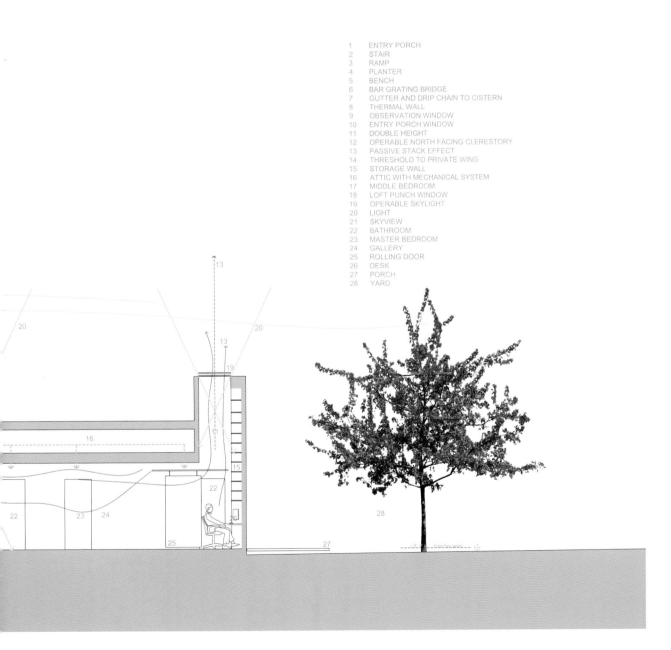

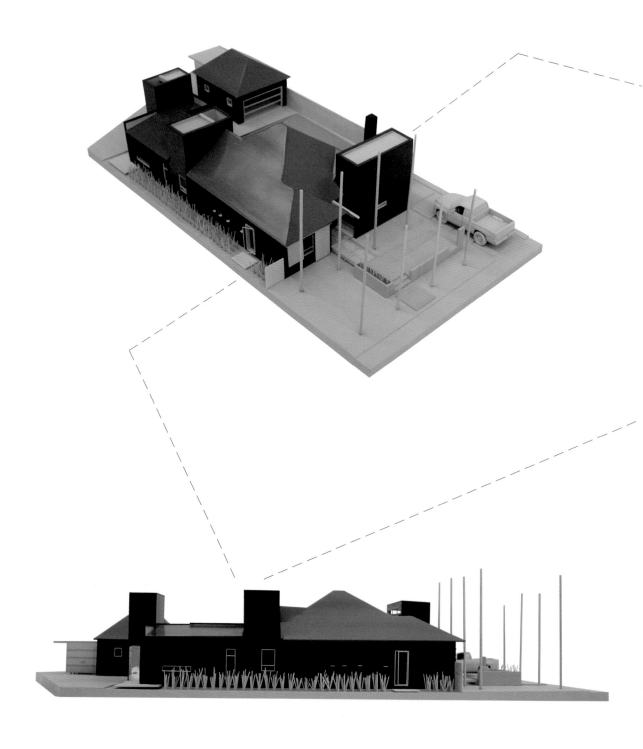

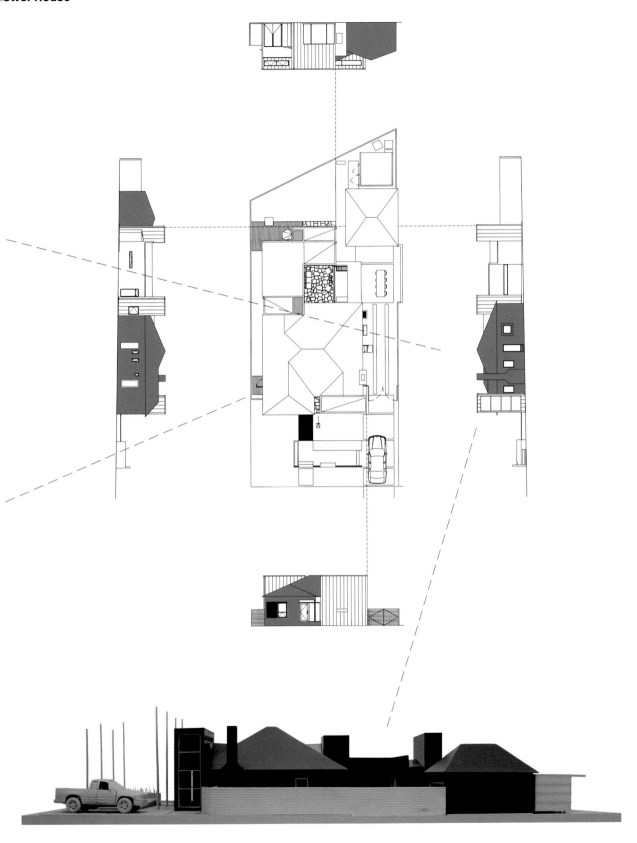

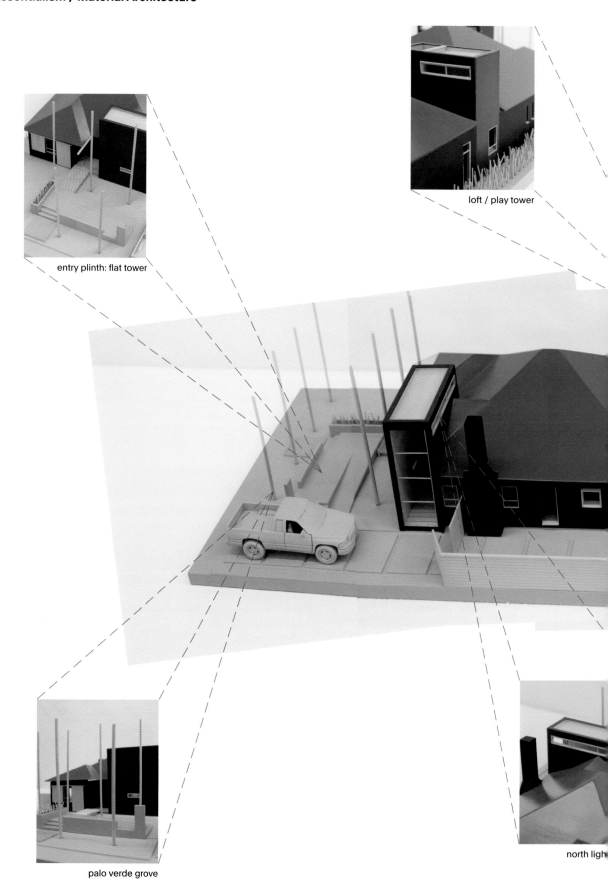

entry plinth: flat tower

loft / play tower

palo verde grove

north ligh

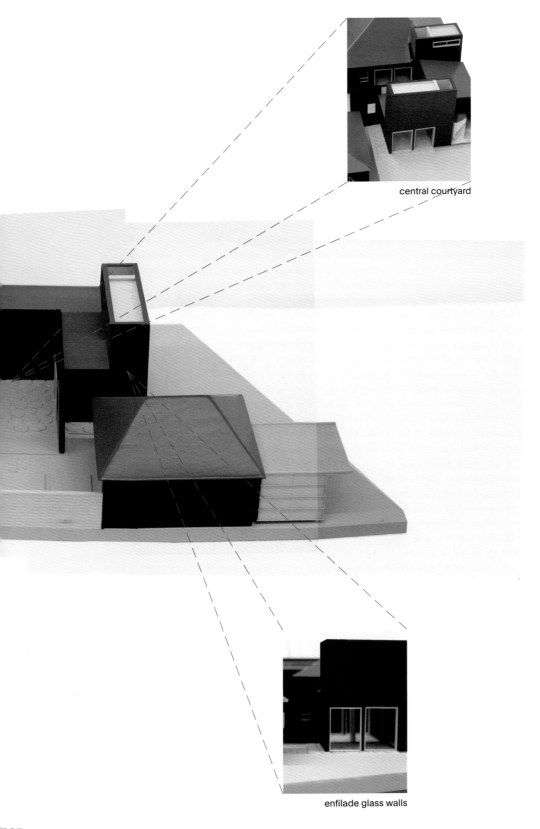

central courtyard

enfilade glass walls

living room expanded into and shielded by south tower towards street

dining room extended towards courtyard

nterior layered enfilade across courtyard

amily room library tower layered toward rear yard

sky oculus

courtyard enfilade

entry porch with milled screen

exterior corridor

north yard

east court

layered family room

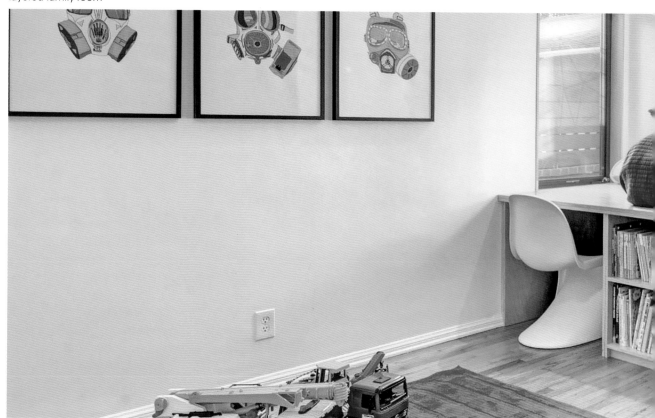

bedroom with loft

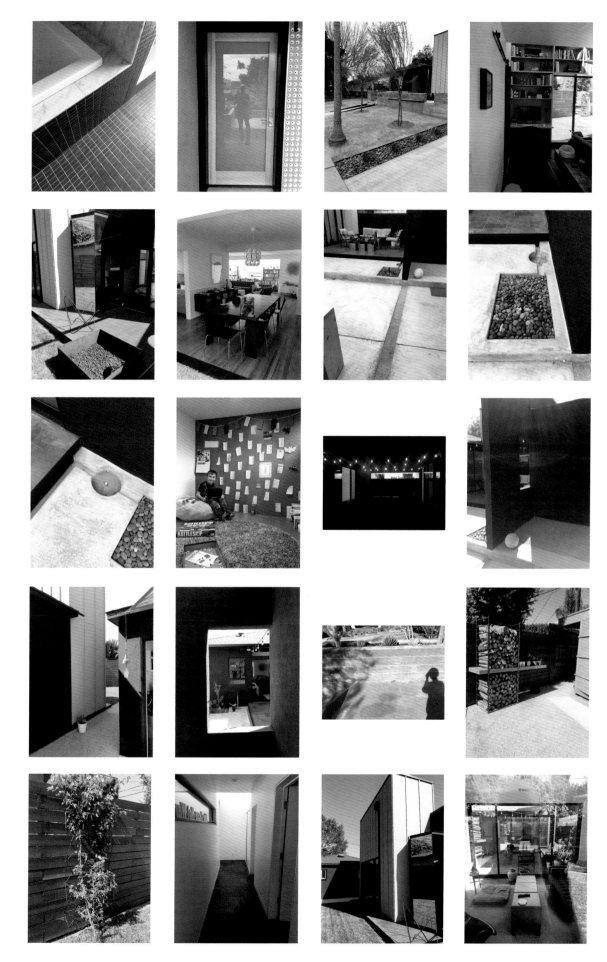

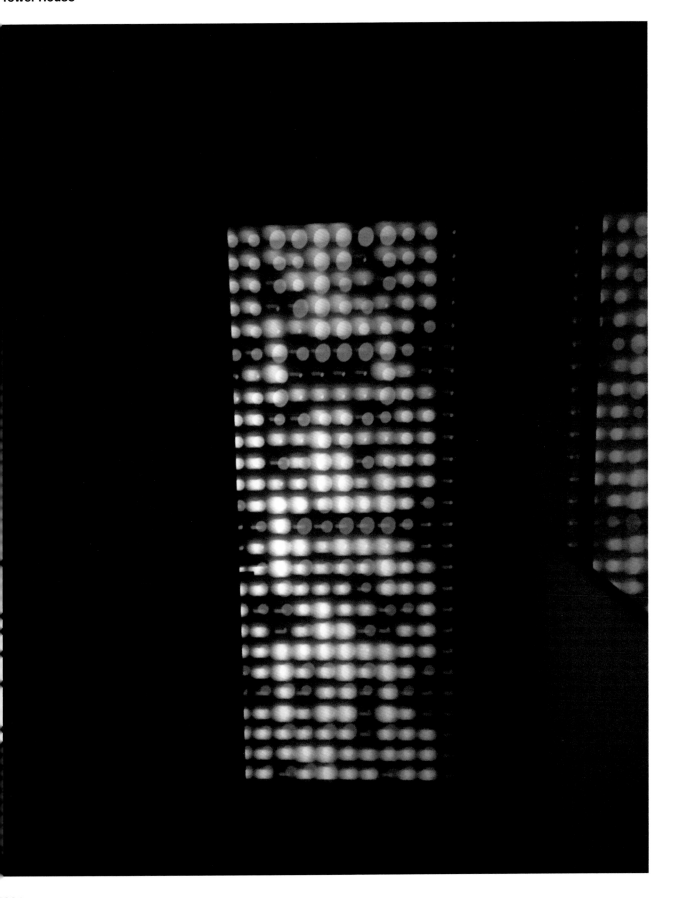

master bedroom with rear expansion and polished stainless steel powder room

rear enfilade

outdoor gallery

front entry

FABRICATING EXPERIENCE THROUGH

MATERIAL
SYSTEMS

MEDIA
Methods of Beginning

ARCHITECTURE AND MATERIALS: MATTER AND MAKING

Architecture and material are intrinsically intertwined. The material matter from which built form is made serves as the media with which designers work. The understanding of the technical constraints must be matched by the sensorial effects. The balance between these elements creates the vocabulary for understanding and wielding material.

Materials receive only cursory attention in design architecture. Issues of form, structure, and geometry have dominated architectural discourse, leaving materiality unattended. Material has remained subservient to form, discussed only in technical terms of construction, yet the history of architecture is the history of material application and invention. The use of new materials and the re-interpretation of existing materials have been at the root of architectural evolution. The thresholds and developments in architecture incurred through material exploration have yet to be fully documented. The role of material precedent, though essential to architectural education, design, and practice has been largely overlooked. The engagement of material precedent (not only from a technical vantage, but as an effectual design catalog of use) provides the opportunity to understand materiality and its essential relationship to architecture.[119]

Prior to the industrial revolution, material was limited by the distance of transport (indigenous locally found building supplies) and the technology of local craft (the traditions of making passed down through cultural generations). This limitation provided a continuity of materiality to form and effect based upon the vernacular architecture. Wood was harvested locally, bricks were fired out of soil found within the area, and stone was taken from local quarries. The connection between the material for making and the act of making was distinctly attached to place and region. With the industrial revolution, infrastructures for movement, combined with expanding populations and the emergence of new material and production technologies shifted the palette and the capability of architecture. The architect was suddenly presented with a selection of materials from which to choose. Considering cost, structure, form, effect, et cetera, materials were selected to ensure the ability to build relative to design intentions. Its limitation and abilities soon became evident and the role of material was foregrounded. Suddenly aesthetics and form were intertwined with material ability. The way skin and structure, frame and enclosure, were handled was suddenly a product of the material selected. Performance and technology as parallel limitations provided

angle of repose
Allison Weise
the form of process

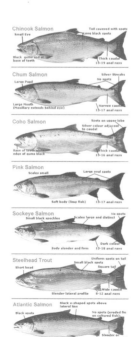

salmon species
iterations of type

expression of design through the tectonic detailing and implementation through construction. The role of architecture was no longer only compositional, but one dependent upon material.

The advent of technology brought advancements to material processes. The expansion of techniques for working with materials liberated glass, steel, and concrete to take on any form. Wood technologies expanded from milling processes to engineered lumbers to accumulate smaller members into any shape and span; even wood chips and sawdust were aggregated into sheet materials (OSB and MDF) shifting the formal consideration from line to plane. Materials can be bent, rolled, and cast with infinite flexibility. The expansion of digital fabrication processes have only accelerated this condition. Anything can be cut with ease and precision. The diversity of options grows logarithmically each day.

At the root of these issues of choice and methodology are the design intentions that aid in material selection, application of process, and the exploitation of how these can effactually and formally be deployed. How a material is used and perceived sits at the root of its application and design. Making architecture is guided by a material's manufacturing process and construction techniques. These systems establish specific boundaries providing the freedom to operate within their systems. Design is not ingenuity of form but rather a collaboration of poetic and rational systems. It is the balance of these two that produce architecture. Perhaps the most famous declaration from Vitruvius in *D'architectura* is: "Well building hath three conditions: firmness, commodity, and delight."[120] It is not any one alone but their synthesis.

Material has tactility and an intrinsic nature. Its visual and emotional characteristics carry an interpretation. Its use establishes an aura and a narrative. The aura comes from the experiential association while the narrative tells the story of its history, fabrication, and application.

The dialog between material and design has become disengaged. Historically there was a definitive relationship between material, place, and form. Technology (through both the diversity of materials currently available as well as the globalism of their availability) has divorced material from form. Any structure can be associated with any shape and associated with any material. Such material application is evident throughout history, from Augustus' attitudes of structure to skin "I found Rome of clay; I leave it to you of marble"[121] to a more recent example of Frank Gehry's Disney Concert Hall changing from stone to metal cladding without affecting the form.[122] Such separation has removed material from the design process positioning it as a finish. Material has lost its foundational premise turning it into a simulacrum. Cesar Pelli states "architecture is the eight inches of the curtain wall,"[123] and Rem Koolhaas goes even farther arguing "our influence has been reduced to a territory just two centimeters thick."[124] The surface is the product.

In opposition to this, the integration of the material with the design is intrinsically present in the works and writing of Louis Kahn who states: "Material should be the fountainhead of form."[125] Similarly in educational curricula, Mies van der Rohe implemented a material based premise as Director of the Illinois Institute of Technology Architecture Program: "In the second year the student learns simple construction in brick, wood, and stone. He learns the properties of these materials and how they can be put together to make simple buildings."[126]

In both of these, the foundational premise is the expression of material as collaboration between design and construction to result in architecture. Putting materials to best use involves an appreciation of their innate sensory qualities as well as their technical potential. This must be at the root of architecture.

REPRESENTATION

Though architecture's ultimate manifestation is humanity's largest physical construct, it originally operates in its most fundamental state as ideas. Their manifestation must translate across diverse modes before it is ever realized. Architecture can be written, drawn, built, and occupied. Different projects exist in and across each of these different modes, states, and categories. All must be experienced.

Drawing: Drawing is the primary method of architectural representation. It is the dominant media of architecture and has deep roots in the history of architectural thinking and practice. The drawing is an essential tool towards how we understand and investigate our discipline. Drawing is a language. It is a way of seeing. It is a way of thinking. It exerts a mood, creates an atmosphere, and represents a sensibility. It establishes rules and cues. The way in which something is visualized (compositionally and through media choice) imprints upon the form it produces. The object is thus indebted to the representation as it is the facilitator of its existence. This endows representation with significant responsibility and relevance.

Different drawings serve different roles. The intention of the author and the compositional impact of the representation are as active as the content itself.

A drawing is real thing in its own right but is also a representation of something else. In this dual role it engages the potential and opportunity of interpretation. It can be precise. It can be artful. It can be technical. It can generate confusion as an oblique view of what it is trying to represent. It can be false. It can trick. It can even lie in its conveyance of information. It can be persuasive. It tells a story and writes its own relationship between occupant and viewer. In all conditions it is active and participatory with content.[127] In its purest state the drawing is an investigation as an exploratory research tool. It tries to understand and describe, to study and to challenge. As a map, the drawing coveys information in diverse ways.[128]

In drawing there has emerged a dichotomy of thinking. There is a distinct division between drawings made for a professional audience and those created for the general public. The dichotomy could be further classified into informatics (that rely upon abstract documentation of larger systems and intentions) versus the representational (trying to present a simulacrum of visual perception). Representation uses methods of description that present a new reality typically bigger than the content itself. The drawing has become a sales pitch while still endowed with the

analytical, the investigative, and the compositional. In all of these modes it is a documentary mechanism coordinating and describing its details and methods of translation into physical being via construction.

Architecture is typically still invested in the hyper-documentation of "the thing." There is an opportunity to move beyond this. Architectural drawing as a genre deserves an investigation and dominance in its own right. The great recession of the early 21st century slowed the opportunities to build. This period facilitated a return to drawing. It created an investigation of the media itself. As a result new categorical methods of thinking have emerged.

The result of the graphic manifestation of the intangible into a visual capacity allows for the physical realization to provide an opportunity to compose. At its purest state, drawing is the practice of thinking through making. This embodies it with the opportunity to serve not only as documentary object but as a conclusive object in its own right that can inspire imagination and challenge perception and propose possible realities. The opportunity of representation resides in this investigative process. How we draw is how we think. The drawing is the manifestation of the architecture. It is the terminus of our discipline's direct making. It is the object endowed with our direct interest. It is a resultant "thing" and idea synthesized. The representation of architecture can be loosely categorized into: Drawing and Medium.[129]

Bird in Space
Constantine Brancusi
frozen motion

DRAWING

Drawing can be described in four (admittedly broad) categories that represent an intent:

(1) Rendering, perhaps most indebted and frequently analogous to realism and photography in the arts.

(2) Representation, informational, and technical drawings exemplified in by section, axonometric, and so on.

(3) Visualization, extending from form to make visible both unseen forces or performances and architecture's response to them.

(4) Diagram, a reduced depiction of a concept or organizational information.

MEDIUM

Specific genres of architectural medium (to be considered in various combinations) include:

(1) Orthographic Projection, or the plan, section, elevation, axonometric, and other drawings that present an analytical depiction of form, approaching composition through both a deep engagement with geometry and the instrumentalization of mathematical principals.

(2) Perspectival Drawing, the pursuit of an (not necessarily embodied) experiential understanding through an analytically constructed methodology that is intrinsically abstract.

(3) Photorealism, or the simulation of (present or potential) reality through methods including photography, rendering, and other pictorial means often tied to the picturesque.

(4) Collage, a compositional and technological articulation through acts of incongruent juxtaposition. It is composition through found elements combined or relatively positioned.

(5) Programmatic Mapping, the functional examination of how things work and optimizing of relationships toward a quantifiably superior solution. Typically rooted in use and function, such analytical relationships facilitate dialogue and engage social or environmental engineering as motivational drivers.

(6) Generative Drawing, in which computational tools become method-based generators of form, indulging tools as generative mechanisms capable of deploying methods with fixed control points and process-based inputs.

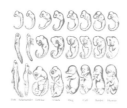

patterns in Paleontology
patterns of growth with
differential results

(7) Information Management and the Parametric techniques embedding "smart" geometries into models for adaptability by way of integrative informatics. This system tends to favor focused, formal rules that produce a simultaneity of iterative difference and similarity through mass-customization.

(8) Expressionism, or formal derivation through an individual compositional will or desire, typically manifested through painterly gesture and aesthetic relativism. This approach often employs iconography engaged through shape, figuration, and metaphor.

(9) Narrative, typically the instrumentalization of historical reference to generate a versioned representation of past architectures often citing typology or morphology.

(10) Experiential, or the documentation of affect, ambiance, environment, and atmosphere. Engaging the sensuous and ephemeral, sensorial methods beyond the visual and spatial including: temperature, moisture, smell, texture, sound, and numerous other difficult-to-represent stimuli.

These two categorical sets, the constructed framework of drawn intentionality, and the methodological approaches taken in drawing generation and interpretation, each offer significant resonance and impact on the ensuing architectural form and product. Tools shape results, and as such architecture must master its methodological underpinnings.

WOVEN
REASON
TISSUE
INTERVENTION
CONTESTED SPACE
BRICOLAGE
POTENTIAL
MONTAGE
CIRCUMSTANCE
IMAGE
PROPOSITION
CONTEXT
STIMULI
REALITY
REVISION
PLANNING
DIAGRAM
SENSE
SCENIC
UNFOLDING
HYBRID
HETEROGENEITY
HAZARDS
SPACE
FORM
VIEW
SUPERIMPOSITION
TRANSITION
DISSOLVE
HORIZONTALITY
VERTICALITY
SURFACE
THICKENED
DEVELOPMENT
PERFORMANCE
SITUATION
CHARACTER
PHYSICAL ATTRIBUTES
CONVENTION
MOVEMENT

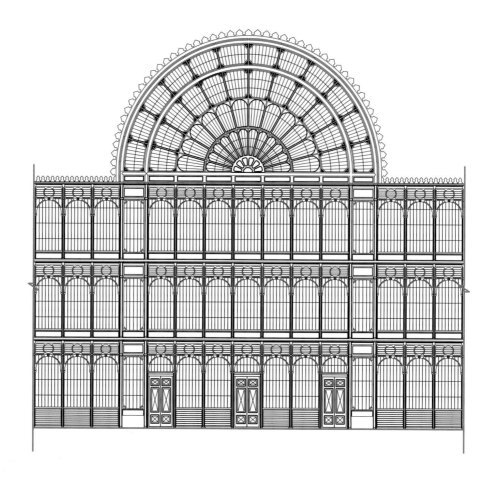

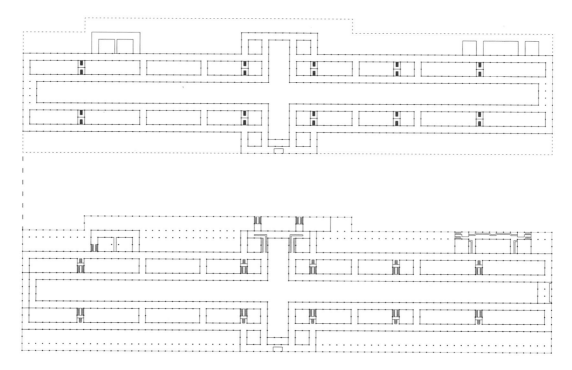

CRYSTAL PALACE

FABRICATION + ASSEMBLY

Plan

The plan of the Crystal Palace illustrates the dominance of the repetitive modularity. The unitized construction established the roots for the scale, speed, and form of the building's construction through the intense efficiency and repetition. The cubic grid creates the base volumetric unit. This spatial module is derivative of the standardized and serial component parts of the plate glass panels and cast-iron structure assembled in modular repetitive arrays. Built into the system at multiple scales are opportunities for variation to allow edges, corners, or multilevel accommodations to iterate subtle performative variations out of the otherwise standard parts. The systemic use of a limited palette of materials deployed in an optimized system created a new sensibility of design rooted in industrialized processes and standardized production. The tectonics became the architecture.

THRESHOLD 5
Fabrication and Assembly

THE CRYSTAL PALACE

"The Crystal Palace was a cast-iron and plate-glass building originally erected in Hyde Park, in London, England, to display examples of the latest technology developed during the Industrial Revolution for the Great Exhibition of 1851."[130] As an open competition, the call was for a temporary, economical design able to be built quickly. Sir Joseph Paxton's winning modular design used repetitive elements and optimized fabrication processes to provide the necessary speed and economic efficiencies. Formally, the building was a massive, terracing "flat-roofed rectangular hall."[131] Measuring 1,848 feet long by 456 wide, with an interior height of 128 feet at its center, the rectangular body was cross cut with a central 72-foot-wide and 168-foot-high barrel-vaulted gallery.[132] With the recent invention of the cast plate glass method in 1848[133] (which allowed for large sheets of affordable yet strong glass) the building centered its design on the production capabilities using the material for all wall and ceiling surfaces. The geometry and dimension of the building was based upon the largest size pane of glass available: 49 inches long by 10 inches wide.[134] Scaling the entire building around these dimensions allowed the entire exterior surface (walls and roof) to be glazed by identical panes. "The economies of scale permitted the manufacturing and assembly of the building parts to be both quick and inexpensive. As each module was identical, fully prefabricated, self-supporting, and fast and easy to erect; all of the parts could be mass-produced in large numbers.[135]" Even when variation was required, parts were optimized to serve multiple functions to further economize the process. The integration of the scale of repetition and seriality of industrial production provided a new sensibility to architecture.

This tectonic unit was serially aggregated into modular panels that composed the structural and spatial module based on a 24-foot-cube. Each volume was structurally self-resolving providing a physical independence that permitted construction to be segmental while allowing for volumes to be removed as needed to respond to functional and compositional requirements. The modular construction allowed for erection as quickly as the parts could reach the site with some sections standing within eighteen hours of leaving the factory.[136] The premise of the multi-directional unit module within a gridded plan allowed for expansion and flexibility. Its massive plan translated into repetitive bays: 77 modules long by 19 wide.[137]

The Crystal Palace represents several significant conceptual thresholds for architecture:

MANUFACTURING DRIVING FORM AND TECTONIC

The shift from a formal and compositional based sensibility to a design emergent from manufacturing and part based sensibility in the Crystal Palace shifted the primary compositional authority towards the material properties and the processes of fabrication and assembly. This process based logic introduced an efficiency of form that required the architecture to provide ingenuity through the assembly and the ordering logics relative to the prescriptive material origins and economies. Requiring an integrative sensibility to how things are made and what things are made out of, the full cycle of production became essential for the architect to master. This fundamental shift repositions the point of departure for design thinking relative to materials and construction.

METHOD OF PRODUCTION AS ARCHITECTURAL TERRAIN

The method of production for the glass components of the Crystal Palace was rooted in an entirely new technological capability. The larger scale and the regularity by which the product could now be fabricated created a mass producible component. The architecture of the Crystal Palace emerged from the serial accumulation of this repetitive part. The application of a "product" (here still in its most primal state as a piece of raw plate glass) shifted the conception of architecture from the true autonomy of formalist creationism to the governing of assemblies of existing systems and products. This shift marks a pivotal moment in architectural production that has only since amplified. Standardization, fuel by economics and the legalities of ensured performance, have regulated architecture to an orchestration of the assembly of pre-existing systems. Innovation or iteration only occurs through an upstream insertion into their processes, understanding materials, construction, and assembly techniques and the fundamental capabilities of tools in the hands of skilled laborers to present innovative opportunities for modification or iteration.

REPETITION OF UNIT AND THE SERIAL PRODUCTION OF COMPONENTS

Shifting architecture from the subordination of the part (where previously segmental construction was a necessity that was masked or ignored) in the Crystal Palace, the repetition of the unit emerged from the serial process of production as a formal and systemic generator. The regimental nature of the system induced the visual reading of the collective field. Out of the individual piece the part to part relationship establishes a geometric field that produces the overall effect of the system. The component (or part) becomes the originating element, establishing form, geometry, and material effect.

TRANSPARENCY

The evaporative nature of glass commenced a long and ongoing engagement with the phenomenological capabilities of the material. At the Crystal Palace, though glass was primarily adopted more for its pragmatic performance and remained bound by the heavy encircling frame, it is still a pivotal moment of dematerialization. Though the building enclosed a massive volume, the use of the transparent cladding allowed for an evaporative effect to its presence. The blurring of the boundary between outside and in; the use of natural light to flood the space; the privileging of the skeletal structural frame made possible by the visual removal of all else; each introduced signifiant opportunities for both literal and phenomenal transparency.[138]

STRUCTURAL EXPRESSIONISM AS THE REMAINING PRESENCE

The articulation of the component provided for the origins of the "high tech"[139] architectural expressionism founded in the celebration of the individually articulated functionalist elements of the building. Revealing and celebrating these technical components, the overtly expressed elements illustrated the collective systems and their overall performance. Each elemental piece (typically serially produced and prefabricated) provided a comprehensive revelation of the functional working of the building. As a result the Crystal Palace foregrounded the structural system by dematerializing all else (enclosure, partitions, ventilation, utilities, et cetera) leaving the frame as the dominant figure.

SKELETAL FRAME AS COMPOSITIONAL FORM

The combined use of a repetitive palette with the transparency of the plate glass material evaporated the presence of the enclosure foregrounding the structural skeleton of the building as the compositional figure. This privileging of the structural frame provided a new reading of the physical forces within a building. Though begun at Chartres with the externalized expression of the buttresses, at the Crystal Palace, the full structural system is extracted from the surrounding composition to read as a standalone systemic element. The physical foregrounding of the force lines into columns, beams, trusses, and arches created an essential formalism that nearly fully eradicated ornament in favor of functional expressionism.

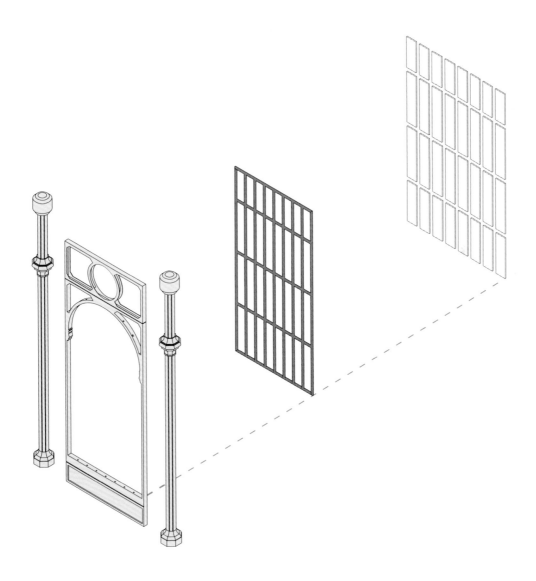

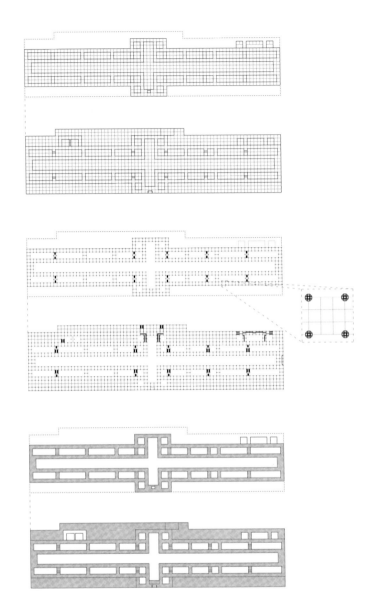

Planametric Modularity

The intense tectonic modularity of the Crystal Palace is evident in the planametric organization. Illustrating both the primary ground level and the upper mezzanine, the plans demonstrate how the standardized grid establishes both a planar and sectional module. Equal in all directions the cubic module is based in the efficiency of production, repetition, and material. The 20-foot by 20-foot structural module creates the caged frame. Relentless and anonymous to the local activities, the grid blankets the field with dominant authority and evenness. Localized decisions of variability of floor plate, sectional expansion, or edge condition are each accommodated through variation within the structural element itself maintaining a seemingly homogeneous quality to the componential construction. Removals of the columns where the spatial expansion occurs from level to level creates clearings within the field and gathers circulation into directional lines. The overall super-structural grid is further divided into a smaller grid to resolve the edge bays of the enclosure.

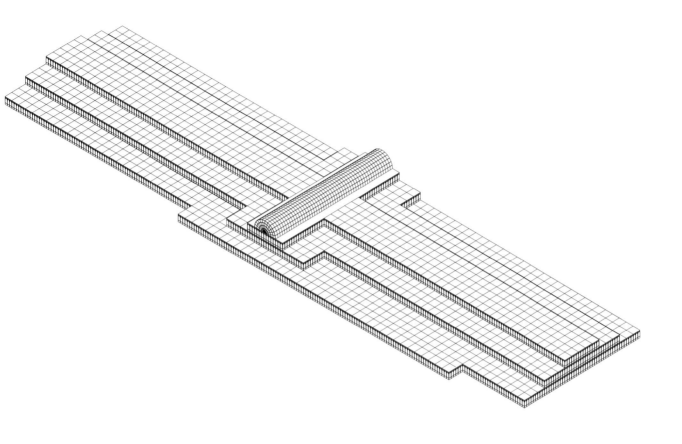

Axonometric

The elemental system of repetitive components of the Crystal Palace is applied in a cruciform plan. With an axial central hall, the configuration allowed for two massive wings with upper mezzanines. The transparency of the glass and the slenderness of the skeletal structural system allowed for the building to read as an evaporative field arrayed through the exhibition space.

The three-dimensional module of the system allowed for a pixelated and terraced bay system that carried the regimented optimization of the local tectonic capability into the collective massing.

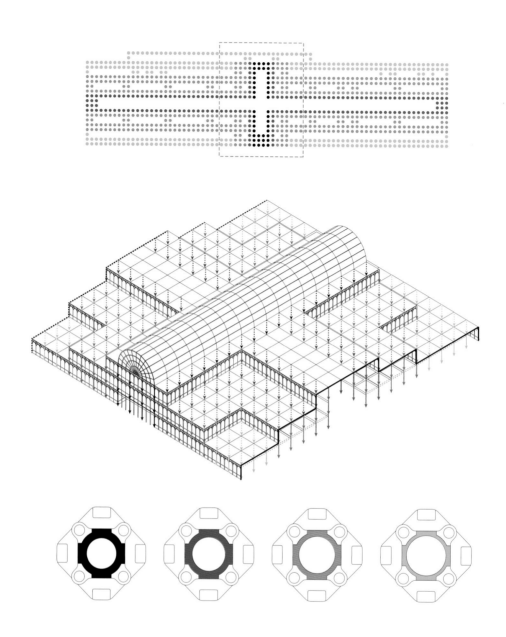

Loading

For the structural system to maintain the regular column field while accommodating the variable sectional heights and multistory configurations required a systemic adaptability. The building plan produced varied intensities of load path due to the terraced form. The columns did not respond with any external differentiation, but rather employed an internal thickening of their material wall. Within the system a series of types emerged with internal performative capabilities. This masking of differentiation remained classical in the desire to create equality. Material and technical prowess allowed identification, prediction, and accommodation through an articulate understanding of statics and material property allowing the architecture to be invisibly responsive with efficiency and optimization.

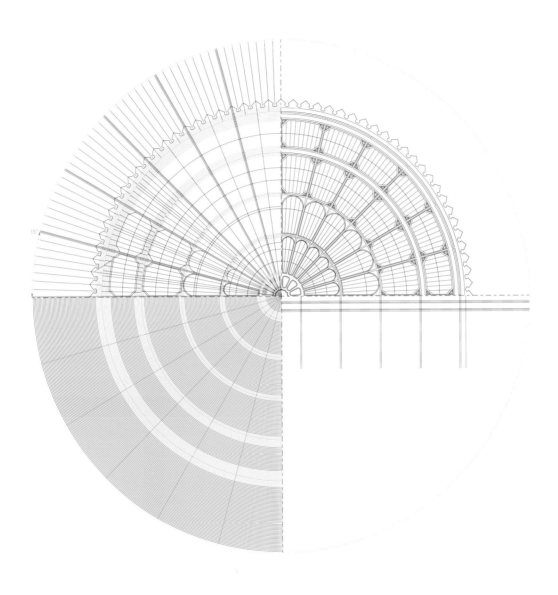

Meridian Geometry

The meridian geometry of the central semicircular ceiling of the Crystal Palace is rooted in a modular extension of the building's primary grid system. Broken into equal subdivisions of arrayed geometry, it is a semicircular composition with an axial symmetry mirroring each quadrant. Broken into six equal segments and four offset and layered rings, the fifteen degree increment allows for repetition of each segment. This scale and subdivision further allows for the columnar module of the rectilinear geometry below to align with the arch geometry of the segments above. This seamless stitching creates structural and visual continuity of the field bent and returned through the atrium arch.

Elemental Components

Each bay of the facade of the Crystal Palace was broken down into an elemental and further serialized system. Articulated by a simultaneous response to the need for repetitive parts born from efficient production, each component of the facade was refined and configured to optimize functional need. Transparency to the skin, operable ventilation, material limitations to the glass production, et cetera, were each determining factors that linked the cycle of production to the functionality of the system. This bridge between manufacturing and architecture shifted the responsibility of the architect into full cycle responsibility as a "master builder" understanding material properties, manufacturing techniques, construction practicalities, and building performance. The new industrialized materials of the skin allowed the fabrication techniques (in all of their limitations and capabilities) to determine the architect's palette and combine production with design.

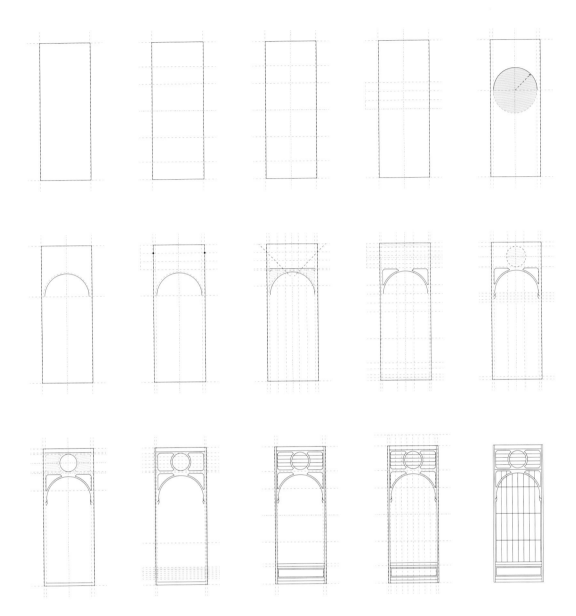

Anatomy of a Panel

The componential construction of the Crystal Palace is emphasized through the layered elements. From the super-structural bay divided into the three panel subdivision, this module is further divided into: (1) columnar edges for structure, (2) frame to hold infill, and (3) infill systems of both glass panels and operable louvers for ventilation. The system was an expression of the aggregated elements. Each piece was articulated as a component of production and functional utility. The revelation of the components eliminated poche dematerializing the wall into an assembly of parts. The anatomy of the panel is revealed through the incremental decisions that sequentially determined its articulation. Based in the sub-module of the super-structural organizing grid, the primary unit is divided into three zones with a top, a middle, and a base. Each zone assumes a different functional and formal articulation. The top and bottom have operable louvers for ventilation while the center is fixed glass allowing for transparency and dematerialization of the wall. Derived by function and articulated through their revealed expression, the building became a performative machine.

LIGHT FRAMES

LIGHT FRAMES
Materials & Applications

This is a project founded in material. Begun with the fundamentals of a material's capability; developing material geometries that efficiently collaborate engaging with a distinct material based processes for generating components; developing material systems out of these components; deploying advanced computational technology to manage the material media; and ultimately deriving form, experience, and effect from the collaboration of all of these systems the methodology comes from an intrinsic dialogue with the physical constraints of making. Deploying the tectonics of materials to generate a light based spatial experience, this project is a methodological assimilation of material technique with design intent.

EXPERIENCE

Upon entry from the street, the viewer is immediately engulfed. The front figure of the conduit tower holds the urban edge of the infill site volumetrically expanding vertically while sitting delicately on the ground spanning from a column to a wall. The nested figure of the two sectionally layered domes generates a double density moiré effect of the superimposed frames. The galvanized surface of the electrical metallic tubing (EMT conduit) reflects and evaporates in the sunlight projecting a bold shadow field below.

As one ascends the existing steps and slides past the fountain, the pneumatic vinyl chapel reaches out its entry. This second figure projects light. The transparent surface of the pneumatic's outer skin reveals the complexity of its inner structure. The geometry evolves from a conical entry, morphed with a curving barrel vault, connecting to an apsidal end and a conical chimney with an open oculus. The reinterpretation and recombination of these iconic shapes generates new forms while providing referential glimpses to historical architectural precedents. These primal architectural forms (typically conceived as gravitational masses) are clad in parametrically controlled PVC. The composition of funneled, reflected, and refracted light produces a sunlit room that transitions through the day. At night the relationship inverts to make the entire structure a glowing projective lantern.

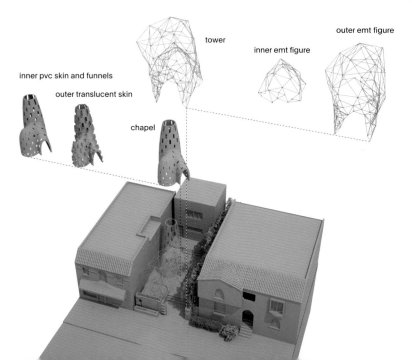

inner pvc skin and funnels

outer translucent skin

chapel

tower

inner emt figure

outer emt figure

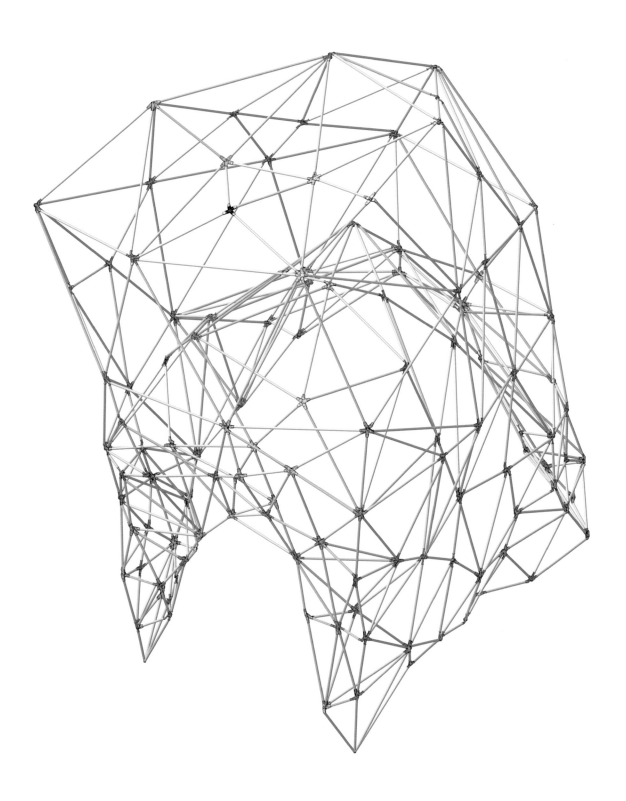

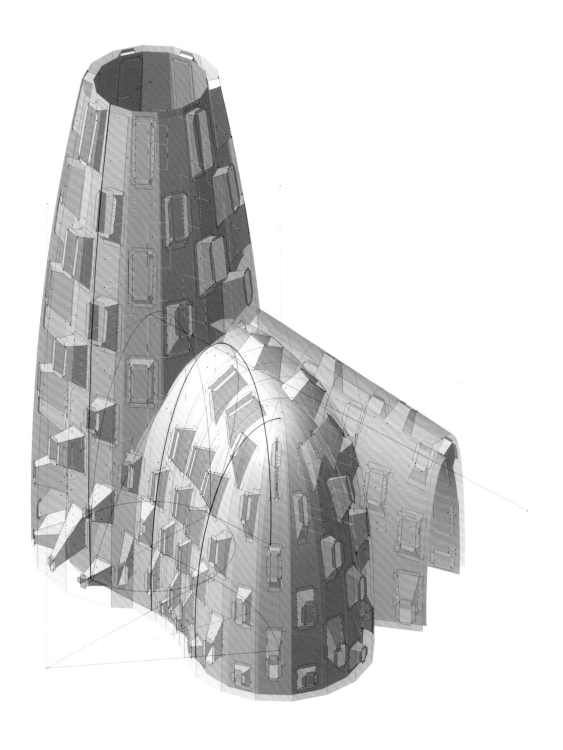

MATERIAL HISTORY AND REFERENCE:

With a limited budget of $6,000, the material selection needed to be hyper efficient. Using compositions of line and plane, the geometry allowed for the creation of large figures that could fill the volume of the urban infill site while minimizing material. These two considerations in conjunction with the material legacy of Los Angeles architecture and material innovation led to galvanized electrical metallic tubing (EMT) and vinyl plastic.

CONDUIT

The use of galvanized electrical metallic tubing (EMT) referenced the galvanized chain link projects of Frank Gehry[140] (the most dominate architectural figure in Los Angeles). As a ubiquitous material, but one that had not been overtly employed as a primary building material as either structure or finish the affordability and off-the-shelf availability of this under celebrated material provided opportunity.

Similar to the effect of the "Two Running Violet V Forms"[141] where Robert Irwin installed a chain-link fence in the canopy of a eucalyptus grove in La Jolla, California to create an evaporatively diffused linear figure; here the density is folded back on itself as a palimpsest figure to allow the layering of the field upon itself. The intricacy of the delicate frame creates a three-dimensional line drawing that allowed density to create open detail in the space. The common tubular material was figured through three-sided fractal elements of variable triangulation using overlapping layers to create visual density. Two implied surface elements create nested inner and outer figurative and structural shapes. The visual interlocking of the two creates a double density.

The linear figure serves as an effectual generator producing a cloud of shadows. The lines of the frame structure project into the space activating the full urban void of the infill site in the powerful Southern California light. The galvanized surface reflects the color of the sky evaporating presence through reflection. The changing effects of natural, street, and internal lighting allows for evolutionary readings of the figure. The result is an immaterial presence.

PVC

The PVC figure is founded in hybridized descriptive geometries. The form is derived from the evolutionary aggregation of a cone, a barrel vault, an apse and an oculus. The specific figure emerges from the inter-relationships of each of these forms and the adaptive responses the individual geometries must make to one another. To provide entry, a truncated cone engages at the knuckle of the vault and the open chimney cone. The barrel vault forks off the entry knuckle and bends to resolve in an apse. The collective form creates a chapel-like enclosure focused on the referential spirituality of these iconic forms and their effects of projected light.

The resolution of the flexible sheet material into a load bearing formal system required the translation of compressive mass into tensile surface through pressurized air. An inner cavity (bound by an interconnected interior opaque surface and exterior translucent surface through a field of variable four-sided

wireframe

joints

pipes

conical windows) creates a stabilized tapering wall. The material, through its: [1] process of creating a shell of vertically stripped bays (derived from the roll of the sheet material) and [2] requirement for incremental lateral connections to respond to the outward force of the pressurized air; required a responsive translation of form to collaborate with the generation of the experience. The projected light effects are facilitated by the systematized understanding of the material.

geometries

surfaces

forms

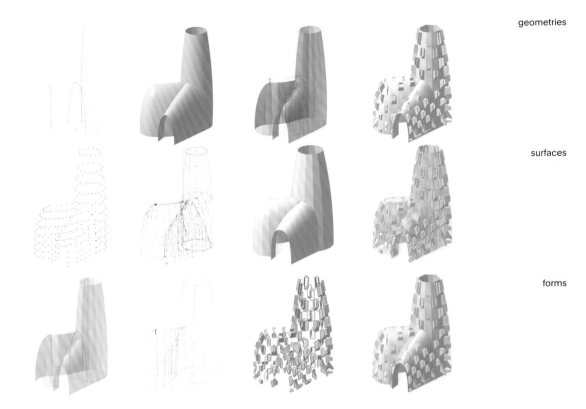

vc chapel system

ransverse section

SPECIFIC THINKING: MATERIAL

The doubling of the material arose from the individual expression of each pavilion and their interrelationship. Chosen for their cultural identities as well as their effectual qualities, their existence in the realm between transparent and opaque, present and absent, began the engagement with their optical potential. Each material instigates diverse light effects with changing relationships between their dialectical conditions endowing them with even further ambiguity of their effectual results.

EMT conduit is a linear material capable of aggregation into segmented field configurations. Vinyl plastic fabric is a continuous planar surface material. It is available with varied levels of transparency and translucency. It readily engages heat welding that lends itself to panelization. These two systems meet to produce a dialogue through their light effects of emissivity, transmission, and shadow. They compose the spaces bound within as well as refracting and reflecting to impact their surrounding context.

MATERIAL TRANSLATION

The development of the tectonic system of each assembly emerged from the intrinsic material properties: plastic as sheet and conduit as extruded line. These foundational material sensibilities and their associative physical properties establish the methods available to derive form.

The galvanized conduit (as a liner system) employed variable densities of triangulation to generate a faceted surface. The formal figure (produced through the structural optimization of the delicate members) required and facilitated the opportunity to engage the density of field through dynamically layered and performatively figured surfaces.

Plastic laminated PVC fabric available as a rolled two-dimensional sheet material and capable of being thermally welded is: [1] a modern material; [2] glossy and reflective; [3] formally flexible; and [4] able to be used as a self-supporting skin. Its material plasticity challenges the traditions of the two-dimensional surface. Reconciling the limitations of the factory-dictated flat dimension with the organicism of an air-inflated structure allows for the rigid geometric framework of the proposed formal system to engage with the flexibility and constantly evolutionary reality of a natural system. Embracing the capability of introducing depth to the material through captured internal air pressure, the weldable fabric provides opportunity for a panelized surface. Referencing the ubiquitous Los Angeles "bouncey castle" deployed for children's birthday parties, the tectonic system was applied to iconic architectural forms.

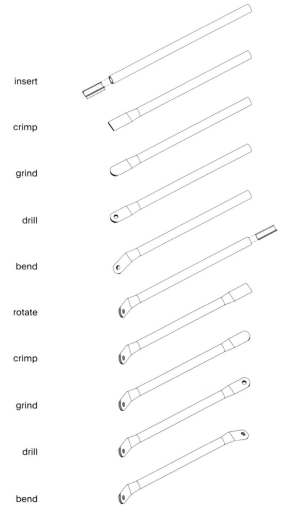

insert

crimp

grind

drill

bend

rotate

crimp

grind

drill

bend

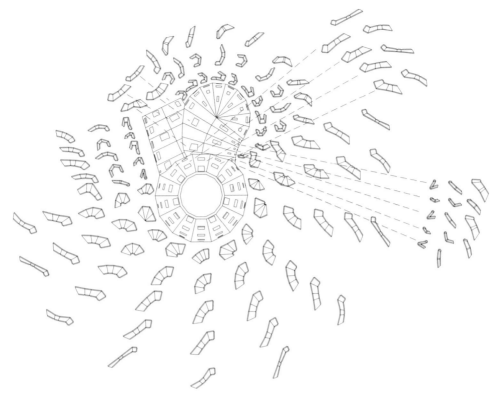

pvc chapel component templates

oints and seams

SYSTEMIZATION

The systemic organization of the material systems comes through their segmental construction and its ability to produce effect. In the conduit tower, the panelization relies upon a triangulated three-sided unit. The local structural requirements of the graduated figure combined with the double domed geometry (one shallow and one highly arced) produces the collective figuration of the whole. The localized composition is determined by both the structural requirements and the tectonic regulation of the assembly system through the joint.

In the inflatable chapel, the four-sided truncated pyramid is used as the individual connective unit. Projecting out of the inner opaque surface, they act as accumulated, variably-figured forms that serve as structural bridges producing aggregated effects through their individuated unitization. Modular in their construction and gradient, they link to inner and outer surfaces that define the overarching forms: conical entry, taper conical open topped drum, and bending barrel vault culminating in an apse.

GEOMETRIC GOVERNANCE

EMT: The conduit tower regulates the three-sided faceted system at the nodal joint. This detail requires an engagement of the overall system to prevent an over complexity of any one connection. Defined by economy of fabrication to minimize complexity, all joints were limited to crimped and bolted connections. The gradient of the length of a member to the density and frequency of members illustrates the aggregation, scale, and scope of the structural forces.

PVC: The PVC chapel was designed and fabricated through parametric models in CATIA.[142] Using a regimented system to allow for diversity of form with simplicity and optimization of fabrication, the system starts with the four-sided, flat sheet of the material. Maintaining planarity with the inner and outer surface, the depth of each cone is determined by the structural taper of the wall. The variability of the cone angle and size gradients was: [1] vertically from more to less wall to allow a visual evaporation of the wall; and [2] from more to less away from the structural overlaps of the primary geometric forms. The parametric digital model allowed for flexibility to be built into the system of formal investigation, allowing for iterative variation without losing the standardization of the units and the synthetic template production.

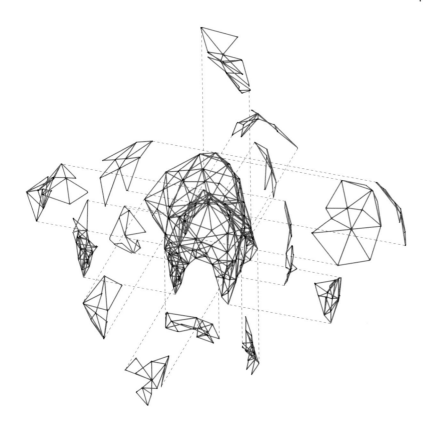

conduit tower prefabrication components
axonometric

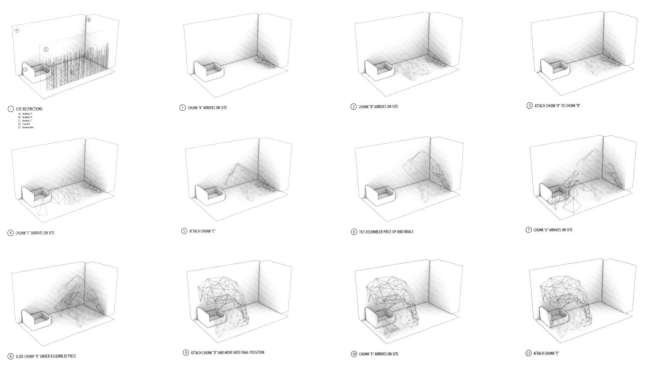

① SITE RESTRICTIONS
   (A) Building "A"
   (B) Building "B"
   (C) Building "C"
   (D) Fountain
   (E) Bamboo Wall

① CHUNK "A" ARRIVES ON SITE

② CHUNK "B" ARRIVES ON SITE

③ ATTACH CHUNK "A" TO CHUNK "B"

④ CHUNK "C" ARRIVES ON SITE

⑤ ATTACH CHUNK "C"

⑥ TILT ASSEMBLED PIECE UP AND BRACE

⑦ CHUNK "D" ARRIVES ON SITE

⑧ SLIDE CHUNK "D" UNDER ASSEMBLED PIECE

⑨ ATTACH CHUNK "D" AND MOVE INTO FINAL POSSITION

⑩ CHUNK "E" ARRIVES ON SITE

⑪ ATTACH CHUNK "E"

assembly sequence

view from conduit tower towards pvc inflatable

PERFORMATIVE REQUIREMENTS

EMT: The conduit tower works with light through reflection and projection. The palimpsest density of the doubled geometric frame generates a reciprocal density of shadow.

PVC: The variable cones of the PVC chapel are governed by the compositional experience of projected light. Creating a reducing scalar dimension and an adjusting angle of repose as they ascend, each of the apertures varies in depth, directional axis, and perimeter frame size. During the day, light is projected into the chamber. At night this reverses projecting light outward into the surrounding context.

FABRICATION / PROCESS / TOOL

EMT: The conduit tower uses simple fabrication techniques: crimping, bending, and bolting. The system is: [1] calibrated digitally; [2] fabricated in individual units; [3] chunked for prefabrication; then [4] grouped for final installation. Base on a triangulated module, the structure generates its density through the layered double domed canopy.

PVC: Using standard controls and geometries derived from the CATIA model, the air inflated structure is buttressed by the large base wall thickness (tapering as the figure goes up) and the tethering interconnections of the inner and outer surfaces through the field of cones. Each piece (both the ribboned surfaces and unfolded conical connectors) is cut from the vinyl fabric and then heat welded to create a continuous surface of enclosure.

INSTALLATION / CONSTRUCTION

The precision of the process permitted the translation of the digital model through templates and fabrication models into final parts and components. The work flow allowed for all output to be direct and accurate. Prefabricated in chunks for transport and then sequentially assembled on site (like a ship in a bottle) the process was precisely mapped and staged.

EXPERIENCE

The experience of the pieces comes through their effectual engagement. The layering of light and shadow; the density of the projected light, funneled light, and cast light; and the translucency and reflectivity of surfaces; aggregate to generate ephemeral visual effects. The installation creates an experience that engages the viewer through the perception of the orchestrated ambient environment. The compositional interplay becomes the experience of light.

conduit tower prefabrication components
plan

model

view through occulus

night view

entry

nterior view at night

apse detail

DENSITY FRAMES

DENSITY FRAMES
USC Religious Center

The Density Frames installation is the iterative cousin of Light Frames. Seeing the original installation, there was a request to reinstall it at the University of Southern California University Religious Center. After examining the small budget available and significant effort required to relocate the structures, it became evident that for the same expenditure, the installation could be iterated and customized to the space. Deploying the same two doppelganger parts: (1) an iterative, variably triangulated structure and (2) a new, transparent (now levitating) inflatable; the configuration and their inter-relationship evolved from the plan based adjacency of Light Frames to a sectionally layered relationship in Density Frames. Stacked and inter-penetrating, the structures negotiate the courtyard of the modernist religious center. Expanding the adjacent glass walled chapel; engaging the exterior ceremonial stair from the lower to upper level; and responding to the scale and nuance of the building's courtyard; Density Frames extended the experiential investigation of light, material, form, and system.

The variably triangulated frame was formed through a combination of structural necessity and site based constraints in dialogue with spatial and effectual goals. As a shallow dome with an ocular void (filled by the penetrating inflatable) the north wall edges the stair and sits on an existing cast-in-place concrete planter wall. Matching the height of the stair landing, the frame folds in the space to create a lattice ceiling that lands on two figurative legs flanking and framing the chapel. The collective table creates a baldacchino form scaling the space and extending the adjacent chapel; and creates a form that serves to catch the deflated drape of the inflatable figure when deactivated.

The levitating inflatable is made of transparent polyethylene plastic. Heat welded joints allow for a clean continuity to the surface and shape. Formed through five arms of transitional tunneling forms, there is an interconnected outer and inner shape. The outer arms align with site constraints referencing historical ecclesiastic architectural forms while circumscribing palimpsest religious symbols into a hybridized figure. The inner shapes serve as projective voids that funnel light, control view, and frame the sky.

A series of faceted benches scatter below the figures. They house the blowers that feed the upper inflatable while providing moments of repose and contemplation. A pressure timer turns on and off the buoyant inflatable shape marking activity and presence in the space.

The collective composition is a dialogue between rigid and fixed against mutable and floating. This conversation emerges from the relative relationship of aspiration and inspiration of physicality versus faith as a basis of religion. The installation becomes a canopy, a chapel, a sculpture, but most importantly an instigator. It is an intervention conceived as an extension of what has always been there unnoticed but now temporarily highlighted and framed.

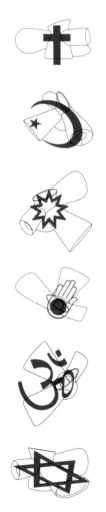

Density Frames

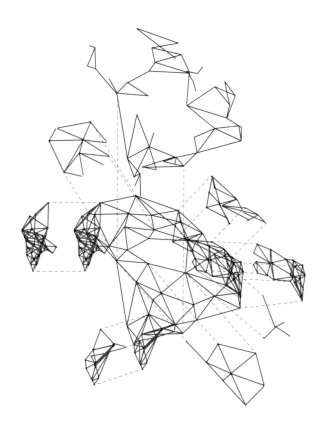

Conduit canopy with reiterated chunks

View from street

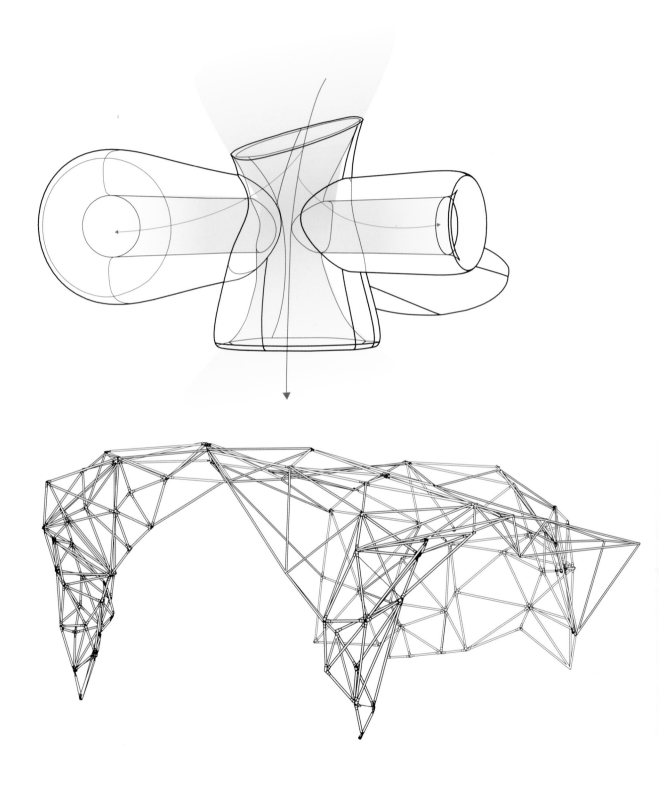

INFLATABLE

CONDUIT

BENCH

NORTH ELEVATION   EAST ELEVATION   SOUTH ELEVATION   WEST ELEVATION

elemental elevations

view from entry to courtyard

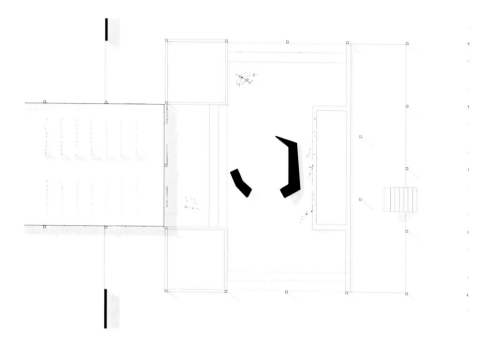

plan

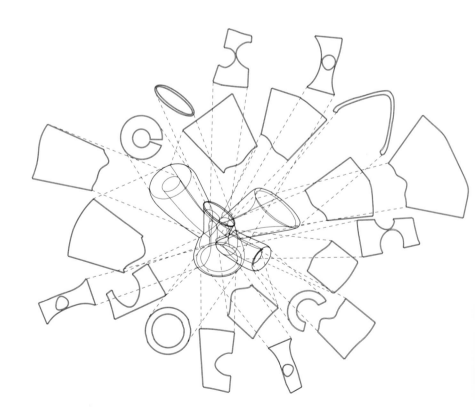

inflatable templates

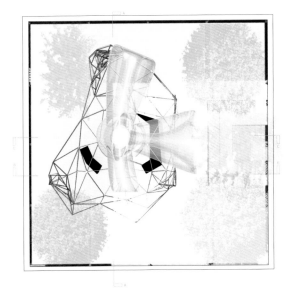

op view

view from chapel

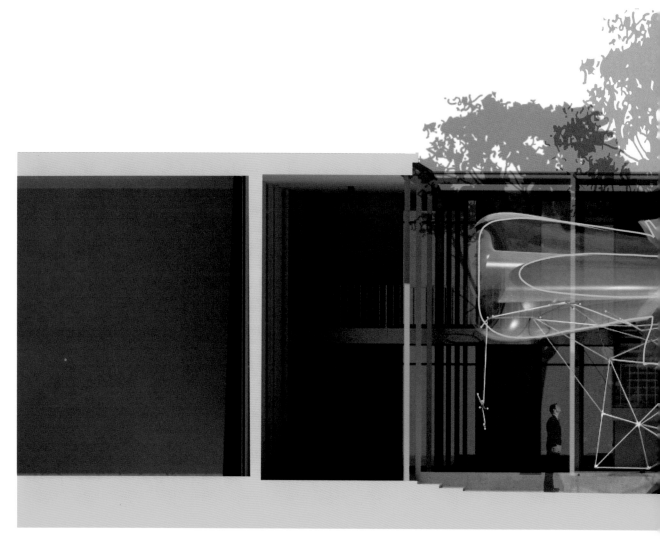

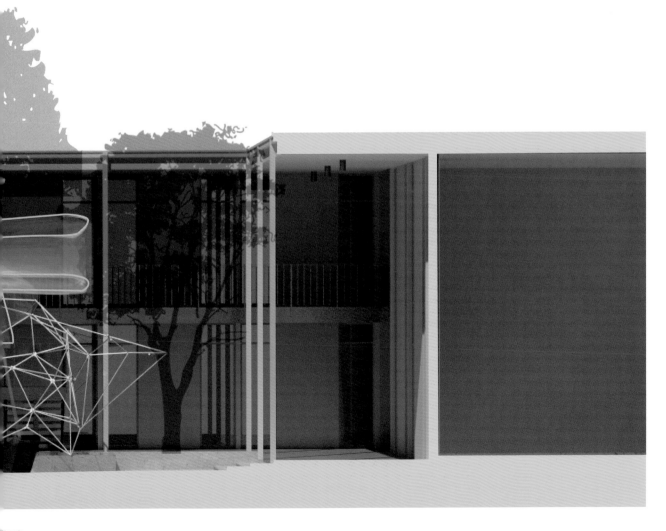

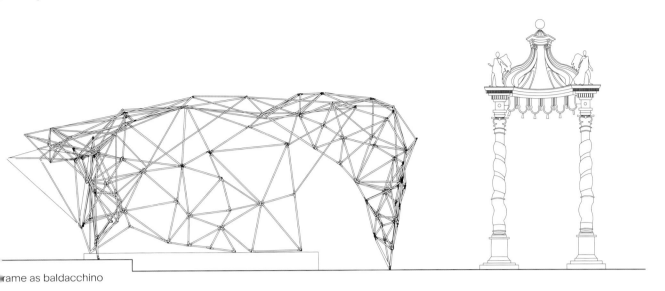

frame as baldacchino

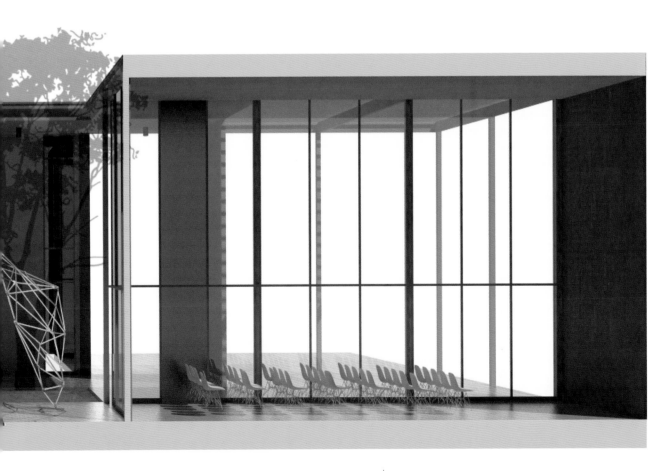

FURLINED

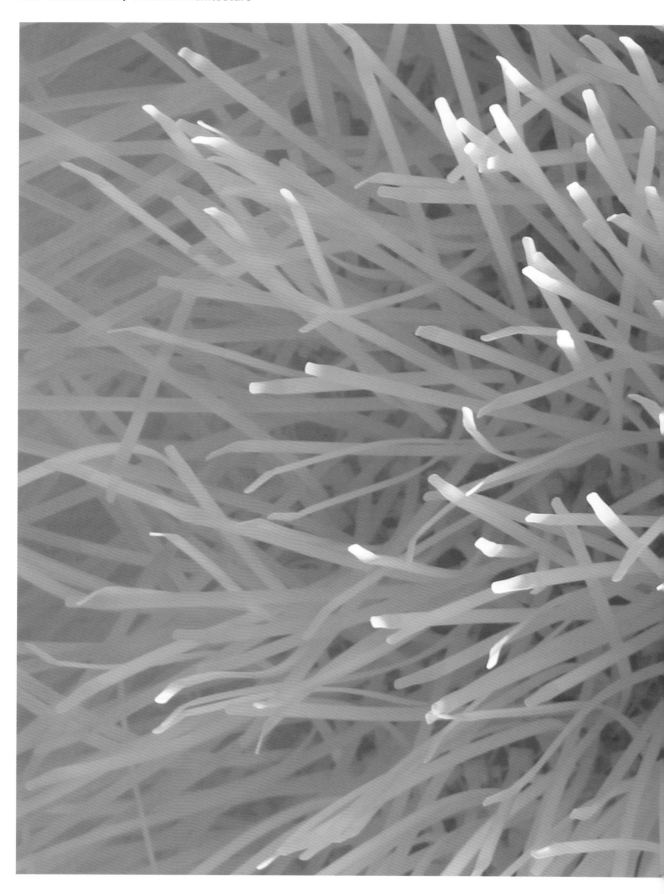

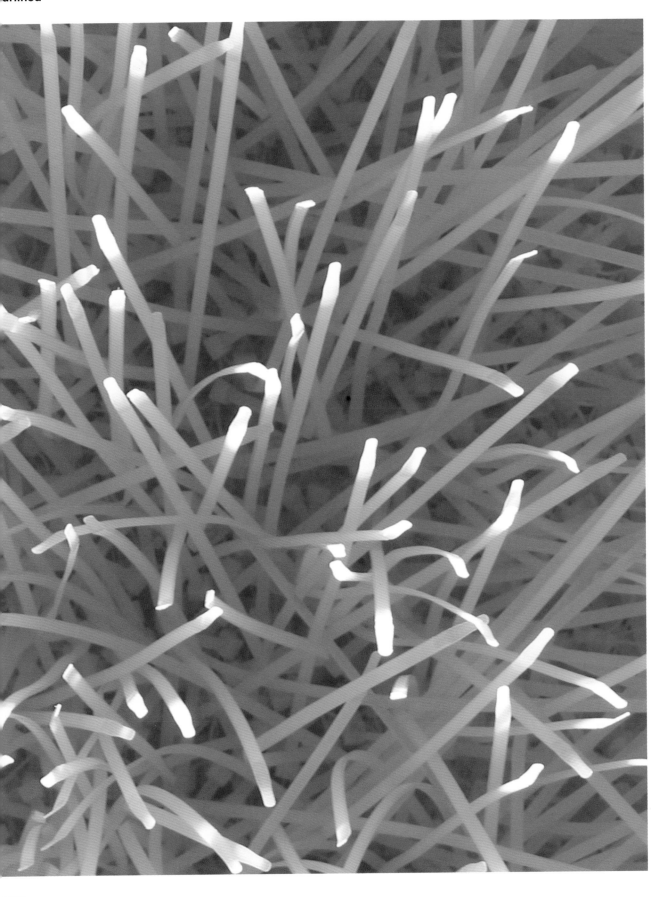

FURLINED
Museum of Contemporary Art [L.A. MOCA]

As a part of the New Sculpturalism show at the Museum of Contemporary Art, Los Angeles, a selection of voices defining the next generation of Los Angeles architecture were identified to design and build an experimental pavilion for the show. Furlined was one of these pavilions.

The legacy of form is derived from the material nature of its tectonics. Fascinated by the fold, artists through the ages have spent time on its form. Michelangelo focused repeatedly on drawings of fabric. They are a way to express feeling through frozen motion without using historicist decoration. In this pavilion, the signature folds of Gian Lorenzo Bernini's flowing drapery in The Ecstasy of St. Theresa inspire the form. They allow for the simulated energy of movement to be applied through representational figuration to harness its abilities in a static form. Through this an abstraction of material and form unite to create an emotive moment.

Building on the postmodernist independence c skin from structure as a disengaged relationshi that is core to Los Angeles architecture, the pavilio accelerates the condition. Three layers, each wit their own material, tectonic logic, and manufacturin technology, engage differentiated skins (inner an outer) blanketing the structural system. Independentl defined and formed components are tasked wit varied experiences. The dialogue between th elements generates a new and dynamic conversa tion. Synthesizing the intention of the fold with th geometry and materiality of pop art, minimalism and geometric abstraction originating in Souther California in the 1960s. The pavilion emerges fron the tectonics of place aligned through this lineage c local architectural thought. Refocused on light an space, the form and material (through their systems become players in a dynamic conversation.

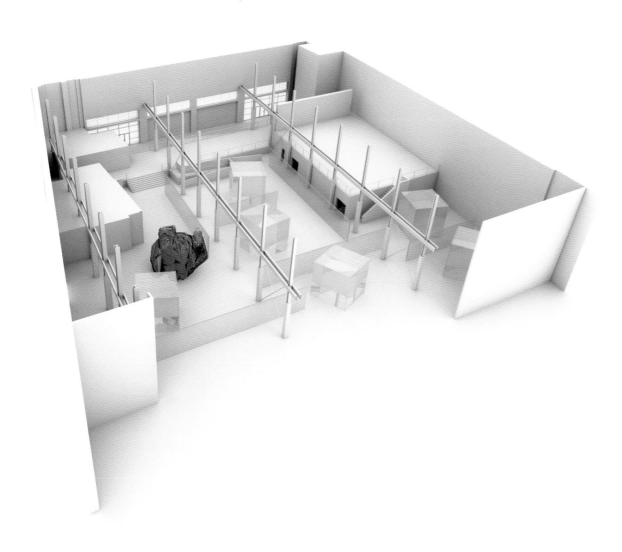

Site | Context

To serve as a foil to the traditions of contemporary art spaces, a series of contrasts are cultivated: [1] white opaque walls are contrasted with transparent colored ones; [2] solid singular surfaces are contrasted with outer layered superimposed skin to central structure to inner lining; [3] illuminated surfaces are contrasted with light emitting forms; [4] orthogonal and quadrilateral are balanced by irregular and triangulated; [5] rigid is contrasted with soft; [6] smooth is contrasted with hairy.

The pavilion is designed to be experienced at a multiplicity of scales and vantages. As the viewer approaches and moves around the pavilion in the X, Y, and Z axes it presents different aspects: an unfolding form, varied levels of detail, and specific experiential effects. From afar, upon approach, adjacent, inside, and upon departure, the understanding and resolution change. In each condition the pavilion enigmatically engages the viewer and evolves in its contextual and material relationships.

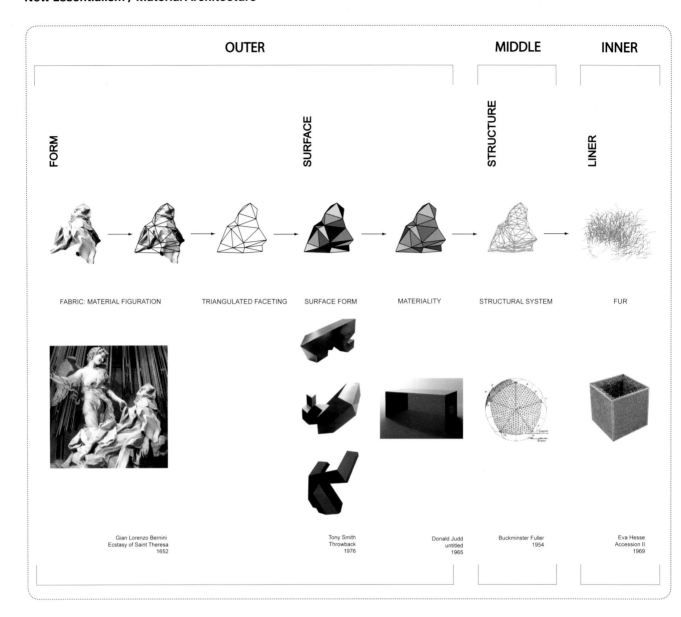

OUTER   MIDDLE   INNER

FORM   SURFACE   STRUCTURE   LINER

FABRIC: MATERIAL FIGURATION   TRIANGULATED FACETING   SURFACE FORM   MATERIALITY   STRUCTURAL SYSTEM   FUR

Gian Lorenzo Bernini
Ecstasy of Saint Theresa
1652

Tony Smith
Throwback
1976

Donald Judd
untitled
1965

Buckminster Fuller
1954

Eva Hesse
Accession II
1969

Evolutionary Thinking

The primary external form evolves from the dynamism of drapery. Physically freezing its motion, the figure translates the sculptural movement of a draped form into a triangulated and faceted network. Dynamically figured but pixelated in its facets, the joints are left open through a recessed panel edge to allow a detachment of panel from panel and highlight the open joint as a graphic line through the resonating colored edge of the Plexiglas.

The structure ghosts and reiterates the outer form, repeating and resonating in line the geometry established by surface. The inner liner emerges from the repetitive rationale of a gridded loop coupled with the dynamic drape and position of the variably extruded and dangling length of the "hair" link. The contrast of the outer figure with the inner texture produces an enigmatic and unexpected world within.

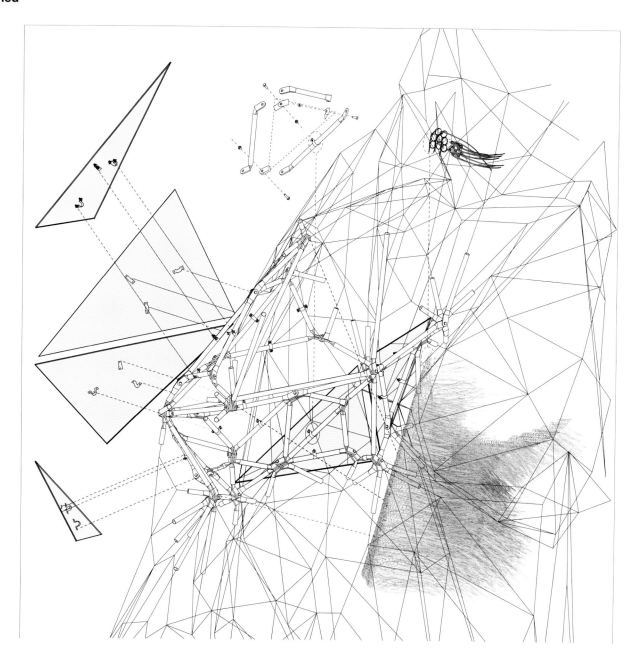

Fabrication | Prefabrication | Assembly

The skin, derived from the supple lines of a curvilinear surface, is faceted and flat milled. CNC milling and heat torching allows for crisp resonating edges and flawless lines in the reflective and transparent Plexiglas. Connected by simple bolting using standard conduit brackets, the three point contact allows a delicate suspension of the transparent surface. Beneath the Plexiglas is a network of optimized structure comprised of a crimped, angled, and bolted conduit frame. Variably triangulated for optimal stability, the galvanized material becomes the skeletal line of networked structure.

The minimal weight and efficient geometry allow for a maximization of strength and stability with optimized presence. Suspended as the inner lining is an artificial fur woven of variable length clear plastic zip ties. The surface embraces the viewer in a furry cocoon varying in thickness and depth. Formed of a backer of 4 inch looped zip ties in parallel succession, these are then linked to their neighbor with zip ties ranging in length from 4 to 14 inches to produce gradients of depth and overlap. The woven pelt creates an artificial fur.

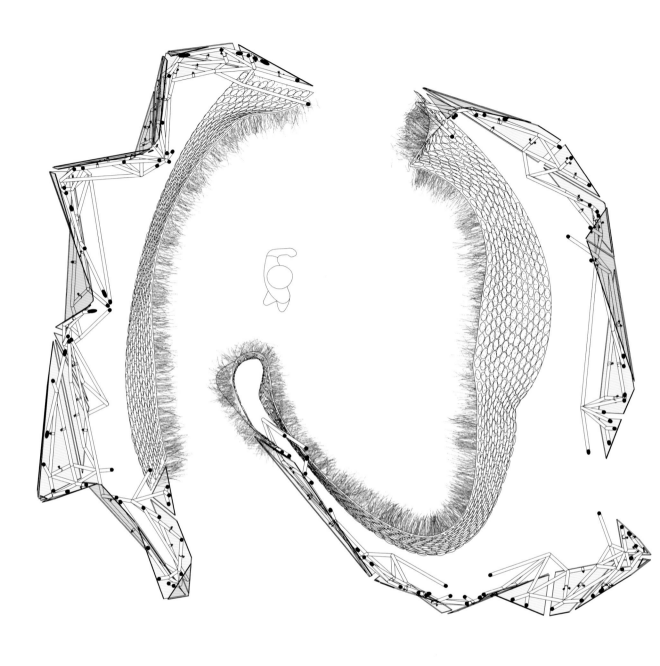

Experience

The pavilion stands as a radiating and hulking figure. A vibrant and lustrous acrylic surface illustrates its precise machined form. A softer inner liner of plastic fur welcomes and invites the viewer in.

Glowing and embracing the dome's fur of plastic hair, the viewer relates to the scale of the unit and piece. The place is made through the material effect.

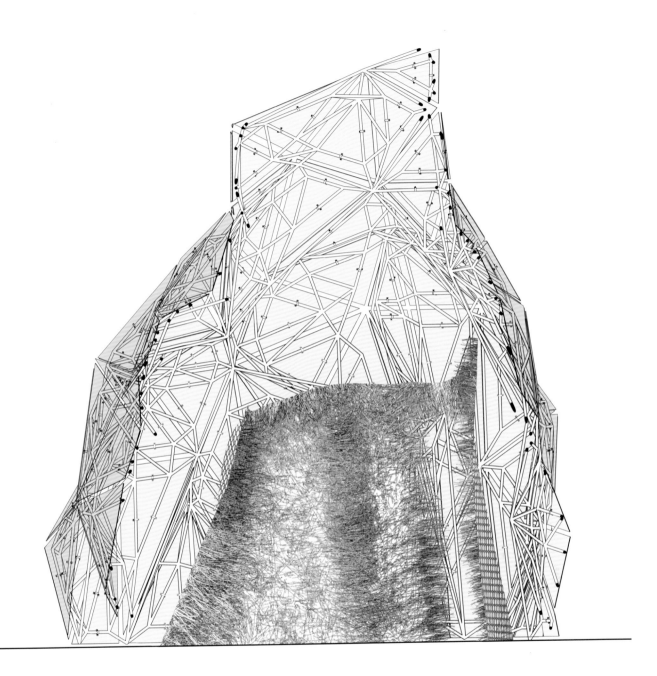

Program

The functional premise of the pavilion is as a reading room. Monographs of the architects featured in the larger exhibit are nestled within the fur lining of the inner skin. Submerged in the depth of the repetitive field the orthogonality of each book is contrasted by its luscious, furry surrounds.

With varied deformations in the surface, the prominence and significance of each architect on the legacy of Los Angeles architecture is depicted through their position and hierarchy in the surface.

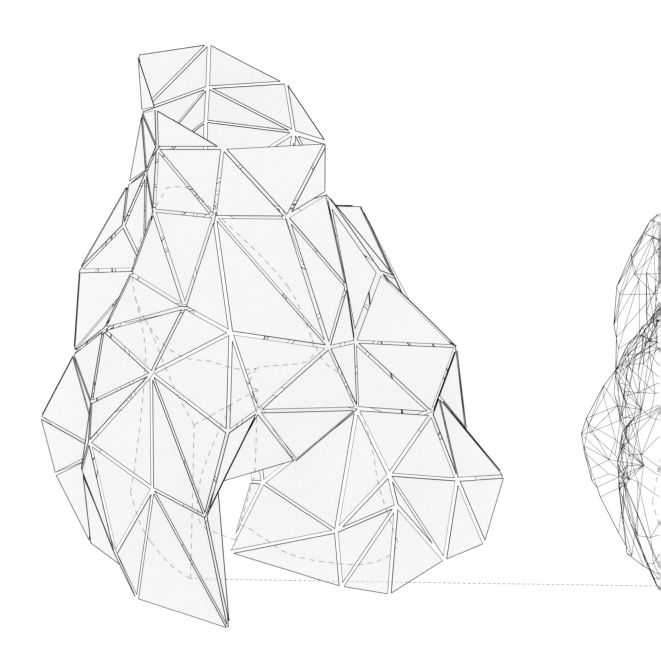

Material Elements

The material palette is three fold: [1] florescent pink acrylic Plexiglas; [2] galvanized one-half inch electrical conduit; and [3] vaiable-length, clear, plastic zip ties. Each forms an independent system with their formal governances interrelating through their layering. Rooted in the exploration of new materials being developed for industrial use in the post-World War II era, the palette extends the legacy of regiona materiality through a re-appropriation of its palette Architecture assumes innovation through adoptio of non-traditional architectural materials.

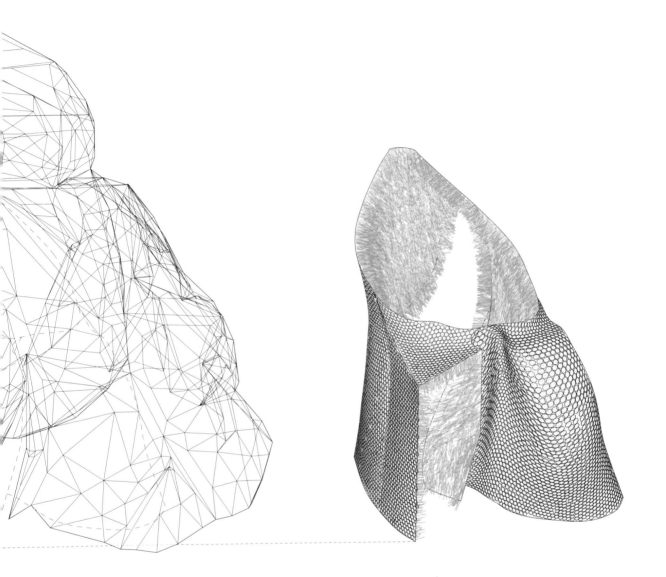

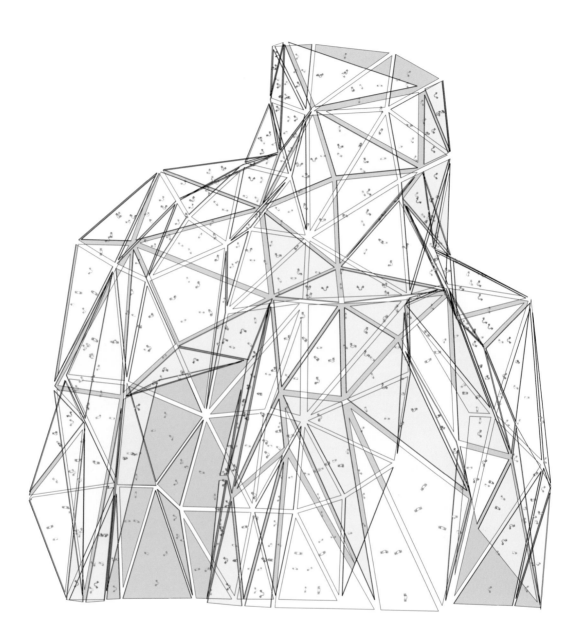

Panels

The neon Plexiglas panels produce a faceted and triangulated veil. Glossy and machined, their color resonates outward and glows inward. The slick, in-organic material references the painted, waxed, and polished surfaces of Southern California automobiles, surfboards, and fiberglass boat hulls.

The prismatic form works in conjunction with the materiality to manifest in a powerful optical emanation

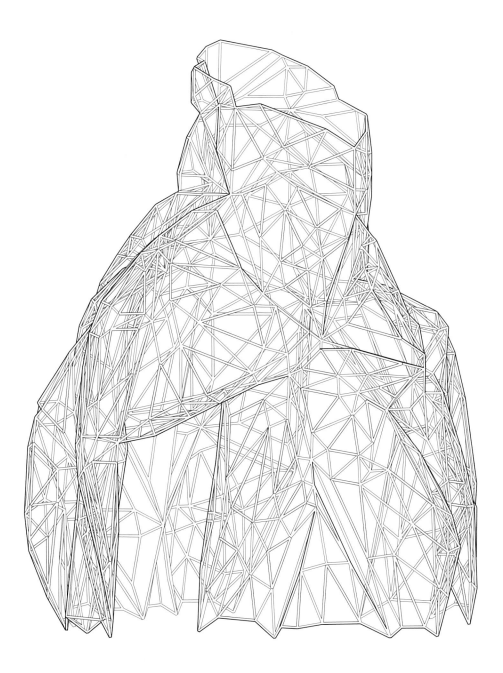

Structure

The structural web is originated in the facet of the surface panels. Translating plane into line, the form reiterates through an offset of the initial surface tri-angulation. This co-planar surface (now defined by line) establishes the point of structural connection. These structural armatures branch backward to create a triangulated web connecting adjacent panels in protruding clusters. When a valley occurs in the form, the density offsets and dives below the surface. The stitching of the chunks is read through the seamed density of the frame. Composed of 1440 bolted pieces, the collective acts like a webbed bloom enveloping the visitor while remaining ghosted by the veil of the inner and outer layers. Made of galvanized electrical conduit with variable triangulated geometries in customized lengths; its reflective surface refracts the light simultaneously creating a density of line through intensity of light and shadow.

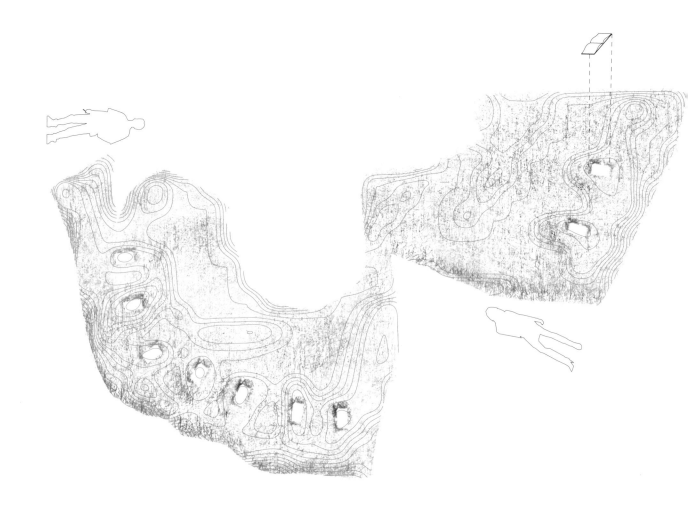

Fur

The inner-most layer is an artificial fur created as a hide of woven zip ties. The surface is from an every-day object, in serial repetition, to produce effectual situations. The zip ties are a woven looping fabric: half cinched circles perpendicularly joining fully cinched zip ties to create the extending field. Varying length ties allow for densities, gradients, and intensities to emerge in the fur depth.

A tactile and enigmatic surface, the open weave allows light to penetrate and reveal the layered construction of the three superimposed layers. The dynamic form allows the visitor to physically engage the architecture, beckoning to be touched, and discover the books that submerge and emerge from its tactile field.

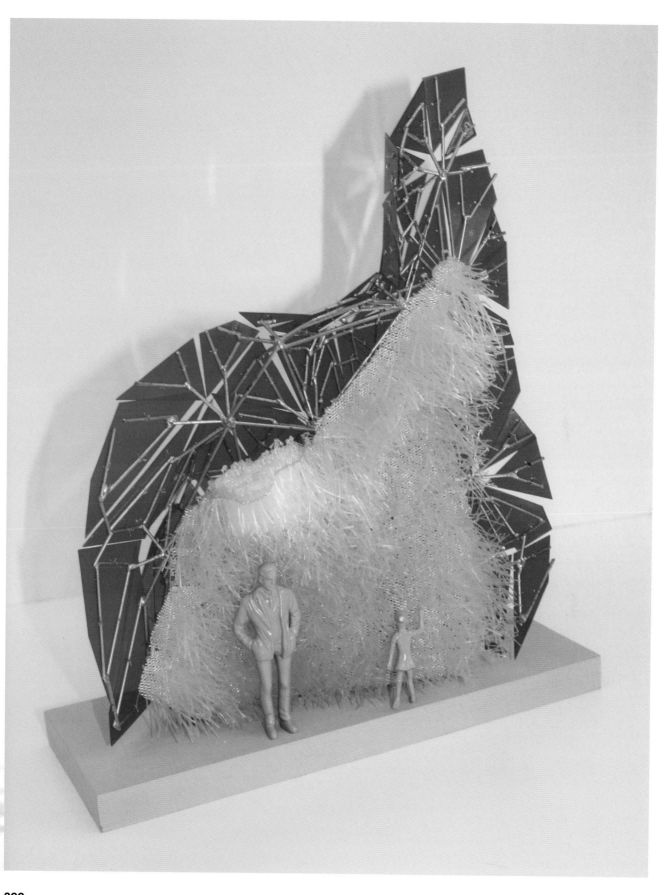

400

POINT — COUNTERPOINT:
Interview

POINT — COUNTERPOINT
Interview

BPG: What is the premise of your architecture?

Gail Peter Borden: Architecture is everything. That is something Lars Lerup (who was the new Dean when I started my architectural education at Rice University) always said. He meant it too with the discourse and pedagogy he pursued. This instilled in me, at the beginning of my architectural education, a fundamentally inclusive method of thinking about architecture and its authority and responsibility and potential. Architecture is not design, it is bigger and Architecture holds the answers to serious problems facing humanity.

BPG: What is the image of the designer for society? Should the primal and individuated vision be made real?

GPB: Fundamentally, I became an architect because I was interested in the creative process but at the scale and resonance of space and building all within the construct of a "profession." The idea that architecture could change the world was always latent. Architecture at any scale is fundamentally a big thing. It takes time and resources and has "some" permanence to it. It also has liability, so everyone involved is serious and focused to make the best thing they can. That means opportunity. I never subscribed to the heroic contrarian like Howard Roark or Frank Lloyd Wright. Those stories are enticing but I am not really interested in the showmanship or brinkmanship that modality requires. I am interested in the work. As far as saving the world, it is our responsibility and it grows into every decision I make as a driving sensibility, but it is also not the sole destination for design. I've always been interested in phenomenology, the experiential aspects of design, right down to the primal way atoms work. I strive for a deeper interest in the poetics of space. This rationale provides more fodder for inspiring the human spirit. This has been with me from the beginning, and only intensified over time.

BPG: What is the role of writing in your architecture?

GPB: In my book *Process*, I present analyses of some of the most important works of architecture from the last century, "unpacking" them through meticulous line drawings and text to reveal the representational and material logics behind them. I look for what's effectual in architecture, how architects use materials and the intentions behind them. As a sweeping journey through architecture, *Process* focuses with analytical precision on buildings more commonly understood through the universalizing wide-angle lens of architectural history and theory. My specific interest lay in the relationship between representation and tectonics; the idea that a drawing could speak towards the craft of construction. That book attempts to build a bridge between the systems of representation (and drawing in particular) and how they can associate with tectonic logics. The goal was to understand the logics of how to draw materiality. *Process* also carries forward the research mission I have been undertaking since I first became interested in issues of materiality. As such it can be seen as part of a body of work reaching back to my experiences in 2004 as an artist in residence at the Chinati Foundation in Marfa, Texas. It was a primal time for me; the landscape, the synthesis of geometry, place, material, and intentionality. Seeing the works of Donald Judd was a moment of clarity. Light is as much a material as concrete. It also goes back to a conference I organized at the USC School of Architecture in 2008, called *Matter*. As stated in the introduction to the related volume I co-edited with Michael Meredith, *Matter: Material Processes in Architectural Production* (2012): the design and application limits of a particular material are no longer seen as inherent within the material itself, but rather as functions of surrounding processes. Because of this, we argue that we find that our nostalgic default material understanding has been fundamentally de-stabilized, thus, we need a new way to conceptualize the status of material in architecture. Architects and architecture are part of mutually interdependent material networks composed of neurons, trees, electricity, finance, et cetera, everything all together. We operate in the context of simultaneous and dynamic forces to which all matter is subject and with which all matter participates, amplifying and mitigating and being amplified or mitigated in turn. In essence, matter *"matters"* and materials in architecture can once again have agency. This positions materiality as a procedural medium in which and through which we work. In other words, design is a manipulative process in which material, or matter, is a key generative participant. This re-assertion of the vital and dynamic role materials play in design as a process is the main premise that underlies *Process* and two other volumes I have written: *Material Precedent: The Typology of Modern Tectonics* (2010) and *Architecture Principia: Architectural Principles of Material Form* (2014) co-authored with Brian Delford Andrews. This book (*New Essentialism*) is a different approach. It is expansive as a manifesto; analytical through historical thresholds; and then cataloging demonstrative projects that present a vision and methodology.

BPG: Speak about materiality?

GPB: Materials have always interested me. How things work and are made and how assemblies can be expressive of the part in the whole. As a child I was very involved in making; from model kits to construction projects. I used to rearrange the furniture in my room two or three times a week. I would do it without my parents knowing, sliding things, and moving art, carpets, et cetera. They would come to my room and it would all be different. This provided me with programmatic analysis, iterative design and the opportunity to engage a space through repetitive design. Materials developed early on in my architectural education. In addition to architecture I simultaneously pursued a degree in fine arts. Making on all levels was of great interest. I started as a sculptor (welding, casting, milling) and though ended more in painting, was always interested in the object, how it was made and the relationship of this physical nature to the final effectual result. In architecture the inspiration of material spoke a lot towards form and provided a unique opportunity for expressionism innate to the process of building. As an academic, it emerged as a connective tissue that allows for the theoretical, intellectual, and methodological but also connects with practice. The conversation with architects can always find commonality in the tools and techniques of how we make. This essentialism, in combination with my more pragmatic personality linked in my process an interest in how things should be formed or articulated. I have a deep connection to what things are made of. Architecture for me is about the celebration of inevitabilities and embracing the true nature of materials. As things, their opportunity is in their very being. Materials are a beginning and an end and thus have tremendous opportunity.

BPG: What's the basis of your practice?

GPB: Practice has always been an aspiration and primary goal. When I became an architect, the hope was always to have enough opportunities to keep busy and engaged. When I graduated, the next day I think I hung out my shingle. I was not licensed at the time so could not call myself an architect so instead used Borden Partnership as a philosophical and inclusive name knowing that good design emerges out of the collaboration of a community of design professionals, material manufacturers, builders, makers, users, and client. It really takes all of these things firing in collaboration with one another to realize a project well. Built work is where ideas are tested. I use unbuilt work as an essential tool to investigate architectural thinking and interrogate the principles of what architecture should be independent of the pragmatic realities and specifications of a client-driven, need-based project. These works need to be challenged. They need to be made. Only through this process of idea becoming manifest can the touchstones of architecture be engaged. Space and the experience of material driven environments in light are where the architect composes uniquely. I frequently operate in the realm of fine arts where the drawing or the object are the final destination of an idea. I have no fear or animosity of this condition, but the ability to manifest beyond (into the installation and even more permanently into architecture) this is another level of transcendence. So few projects get there. Even good architects do lots of work that cannot make it there. I am trying with every project for this. To create something that is so powerful that the use and the pragmatics are sidelined to just being there. This is hard to achieve. Kahn achieved it with regularity, but there are alternate methods of getting there that interest me and build on his vision. I think we got there in the Tower House, but even then, the budget and scope was so limited. This little addition with so many constraints on the existing was saddled and handcuffed, but it is a space that changes and resonates differently daily and this provides hope that the conceptual organization alongside the formal composition and material articulation provide a regularizing but unique experiential opportunity. This is the hope for practice and the optimism that one must enter every project with. This same optimism however has proven that not every project has the opportunity you hope it might. That's what makes architecture hard, on so many levels, also what makes it exciting. My practice takes on different modes concurrently: compositional studies, furniture, books, installations, and commissions. I have particularly focused on the single family house as a basic building block and serial experimental type. In the last 3-4 years I have taken on two dozen of these (none of which are included here for space and timing... that will be the next book) in different scales and

budgets and scopes. Many are more pragmatically and service driven but each represents an opportunity to develop and learn and test. Practice is that: practice. It needs a lot of serial building to get the skills and experience to know which battles to fight and have a collection of details that are explorations, yet pragmatic articulations.

BPG: What is your relationship to academia?

GPB: Academia is both an arena in which you can engage the touchstones of architecture through a constant replenishment of the overarching aspirations of architecture; but also a place to affect the built environment. Like a farmer cultivating seeds, the ability to make more than you build by fertilizing the profession with fleets and waves of iterative thinkers is a potent and powerful opportunity and ultimately responsibility. This desire to better the world through built form is what I believe in and where and how I think we need to operate to advance humanity. Architecture is a powerful and critical tool and modality in creative production. Humanity is faced with serious challenges that only architecture can respond to. It takes a collective. Academia provides the forum and mechanism. At times I feel guilt and sadness that I am actively creating generations that have to fight and convince and toil for change, but then I am assured that they are endowed with the greatest opportunity to engage themselves through changing the world. Their mission is not easy (it comes back to how hard architecture is) but it is essential and there is little more that one can hope for in this world: purpose, need, requiring creative innovation and vision towards the advancement of humanity. That is powerful stuff. The old saying: "teach a man to fish. ... " My hope is to have even more impact than just being a prolific builder through instigating and affecting waves of prolific builders. The change is upon us, perhaps perpetually.

BPG: Talk about tools and computation specifically.

GPB: Computation is an amazing development in tools. I was educated in a pre-digital era and a post digital era. I have experience (and I like to think prowess) on both sides. I do not feel indebted to it, which is a new modality that current generations get so baptized in that their process becomes overly intertwined and sometimes off kilter as a result. The tools themselves offer tremendous opportunity for precision, efficiency, complexity, and integration with fabrication. It is not really something you can chose to engage it is just a defacto participant, but I am not interested in it as a generator. The idea of coding a building or using formal tricks of the software to make spaces for people does not interest me. The distance from the body, the experience, the material, the light, the use, et cetera, is just too far. It actually interferes, so though I am often enticed to build elaborate formal models, generate photo-realistic renders, animations, scripts, and interactive software to deeply engage the data, tools, robots, and machines for three-dimensionally realizing complex things, but I have to focus my time and become an innovative user not an inventor in those categories as they move away from buildings and architecture. I want to make the objects and have to thus temper my interest in the tools to avoid them becoming a destination in their own right.

BPG: How do you insert and position your work within architecture?

GPB: The premise of this book is to look back and identify origins of the now and project forward the principle methods of thinking for the future. This is cataloged in these five methodologies and modalities of working. They present collectively an analysis of where things have come from, where they are heading, what I believe is the conceptual path forward, and provide a demonstration through creative production of possible outcomes. The future is thus represented in the holistic process and thinking to draw out a possible path for architecture. It is still just a beginning.

BPG: Describe your creative process.

GPB: I am inspired by a lot of things. Materials come with associative opportunities. They speak towards tools and methods of engagement, but I am also interested in typologies: house types, furniture types, et cetera. Typically my design inquiries come out of the combination of these two: a specific opportunity to engage a type and then its articulation emerges out of a material that projects a logic and process of working that develops a form and response. The differentiation occurs when one of the two (typology or material process) comes first and instigates the inquiry. There is also always a desire to work in series. Early on in my painting, I adopted a method of always working on a minimum of three canvases at a time. It created a dialogue between the works but also allowed for movement if one piece was either stalled or too wet to work into, I could continue and respond in another. During my last residency at the MacDowell Colony I took on an even more exaggerated version of this with a half dozen tables, stations, and media. One collage, one drafting, one computation, one a chronological narrative, one triangulated facet surfaces, et cetera. This collective series of methods allowed for a multiplicity of engagements. Within a media I am also interested in series as each medium provides a technique and it takes iteration to engage the potentials. At each table there were then multiple stations. The exploitation of the technique allows for familial investigations. The families have a presence even if not together. This method applies to objects, drawings, theoretical work, books, and commissioned projects. They are collectively a spectrum of opportunities.

BPG: What are your influences and their significance?

GPB: There are myriad influences from modernism to minimal art; powerful and iconic natural landscapes that resonate as contrasting environments; material palettes of varied qualities; furniture and object design; geometry; Architects like Le Corbusier, Mies van der Rohe, and Louis Kahn, as well as contemporaries like Peter Zumthor and John Pawson; but also artists like Donald Judd, Richard Serra, James Turrell, Robert Irwin, Agnes Martin, and then also the cleverness of Nendo and others. They each represent something different but I think they collectively are endowed with a minimal quality (deploying minimal means for maximal effect) and the idea of systemic logics (rule based rationales that provide a differentiation through deployment). These rigors engage an opportunity that is truly pure in logic and result.

BPG: Materiality is a consistent theme in your work and writing. Can you talk about its origins and how you came to this?

GPB: For me materiality is very different from materials. Materials are technical and actual. They engage the realities of physics and the techniques and trades of tradition and best practices. Materials are tools and assemblies and construction in all of its capacities. Materiality is also these but it adds the effectual. It brings the aspirational, the experiential, the perceptual, and the emotive. This is the design of architecture. The construction of a mood and an environment through the physical things that we build out of. This collective collaboration provides for materiality to be an active participant as a facilitating system.

BPG: Talk about your interest in the sensorial?

GPB: The sensorial is really where we are able to engage our physical selves with the constructed world. I think this territory engages me because it is centered in that liminal state between fine arts and architecture. It engages the individual through their senses to be able to experience and personally reconcile a relationship of the inner-self with a physical object. It is the root of realized/built architecture to impact that which we feel. Thus the sensorial has myriad ways of being expressed, but fundamentally is *the* highest aspiration. Now the next immediate question becomes what type of experience do you want to facilitate? How do you curate what elements you use to construct a mood or an environment? A light condition? A sequence? A narrative through the architecture? The answer to these is design. A coupling question is if experience can exist independently of architecture? Yes, experience exists in everything we do; that is why we have bad experiences, that is why we have interfaces all the time that are engaging with the world and other people yet we don't recognize or notice them. The problem with these experiences is that they are not considered. They are not curated. They are not aspirational. They are not intentional. As a result they are also not liberating. There is no ability for those experiences to enlighten us; to be poetic. That poetry, that curation and consideration, this is where we find architecture. The difference between sound and music is the difference between objects in the everyday experience and the sensorial in architecture. This is where we are able to enlighten the human spirit, to affect the trajectory of the actions that we undertake on a daily basis through our constructed environments. That is the noblest cause that one can hope for in making something. The sensorial is at the root of this.

BPG: Does that mean picturesque?

GPB: Picturesque is something different entirely to me. It is related through the idea that you can compose and through this composition instill an idyllic and even romantic ideal about what the perceptual environment can provide, but the picturesque at the same time holds it small because I think it is quagmired in 18th-century ideals of a romantic or even nostalgic sensibility of shared beauty. This brings us into a much more complicated conversation about "what beauty is"? about how we perceive and evaluate things and if aesthetics is even a necessary echanism by which to discuss architecture. There a moment in the personalization, a transition into evaluative structure, as to whether or not something is "good" or "bad." This is not really necessary errain for architecture to engage. Instead it should mply be confronting ideas about how and what the opportunities for experience can be and how those xperiences can differentiate themselves and enghten the occupant overtly or covertly. So to answer he question more directly there is something about he terminology of the picturesque that holds the opportunities for experience small. The underlying ensibility is very powerful terrain.

PG: With materials comes a discourse about tools and ltimately process. Can you describe this?

GPB: Yes. I think this association is at the remise of what I believe is the opportunity and he personal interest in what materials are in the esign process. Every material has a mastering set f physical qualities. As a result it can be worked: ut, bent, joined, et cetera with different but specific ensibilities that are derivative of the tools by which hat material can be worked. Thus the tool becomes n imprint upon the material, and the action of the ol becomes the process by which you engage the aterial. The combination of the three: [1] tool, [2] rocess (or technique), and [3] material, becomes directly generative driver of form. The form as this anifestation of the material is then perceived and ead through all of these previous steps. Material process, through a tool, into a form governs the xperience. Thus the designer's greatest opportunity to insert themselves as far upstream as possible all of these conversations to provide for both an pportunity to manipulate the resultant but also collaborate with the intrinsic systems as to how omething can be and should be worked. What is teresting about this is that there is an intrinsic morality the process that emerges from the specific things e make and how we make them. This relationship thus critical in the dialogue and transition from an dea to form. It is architecture.

PG: Does materials mean tectonics? The physical ssembly of parts? Seems like your time in Renzo Pino's office may have been influential in this capacity?

GPB: Though linked, materials and tectonics are fundamentally different things. They share a ensibility as materials are the raw matter from which e make things and tectonics is the methodology y which we join part to part to create a language. hus matter and materials require tectonics, and ectonics require materials and matter, but they ave fundamentally different underpinnings. Teconics and the expression of the way in which we nake collective composition out of individuated arts (something intrinsic to all architecture as it is evitably componental construction) is something hat definitively resonates in the work of Renzo Piano. My time in his office was a submersion into such a ensibility both in his work done to date as well as projects that I was active in producing. There was owever a dissonance that existed between this nethod and compositional technique and what I hought architecture could and should be. Materials offer something more, something spiritual, and omething unique. The celebration of the beauty of he actual is a dynamic thing. The sensibility of the

material resonates with me as a way in which one can articulate logic and a methodology of making through the assembly of diverse pieces. On some levels this is what architecture is about. To make something big, it needs to be assembled out of smaller parts and thus the parts we choose (our materials) and the way we assemble (the tectonics) unify in this collective composition to create the ultimate form that becomes space and building. This language of assembly is latently expressed in the final product no matter how much we try to subordinate it. To celebrate it through collaboration with it as a premise for the making of architecture is an opportunity. The rationale of this logic is where the systemic understanding of part to whole can create a collective composition.

BPG: Beyond materials there is also a strong interest in precedent and history, can you describe this?

GPB: As architects we are always generating and what we currently make is read relative to what we have made in the past. Thus whatever we produce now is a step in the lineage of what has come before. Understanding history is critical. It endows us with a body of knowledge and gives us a framework against which to move forward. History is a language and the syntax and context in which we operate. For me it is interesting to see how others approach and perceive the different stages of historical and technological knowledge. The evolution over time of what architecture can be and has been establishes a ladder that is evolutionary and clearly derivative of the sequence of development and its past. My interest in looking at history is finding these moments and thresholds in which innovation and transformative shifts have occurred. I am not particularly interested in any direct historical documentation of the past in my work but rather an analytical look at that which is come before as a creative designer to understand how we can feed and inform movement forward. This is why my books are founded in analytical drawings. I am trying to understand and unpack and pro-actively represent significant moments in historical production that resonate into a new sensibility of what architectural material reading can be. To look backward allows us to look forward. To understand the past allows us to envision the future.

BPG: The role of typology plays into this?

GPB: Typology builds on the idea of precedent, but narrows it down through the lens of a specific building function. It represents a purity of thinking that has evolved within a distinct legacy. It demonstrates discrete and differential ways of engaging organizational tactics, conceptual tactics, and formal tactics in precise ways to iterate diverse outcomes. Typology demonstrates through the nature of its lineage a series of things that resonate with me: multiplicity and iteration of the specific compositional form of a functional type; it privileges and illuminates precedent through the story of history and previous models as springboards to develop a language against which you respond; and it suggests that you have a family of discourse to which architecture must join and respond. These three together make typology an incredibly interesting legacy in which to operate. I think it's also important simply from the vantage of being disciplinarily proficient (i.e. being aware of diverse types and being able to recognize those types as pristine models that differentiate from one another under very specific constraints and rationales) to provide for the ability to operate relative to those. I don't think it implies a subscription or simply a selective catalog of preordained answers but rather provides a context and a legacy of thought in which an architect should be schooled and then be able to respond with their own design decision adopting, building on, or contradicting type.

BPG: How about the significance of vernacular and the surrounding buildings of a specific site?

GPB: Vernacular again is another iteration of precedent. There are vernacular typologies. There are also vernacular principles that have emerged out of material and construction techniques, cultural preferences, historical evolutions, and a broad variety of influences. What's important about vernacular that there is a purity and the rationale that has evolved over time, emerging out of a precise relationship with a place, and has manifest itself in iconographic and ultimately formal results that are discretely architectural. As a result, this provides a specific dialect within architectural language that is tailored to place and has a sensibility that is linked with the locale from a rational legacy of iterative historical approaches. That is a powerful thing. I think it has to become a place of departure and understanding. It represents the things that an architect would begin to respond to in some capacity either through a resonance or an amplification of what's there, or an overt contradiction to what's been done for a very purposeful rationale. I think collectively the trifecta of: precedent (which really is simply looking at historical models of all genres) in combination with typology (which now focuses on a specific functional legacy that might transpose across diverse locations, construction types, and cultural milieus) and then finally vernacular (which emerges out of a very specific association with place and culture and construction); these three together are important vantages to begin to understand a project. These, in collaboration with touchstones like function (program); or site (which sets a very specific context and nature of where something will be); and ultimately material (what that thing will be made out of); the collective is a powerful conversation and historical condition into which one is inserting and operating. These things together are the responsibility and power of an architectural education and I think represent the necessity of what we have to endow generations of designers with as tools and approaches. To come from this vantage, armed with this body of knowledge, and responsive with a creative lens; architects become indispensable visionaries for the future.

BPG: That's a really good place to stop ... or start.

DYNAMICS
COMPOSITE VIEWS
REFERENCE
REPRESENTATION
PROSPECT
CONNECTIVE TISSUE
ORGANIZATION
UNFOLDING EVENTS OVER TIME
STAGING
BUNKER
OBSTACLE
RECREATIONAL
PRIVATIZED
COEXISTING
BYPRODUCT
PRESERVATION
SUSTAINABLE
ACTIVITY
APPROPRIATION
TIME
USE
SAFETY
WEAVE
ROLE
BODY
AESTHETIC
CONVENTIONAL USAGE
INVENTORY
ELEMENTS
SHARE
RUIN
OBSTACLE
INFRASTRUCTURE
FENCE
LINE
LOOKING
SURROUNDING
TRANSITION
DISCOVERY

SELECT ADDITIONAL WORKS

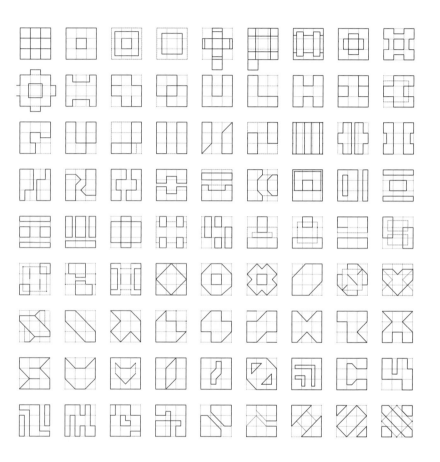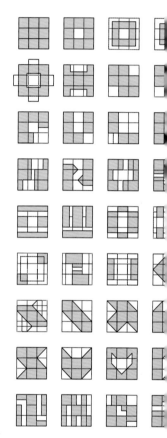

9 Square Houses
2017

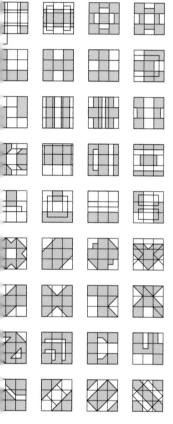

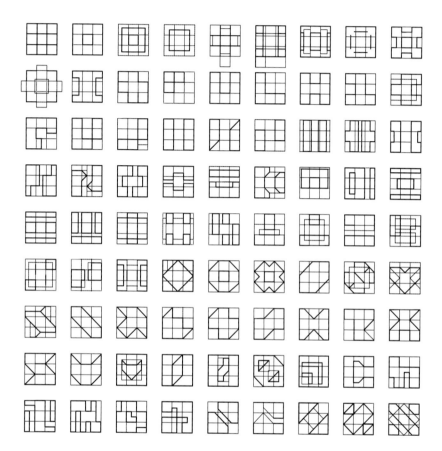

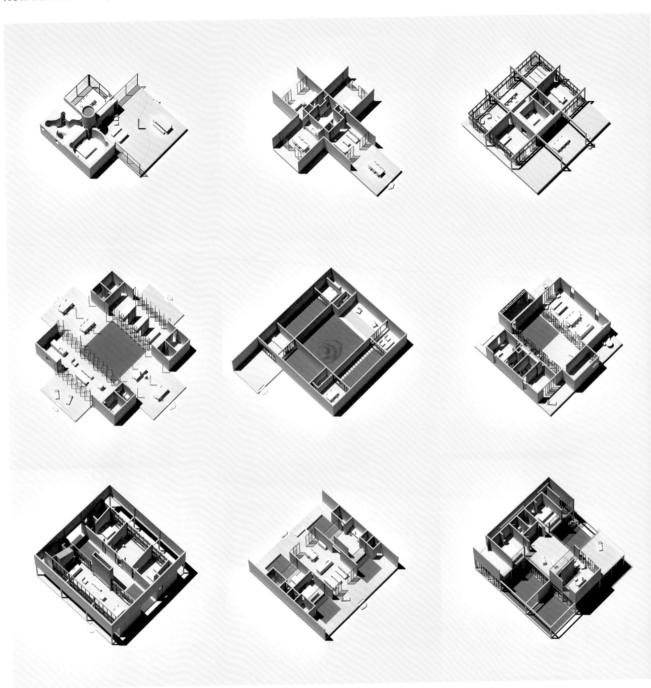

New Essentialism / Material Architecture

House La Jolla 2
Los Angeles, California
2015-2017

exhibition design
Dalllas Art Fair
Dallas, Texas
2015

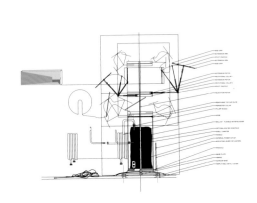
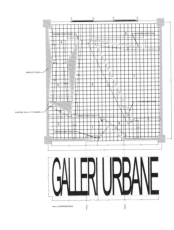

wedding chapel
Jade Mountain,
China
2015

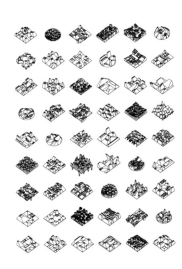

Select Additional Works

stump stool series
2015

triangulated table
Los Angeles, California
2015

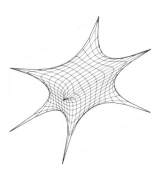

House La Jolla
Los Angeles, California
2014-2015

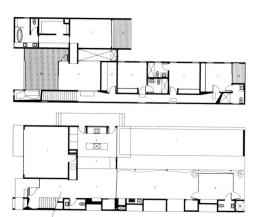
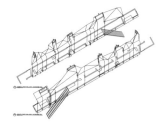

New Essentialism / Material Architecture

perspectival frames
2015

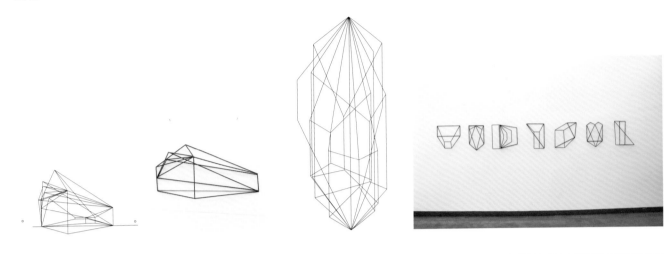

House K
Los Angeles, California
2014-2016

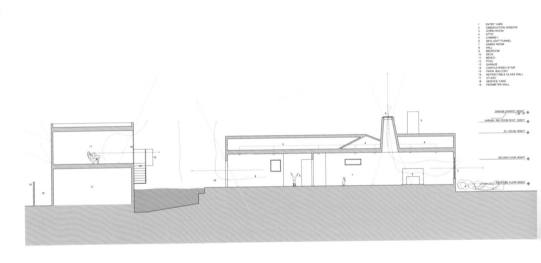

Palm Springs Sisters
Palm Springs, California
2014-2016

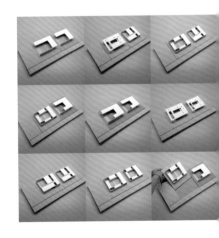

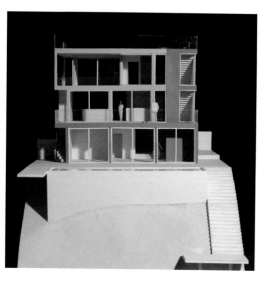

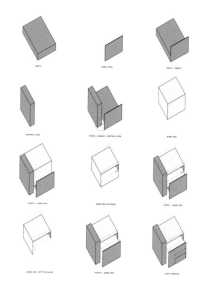

2626 Creston
Hollywood, California
2013

charter high school
Los Angeles, California
2013

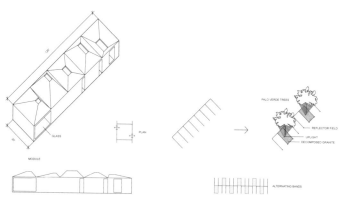

villa [x3]
Jinhai Lake, China
2013

906 Wellesley
Brentwood, California
2013-2014

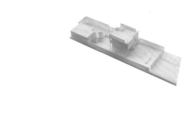

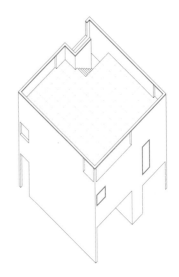

House M
Hollywood, California
2013-2014

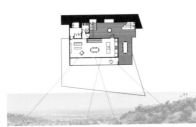

House 79
Los Angeles, California
2013-2015

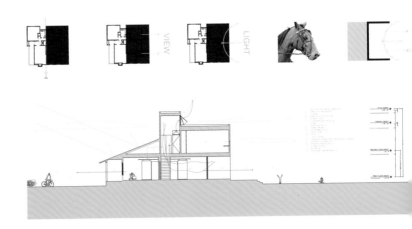

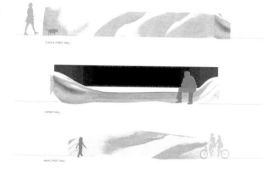

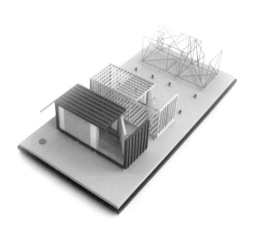

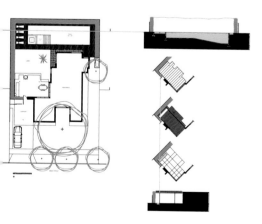

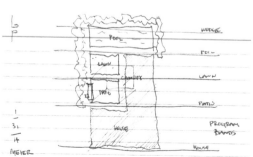

House N
Los Angeles, California
2012-2015

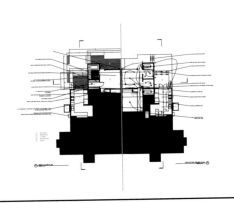
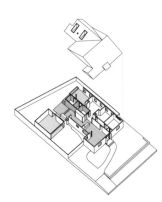
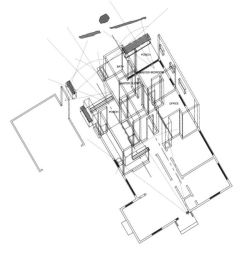

future lunch party
Warner Center, Woodland Hills, California
2011

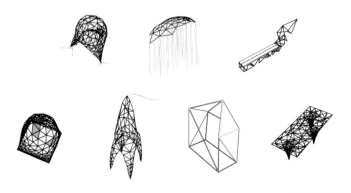
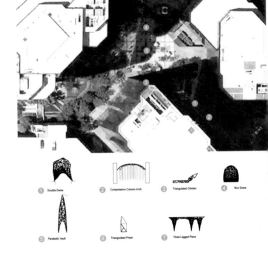

MacDowell Colony Artist Studio
Peterborough, New Hampshire
2011

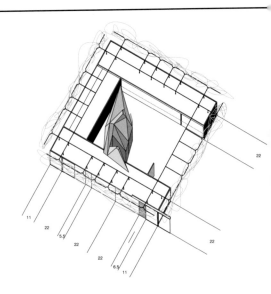

L.A> Tower: vertical campus
Los Angeles, California
2010

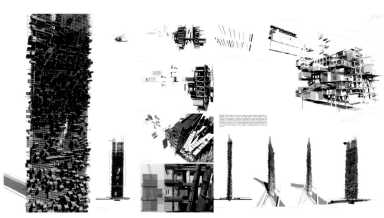

Air Force Village Chapel
San Antonio, Texas
2010

USC DATAshop
USC School of Architecture
Los Angeles, California
2010

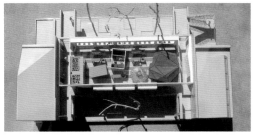

chair bookcase, bookcase chair
plywood chair
2010

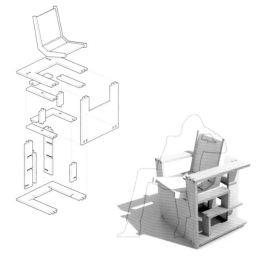

rider field
Raleigh, North Carolina
2009

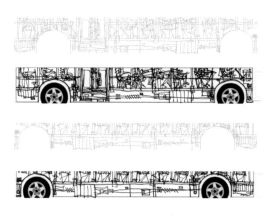

sun shelter
Phoenix, Arizona
2009

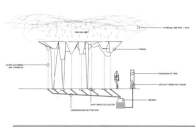
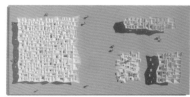

TOGS
(Temporary Outdoor Gallery Space)
Austin, Texas
2008

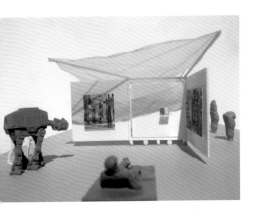
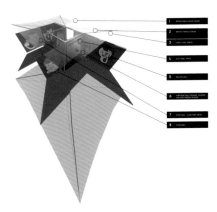

L.A. Liner
Hollywood Boulevard
Los Angeles, California
2008

99K House
Houston, Texas
2008

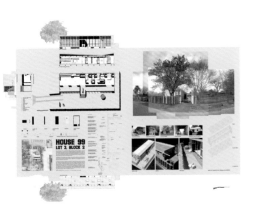

Qingyang Lvshou Park
Chengdu City
Sichuan Province
China
2008-2010

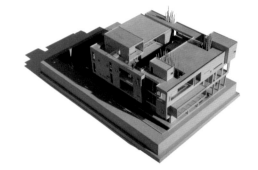

city hall art project
City of Delray Beach,
Florida
2008

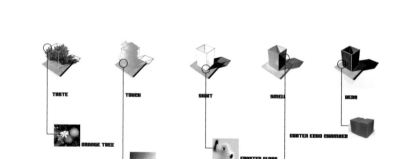

L.A. MARKINGS
rail
Los Angeles, California
2006

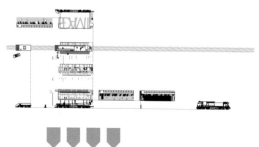

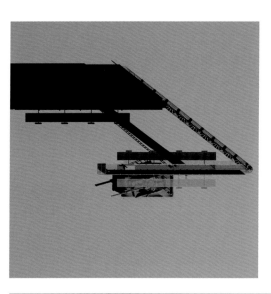

L.A. MARKINGS
billboard
Los Angeles, California
2006

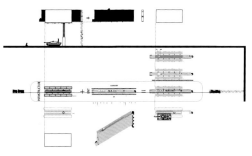

L.A. MARKINGS
lifeguard
Los Angeles, California
2006

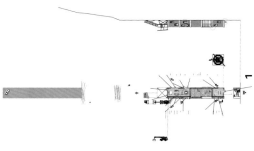

L.A. MARKINGS
powerline
Los Angeles, California
2006

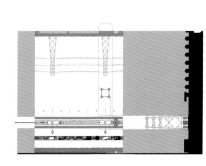

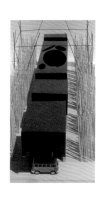

Stockholm Public Library Addition
Stockholm, Sweden
2006

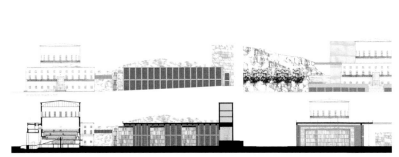
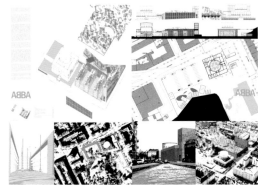

Low Country Line House
Gordon County, Georgia
2007

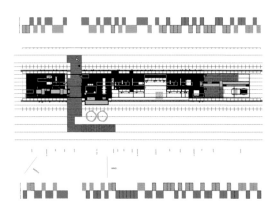

Morton Family Foundation
Western Center for American Studies
Grand Tetons, Idaho - Montana
2005

Select Additional Works

OP1 - Loop House
Oak Park, Raleigh, North Carolina
Hometta
2005

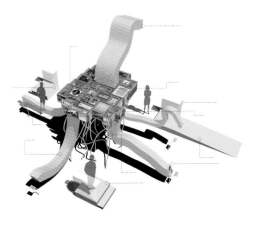

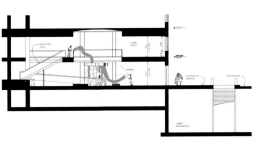

IN[formational] FA[cilitator]
Monument to the First Amendment
Chicago Tribune Building
Chicago, Illinois
2004

LANDed *BLUR*
Philbrook Museum
Tulsa, Oklahoma
2004

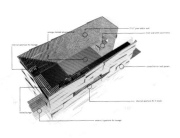

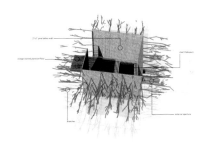

pedestrian bridge
Seaside, Florida
2002

Rubber-Banded House
Raleigh, North Carolina
2002

 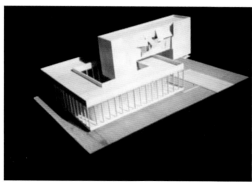 

Anywhere House
urban
Atlanta, Georgia
2000

  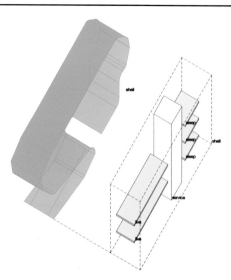

Anywhere House
suburban
Houston, Texas
2000

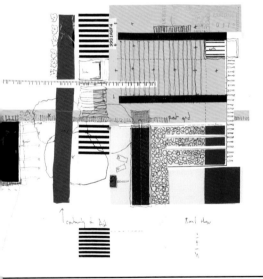

Anywhere House
rural
Fluvanna, Virginia
2000

farm for a gentleman
Fluvanna, Virginia
1998

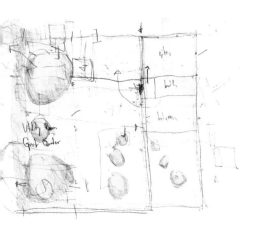

faceted figure
(from series)
2010

perspectival figure
(from series)
2010

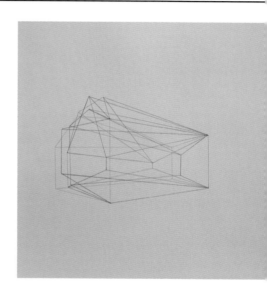

triangulated figure
(from series)
2010

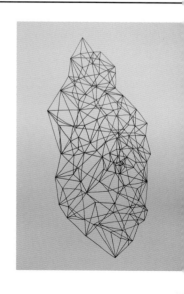

Select Additional Works: drawing

faceted figure
(from series)
2010

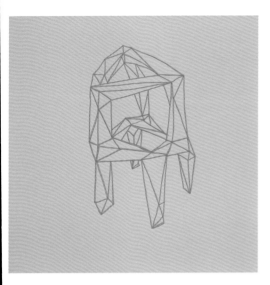

collage figures
(from series)
2010

triangulated figure
(from series)
2010

shallow spaces
2016

shallow spaces
2016

shallow spaces
2016

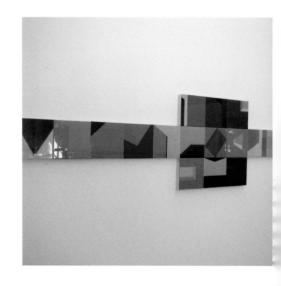

shallow spaces
2016

shallow spaces
2016

shallow spaces
column
2015

faceted figures
2016

totems
2015

wall boxes
2015

robot
2011

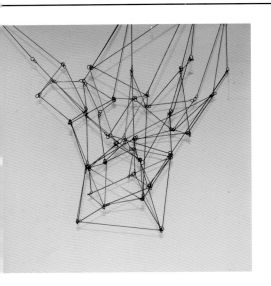

stool series
2013 and 2016

stool
2013

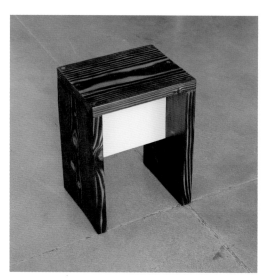 

stool
2013

 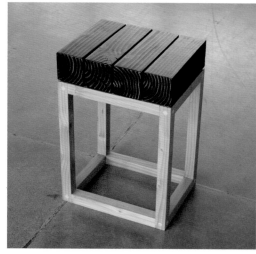

coffee table
2013

sorting table
2013

trellis
2015

ENDNOTES

ENDNOTES

1 Strickland, Edward. *Minimalism: Origins*. Indiana University Press, 2000.

2 Ibid.

3 Ibid.

4 Ibid.

5 Ibid.

6 David Burluik on John Graham's exhibition at the Dudensing Gallery.

7 Strickland, Edward. *Minimalism: Origins*. Indiana University Press, 2000.

8 Ibid.

9 Ibid.

10 "A belief that things have a set of characteristics that make them what they are, and that the task of science and philosophy is their discovery and expression; the doctrine that essence is prior to existence. " - *Oxford Dictionary* "essentialism"

11 The structure uses Strickland's thematics for the evaluation of minimalism as an armature.

12 The title itself suggests that the production of words is intended to illuminate methods that generate objects. This linkage through the same individual is fundamental to the total consideration and cohesiveness of the result. Though each (loosely termed: intent, design, and making) have intrinsically differential bodies of knowledge and physical modus operandi, they must become intrinsic cousins of one another: simultaneously none of them, but all of them.

13 Percy, Walker. *The Moviegoer*. New York: Alfred A. Knopf, 1961.

14 See *Ultramodern: Cultural Context: The Time and Place of Operation - Americanism and the late 20th Century.*

15 Wittgenstein, Ludwig and G. E. M. Anscombe, ed. (Gertrude Elizabeth Margaret), and Wright, G. H. von ed. (Georg Henrik). *Zettel #452*. Berkeley: University of California Press, 1967.

16 Borden, Gail Peter and Brian Andrews. *Principia: Architectural Principles of Material Form*. Pearson Press, 2013.

17 Reference to the Vitruvian elements: *firmitas, utilitas,* and *venustas (translated by* Henry Wotton into "firmness, commodity, and delight"). Firmness establishing structural integrity; Commodity providing function; and Delight the aesthetic beauty.

18 APOD: 19 August 2007 - A Sonic Boom. Antwrp. gsfc.nasa.gov. 2010.

19 Like Marcel Duchamp's "readymades" where ordinary manufactured objects were selected by the artist and modified. By the act of selection or juxtaposition or a repositioning, along with titling and signing it, the found object became art.

20 Richard Serra MOCA catalog, p. 195.

21 Based on an architectural interpretation of Serra's statements on his arguments to preserve Tilted Arc.

22 Richard Serra, "Verb List Compilation: Actions to Relate to Oneself" [1967-1968] http://www.neromagazine.it/magazine/index.hp?c=articolo&idart=1069&idnum=41&num=31

23 Krauss, Rosalind. *Richard Serra Sculpture*. Catalog edited and introduced by Laura Rosenstock. New York: Museum of Modern Art, 1986, pp. 19, 29, 32-33, 37.

24 Taylor, like Krauss, quotes Serra's term "field force." See Mark Taylor, "Learning Curves," in Torqued Ellipses. New York: Dia Center for the Arts, 1997, p. 41.

25 Ibid, p. 48.

26 As an extension of Rene Descartes: "I think therefore I am."

27 Semper, Gottfried. *The Four Elements of Architecture and Other Writings*. Cambridge, 1989.

28 Ottman, Klaus. "Spiritual Materiality: Contemporary Sculpture and the Responsibility of Forms." Sculpture Magazine, April 2002.

29 Greenberg, Clement. "Avant-Garde and Kitsch," in *Art and Culture*. Beacon Press, 1961, p. 3–21.

30 Barthes, Roland. *"Disgressions,"* in *The Grain of the Voice: Interviews 1962-1980,* p. 115.

31 Ibid.

32 *Journal of Contemporary Art*-ONLINE - http://www.jca-online.com/horn.html

33 Frampton, Kenneth. *Towards a Critical Regionalism: Six points for an architecture of resistance,* 1981.

34 Norberg-Schulz, Christian. *Genius Loci: Towards a Phenomenology of Architecture.*Rizzoli, 1979.

35 Frampton, Kenneth. *Towards a Critical Regionalism: Six points for an architecture of resistance,* 1981.

36 Ibid.

37 Kuh, Katharine. *The Artist's Voice: Talks with Seventeen Modern Artists*. 1st Da Capo Press ed. New York: Da Capo Press, 1999.

38   Sullivan, Louis. The Tall Office Building Artistically Considered. 1896.

39   Weschler, Lawrence, Robert Irwin and Moshe Lazar. *Seeing is Forgetting the Name of the Thing One Sees: A Life of Contemporary Artist Robert Irwin.* Berkeley: University of California Press, 1982.

40   Role of Socratic questioning.

41   Norberg-Schulz, Christian. *Genius Loci: Towards a Phenomenology of Architecture.* Rizzoli, 1979.

42   http://www.zva.cc/

43   By localized the reference is to both regional one-off stores or chains; but also referring to specific limited product selection stores: i.e. shoes; a focused subset of product.

44   Following the purchase of the Louisiana Territory came the associated challenges of subdividing, selling, and occupying it. Thomas Jefferson devised a system that would make platting and selling achievable through the implementation of a grid in the Land Ordinance of 1785.

45   Here the reference to "40 acres and a mule" was attributed to Union General William T. Sherman's Special Field Order No. 15, issued on Jan. 16, 1865. This is only half-right as Sherman prescribed the 40 acres in that order, but not the mule.

46   A movement in the period from 1800 to 1830 expanded the right to vote to include all white men. Keyssar, *The Right to Vote: The Contested History of Democracy in the United States* (2009) Chapter 2.

47   REI- Recreational Equipment Incorporated.

48   *Fight Club.* Twentieth Century FOX. Directed by David Fincher. 1999. 139 min color. R.

49   Margulis, Lynn and Dorian Sagan. *What is life?* New York: Simon+Schuster, 1995.

50   Higgins, Tom. *NASCAR's Greatest Races: The 25 Most Thrilling races in NASCAR History.* New York: Harper Entertainment, 1999.

51   Dave Hickey eloquently describes this concept through the democracy of Basketball in an article entitled *"The Heresy of Zone Defense"* where football is represented as the predominate metaphor of warfare, entirely based on a physical occupation of space based upon might. Hickey, Dave. *Air Guitar: Essay's on Art and Democracy.* Los Angeles: Art Issues Press, 1997.

52   McNair, James D, III. *New Home Plans for 1997: Featuring 250 Top Selling Designs.* Waterloo, Canada: The Garlinghouse Company, 1996.

53   Old Navy to the Gap to Banana Republic is one example of brand hierarchy in cost, formality and associated class.

54   The seeming expansion of culture is counterbalanced by a repetition of types. Despite the increase in information, its contents are stereotypical. Single types repeat and reflect themselves to produce more of the same.

55   Plastic Column: FRP Classic. Non-load Bearing Fiberglass Columns. Melton Classics Inc.

56   For a Virtual Tour visit: http:/www.caesars.com/palace

57   Pella Window formation: Sweet's General Building & Renovation Catalog File. Pella Corporation.

58   Plastic Shutters: Plastic "Style-A-Panel" and "Style-A-Louver" Mid-America Building Products. A TAPCO International Company. Plymouth, Michigan. USA.

59   Teyssot, Georges. *The American Lawn.* Princeton Architectural Press, 1999.

60   http://www.streetofdreams.com/

61   *American Beauty.* DreamWorks. Directed by Sam Mendes. 1999. 121 min color. R.

62   Mitchell, Margaret. *Gone With the Wind.* Directed by Victor Fleming. A Selznick International Picture. A Metro-Goldwyn-Mayer Release. 1939.

63   *Fight Club.* Twentieth Century FOX. Directed by David Fincher. 1999. 139 min color. R.

64   Garreau, Joel. *Edge Cities: Life on the New Frontier.* New York: Anchor Books–Random House, 1988.

65   Lynch, Kevin. *The Image of The City.* MIT Press: Cambridge, Massachusetts, 1960.

66   Gap, J Crew, Banana Republic, Abercrombie and Fitch, Old Navy (among others).

67   CBS, ABC, NBC, FOX (among others).

68   Wal-Mart, Home Depot, K-Mart, Target, Lowes, Borders (among others).

69   McDonalds, Starbucks, Taco Bell, Olive Garden (among others).

70   Washington DC and the legacy of Frenchman Pierre L'Enfant's Baroque plan

71   *Houston, New York City, et ceter.* Celik, Zynep, Diane Favro, and Richard Ingersoll. *Streets: Critical Perspectives on Public Space.* Berkley: University of California Press, 1994.

72   The Menil Museum, The Contemporary Arts Museum, The Glassell School, Mies van der Rohe's original Museum of Fine Arts and Raphael Moneo's recent addition, Robert Venturi's Children's Museum, et cetera, Pope, Albert. *Ladders.* New York: Princeton Architectural Press, 1996.

73   The premise of the tourist object as the principle definition of popular identity (formalized in snow globes, paperweights and projected maps) the tourist attraction as spectacle becomes landmark.

74   The legacy of the traditional monument. Benevolo, Leonardo. *The Origins of Modern Town Planning.* Cambridge, Massachusetts: MIT Press, 1967.

75   Duany, Andres, Elizabeth Plater-Zyberk, and Jeff Speck. *Suburban Nation: The Rise of Sprawl and the Decline of the American Dream.* New York: North Point Press, 2000.

76   I use such a democratic term very loosely. Lang, Peter and Tam Miller. *Suburban Discipline.* New York: Princeton Architectural Press, 1997.

77   Two shows from the inception of Walt Disney's corporate birth and flourishing.

78   Robert Venturi, Denise Scott Brown and Steven Izenour. *Learning from Las Vegas.* Cambridge, Massachusetts: MIT Press, 1977.

79   Hickey, Dave. *Air Guitar.* Los Angeles: Art Issues Press, 1997.

80   Hickey, Dave. *In the Palace of the People: New Lessons from Las Vegas.* Three Lectures given by the Visiting Cullen Professor in Architecture at Rice University School of Architecture, fall 1997.

81   John Nash and Karl Marx to name some primary figures.

82   Taeyoung, S. et al. *A cat cloned by nuclear transplantation.* Nature advanced online publication, 2002.

83   The relative positioning of event with the collective iconography of presence determines the suggested role. The stereotype is in fact devoid of anything but rumor as the individual each determines the quantified clarity of reasoning. The object is independent of association while in debt to both creator and owner/employer.

84   One of the Seven Wonders of the Ancient World.

85   Pedley, John. *Sanctuaries and the Sacred in the Ancient Greek World.* Cambridge University Press, 2005.

86   Pliny the Elder. *The Natural History.* 16.79.213-16, http://www.perseus.tufts.edu/hopper/text?doc=Plin.+Nat.+toc

87   Translated by Morris Hickey Morgan. *Vitruvius: The Ten Books on Architecture.* Dover Publications, 1960, Book III.2.7.

88   At the artillery sheds of the Chinati Foundation, Marfa, Texas, 1982-1986.

89   Lawrence Weschler, Robert Irwin, and Moshe Lazar. *Seeing is Forgetting the Name of the Thing One Sees: A Life of Contemporary Artist Robert Irwin.* Berkeley: University of California Press, 1982.

90   Ibid

91   Pomerantz, James R. "Perception: Overview." In: Lynn Nadel (Ed.). *Encyclopedia of Cognitive Science,* Vol. 3. London: Nature Publishing Group, 2003, pp. 527–537.

92   Gilles Deleuze and Felix Guattari. *What is Philosophy?* Columbia University Press, 1996.

93   Kirsch, David and Paul Maglion, University of California San Diego. "Perceptive Actions in Tetris." AAAI Spring Symposium on Control of Selective Perception. Stanford University. March 1992.

94   Steven J. C. Gaulin and Donald H. McBurney. *Evolutionary Psychology.* Prentice Hall, 2003, pp. 81–101.

95   Bernstein, Douglas A. *Essentials of Psychology.* Cengage Learning, 2010, pp. 123–124.

96   Wolfe, Jeremy M.; Kluender, Keith R.; Levi, Dennis M.; Bartoshuk, Linda M.; Herz, Rachel S.; Klatzky, Roberta L.; Lederman, Susan J. "Gestalt Grouping Principles." *Sensation and Perception* (2nd ed.). Sinauer Associates, 2008, pp. 78, 80.

97   Kushner, Laura H. *Contrast in Judgments of Mental Health.* ProQuest, 2008.

98   http://www.crystalinks.com/romebaths.html

99   Marina, Piranomonte. *The Baths of Caracalla.* Mondadori Electa, 1998.

100   https://en.wikipedia.org/wiki/Baths_of_Caracalla

101   Ibid.

102   Rafael Moneo, *Theoretical Anxiety and Design Strategies in the Work of Eight Contemporary Architects.* Cambridge, Massachusetts: MIT Press, 2005.

103   http://hockney-optics.brandeis.edu/issues/hockney.php

104   http://www.zoharworks.com/artandoptics/afterthoguhts/after_fs.html

105   Branner, Robert. "Chartres Cathedral." *Norton Critical Studies in Art History,* 2nd Edition, W. W. Norton & Company, 1996.

106   https://en.wikipedia.org/wiki/Chartres_Cathedral#Plan_and_elevation

107   Ibid.

108   Known as pilier cantonné.

109   Each bay was equally split into four webs by two diagonally crossing ribs.

110   https://en.wikipedia.org/wiki/Chartres_Cathedral#Plan_and_elevation

111   https://archive.org/stream/reportonarttechn00losa_/reportonarttechn00losa#page/n0/mode/2up

112   Sullivan, Louis. *The Tall Office Building Artistically Considered.* 1896.

113   Koolhaas, Rem. *Delirious New York. Definitive Instability.* 1978.

114   Maurizio Naldini and Domenico Taddei, *La Piazza, La Loggia, Il Palazzo Rucellai,* Edizioni Medicea, 1989.

115   https://en.wikipedia.org/wiki/Palazzo_Rucellai

116   The Rucellai family was a powerful in Florentine banking.

117   https://en.wikipedia.org/wiki/Palazzo_Rucellai

118   Ibid.

119   Borden, Gail Peter, *Material Precedent: The Tyology of Modern Tectonics,* Wiley Press 2010.

120   This quote is taken from Sir Henry Wotton's version of 1624, and is a plain and accurate translation of the passage in *Vitruvius* (I.iii.2): 2. Haec autem ita fieri debent ut habeatur ratio firmitatis utilitatis venustatis. firmitatis erit habita ratio, cum fuerit fundamentorum ad solidum depressio et quaque e materia copiarum sine avaritia diligens electio, utilitatis autem, cum emendata est sine inpeditione usus locorum dispositio et ad regiones sui cuiusque generis apta est commoda distributio, venustatis vero cum fuerit operis species grata et elegans membrorumque commensus iustas habeat symmetriarum ratiocinationes.

121   Caesar Augustus from *Cassius Dio* 56.30.3 - At his death-bed.

122   "However, construction of the concert hall itself stalled from 1994 to 1996 due to lack of fundraising. Additional funds were required since the construction cost of the final project far exceeded the original budget. Plans were revised, and in a cost saving move the originally designed stone exterior was replaced with a less costly metal skin. The needed fundraising restarted in earnest in 1996—after the real estate depression passed—headed up by Eli Broad and then-mayor Richard Riordan and groundbreaking for the hall was held in December 1999." Gehry, F. *Symphony: Frank Gehry's Walt Disney Concert Hall.* Harry N. Abrams: 2003.

123   Cesar Pelli, 1056 Chapel Street, New Haven Connecticut 06510.

124   Rem Koolhaas, "Fundamentals," Biennale Architecttura 2014, 7.06-23.11

125   *Louis Kahn*

126   *A Curriculum of Ideas, Reginald F. Malcolmson, Journal of Architectural Education (1947-1974), Vol. 14, No. 2, ACSA-AIA Seminar: The Teaching of Architecture (Autumn, 1959), pp. 41-43.*

127   *Contemporary media has been accelerated by computational tools. Much of current architectural representation is digitally produced and offers easy and seductive imagery.*

128   Tufte, Edward. *The Visual Display of Quantitative Information.* Graphics Press, 2001. provides an extensive examination of representation and information.

129   An extended discussion from introduction of: Borden, Meredith. *Lineament: Material, Representation and the Physical Figure in Architectural Production.* Routledge. 2017

130   https://en.wikipedia.org/wiki/The_Crystal_Palace

131   Ibid.

132   McKean, John. *Crystal Palace: Joseph Paxton and Charles Fox.* Phiadon, 1994.

133   https://en.wikipedia.org/wiki/The_Crystal_Palace

134   Ibid.

135   Ibid.

136   McKean, John, *Crystal Palace: Joseph Paxton and Charles Fox.* Phiadon, 1994.

137   https://en.wikipedia.org/wiki/The_Crystal_Palace

138   Colin Rowe and Robert Slutzky. *Transparency: Literal and Phenomenal.* Perspecta, 1963.

139   High tech architecture as a genre come from Joan Kron's and Suzanne Slesin's, *High Tech: The Industrial Style and Source Book for The Home.* New York: Clarkson N. Potter, 1978.

140   Gehry Residence, Santa Monica 1978 (for example) http://www.archdaily.com/67321/gehry-residence-frank-gehry

141   Two Running Violet V Forms, Robert Irwin, 1983 http://stuartcollection.ucsd.edu/artist/irwin.html

142   CATIA stands for: computer aided three-dimensional interactive application, developed by the French company Dassault Systèmes.

IMAGE

CREDITS

IMAGE CREDITS

P24 upper — http://www.rollanet.org/~conorw/cwome/article5. htm Originally from: Bretz, J. Harlen. Caves of Missouri. Sotina Publishing, 2012.

P24 lower — http://windsox.us/Building_With_Logs/Contents. html

P25 upper — https://www.youtube.com/watch?v=0sMVrmnuf-Po

P25 lower — Motherwell, Robert. *Elegy.*

P26 upper — http://www.badgerairbrush.com/library/Paint%20 Chart%20Images/Railroad%20Colors.gif

P26 second — http://socks-studio.com/2011/11/03/kitchen-actions-diagrams/

P26 middle — http://www.patheos.com/blogs/filmchat/2014/10/ the-thematic-and-visual-links-between-noah-and-darren-aronofskys-earlier-films-a-gallery.html

P27 upper — Adapted from: Gill, Robert W. *Perspective: From Basic to Creative.* Posted by: Carr, Joey. 2011. On http://alltheworstideas.blogspot.com/2011/06/ construction-of-rectangular-prism-from.html

P27 middle — By Borden, Gail P.

P27 lower — http://ffffound.com/image/261adb3a1e-f09831a33a443bfeac12c1759311ae?c=1333747

P28 lower — Frontispiece for: Laugier, Marc-Antoine. *Essay on Architecture.* London: Printed for Stanley Crowder and Henry Woodgate, 1756.

P29 upper — Campbell, Bradley J. *Blowerless Air Conditioning System.* Nordyne, Inc., assignee. Patent US6457653 B1. 1 Oct. 2002.

P29 middle — http://www.taubaauerbach.com/view.php?id=124

P30 upper — Duchamp, Marcel. *Fountain.* San Francisco Museum of Modern Art, 1917.

P30 lower — http://dylanpbentley.blogspot.com/2014/09/ whats-difference-between-mussels-and.html

P31 — http://ffffound.com/image/9060004673a0e5d1 bb298cdcfad3104d2e206272

P36 upper — Heizer, Michael. *Double Negative.* Museum of Contemporary Art, Los Angeles. Photo Courtesy of Virginia Dwan. http://www.ampersandla.com/ soil-of-creation-michael-heizers-double-negative/

P36 lower — http://mhsartgallerymac.wikispaces.com/Larry+Poons

P37 middle — Albers, Josef. *Study for Homage to the Square: in Stucco.* Private collection, Boston, 1959. http:// www.bu.edu/art/2010/02/05/the-shape-of-abstraction/josef-albers-study-for-homage-to-the-square-in-stucco/

P37 lower — Albers, Josef. *Homage to the Square: Blue Reminding.* Hirshhorn's collection, 1966. http:// newsdesk.si.edu/photos/homage-square-blue-reminding

P38 upper — http://www.architekwiki.com/wiki/masonry-coursing-concrete-block

P39 — http://artobservations.blogspot.com/2009/01/ michael-heizer-at-dia-beacon.html

P40 — http://www.eatonfineart.com/blog/2015/6/3/ artspiration-donald-judd

P41 upper — http://householddaily.blogspot.com/2005_11_01_ archive.html

P42 — https://www.math.unl.edu/~mbrittenham2/ldt/ knots.html

P43 upper — http://www.archivedauctions.com/s/341200/ clement-meadmore-hereabout/

P43 lower — Durer, Albrecht. *Perspective machine.* 1525. https://psicologiadearte.wordpress.com/ciencia-na-arte-e-arte-na-ciencia-2/

P44 — http://www.gujaratweather.com/wordpress/?tag=odisha

P45 — http://www.engr.psu.edu/mtah/projects/millstones.htm

P46 upper — https://wordsonwordsonwords.wordpress. com/2013/07/28/the-work-of-kid-zoom-ian-strange/

P46 lower — http://www.searspartsdirect.com/model-part/ iud4000rq0/3259/0130000/w0503223/00003.html

P47 — http://architizer.com/blog/the-largest-landscape-the-grid-of-american-agriculture Image by Knight, Paul via thegreatamericangrid.com

P48 — https://www.creativereview.co.uk/design-museums-designs-of-the-year-shortlist-revealed/

P49 — http://www.lepoint.fr/automobile/sports-et-reves/les-detournements-de-la-coccinelle-par-l-art-contemporain-07-11-2014-1879361_658. php#xtor=CS1-235

P51 — Originally from: http://www.swissinfo.ch/eng/ art-takes-a-holiday/2040 Photo courtesy of Offentliche Kunstsammlung Basel/Martin P. Buhler, © 2009 Pro Litteris, Zurich. Collage by: Borden, Gail P.

P60 — http://www.earthlymission.com/cross-section-x-ray-of-a-spacesuit/

P70-71 — Originally from: http://www.pics4world.com/vb/ showthread.php?t=5582 Redacted by: Borden, Gail P.

P128 upper — https://missmotion.wordpress.com/page/4/

P128 middle — http://mymodernmet.com/tara-donovan-styrofoam-cup-sculpture/

Image Credits

P129   http://www.returnofkings.com/39492/the-masculinity-and-art-of-jackson-pollock

P128   http://www.flgallery.com/edgar-orlaineta.html

P144-145   Originally from: http://jeffhottinger.com/niemeyer.php Photo credit to Flickr user End User. Redacted by: Borden, Gail P.

P148 upper   http://www.voicesofeastanglia.com/2014/09/walter-pichler-austrian-avant-garde-architectural-artist.html

P150 middle upper   Originally from: https://commons.wikimedia.org/wiki/File:G-AWZI_HS_Trident_3_Joiner_(10894988786).jpg

P148 lower   Originally from: http://www.todayandtomorrow.net/2009/07/28/jan-dibbets/

P230   https://www.reddit.com/r/HistoryPorn/comments/2n12y8/the_cathedral_of_amiens_during_ww_ii_france_1940s/

P231   Croucher, Meredith W., Jr., James M. Fisher, Richard Letizia, LeRoy A. Lutz, Ralph F. Makowski, Richard L. Moyse, Richard W. Osgood, John N. Rave, Ward A. Wickwire, and James F. Zillmer. *Structural Joint Members for Space Frame System.* Inryco, Inc., assignee. Patent US4863303 A. 5 Sept. 1989.

P232   http://s9.photobucket.com/user/Toad69n/media/freeshell/pics/geometry/mag14ba.jpg.html?sort=3&o=8

P244-245   Originally from: http://www.ncmodernist.org/gehry.htm Redacted by: Borden, Gail P.

P268   http://andreasangelidakis.blogspot.com/2007/08/aldo-van-eyck.html

P269   https://courses.byui.edu/art110_new/art110/week01/pitch.html

P282-283   Redacted by: Borden, Gail P.

P328 upper   Wiese, Allison. *Angle of Repose.* 2009. http://allisonwiese.com/angle-of-repose/ Image by Davenport, Bill.

P328 lower   http://www.baitrodreel.com/different-types-of-salmon-an-introduction-to-the-salmon-family/

P329   Brancusi, Constantin. *Bird in Space.* Philadelphia Museum Of Art, 1923.

P330   Richardson, Michael K. and Gerhard Keuck. *Haeckel's ABC of evolution and development.* Biological Reviews of the Cambridge Philosophical Society, 77, 2002, p. 516.

P542-543   Originally from: http://interactive.wttw.com/blog/10-that-changed-america/eames-house Photo courtesy of Eames Foundation and © 2014 Eames Ofiice, LLC Redacted by: Borden, Gail P.

All other images in blue tint are open source images.

Select photography of Intensity Frames, Light Frames, and Denisty Frames on pages: 248, 254-255, 340, 353 (lower), 356, 358 (lower), 359 (lower), 360, 372-373, 374, 375 are courtesy of Luke Gibson Photography.

All other images are credited to Gail Peter Borden.